NEW DEVELOPMENTS
IN
AUSTRALIAN
POLITICS

NEW DEVELOPMENTS IN AUSTRALIAN POLITICS

EDITED BY

BRIAN GALLIGAN
UNIVERSITY OF MELBOURNE

IAN McALLISTER
AUSTRALIAN NATIONAL UNIVERSITY

JOHN RAVENHILL
AUSTRALIAN NATIONAL UNIVERSITY

First published 1997 by
MACMILLAN EDUCATION AUSTRALIA PTY LTD
107 Moray Street, South Melbourne 3205

Associated companies and representatives
throughout the world

National Library of Australia
cataloguing in publication data

New developments in Australian politics.

Bibliography.
Includes index.
ISBN 0 7329 4304 3.
ISBN 0 7329 4307 8 (pbk.).

1. Australia – Politics and government – 1990– .
I. Galligan, Brian, 1945– . II. McAllister, Ian, 1950– .
III. Ravenhill, John.

320.994

Typeset in Times by
Typeset Gallery, Malaysia

Printed in Hong Kong

Edited by Elizabeth Watson
Cover design by Dimitrios Frangoulis
Index by Fay Donlevy

Contents

PART II: CONTEMPORARY ISSUES

Contributors

Clive Bean is a Senior Lecturer in the School of Social Science at Queensland University of Technology. He has published numerous articles on Australian political behaviour and has been the editor or joint editor of book length accounts of the last three Australian federal elections.

Graeme Cheeseman is a Lecturer in Politics and Defence Studies at the University College, The University of New South Wales. He is the author of *The Search for Self-Reliance: Australian Defence Since Vietnam* (1993) and co-editor of *Discourses of Danger and Dread Frontiers: Australian Defence and Security Thinking After the Cold War* (1996).

Glyn Davis is Associate Professor in Politics and Public Policy, Griffith University. He previously held a range of senior government posts, most recently as Director-General with the Queensland Office of the Cabinet. He is the author of *A Government of Routines: Executive Coordination in an Australian State* (1996).

Brian Galligan is Professor of Political Science and Director of the Centre for Public Policy at the University of Melbourne. Before taking up this position in 1995 he was Professor and Director of the Federalism Research Centre in the Research School of Social Sciences at the Australian National University. His main areas of research are Australian constitutional politics and political economy. His recent books include *A Federal Republic: Australia's Constitutional System of Government* (1995) and, with Ann Capling, *Beyond the Protective State* (1992). His current research is on the politics of rights in Australia, with Ian McAllister, and the institutional definition and development of Australian citizenship, with John Chesterman.

Helen Irving is a Senior Lecturer, teaching Australian politics and political theory in the Faculty of Humanities and Social Sciences, University of Technology, Sydney. She is the author of *To Constitute a Nation: A Cultural History of Australia's Constitution* (1997), and the editor of *A Woman's Constitution? Gender and History in the Australian Commonwealth* (1996). She comments frequently in the media on republicanism and constitutional reform.

Chandran Kukathas has taught courses in Politics and in Philosophy at Oxford University, the Australian National University, and the Australian Defence Force Academy. He is the author of *Hayek and Modern Liberalism* (1989), *Rawls. A Theory of Justice and its Critics* (1990) co-authored with Philip Pettit, and *The Theory of Politics: An Australian Perspective* (1990) co-authored with Ian McAllister, David Lovell and William Maley. He has edited *Multicultural Citizens: The Philosophy and Politics of Identity* (1993), and is founder and co-editor of *The Journal of Political Philosophy*.

Ian McAllister has been Professor of Government at the University of Manchester since March 1996, and prior to that was Professor of Politics at the Australian Defence Force Academy. He has written extensively on political behaviour and public opinion, immigrants and ethnicity, and drug use. His most recent books are *Dimensions of Australian Society* (1994), second edition with Brian Graetz, and *Russia Votes* (1996), co-authored with Stephen White and Richard Rose. He is currently working on the politics of rights in Australia with Brian Galligan.

Deborah Mitchell is a Fellow in the Research School of Social Sciences at the Australian National University. She has published widely on the welfare state, women and the labour market, and poverty and inequality. At present her main research interests are the impact of globalisation on the welfare state and the interaction of the life course with social policy.

Martin Painter is Associate Professor and Head of Department of Government and Public Administration, University of Sydney. He teaches in public policy and his current research interests are in federalism, intergovernmental relations in Australia, and the transformation of the public sector.

Elim Papadakis is Professor of Modern European Studies at the Australian National University. He was previously Professor of Sociology and Head of Department at the University of New England and Visiting Fellow in the Political Science Program, Research School of Social Science at the Australian National University. His recent publications include *Environmental Politics and Institutional Change* (1996) and *Politics and the Environment: The Australian Experience*.

John Ravenhill is Senior Fellow in the Department of International Relations, Research School of Pacific and Asian Studies, at the Australian National University. He taught previously at the University of Virginia and University of Sydney and in 1995 was Visiting Professor at the University of California, Berkeley. He has written widely on international political economy and on Australian foreign policy. He is the chair of the Research Committee of the Australian Institute of International Affairs, a past editor of *Australian Journal of International Affairs*, and currently edits the Cambridge Asia–Pacific Studies series.

Shirley V. Scott worked as a Research Assistant and Lecturer at the University of Southern Queensland before taking up an appointment in the School of Politics, University College, The University of New South Wales. She currently teaches and undertakes research on the politics of international law, international institutions and international security regimes.

Campbell Sharman is Head of the Political Science Department at the University of Western Australia. He has had a long interest in Australian state politics, patterns of partisan competition, and the operation of the federal system.

Russell Trood is Associate Professor of International Relations and Director of the Centre of the Study of Australia–Asia Relations, Faculty of Asian and International Studies, Griffith University.

John Uhr is a Senior Fellow in the Political Science Program at the Australian National University. In 1995 he served as the last Director of the Federalism Research Centre, the Australian National University. Prior to that he has taught public policy and management, and ethics in government. He is editor of, and contributor to, *Ethical Practice in Government: Improving Organisational Management* (1996), and co-editor of, and contributor to, *Evaluating Policy Advice: Learning from Commonwealth Experience* (1996). He has also published extensively on Australian government and public management, with a special focus on ethics in government.

Introduction

Australia has an enviable history of political stability for almost a century as a federal state, and before that for fifty years as a continental collection of self governing colonies. But stability has also been accompanied by significant change and development, usually evolutionary and gradual, although occasionally rapid and dramatic. In recent years many of the certainties of Australian political economy that structured political debate have come under critical scrutiny or have been abandoned altogether. These include 'settled policies' of protection for manufacturing industries, national arbitration for setting wage levels, and extensive state action in providing public utilities. The Australian public sector is undergoing a revolution as new practices of managerialism and marketisation, drawn from the private business sector and the discipline of economics, replace older orthodoxies of public administration and government provision of services. The 'state socialism' of earlier decades and the 'big government' of the postwar period are being replaced by the 'contract state'.

Australia's ongoing restructuring of national policies and the public sector are in response to the challenges and opportunities of global change. No longer able to command a premium for its natural resources and primary production, the Australian economy has become internationally competitive in a world where rapid technological change is transforming productive processes and the economies of neighbouring Asian countries. Australian trade, particularly on the export side, has led the reorientation of the economy and national attention away from Britain and Europe to the Asia Pacific region. The recent public debates about whether Australia is part of Asia, and whether Australians are Asians, have highlighted the awkwardness of articulating the country's changed economic and perceptual place in the world.

Australian politics have also had to contend with new social movements and issues. These new perspectives are not derived from the old social divisions of left and right, capital and labour, or regional divisions based on states. By contrast, they are based on the new politics of human rights, the environment, feminism and Aboriginal entitlement to land and self determination – all issues that have been at the forefront of political debate during the 1990s. These new perspectives have expanded the agenda of

Australian politics and have had a substantial impact on political coalitions and public policy making, particularly among the major political parties. The goal of this book is to provide a comprehensive overview of contemporary issues and problems in Australian politics. While our time perspective is mainly the past five years, we also examine these issues and problems in long-term perspective, since many can only be properly understood by placing them in their historical context. This is particularly important where trends in elections or in political behaviour are concerned. But it is also important in evaluating institutions such as the constitution, which was devised a century ago but which has, of necessity, to deal with contemporary challenges of governance. Similarly, a review of Australia's place in the global economy has to begin with an examination of the legacy of ninety years of public policy since federation.

Along with issues and problems concerning Australian domestic politics, we consider it important to examine the international dimension. For too long international relations has been regarded as an endeavour that is separate from the study of Australian political institutions or political behaviour. As Australia moves towards greater engagement with the world economy in general, and the Asia–Pacific region in particular, in the twenty-first century, the international dimension is likely to become more closely integrated with domestic politics, as is the case in many other countries.

Part I examines the operation of the political system and the political culture within which it is imbedded. One of the legacies of the Keating Labor government was to initiate a popular debate about Australia's national identity. This was reflected in Paul Keating's personal commitment to severing the remaining constitutional links with Britain and creating a republic. But the debate has also raised fundamental questions about Australia's identity in the twenty-first century, the obligations that link citizens and the state in an ethnically plural society, and the role that governments can and should play in fostering civic knowledge. Ian McAllister examines these themes by analysing how Australian voters feel about their national identity, what they see as the key elements of citizenship, and the extent of their political knowledge. Although Australians' sense of national pride is exceeded only by citizens of the United States, the components of that pride are more likely to focus on sporting prowess than on literary or technological achievements. In line with their pluralistic origins, Australians see citizenship in terms of achieved rather than ascribed characteristics, but their political knowledge is limited. Fusing these disparate elements into a cohesive national identity will be the major challenge of the twenty-first century.

Central to the institutional definition of the Australian nation is the constitutional system, the legitimating basis of which became an issue after residual links with Britain were formally terminated in the Australia Acts of 1986. In response, the High Court began developing a new jurisprudence grounding the Australian constitution on the Australian people. Further-more, in a series of bold decisions in the 1990s, the High Court ruled that there were certain implied political rights inherent in the requirement of representative democracy embodied in the constitution. In Chapter 2, Brian Galligan assesses these new developments in constitutional thinking and interpretation. He argues that, important as the more adventurous decisions of the Mason Court may have been, the constitutional system changes more through political practice, including innovative developments in the use of powers and changing arrangements in intergovernmental relations. The federal system of multiple governments with concurrent jurisdiction in major areas is, he argues, an appropriate institutional one for enhancing democratic participation, dealing with policy complexity and responding to global challenges.

The states remain a key part of the constitutional system. As Campbell Sharman reminds us in Chapter 3, they account for much of the ongoing politics and policy making of Australian government – delivering most of the services, promoting development and ensuring law and order. Typically conservative and highly pragmatic, state politics have had to cope with an increasingly rapid rate of change in recent years because of changes in federal politics, spectacular failures in economic and commercial manage-ment in three of the states, and institutional shortcomings associated with those failures in tackling public and police corruption. Despite all of this turmoil, Sharman documents continuing political stability measured by partisan support for the major parties. While there is evidence of some weakening of the Labor vote in several of the states and of influential activists not joining traditional parties, it is too early in the electoral cycle to identify continuing trends. The challenge to, and relative stability of, the party system are examined further in Chapter 6 by Clive Bean.

At the centre of national politics is the Commonwealth parliament which, as John Uhr details in Chapter 4, is undergoing considerable change. There is a continuing injection of multi-party decision making because of the controlling position of minor parties and independents in the senate which has forced changes to the orthodox model of responsible party government. This increased role of the minor parties has led in recent years to some effective resistance to executive domination evident in enhanced senate scrutiny of, and forced modification to, important legislation. Uhr emphasises that parliament is not one unified and coherent political insti-tution but rather a series of overlapping institutions, a feature also of the core executive, as Glyn Davis explains in Chapter 5.

While more central than parliament in the process of governing, the core executive has less constitutional definition, being almost entirely structured by conventions and evolving practices. In considering these, Glyn Davis examines not only the prime minister and cabinet, but the wider set of institutions involved in governing. His account is structured around three interconnected concerns of government: the political need of those who govern to pursue their interests and those of their constituents; the policy need to develop and implement their policies; and the administrative need to ensure the public sector is working efficiently and effectively towards the goals set by cabinet. New managerialist techniques have provided the core executive with greater reach over departmental activity in recent years, rendering older public service practices obsolete. The core executive is of course selected through the electoral process.

Political parties competing in free, competitive national elections are at the heart of modern democracy. In the past two decades, Australia has departed from international trends by sustaining a strong, stable party system where the major parties have attracted the vast majority of votes from election to election. In the 1990s, however, there is some evidence that Australia may be experiencing the partisan dealignment that has afflicted many other advanced democracies, with voters defecting in increasing numbers from the major parties to minor parties and independent candidates. Clive Bean assesses the evidence for and against this proposition by examining federal and state election results, party membership statistics, and the level and strength of partisanship within the electorate. He argues that while the results are mixed, there is some evidence from the most recent elections to support the argument that the main political parties are losing their electoral hegemony. But he also cautions that the major parties have proved themselves highly adaptable in dealing with such challenges in the past.

Part II turns to an examination of a select number of contemporary political issues that have had special significance in recent years. The first is republicanism and citizenship, which Helen Irving discusses in Chapter 7. Although debated sporadically before, only in the 1990s did the republican cause seem likely to succeed. Nevertheless, as Irving documents, just what republicanism entails, how it should be achieved and whether it entails a substantial or largely symbolic change are all contested in the flurry of recent writing and debate. The 'minimalist' position broadly favoured by Mr Keating and his Republic Advisory Committee entailed changing as little as possible regarding the office of head of state in order to facilitate the change. But many are uneasy with leaving the executive power unspecified – the constitution gives the queen and vice-regal surrogate unlimited power and makes no mention of the prime minister and cabinet – and advocate defining the powers of the head of state including the so-called 'reserve' or discretionary powers. Moreover, there is strong popular support for electing the head of state, whereas most elites are horrified by such a proposal. Feminists and Aboriginal people are among those who seek to broaden the republican debate and link it with citizenship concerns which have also become fashionable in the 1990s. This linking of republicanism and citizenship promises to be a rich stimulant to continuing public discussion and debate about Australian politics.

The next issue selected for detailed consideration is the reshaping of the public sector, relying upon the new orthodoxy of economic or market liberalism. As Martin Painter points out in Chapter 8, the public sector is in the process of being 'marketised' in the name of a more competitive economy and efficiency in provision of services. Significant restructuring of the public sector, both of the Commonwealth and the states, has occurred; and a continuing agenda of microeconomic reform has been prominent on the agenda for intergovernmental relations. Painter sees the states as losing out in the brave new world of principal–agent relations where control by individual states is being pooled or by-passed in national arrangements. The process of marketisation, which is transforming the Australian public sector, Painter suggests, is part of the wider transformation of political and administrative arrangements in post-industrial society.

Human rights are of central concern to the new politics of post-industrial societies and, as outlined in Chapter 2, became a political issue with the High Court's implied rights decisions of the 1990s. In Chapter 9, Chandran Kukathas makes a critical examination of cultural rights. As a political system based on the traditions of liberal egalitarianism, Australia's legal institutions have historically been colour- or culture-blind. However, the more explicit recognition of cultural diversity in political debate in the 1990s – through the policy of multiculturalism and Aboriginal land rights – has brought the role of legal institutions on matters of culture into focus. Kukathas opposes the argument that there should be special rights for cultural groups and argues instead that such measures represent an unwarranted politicisation of culture. He argues that government responses to cultural diversity must stick to the original liberal idea of individual rather than group rights.

In Chapter 10, Deborah Mitchell examines the government response to changes in family arrangements in the 1990s. Government policies designed to meet the needs of families represent the fastest growing area of social policy in Australia. Mitchell argues that during the 1980s, family policies were introduced with comparatively little consideration being given to their overall coherence. In many cases, these policies were responding to needs generated by the changing labour market position of women, but the social consequences of no-fault divorce, introduced by the Whitlam Labor government, as well as rising unemployment among men were also factors. The result is a complex set of social policy arrangements, many of them overlapping, which represent a major cost to government. Mitchell argues that the next challenge in social policy will be to devise policies which properly reflect the transition in women's lives from being home-makers and full-time carers in the 1960s and 1970s to breadwinners and working mothers in the 1990s.

Following its pivotal role in determining the outcome of the 1990 federal election, the issue of the environment was less prominent in the 1993 election, only to regain its importance in the 1996 election. Elim Papadakis traces the origins of popular concerns about the environment to 1983 and the federal government's intervention to halt the damming of the Franklin River in Tasmania. But popular concerns about the environment did not begin to influence the priorities of political organisations until the late 1980s, when these concerns grew significantly. An analysis of party policies on the environment and mass media coverage of environment issues spanning nearly half a century demonstrates how the presentation of the issue has changed. The overall trend has been for public opinion, the media, policy makers and political parties to focus increasingly on resolving the tension between the environment and development. Both green groups and the major political parties have acknowledged the need to link employment with environmental protection. Resolving these two apparently irreconcilable goals will be a central public policy priority over the next decade.

Part III of the book turns to the international dimensions of Australian policy-making. The international environment faced by Australian foreign policy decision-makers changed dramatically at the end of the 1980s. The collapse of the Soviet Union and its allied Communist regimes in Eastern Europe brought the most fundamental change to the structure of the international system since the postwar settlement in 1945. With the end of the Cold War, countries had to adjust to a new system in which there was only one superpower – the United States. Yet if the United States enjoyed unprecedented military hegemony, its dominant position in the global economy had increasingly been eroded by the rise of the European Union and of Japan and the East Asian newly-industrialising countries. The relative decline of the US economy, coupled with the complexities of conflicts in the post Cold War era (often civil rather than inter-state wars), and the reluctance of domestic opinion in the US to risk American lives in conflicts where core US interests did not appear to be threatened, caused uncertainty over the continuing capacity and will of Washington to underwrite its allies' security.

Australian foreign policy decision-makers faced a number of critical challenges in the first half of the 1990s. The first was how to re-shape defence and foreign policies to respond to the post Cold War international environment. The second was how to promote domestic adjustment and to redirect foreign economic relations to cope with the increasing impact of globalisation on the Australian economy. Increasingly, the Australian government looked to East Asia, not only as a market and source of foreign investment, but also as a partner in reshaping economic and security regimes.

Graeme Cheeseman discusses the response of Australia's defence community to the changing international environment in the first half of the 1990s. He argues that the manner in which the post Cold War security environment has been interpreted by Australian defence planners has privileged traditional realist concepts of security, and attempted to advance the claims of the defence forces to scarce budgetary resources. Defence planners were slow to adjust to the ending of the Cold War, at first arguing that it had exerted no significant impact on Australia's security environment or on the country's basic approach to defence and security issues. Subsequently, however, planners have placed emphasis on the possible threatening dimensions of political and economic change in the Asia– Pacific region, in particular, on how rapid economic growth was facilitating forced modernisation in many Asian countries. The response of Australian security planners to the new environment has been threefold: arguments for increased defence expenditures in support of a traditional role for Australian forces; continued reliance on the alliance with the United States (re-emphasised by the Coalition government after the March 1996 election); and new engagement with neighbouring countries through increased cooperation between the Australian Defence Forces and their regional counterparts.

Developments in the economic realm in the first half of the 1990s, John Ravenhill argues, were less dramatic than in that of defence. This period was one of consolidation, in which the government built on many of the initiatives taken by the Hawke Labor government in the 1980s. These initiatives had attempted to address four principal problems in Australia's relations with the global economy: the high levels of protectionism accorded to domestic manufacturing and the consequent failure of much of this sector to compete in world markets; the relative closure of the Australian economy at a time when the share of trade in the economies of most industrialised countries was expanding rapidly; the growth of agricultural protectionism in the world economy; and, finally, a fear that the world economy would fragment into rival regional trading blocs. To a considerable extent, the government increasingly looked towards Asia as providing a solution to both internal and external dimensions of its economic difficulties. Ravenhill suggests that government policies enjoyed success in a number of areas. The composition of Australian exports changed dramatically between the mid-1980s and mid-1990s with rapid growth in the share contributed by elaborately transformed manufactures. Coalition building in support of trade liberalisation – through the Cairns Group and the Asia–Pacific Economic Cooperation grouping – enabled Australia to exert much greater influence on international negotiations than if it had acted alone. The outcome of the Uruguay Round of GATT negotiations, however, was far from fully satisfactory for Australian interests, and underlined the relative powerlessness of a small player in the world economy.

Globalisation not only impinges on the Australian economy but also on other dimensions of domestic and foreign policies. The increasing interaction between international and domestic aspects of policy has generated

Introduction

increasing controversy over Australia's participation in international institutions and treaties, and the extent to which international obligations should be permitted to impinge on the balance of constitutional power within Australia. Shirley Scott's chapter, which focuses in particular on the chemical weapons convention and on the Antarctic Treaty System, discusses three of the principal elements of this debate within Australia. These are the growing fears of a loss of sovereignty; concerns about a 'democratic deficit' given the limited scope for public and parliamentary (either Commonwealth or state) debate of international treaties; and the impact of Australia's international commitments on federal–state relations. Scott concludes that these concerns have generally been overstated, and that in any event the Coalition government elected in 1996 is likely to show greater sympathy with state concerns over erosion of their powers.

Russell Trood evaluates how successful Australian governments have been in their efforts to engage the country more closely with Asia over the last decade. Although engagement with Asia had occurred under previous Coalition governments, it had never received the prominence accorded it first by Prime Minister Bob Hawke and then by his successor, Paul Keating, and by the Foreign Minister in the Labor government of the 1990s, Gareth Evans. Although engagement with Asia is most often conceived in terms of economic interdependence, Trood emphasises that the economic dimension is but one of three that have been prominent in government policies in the last decade. The other two dimensions are various policies aimed at making the country more Asia-literate, and cooperative engagement in the area of defence. Trood notes the difficulties faced by Australian governments in seeking closer engagement with Asia – the diversity of Asia itself, Australia's lack of historical and cultural ties with the region, and differences on key political issues such as respect for human rights. Nevertheless, he argues, the government's push for closer relations with Asia has enjoyed significant success in the last decade, particularly in the realms of economics and defence cooperation.

We are grateful to a wide range of individuals for their assistance in making this book possible. Peter Debus, from Macmillan, gave us strong support. Roger Jones made available at short notice a preliminary version of the 1996 Australian Election Study (AES) survey conducted after the March 1996 federal election.[1]

Brian Galligan
Ian McAllister
John Ravenhill

Note

1 The AES is directed by Ian McAllister, David Gow and Roger Jones and funded by the Australian Research Council. The data are publicly available from the Social Science Data Archive at the Australian National University. The 1996 AES had a response rate of 61.5 per cent and was used in several of the chapters.

PART I

The political system

1

Political culture and national identity

Ian McAllister

Until recently, there was comparatively little interest in Australian political culture or national identity. Australians were viewed as a fragment – albeit a distant one – of their British forebears, and their roles in the First and Second Word Wars had cemented their essentially British character. While the particular circumstances of white settlement – the transportation of convicts, the frontier conditions, and the physical remoteness – all helped to mould a distinctive Australian culture, it did not detract from the British symbols, beliefs and values which lay at its core. Moreover, the absence of any physical threat – with the exception of the threat of Japanese invasion early in the Second World War – nor of any major economic or political crises, meant that the political culture was not subjected to the scrutiny that had occurred in many other countries.

In the postwar years this began to change. In the first place, Britain's entry into the European Community in 1972 weakened the traditional political and economic links between Australia and Britain, and formalised a situation which had been evident to many for more than a decade. At the same time, the post-1947 immigration program, which had brought non-English speaking immigrants into the country in large numbers for the first time, finally began to impact on cultural identity and, in a more limited way, on the formal political institutions of the state. Finally, the large scale Asian immigration that commenced after the end of the Vietnam War in 1975 emphasised the incongruity between political symbols which were largely of British origin and what was, in effect, an ethnically plural society.

The past decade has seen more discussion about Australia's political culture and sense of national identity than at any time since white settlement. In old societies, these facets of the society are accepted and established; embedded in history and based on common symbols, shared experiences and similar values, they are stable and subject only to the most limited amount of change. By contrast, in new societies, the absence of shared experiences and a system of collective values means that political culture and identity can be reconstructed more easily, particularly when the existing structures appear to have little relevance to contemporary circumstances. It was the apparent irrelevance of political symbols to the reality of Australian society which enabled the republican question to emerge as a major political and election issue in the early 1990s (Lawson and Maddox 1993; Leithner 1994).

This chapter examines contemporary debates about Australian political culture and national identity, with particular reference to their reflection in and likely impact on political behaviour. The debates were brought into perspective by the republican issue, raised by Paul Keating in the early 1990s, but they were given added impetus by debates concerning the nature of Australia's political institutions and the relationship between the federal government and the states, as well as what has largely been an elite-driven move to establish links between Australia and the other nations in the Asia–Pacific region. The first section of the chapter examines the concepts of culture, identity and citizenship, while the second section focuses on Australian political culture. The third section explores changes in national identity and citizenship, while the fourth section analyses government moves to increase political knowledge through civic education.

Culture, identity and citizenship

The activities that are generally considered to be political within a society are moulded by the culture of the society within which they take place. Political culture, in turn, represents the accumulation of all of the shared experiences and historical events that have occurred within a society and which have evolved to shape that society's character and outlook on the world. It is this collective memory, passed down through the generations, which provides the distinctive character that makes one society different from another. The importance of political culture in shaping political outlooks has long been recognised. In *The Republic*, Plato spoke of states being composed less of 'oak and rock' than 'of the human natures which are in them'. In the nineteenth century, historians talked about 'national character' or 'sentiment' when they tried to explain the political distinctiveness of a society.

The concept of political culture was first given widespread currency in political science in 1963 with the publication of Gabriel Almond and Sidney Verba's *The Civic Culture*. Using opinion surveys collected in Britain, Germany, Italy, Mexico and the United States, Almond and Verba identified a range of citizen orientations towards politics and related those orientations to political stability. They argued that Britain and the United States most approximated to a 'civic culture' within which potentially destabilising elements were held in check. By contrast, they found that Germany, Italy and Mexico lacked these moderating balances, causing political instability. Attempts to explain political behaviour using political culture fell into disfavour in the 1970s (see Almond and Verba 1980), but more recently it has experienced a renaissance, mainly as a result of greater sophistication in cross-national survey research, as well as more theoretical rigour in defining exactly what political culture is (Inglehart 1990).

National identity is the feeling of being associated with a national group, defined by common heritage which may be based on many attributes, the most common being race, territory, language and history. Historically, nationalism was once viewed as a nineteenth century invention which political elites used to mobilise the loyalty of the masses, a function which became more pressing in the age of democratisation at the turn of the twentieth century. It was generally believed that economic modernisation in the twentieth century would undermine nationalism, as economic competition and international trade weakened national sentiments. Contrary to these predictions, the emergence of regional ethno-nationalism in many societies in the 1960s and 1970s demonstrated that feelings of national sentiment remained a potent source of division (Smith 1981). There is some evidence, however, that value change in western societies may be eroding the popular sense of nationalism and patriotism in many countries (Inglehart 1990: 408).

Citizenship confers certain legal rights as a consequence of being a member of a nation. Citizenship is usually granted by birth or descent, but it can also be conferred by adoption or naturalisation, as in Australia. Traditionally, these legal rights have been interpreted as political in nature, such as voting and the right to stand for election to political office, as well as certain military obligations such as conscription. However, the twentieth century has seen a trend towards what Gans (1968) has called the 'equality revolution' in citizenship. In Gans' view, the state has legislated increasingly to preserve political and social equality as a natural extension to legal rights. The net result of this revolution has been an extension of fundamental rights to cover ever widening activities, behaviours and social groups (Marshall 1964).

These three concepts are closely related. The political culture and national identity of a country are both shaped by shared experiences and common symbols. While culture helps to shape the processes that take place within a society, it also has some impact on the collective national identity. In turn, the way that the country views itself will also help to mould that culture. Of the three concepts, citizenship is perhaps the easiest to identify and define, since it is primarily an attribute that is formalised in law. However, as noted above, citizenship – both in terms of rights as well as responsibilities – now has a much more diverse meaning, as is illustrated in the discussion of multiculturalism later in the chapter.

Australian political culture

Although there has been much written about Australian political culture in recent years, its contours have remained elusive. In part, this is because of the abstract nature of culture, and of the different approaches and methodologies that have been used to try and map it. In part, too, it is a consequence of the fact that much of the cultural underpinnings for social and political behaviour are taken for granted, and it is only when there is a significant event or a profound change that we gain a fragmentary glimpse of the cultural foundations. The task of understanding and explaining the origins of Australian political culture has been mainly one for historians. The most influential work is probably W. F. Hancock's *Australia*, published in 1930. In turn, the roots of Australia's political culture stretch back to the circumstances surrounding Australia's white settlement and the colonial 'fragment' that was separated from Britain and which took root in Australia (Hartz 1964).

Various interpretations of Australian political culture have identified themes which have their expression in institutions, rules, procedures and in the everyday life and patterns of behaviour of ordinary Australians (see for example, Bean 1993a; McAllister 1992; Aitkin 1986). Two common themes emerge from these studies, under different titles and with different interpretations placed on them, which encapsulate the Australian ethos: egalitarianism and the role of the state, the latter rooted in utilitarianism. Moreover, each has undergone significant changes in the ways in which it has been reflected in politics in the postwar years.

The notion of equality in Australian society has its origins in the frontier tradition which emerged in the early years of white settlement, and the reliance of the early settlers on their friends and neighbours for support – what was later termed 'mateship' (Ward 1958). This frontier spirit was also present in other immigrant societies, notably the United States, Canada and South Africa, but the Australian frontier experience – with fewer people and in many ways a harsher environment – fostered a degree of egalitarianism far beyond that found in the other colonial societies. As the 1853 *Emigrant's Guide to Australia* commented, 'the equality system here would stun even a yankee ... all are mates' (quoted in Thompson 1995: 9). Equality was also fostered by the convict heritage and since few convicts wanted to return to Europe, most had the goal of establishing an open, less privileged and meritocratic society, very different from the one that they had left behind.

How these experiences and heritages have shaped popular beliefs and equality in the present day can be seen in Table 1.1, which examines the importance that survey respondents ascribe to six different aspects of equality of opportunity in Australia, Britain, Canada, New Zealand and the United States. The responses show the proportion of the survey respondents in each country who regarded each of the six qualities as 'essential' for getting ahead in their own country. The results show that while inherited privilege – represented here by having a wealthy family and educated parents – and status – represented by knowing the right people and having political connections – are of modest importance, merit is much more highly valued. Moreover, it is hard work which is seen as being more important than ability, although to a lesser degree in Australia than in the other three countries.

TABLE 1.1   *Public opinion towards equality of opportunity in the Anglo-American democracies**

| | (% say 'essential' to get ahead) | | | | |
	Australia	Britain	Canada	New Zealand	United States
Inherited privilege					
Wealthy family	6	3	3	5	6
Educated parents	6	4	4	5	6
Merit					
Ability	18	12	9	13	10
Hard work	33	34	36	42	38
Status					
Knowing right people	15	11	11	8	9
Political connections	7	2	4	3	4
(N)	(2,203)	(1,066)	(1,004)	(1,239)	(1,273)

* 'To begin with, we have some questions about opportunities for getting ahead. Please tick one box for each of these to show how important you think it is for getting ahead in life ...'

Source: International Social Survey Project, 1992, Social Inequality II.

Once egalitarianism was firmly established in social relations, demands grew for it to be applied to political institutions as well. Throughout the 1850s, a range of political reforms were introduced in the colonies which were far ahead of those of any other country in the world, with the possible exception of New Zealand, which, in any event, shared some of the same characteristics as Australia. By 1859 all of the colonies, with the exception of Western Australia and Tasmania, had introduced universal manhood suffrage (Table 1.2). In Britain, by comparison, the franchise was extended in 1884 to working men, but it was not properly universal until 1918, almost sixty years after its introduction in Australia. New Zealand led the world in granting votes for women, in 1893, with most of the Australian colonies following shortly after. Once again, Britain and the United States lagged behind their Australasian counterparts. The nineteenth amendment to the United States constitution gave women the vote in 1920, while

British women had to wait until 1928 in order to vote on the same basis as men.

TABLE 1.2   *The pace of democratic reform in Australia, New Zealand, the United Kingdom and the United States[a]*

	Manhood suffrage	Votes for women	Abolition of plural voting	Secret ballot	Payment of members
Australia					
NSW	1858	1902	1894	1858	1889
Victoria	1857	1909	1899	1856	1870
Queensland	1859	1905	1905	1859	1886
South Australia	1856	1894	–[b]	1856	1887
Western Australia	1907	1899 1907[c]	1907	1877	1900
Tasmania	1901	1903	1901	1858	1890
Commonwealth	1901	1902	–[b]	1901	1901
New Zealand	1879	1893	1889	1870	1892
United Kingdom	1884 1918	1918 1928[d]	1948	1872	1911
United States	1870	1920	–[b]	1893	1883

a   Reforms are for the lower house in Australia, the UK and the US.
b   Plural voting never existed.
c   Women received the vote in 1899 on a restricted franchise.
d   On the same basis as men.

Sources: (Australia) *Joint Select Committee on Electoral Reform, First Report*. Canberra: AGPS, 1983; (New Zealand) J.O. Wilson, *New Zealand Parliamentary Record, 1840–1984*, Wellington, Government Printer, 1985; (United Kingdom) David Butler and Gareth Butler, *British Political Facts*, London: Macmillan, 1995; (United States) various.

In addition to widening the franchise, a range of other democratic reforms were also introduced in Australia, far in advance of the other English speaking democracies. Plural voting was abolished in the colonies and states around the turn of the century, half a century before Britain, and when the Commonwealth was established in 1901, the electoral system was based on the principle of one man, one vote. The secret ballot is usually regarded as a cornerstone of democracy, since without it there is scope for bribery and intimidation. Australia was the first country in the world to introduce secret voting, and it had been introduced in all but one of the colonies by 1859. By contrast, Britain did not introduce the secret ballot until 1872 and the United States until 1893. The principle of payment for elected representatives was also established early – in 1870 in Victoria, with most of the remaining colonies following by 1890.

In addition to quickening the pace of democratic reform and consolidating the innovations that were made, egalitarianism was also important in providing a utilitarian expectation about the proper role of the state. Utilitarianism is the desire to see everyday problems resolved efficiently by the use of whatever methods are available and at whatever cost. As Hancock (1930: 69) observed in a famous statement: 'Australians have come to look upon the state as a vast public utility, whose duty it is to provide the greatest happiness for the greatest number.' In other words, the state exists primarily in order to resolve problems and disputes, not to preserve individual liberty. The hand of utilitarianism is seen in the desire to accommodate conflict bureaucratically, without necessarily resolving it. For example, the Industrial Relations Commission was established to weaken class conflict, rather than to resolve it, while the *Mabo* legislation was designed to mute Aboriginal land claims.

The prime example of utilitarianism in politics is compulsory voting. Since democracy seeks to give all citizens a role in decision-making, the utilitarian method of achieving this 'right' is through compulsion and legal enforcement. Australia, Belgium and some South American countries are the only democratic countries in the world to force citizens to vote in this way in national elections. Peoples' views of compulsory voting have under-

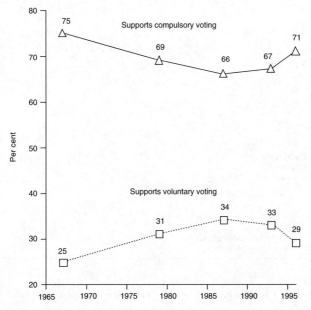

FIGURE 1.1   *Attitudes to compulsory voting, 1967–96*

Sources: 1967 and 1979, Australian National Political Attitudes surveys; 1987, 1993 and 1996, Australian Election Study surveys.

gone change over the past three decades, albeit gradually (Figure 1.1). In 1967, three-quarters of the electorate supported compulsory voting, a figure which declined to 69 per cent in 1979 and 66 per cent in 1987. Since then, perhaps in response to discussions among some of the state Liberal parties about abolishing it, support for compulsory voting has increased, to 71 per cent in 1996. Nevertheless, these levels of popular support remain remarkably high, given the apparent contradiction between democracy and compulsion. They confirm that the roots of the system lie in the mass utilitarian culture which grew up in the nineteenth century.

Notions of egalitarianism in economic views have experienced more change over the period since 1967 (Figure 1.2). In the 1960s, there was majority support for the view that both trade unions and big business had too much power, though with business being more heavily sanctioned by voters than the unions. Popular support for this view increased during the 1970s and 1980s, and since 1990 about eight out of ten have considered that both groups had too much power, though with business experiencing more opposition than the unions. Judged against the slow changes that

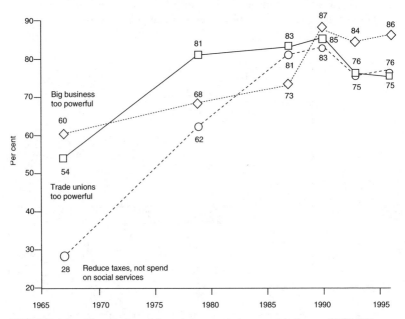

FIGURE 1.2   *Changes in public opinion towards economic issues, 1967–96**

*Estimates exclude middle categories

Sources: 1967 and 1979, Australian National Political Attitudes surveys; 1987–96, Australian Election Study surveys.

usually take place in such attitudes, these are substantial changes. At the same time, notions of egalitarianism, as reflected in the provision of social welfare rather than reduced taxes, have decreased. In 1967, only 28 per cent supported the individualist view that taxes should be reduced rather than more money spent on social services; by 1979 this had more than doubled, to 62 per cent, rising further to 81 per cent in 1987.

These changes are at least partly a consequence of short term shifts in the prevailing economic climate, away from state collectivism and towards a less regulated economy, which are the result of changes in the party in power and hence in the priorities of public policy. This has occurred across a range of societies over the same period, notably in Britain and the United States, where Margaret Thatcher and Ronald Reagan gave their respective names to a new and radical form of free market competition (Cooper, Kornberg and Mishler 1988). But the changes are also a result of longer term changes in the political culture, a conclusion which is further confirmed by the fact that the move away from collectivism in Australia and New Zealand was initiated by social democratic governments, who in principle should be most opposed to such a change (Castles, Gerritsen and Vowles 1995).

National identity and citizenship

During the nineteenth century, the prevailing sense of Australian national identity was British. Britain was responsible for the defence of Australia and for her external relations; there was a steady and frequent movement of the middle classes between the two countries; and the bulk of Australia's trading relations were with Britain. In the twentieth century, the sense of national identity was also British, but tempered with a greater awareness – following the experiences of the Second World War – that Australians were both part of Britain and separate from it. It was this apparent contradiction that provided the basis for the new concepts of Australian identity which began to emerge in the 1970s and 1980s.

This more pragmatic sense of Australian national identity was based on several changes in Australia's circumstances. The earliest change was the new reliance on the United States for defence, emphasised by Britain's inability to defend Australia during the Second World War and epitomised most dramatically by the fall of Singapore to the Japanese. Inevitably, American influence has permeated other aspects of Australian society, notably in the commercial sector. The postwar generation, which had grown up with these new strategic realities, came to believe that Britain no longer fulfilled Australian cultural aspirations. The post-1947 immigration of non-British settlers also gradually began to change the character of many Australian cities, though its impact on political institutions and public policy was, until comparatively recently, negligible. Finally, Britain's entry into the European Community in 1972 formalised the shifting trade relationships; Australia now had to seek a wider range of trading partners to survive in the modern world.

Despite the changing nature of Australian national identity in the 1970s and 1980s, the survey evidence suggests that popular feelings of national pride in Australia are higher than in any other country in the world, with the exception of the United States (Figure 1.3). When asked how proud they were to be Australian, no less than 70 per cent of the Australian respondents said that they were 'very proud', compared to 76 per cent of Americans. By contrast, only 54 per cent of the British and 53 per cent of the Irish respondents felt the same way. Levels of national pride are even lower in mainland Europe: the same survey found that only 40 per cent of Italians were very proud of their country, as were only 21 per cent of Germans, obvious legacies of their roles in the Second World War (Inglehart 1990: 411). By any standards, then, Australians have a strong sense of national pride.

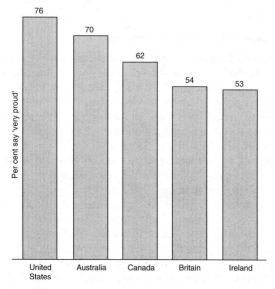

FIGURE 1.3   *National pride in the Anglo-American democracies* *

* 'Would you say that you are very proud, quite proud, not very proud or not at all proud to be [nationality]?' Figures for Britain and Ireland are for 1985, others 1981.

Source: Inglehart 1990: 411

Starting in the 1970s, Australian national identity has experienced two challenges. The first is multiculturalism and the second, to a much lesser extent, Aboriginal nationalism. Multiculturalism was first put forward as government policy in 1972, but its origins lie in postwar non-English speaking migration to Australia. By the late 1960s the prevailing assimilationist policies, by which settlers were expected to conform to the norms of white Anglo-Celtic Australia, were becoming increasingly unworkable and it was left to the 1972 Whitlam Labor government to revise them. In 1973 A. J. Grassby, the Minister for Immigration, produced the new government policy towards immigrants entitled *A Multicultural Society for the Future*. The adoption of the term 'multiculturalism' seems to have had much to do with the Canadian experience, where 'multiculturalism' – 'a policy of multiculturalism within a bilingual framework' (Berry and others 1977: 2) – had been adopted as government policy the year before.

Since 1973, a variety of government organisations and interest groups have popularised the concept of a multicultural society, and a range of policy initiatives have been introduced to promote it. In 1977 the Ethnic Affairs Council adopted a formal statement which advocated a multicultural society based on a diversity of ethnic groups and cultural identities, while recognising the importance of a common core of institutions, rights and obligations. It also made extensive recommendations on achieving equality of opportunity in the labour market, and equal access to government services and resources. Various government bodies were also established to develop government policy on multiculturalism. More recently, the government has defined multiculturalism in terms of cultural identity, social justice and economic efficiency (Office of Multicultural Affairs 1989: 3).

Aboriginal nationalism has had a much weaker influence on Australian national identity. Aborigines were effectively excluded from Australian history until relatively recently, in what has been called 'the cult of disremembering' (quoted in Thompson 1995: 93); indeed, all adult Aborigines were not entitled to vote until 1962 and they did not have the same electoral responsibilities as other Australians until 1984. Aboriginal political influence has been marginal because of their small size (1.6 per cent of the population in 1991); their geographical dispersion across the continent; and the absence of an articulate, educated middle class. By the early 1990s, this had begun to change. Affirmative action policies were producing more tertiary-educated Aborigines, particularly in law, while the 1992 *Mabo* judgment recognised that Aboriginal land ownership pre-dated white settlement. In 1990 the establishment of the elected Aboriginal and Torres Strait Islander Commission provided Aborigines with a degree of self-determination.

What do Australians see as being the major component of their national identity? The 1996 Australian Election Study survey asked respondents how important they considered seven characteristics were to being 'truly Australian', and how proud they were of Australia in eight areas of national endeavour. Table 1.3 shows that the most important prerequisite for being 'truly Australian' is considered to be respecting political institutions and laws; seven out of every ten respondents saw this as being very important. Three other achieved attributes are rated highly by the respondents – being able to speak English, feeling Australian, and having Australian citizenship. By contrast, ascribed attributes such as being Australian by birth or being Christian are not rated as highly. Consonant with an immigrant society, then, the sense of Australian national identity is one in which achieved attributes such as obeying laws or becoming a citizen are seen as much more important than an ascribed identity, gained through birth or descent.

TABLE 1.3   *Public opinion towards Australian national identity**

Very important for being Australian	(%)	Very proud of Australia	(%)
Achieved		*Cultural*	
Respecting Australia's political institutions and law	70	Its achievement in sports	69
Being able to speak English	69	Its scientific and technological achievements	46
Feeling Australian	69	Its history	39
Having Australian citizenship	62	Its achievements in the arts and literature	38
Ascribed		*Institutional*	
Being born in Australia	33	Australia's armed forces	28
Living in Australia most of one's life	32	The way democracy works	30
Being Christian	18	Its social security system	16
		Australia's economic achievements	11
		Its political influence in the world	9

* 'Some people say the following things are important for being truly Australian. Others say they are not important. How important do you think each thing is?' 'How proud are you of Australia in each of the following?'

Source: 1996 Australian Election Study survey.

The second part of Table 1.3 shows that the Australian sense of national pride has eclectic roots. While the overall sense of pride is high, as was demonstrated above, with the exception of sporting achievements, the foundations on which that pride rests do not receive widespread endorsement. For example, just under half of the respondents feel very proud of Australia's scientific and technological achievements, but only three in ten feel the same way about the operation of democracy, and only one in ten about economic achievements or Australia's influence in the world. Once again, national pride divides into two categories (as in the first part of the table based on a factor analysis of the items), this time broadly identifiable as cultural and institutional, with cultural pride being rated more highly than institutional pride.

It is these feelings of an achieved national identity which are at the heart of multiculturalism, since it emphasises the ability to become Australian by adoption, rather than excluding from the nation all those who have not been born in the country. At the same time, Labor's policies have been aimed mainly at fostering a sense of institutional pride in Australia's political, social and economic achievements. However, the relationship between these four measures and the vote shows that the only one which has a significant impact is institutional national pride, and those who take most pride in this aspect of Australia were also significantly more likely to vote Labor in 1996. By contrast, the remaining three measures are negatively related to Labor voting, though the relationships are not of the same magnitude. Labor was obviously able to mobilise voters on institutional pride, but was less effective in gaining popular support for an achieved sense of national identity.

In the past decade, attempts to generate a new sense of Australian national identity have been given expression in republicanism. Although republican sentiments have existed since white settlement, and surfaced briefly after the 1975 dismissal of the Whitlam Labor government by the Governor General, Sir John Kerr, they remained largely dormant until 1986 when the passage of the Australia Act ended the United Kingdom's power to legislate on Australian affairs. The debate received a further impetus in 1991 when Labor's centenary conference voted to establish an Australian republic. The idea of a republic gained its most powerful sponsor in Paul Keating, who saw the monarchy as a relic of Australia's colonial past and the creation of a republic as a logical step in cementing Australia's identity among its Asian neighbours.

In terms of public opinion, moving the constitutional issue of the head of state into party politics in the early 1990s has had the effect of increasing support for an Australian republic (Figure 1.4). Throughout the 1980s, just over four in ten voters were in favour of a republic, with little or no change in opinion. In 1993, support increased to 58 per cent, with a more modest increase to 60 per cent in 1996. This is a substantial shift and one which can only be explained by Labor's politicisation of the issue. Indeed, the issue is now strongly correlated with the vote, although Labor supporters are more united in their support for a change than are Liberal–

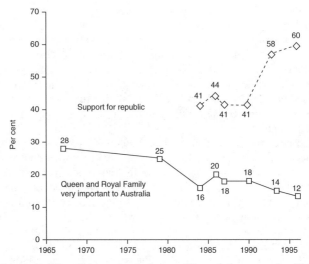

FIGURE 1.4   *Public opinion towards the republic and the monarchy, 1967–96* *

*Question wordings differ between surveys

Sources: 1967 and 1979, Australian National Political Attitudes surveys; Bean 1993b; 1987–96, Australian Election Study surveys.

National supporters for the maintenance of the *status quo* (Bean 1993b). At the same time, the belief that the Queen and royal family are very important to Australia has declined, to 12 per cent in 1996. The republican issue, together with the domestic travails of the family itself, have seen an unprecedented decline in their popular standing.

Political knowledge and civic education

As one of the major responsibilities of citizenship, democratic participation is predicated on the assumption that voters are sufficiently informed and knowledgeable about the political process to make balanced judgements. The perennial dilemma for democrats, however, is that there is often empirical evidence to show that this prerequisite is not met. The early roots of this democratic tradition are to be found in the work of Jean-Jacques Rousseau, Alexis de Tocqueville and John Stuart Mill. In the nineteenth century, it was feared that the tyranny of the ill-informed majority in a democracy would overwhelm vulnerable minorities. To cope with this problem, Mill advocated various electoral devices, such as plural voting for the educated and literacy tests for citizenship, while Tocqueville emphasised the American experience of pluralism, with the decentralisation of government administration and the widespread involvement of citizens in local decision making.

In the twentieth century, the experience of fascism and the results of the first opinion polls appeared to support the view that mass publics were largely ignorant of their civic responsibilities and open to persuasion by demagogues. This gave rise to the notion of democratic elitism, whereby citizens were charged with choosing between competing elites, and it was elite competition which provided the democratic element within modern societies, not political participation. As Schumpeter (1987: 295) argues in *Capitalism, Socialism and Democracy*, voters should elect an individual and then leave decision making to them: 'once they have elected an individual, political action is his business and not theirs.' Since the 1960s, this view has changed once again, and it is increasingly viewed as the state's responsibility to ensure that citizens are sufficiently informed to take political decisions.

Australia has followed the United States, France and some other countries by placing civic education in the mainstream of the educational curriculum. In 1994 the Labor government established a Civic Experts Group (CEG) chaired by a historian, Stuart MacIntyre, 'to prepare a strategic plan for a non-partisan program of public education on civic issues' (CEG 1994: 3). The CEG proposed an extensive program of civic education, which would take place mainly in schools; the government supported the majority of the CEG's recommendations and allocated $25 million for 'a comprehensive civics and citizenship education program' (Commonwealth Government 1995). The CEG viewed civic education largely in terms of knowledge about government machinery and processes, rather than in its social context, by emphasising community involvement and responsibility (Colebatch 1995).

The CEG commissioned a national opinion survey to ascertain the extent of civic knowledge. The results of the survey found that there was widespread ignorance about the workings of government, and about constitutional, citizenship and civic issues (CEG 1994: 132). While the survey found that there was a reasonable level of knowledge about voting and elections, most of the respondents knew little about the operation of the federal parliament, or about the legal system. As many international studies have demonstrated, the least well informed tend to be the young, those who have low levels of educational attainments, were born overseas, or who are women involved in home duties (CEG 1994: 135).

These results are largely confirmed by the 1996 Australian Election Study survey, which asked respondents whether nine factual statements about political institutions were true or false. Table 1.4 shows that while almost all knew that John Howard was leader of the Liberal Party, only about one in three knew that the House of Representatives does not have

75 members, that a deposit is required to stand for federal parliament or that federal parliaments are not elected every four years. Overall, the average voter could correctly answer only 2.8 out of the nine statements and only 7 per cent of the electorate correctly answered five out of the nine statements, with no one scoring more than five.

TABLE 1.4   *Basic political knowledge in the Australian electorate**

		correct	% answering: incorrect	don't know
1	John Howard is leader of the Liberal Party (T)	98	1	1
2	Australia became a federation in 1901 (T)	65	3	32
3	Parliament must be consulted before Australia signs a treaty (T)	47	19	34
4	The Senate election is based on proportional representation (T)	45	10	45
5	Senators may not be members of the Cabinet (F)	41	18	41
6	The constitution can only be changed by the High Court (F)	37	29	34
7	No one may stand for federal parliament unless they pay a deposit (T)	31	36	33
8	The longest time allowed between federal elections for the House of Representatives is four years (F)	31	55	14
9	There are 75 members of the House of Representatives (F)	21	30	49

* 'And finally, a quick quiz on Australian government. For each of the following statements, please say whether it is true or false.'

Source: 1996 Australian Election Study survey.

The main problem with any form of civic education designed to improve political knowledge is that it concentrates on increasing the factual base of knowledge within the electorate, rather than inculcating an awareness of how and why the democratic system works in the way that it does. In part, this stems from the fact that civic education is usually initiated by politicians, who wish to be noticed and to gain esteem. In part, too, it is a consequence of the belief that once simple factual knowledge gains root, other questions about the workings of the system will inevitably arise

(Colebatch 1995). Nevertheless, the experience of the United States has demonstrated that the sense of citizen duty has changed little in the past forty years, while by contrast turnout and political trust have declined dramatically. Citizen duty and knowledge of politics may be related to some aspects of political behaviour, but they have little influence on how the majority of citizens view and use the electoral process.

In the Australian context, the legacy of an enhanced level of political knowledge within the electorate is a strengthened national identity. However, it is not ascribed national identity which increases with political knowledge – in fact, it decreases – but achieved national identity. Thus the correlation between political knowledge and ascribed national identity is -0.08, while the correlation with achieved identity is 0.10. As the previous section outlined, it is achieved national identity – the belief that someone can acquire group membership, rather than inherit it through birth – which is at the core of multiculturalism. In theory at least, more political knowledge within the electorate should foster such pluralistic beliefs about the organisation of Australian society.

Conclusion

Of all of the aspects of a civil society, political culture and national identity are perhaps the most difficult to define, let alone to shape and direct, but they are also undoubtedly the most important for political stability. Political culture – what the British constitutional historian Walter Bagehot called 'the dull traditional habit of mankind' – controls the exercise of political authority, as well as defining the rights and obligations of citizens. A country with democratic institutions cannot sustain them for any period of time unless they are embedded within a democratic political culture. National identity, though linked to culture, is more likely to have implications for a country's external relations. A country that is uneasy with its national identity will be an unstable partner within the world of nations. We need only look as far as the history of Europe in the twentieth century to see the major problems that such circumstances can generate.

Australia has been fortunate in inheriting most of its political culture and the symbols of its national identity from Britain. The independence of the judiciary, the operation of free, competitive elections, and the peaceful handing over of political authority from one government to the next are all part of the British political heritage. Equally, by adopting British monarchical political symbols and practices, Australia has avoided the constitutional crises that have plagued many new democracies, as contemporary events in Russia aptly demonstrate. But in the late twentieth century, Australia stands on the threshold of a period of intense change in its views of itself and of its role in the wider world. Ironically, while it was immigration that gave Australian democracy and national identity its early stability, it has also been immigration – this time from countries outside the British political tradition – that has been the vehicle for change.

The components of the political culture are strong and to the extent that there has been any discernible shift, it is in the views of how interest groups such as trade unions or big business operate, or in how public policy should favour one or other group.

Other, less partisan aspects of the culture, such as opinions about compulsory voting, have been remarkably stable, suggesting that the transmission of these values from generation to generation remains effective. At the same time, there is most popular support for an achieved rather than an ascribed sense of national identity, and it is likely that this trend will continue as the proportion of non-English speaking immigrants and their Australian-born children within the population increases. However, while a generalised sense of national pride in Australia is one of the highest in the world, the only aspects of Australian society which people express great pride in is its sporting achievements. Fostering national pride in the other areas where Australia has truly excelled will be one of the challenges for civic education in the twenty-first century.

Note
My thanks to Clive Bean for his comments on an earlier draft of this chapter.

References
Aitkin, D. (1986), 'Australian Political Culture', *Australian Cultural History*, 5: 5–11.
Almond, G. and Verba, S. (1963), *The Civic Culture*, Princeton, NJ: Princeton University Press.
Almond, G. and Verba, S. (1980), *The Civic Culture Revisited*, Boston: Little, Brown.
Bean, C. (1993a), 'Conservative Cynicism: Political Culture in Australia', *International Journal of Public Opinion Research*, 5: 58–77.
Bean, C. (1993b), 'Public Attitudes on the Monarchy-Republic Issue', *Australian Journal of Political Science*, 28 (Special Issue): 190–206.
Berry, J. W. and others (1977), *Multiculturalism and Ethnic Attitudes in Canada*, Ottawa: Canadian Government Publishers.
Castles, F., Gerritsen, R. and Vowles, J. (eds) (1995), *The Great Experiment*, Sydney: Allen & Unwin.
CEG (Civics Expert Group) (1994), *Whereas the People: Civics and Citizenship Education*, Canberra: AGPS.
Colebatch, H. (1995), 'Political Science and Civic Knowledge', Paper presented at the Annual Conference of the Australasian Political Studies Association, Melbourne, September.
Commonwealth Government (1995), *Commonwealth Government Response to the Report of the Civics Expert Group*, Canberra: AGPS.
Cooper, B., Kornberg, A. and Mishler, W. (eds) (1988), *The Resurgence of Conservatism in Anglo-American Democracies*, Durham, NC: Duke University Press.
Gans, H. J. (1968), *More Equality*, New York: Random House.

Hancock, W. K. (1930), *Australia*, London: Ernest Benn.

Hartz, L. (1964), *The Founding of New Societies*, New York: Harcourt, Brace & World.

Inglehart, R. (1990), *Culture Shift in Advanced Industrial Society*, Princeton, NJ: Princeton University Press.

Lawson, S. and Maddox, G. (eds) (1993), 'Australia's Republican Question', *Australian Journal of Political Science*, Vol. 28 (Special Issue).

Leithner, C. (1994), 'Popular Support for Mr Keating's Republic', *Australian Journal of Political Science*, 29: 354–60.

Marshall, T. H. (1964), *Class, Citizenship and Social Development*, New York: Doubleday.

McAllister, I. (1992), *Political Behavior*, Melbourne: Longman Cheshire.

McAllister, I. (1993), 'Immigration, Bipartisanship and Public Opinion' in J. Jupp, and M. Kabala (eds), *The Politics of Immigration*, Melbourne: Bureau of Immigration Research.

Office of Multicultural Affairs (1989), *Multicultural Policies and Programs*, Canberra: AGPS.

Schumpeter, J. A. (1987) (originally published in 1943), *Capitalism, Socialism and Democracy*, London: Allen & Unwin.

Smith, A. D. (1981), *The Ethnic Revival*, Cambridge: Cambridge University Press.

Thompson, E. (1995), *Fair Enough: Egalitarianism in Australia*, Sydney: University of NSW Press.

Ward, R. (1958), *The Australian Legend*, Melbourne: Oxford University Press.

2

The constitutional system

Brian Galligan

As Australia approaches its constitutional centenary in 2001, there is a good deal of public interest in the constitution: in how well it has served the nation in the past century and how adequate it is for the future. That is too large a task for this chapter, which concentrates on recent developments in constitutional law and governance in the 1990s, and suggests that the constitutional system is capable of meeting contemporary challenges from globalisation and the new politics of human rights, Aboriginal peoples and the environment. Australia's constitutional system is both complex and flexible, allowing subtle and sophisticated developments over time. In any case, most of the pressing problems and challenges facing Australia today are not constitutional ones requiring constitutional change but political, economic and public policy ones requiring policy design, political will, popular mobilisation and some institutional restructuring, but mainly at the sub-constitutional level.

Current constitutional politics are inevitably shaped and constrained, although of course not entirely determined, by past institutional design and by established political practices, conventions, procedures and mind sets. Indeed, a constitutional system is a structural attempt to meet and process new political challenges by using and adapting old institutions and practices which preserve historic agreements and incorporate basic political values. Hence we begin with an examination of the constitutional system, focusing on the design features that are of contemporary interest or relevant to issues dealt with in this and subsequent chapters. The chapter has three main themes that are addressed in three sections: constitutional architecture, constitutional change and constitutional challenges. The focus is partly on the broader constitutional system and partly on the written document which is interpreted by the High Court.

Constitutional architecture

As I have argued at length elsewhere, Australia's constitutional system is fundamentally federal and republican rather than parliamentary and monarchic (Galligan 1995a). That is not to say that the parliamentary and, to a lesser extent, the monarchic parts are not important but rather that they are subservient to the overarching federal and republican parts. The arguments are summarised briefly here.

Federalism divides the totality of domestic political power between two spheres of government, Commonwealth and state, and thereby creates a system of multiple governments, each with limited powers. The broad division of powers and key institutions of government, including the branches of the Commonwealth government in some detail and state constitutions and their residual powers by way of guarantee, are specified in Australia's written constitution. Obviously, federalism precludes parliamentary sovereignty of the strong Westminster kind whereby it is said, with certain exaggeration, that parliament is supreme and can make virtually any laws it likes. In a federal system such as the Australian, governments have limited spheres of jurisdiction specified by the constitution and authoritatively interpreted and enforced by the High Court. Parliaments can only make laws within their allocated areas of jurisdiction. In view of this, it is surprising that there has been so much talk of parliamentary sovereignty among Australian judges, constitutional lawyers and political scientists. Apart from straight out misunderstanding that has been rife, claims of parliamentary sovereignty made about Australian parliaments, whether Commonwealth or state, can only mean the full exercise of legislative power within defined jurisdictional limits for governments, or the plenary extent of specific enumerated Commonwealth powers. But since neither of these usages entails sovereignty *per se*, it would be better to abandon altogether the pseudo-Westminster talk in favour of a constitutional discourse that suits the Australian federal system.

If Australian parliaments are not sovereign, then where does sovereignty lie? The answer that used to be given, before the passage of the Australia Acts in 1986 and various High Court decisions concerning implied rights in the early 1990s, was with the British parliament at Westminster. That august body had sovereignty which was recognised by the courts in Australia as well as in Britain. Where Westminster got its sovereignty from was not queried because that would have opened up an insoluble regression. Instead, it was acknowledged that Westminster was sovereign simply because it enjoyed political supremacy and that was recognised by the courts, or because the courts said parliament was sovereign and that established sovereignty as a legal attribute. This simple but deft conceptual solution, with its delicious ambivalence, satisfied the interests of both British and imperial politics and law: parliament was supreme politically and, in formally recognising that, the courts established a clear first principle of constitutional law. At the same time, the courts asserted their own primacy over constitutional law: in formally sanctioning parliament as sovereign, the courts affirmed their own special role as the authoritative sanctioners of sovereignty.

Surprisingly, for Australian constitutionalists until quite recently, extension of this flimsy theory of Westminster's parliamentary sovereignty was considered sufficient grounding for Australia's constitutional system. The Commonwealth constitution had legitimacy because it was an act of the sovereign Westminster parliament, it was said; and the states either derived their legitimacy from being incorporated into the Commonwealth constitution or from the continuation after federation of their colonial status which had been granted by Westminster statute in the nineteenth century. After the passage of the Australia Acts in 1986, which formally terminated any residual links with the British parliament, a new basis had to be found for the Australian constitutional system. This was found, belatedly, by the High Court in the sovereignty of the Australian people which was always available and in fact had been the real legitimating basis of the Australian constitutional system from the beginning. It is in this sense that it can be said Australia has a republican system: the sovereign people constituted themselves as a civil society with a complex set of governmental institutions, including formal monarchic executives, all subject to their constitution which is the supreme law. History as well as common sense confirms this view.

The people's constitution

One hundred years ago, in 1897, delegates elected by the people of the Australian colonies met in Adelaide to begin drafting the federal constitution. This was a second beginning because delegates appointed by the colonial parliaments had met at an earlier Sydney convention in 1891 and produced a draft constitution which was not adopted. While the Sydney convention was an important precursor and the 1891 draft provided something of a blueprint for the Adelaide convention, there was the fundamental difference of popular sovereignty that remains significant one hundred years later. The 1891 draft constitution was aborted because there was no political imperative for its implementation: it lacked popular support and colonial politicians were diverted to local issues such as, in New South Wales, fighting elections and accommodating Labor as a new force in colonial politics. Federation was revived with popular support for the cause and the elected delegates to the 1897–98 series of conventions beginning in Adelaide, although invariably established colonial politicians as had been the case in 1891, now had a popular mandate for their task. This provided both a motivation for, and a constraint upon, their work: the instrument they produced had to be acceptable to the people of the Australian colonies. After preliminary vetting by colonial parliaments and consideration of their proposals at a final Melbourne session in 1898, the draft constitution was submitted to popular referendum not once but twice. When a designated special majority was not achieved in New South Wales first time round certain amendments were made, including location of the capital in that state, and the amended draft was again submitted to the people and this time adopted. It was then sent to Westminster for formal enactment by the British parliament.

This switch to popular sovereignty between 1891 and 1897 was of fundamental significance for Australian constitutional theory and design. The constitution was in a very real sense the people's constitution because it had been drafted by their elected delegates and endorsed by them. Enactment by Westminster did not change that, nor did such enactment imply that the British parliament was sovereign and the Australian people subservient. These are fictions based on implausible notions of formal sovereignty as a single and indivisible source of legitimacy. The Australian colonists could have broken the tie with Britain by formally enacting the constitution in some local way, but that was not on the agenda. Many had personal ties with Britain, and there were sound geopolitical and economic, as well as strategic, reasons for remaining formally within the protective umbrella of the British empire.

Despite being passed by Westminster, the Australian constitution had all the essential attributes of federal republicanism from the beginning with the people controlling, through a written constitution, all the institutions of government. This was reflected in the constitution's amending formula, section 128, which required a majority of electors overall and a majority in a majority (four out of six) of the states. As parts of the constitution, parliaments and executives along with their formal vice-regal heads, were subject to the supreme will of the people. If the people so decided, the powers of the Commonwealth and state parliaments could be changed, for example constrained through adopting an entrenched bill of rights, and the formal trappings of monarchy entirely jettisoned. In this fundamental sense, the Australian system of government is comparable with the American, which, as Samuel Beer points out, is 'irreconcilably in conflict with the principle of hierarchy which ... necessarily implied parliamentary sovereignty over a unitary system' (Beer 1993: 137). The Australia Acts of 1986 were relatively trivial exercises in formal tidying up – manifestation of the autonomy and sovereignty of the Australian system rather than milestones in their realisation.

Australia has been characterised by strong constitutional practice but a poorly articulated constitutional culture. Despite almost a century of stable constitutional government, which has seen the flexible development of the constitutional system keep pace with the growth of nationhood, there has been surprisingly little attention to, or celebration of, the constitutional system. Increasing recognition of the republican attributes of the constitution based upon the sovereignty of the Australian people should enhance an appreciation of constitutionalism. That should also help in putting parliamentary responsible government into proper perspective.

Parliamentary responsible government and rights protection

The conventional wisdom of Australian political culture and of Australian political science has been the paradigm of 'party responsible government' (Parkin 1980). This was reinforced by public and professional interest which was drawn to the institutions and events of ongoing politics: the clash between political parties which have dominated Australian politics since 1910 and reinforce a Westminster-style adversarial model; an increasingly dominant executive controlling parliament, or at least the House of Representatives, through tight party discipline; big government, especially in the postwar era, served by a burgeoning bureaucracy; and prime ministerial dominance over both party and parliamentary politics. Political scientists and historians who commented upon or wrote about Australian politics in the postwar period typically disliked the constitution and federalism, and painted the states as colonial relics and political backwaters.

An important reason for the persistence of exaggerated notions of parliamentary responsible government was the omission of a bill of rights from the Australian constitution. Such omission was despite the fact that the Australian founders were strongly influenced by the American constitution: they copied its basic federal structure, incorporated a powerful Senate elected on a state franchise as part of the bicameral national legislature, and entrenched the judicature as the third branch of government. The High Court was made the 'keystone of the federal arch' with the role of authoritatively interpreting the constitution and keeping the Commonwealth and state governments and the various branches of government within their constitutionally designated areas. But the High Court was not given the additional role of enforcing an entrenched bill of rights which has become such a prominent part of rights protection in the United States and, more recently, Canada.

According to the mind of the founders, rights protection was more than adequately covered through the continuation of British and colonial institutions and practices which were preserved in the Australian constitutional system. The existing colonies were incorporated into the new federation as states and their constitutions and residual powers guaranteed. The conventional forms and practices of parliamentary responsible government were adopted for the new Commonwealth executive. In addition, there was the strong Australian tradition carried over from Britain and from colonial practice of an independent judiciary and the common law. Moreover, legal and political links with Britain were not entirely severed in the new constitutional founding and, especially after the 1920 *Engineers* decision, British legal and constitutional theory continued to influence Australia's practitioners.

Public confidence in the adequacy of parliamentary responsible government and the common law for protecting human rights continued into the 1960s with leading judges and politicians alike celebrating the efficacy of such a system. Sir Owen Dixon, a dominant influence on the High Court from his appointment in 1929 and chief justice from 1952 to 1964, defended Australia's steadfast faith in responsible government as an alternative to an American style bill of rights. Sir Robert Menzies popularised Dixon's defence of the Australian system of rights through the democratic accountability of the prime minister and ministers to parliament at every sitting. Menzies boasted that 'the rights of individuals in Australia are as adequately protected as they are in any other country in the world' because of 'our inheritance of British institutions and the principles of the Common Law' (Menzies 1967: 54; Galligan 1995b).

Menzies' defence of the Australian system was seriously flawed in a number of respects. The independence of parliament, particularly the House of Representatives, had been undermined by disciplined political parties so that the prime minister and his senior ministers controlled the house and not vice versa. Whether a minister resigned depended on retaining the prime minister's and not parliament's confidence, provided the prime minister retained control of his ruling party. The growth of 'big government' served by large bureaucracies meant that government had become more pervasive with many policy decisions being taken in the executive branch outside parliamentary scrutiny. In other words, parliament was no longer a sufficient check on prime ministerial and ministerial conduct nor an adequate means of protecting rights, despite Menzies' claims.

Discrimination against Aboriginal peoples

For Australia's own indigenous peoples, parliamentary responsible government had never been an adequate safeguard of rights; on the contrary, it had been the means of their denial. Quite deliberately, the Australian founders had not included any core statement of Australian citizenship or declaration of rights and entitlements in the constitution. There were a number of reasons for this besides confidence in the institutions of parliamentary responsible government and the common law inherited from Britain. One was respect for the states, which were left with jurisdiction over key areas of citizenship and rights, including police and criminal law as well as many of the human services and their own electoral and political systems. The states' established laws and practices regarding citizenship would continue after federation.

Another less honourable reason for eschewing citizenship rights or core values in the constitution was to allow deliberate discrimination against Aboriginal peoples and racial groups such as the Chinese. Most coloured aliens were to be ruthlessly excluded from entering Australia by the immigration power: legislation was swiftly passed and applied on racial grounds using elaborate dictation tests to exclude non-whites. But non-white people within Australia, most notably Aborigines and Torres Strait Islanders, would be systematically denied basic human rights and entitlements by both the states and the Commonwealth until the 1960s. The founders were reluctant to place any constraints upon the states' right to discriminate against Aboriginal people or other non-white minorities. Two of the states, Western Australia and Queensland, denied 'Aboriginal natives' the right to vote, and most of them had restrictive control regimes under the guise of 'Aboriginal protection'. There was also widespread discrimination against non-white aliens.

The new Commonwealth parliament was soon to follow worst state practice in actively discriminating against Aborigines. In one of its first major pieces of legislation, the 1902 Commonwealth Franchise Act, which is celebrated because it enfranchised women, Aboriginal natives of Australia as well as Asia, Africa and the Pacific Islands (except New Zealand) were denied the vote. This exclusion was routinely included in subsequent legislation granting social benefits and entitlements such as sickness and disability benefits and the maternity allowance. Successive Commonwealth governments, parliaments and bureaucrats maintained and extended this exclusionary regime: Aboriginal peoples were denied basic human rights, social entitlements and economic benefits, and were subjected to oppressive regulatory practices restricting marriage, movement and employment. Perhaps the most notorious example was the wholesale removal of children from their Aboriginal mothers, the tragedy of which is only now coming to public notice through the 'Stolen Generation' commission. Moreover, the Commonwealth's administration of the Northern Territory, which it took over from South Australia in 1911, was entirely consistent with that of the most oppressive states.

The denial of basic citizenship rights and benefits to Aboriginal peoples was not mandated by the constitution but done through legislative and administrative action on the part of the Commonwealth and the states. The constitution did not prevent this because it included no positive core definition of citizenship to which Aborigines could appeal, nor did it enumerate citizen rights and privileges that might have protected them. Rather, the constitution left such citizen rights and benefits to be legislated by Commonwealth and state parliaments which chose to exclude 'Aboriginal natives' and discriminate against them until the 1960s (Chesterman and Galligan forthcoming).

Australia's treatment of its indigenous peoples gives the lie to Menzies' boastful defence of our record in rights protection and was beginning to become an international embarrassment at the time. Nevertheless, the Menzies government had begun to change the exclusionary regime, amending the Franchise Act to allow Aboriginal people to vote in 1962 and putting the Aboriginal referendum in 1967 which gave the Commonwealth a power to make laws specifically for Aboriginal people and deleted from the constitution the exclusion of Aborigines from being counted in the census. The continuing disadvantaged status of Aboriginal peoples, however, has shown that removing discrimination and having special government programs and grants is not enough. While they remain the most disadvantaged group of Australians, indigenous people are now invoking international standards and using international forums to advance their cause, including demand for self determination, while institutions like the High Court are also relying upon international norms in weeding out discriminatory doctrines such as *terra nullius* from Australian law.

Labor and the constitution

In the past, the main challenge to Australia's federal constitution came from the Australian Labor Party (ALP) which, until the 1960s, was formally committed to the abolition of federalism and its replacement with a unitary system of government. The thirteen years of Labor government under prime ministers Hawke and Keating ending in 1996 showed how complete Labor's reconciliation with the federal constitution has been. The predominant party of government for both the Commonwealth and states during most of the 1980s and early 1990s, Labor wasted little time on trying to change the constitutional system, opting instead to improve the working of federalism and streamline intergovernmental arrangements.

Whitlam (1978) had confirmed after his less-than-satisfactory period in office, 1972–75, that the major obstacles against a program of reform were no longer constitutional but political. The subsequent Hawke and Keating Labor governments adopted the now orthodox policies of marketisation, preferring deregulation and market solutions to traditional state action and regulation. While federalism slowed the implementation of such policies compared with say New Zealand, Australia's more complicated constitutional system ensured more consensual action. One significant consequence is that there has not been the popular backlash experienced by New Zealand in the adoption of the 'mixed member proportional' (MMP) system, which puts in place an electoral system designed to fragment party representation and ensure coalition politics, thereby putting a break on party and executive dictatorship.

The challenges that Australia's constitutional system has to meet in the 1990s are not therefore the traditional ones of 'Labor versus the constitution', but whether it is an appropriate instrument for dealing with globalisation and the new politics of rights, Aboriginal people and the environment, and whether it allows effective and efficient public policy. Labor's reconciliation with the constitution was due partly to the transformation of the ALP: from a trade-union-based party, pledged to centralise power for purposes of statist intervention and economic control, to a party of public managers and economic rationalists, committed to greater reliance on the market and more effective targeting of welfare policies. But it was also partly due to the ability of the constitutional system to develop and change as a flexible instrument of government. This is taken up in the next section.

Constitutional change

In completing a path-breaking book on the High Court's development of the constitution by means of judicial review, Geoffrey Sawer concluded that Australia remained 'constitutionally speaking ... the frozen continent' (1967: 206). That was a surprising, and indeed an incorrect, conclusion because Sawer's book showed just how extensive judicial development of the constitution had been since federation. Others have repeated Sawer's pessimistic conclusion but usually in reference to Australia's supposed poor record on constitutional change through referendum. In reviewing Australia's record on constitutional change, we need to confront this weight of critical assumption.

There are three main ways in which the constitution can change: the first is by referendum; the second is by judicial review; and the third is through political innovation. The first two are well known but the third perhaps needs some explanation. The constitution may change because governments make novel use of available powers, or take initiatives which extend and develop established powers and are not challenged. Indeed, the significance of the first two more formal means of changing the constitution usually depends on governments taking advantage of the changes by using the new powers. For example, the constitution did not develop much during the 1920s because the conservative Bruce-Page government did not take advantage of the new vistas of Commonwealth power that the High Court opened up in the *Engineers* decision (1920). Another example is the use of the Commonwealth's section 96 power to make financial grants to the states on the terms and conditions the Commonwealth sees fit. This has allowed the Commonwealth to expand into social policy areas of education, health and community services, which are otherwise within state jurisdiction. As Whitlam put it, section 96 became Labor's 'new charter for socialisation'.

Referendums

There was no constitutional change by referendum during the Hawke and Keating Labor governments, although referendum proposals were put to the people in 1984 and 1988. Such negative results were perhaps surprising because the previous Fraser Liberal–National Party Coalition government had carried three out of four referendum proposals – on filling casual Senate vacancies, setting retirement ages for judges and allowing Territorial votes – in 1977. The earlier Whitlam government record, however, was one of failure to carry any proposals either on electoral machinery and recognition of local government in 1974 or power to set prices and incomes in 1973. But in 1967 there had been a record 90.77 per cent support for the Aboriginal proposals deleting exclusionary clauses from the constitution.

The 1984 proposals were for simultaneous elections for both houses of parliament and interchange of powers. The former proposal had been put previously by Whitlam and lost in 1974. This time it did slightly better, winning a bare majority of 50.60 per cent overall and two of the states, New South Wales and Victoria. People in the smaller states, however, were concerned about weakening the Senate's independence by making its electoral cycle the same as that of the House of Representatives.

The 1988 slate of referendums was hopelessly defeated, with all proposals securing only about one-third of the votes overall and winning in none of the states. The abysmal result in 1988 put paid to Labor's ambitious plans for more sweeping constitutional change to mark the bicentenary of European settlement in Australia, and in the 1990s made Prime Minister Keating cautious about putting his republican proposals to the people. Therefore it is worth considering what was proposed in 1988 and why the proposals failed so badly.

One proposal was for recognition of local government which had already been put and lost in 1974, and two others concerned parliamentary terms and 'fair' elections. These latter two would have made the Senate's term the same as that of the House of Representatives and controlled state electoral autonomy, both hard to sell to the Australian people who prize federalism and the states. The fourth proposal was for a so-called 'mini bill of rights': extending modest guarantees of rights which already apply to the Commonwealth to also apply to the states. There are three such guarantees: non-establishment of religion, paying just compensation for property acquired by government, and trial by jury for indictable offences. The massive defeat of all the 1988 referendums is readily explained by political circumstances: the Labor government was pre-empting more substantial proposals of the Constitutional Commission which would recommend putting a whole bill of rights into the constitution; and the government's support was in any case half-hearted – this invited opportunistic opposition from the Coalition parties and hostile state premiers who could see an easy victory in defeating the proposals. In any case, the Australian people have always been wary of proposals coming from the Commonwealth that impinge on the states and might alter the *status quo* in ways that are not fully apparent.

Far from showing that Australia is 'constitutionally speaking ... the frozen continent', the recent referendums are classic examples of incompetent attempts to achieve change which failed for predictable reasons. As Ackerman has emphasised in the American context, constitutional change quite properly requires special conditions of exhaustive discussion, persuasion, consensus and mobilisation to achieve the 'enhanced legitimacy' appropriate for 'higher lawmaking' (1991: 6). None of these special conditions were satisfied in 1988: the Labor government was pre-empting the final report and recommendations of its own commission; the opposition parties and key state premiers were hostile to the changes; there was little grass roots support, and certainly no popular movement, as in the highly successful 1967 Aboriginal referendums. In any case, the Australian constitution is usually changed more by judicial review than by formal referendum, and that has continued to be the case in recent times.

Judicial review

One significant development in constitutional politics has been heightened public awareness of the High Court's key role in making public and constitutional law. Previously the doctrine of 'strict and complete legalism', championed by Sir Owen Dixon, chief justice from 1952 to 1964, and insisted upon, somewhat implausibly, by his successor Sir Garfield Barwick, chief justice from 1964 to 1981, had masked the High Court's creative role in interpreting and developing the constitution. Such a role was clearly intended by the constitutional founders and periodically the High Court had been highly activist in making and changing constitutional law.

For example, in 1920 the court adopted a new method of constitutional interpretation in the *Engineers* decision which reversed the method of the previous two decades and opened up enormous scope for expansion of the Commonwealth's powers regardless of the effect on the states. Again in the 1940s a conservative High Court fashioned the section 92 guarantee of freedom of interstate trade into a constitutional right protecting private interstate traders, and used this to overrule the Chifley government's airline nationalisation and bank nationalisation legislation. In making such bold decisions, which reshaped the constitutional powers of government and shaped Australian politics and public policy, the High Court insisted it was only reading the letter of the constitutional text literally and applying it regardless of social considerations and policy consequences.

The Mason Court – Sir Anthony Mason was chief justice from 1987 to 1995 – changed all that, being both activist in a series of major decisions and realist in openly avowing its law making role. As Mason admitted: 'In Australia we have moved away from the declaratory theory and the doctrine of legalism to a species of legal realism' (Mason 1993: 164). Sir Gerard Brennan, who wrote the leading opinion in *Mabo* and succeeded

Mason as chief justice in 1995, acknowledged: 'The rhetoric based on strict and complete legalism masked the truth of the judicial method' (Brennan 1993: 213).

External affairs, treaty making and implementation

Mason and Brennan had led the High Court majority of four judges in the *Tasmanian Dam* case (1983) which gave the Commonwealth an enormous fillip of power by interpreting the external affairs power in a full and plenary way. Because of increasing globalisation and the High Court's generous interpretation of 'external affairs' in that case, as Mason pointed out, 'there are virtually no limits to the topics which may hereafter become the subject of international cooperation and international treaties or conventions' (*Tasmanian Dam* case 1983: 486). The result, as Brennan summed up the consequences of applying the interpretive method of *Engineers*, was that 'the position of the Commonwealth ... has waxed; and that of the states has waned' (*Tasmanian Dam* case 1983: 475).

In a string of subsequent decisions, the High Court affirmed and re-affirmed an extremely wide interpretation of the external affairs power which enables the Commonwealth to pass laws implementing treaties regardless of their subject matter or whether they intrude deeply into traditional state jurisdiction. Key decisions in the *Lemontyne Forest* case (1988), the *Queensland Rainforest* case (1988), *Polyukovich* (1991) and *Horta* (1994) affirmed the Commonwealth's expanding power over environmental policy and human rights. For its part, the Commonwealth Labor government was somewhat constrained by political considerations in extending its environmental and human rights initiatives. For example, despite flirting with the idea, Labor did not proceed with legislating a bill of rights based on the International Convention on Civil and Political Rights to which Australian was a party. This further illustrates the point that the expansive interpretation of Commonwealth powers by judicial review provides only the potential for political change: governments still have to occupy the field. And in the environmental area, the Commonwealth has been pursuing a more cooperative partnership with the states in working out new arrangements through COAG (Council of Australian Governments).

Under Australia's constitutional system, legislating to implement treaties into domestic law is entirely separate from treaty making, which is solely an executive function. That is in contrast to the United States where treaties have to be ratified by the Senate. Leaving treaty making solely as an executive function without restriction derives from its origins as a royal prerogative of the monarch. At federation, treaty making was still an imperial power so no special provision was made for it under the new Australian constitution. With the demise of the British empire and Australia's assuming full responsibility for its own affairs, treaty making became the sole prerogative of the Commonwealth government. Given increasing globalisation and the High Court's expansive interpretation of the external affairs power enabling the Commonwealth to legislate for the implementation of virtually any sort of treaty into domestic law, treaty making therefore becomes an easy way for the Commonwealth to build up an inventory of laws-in-waiting.

Labor and its ambitious Minister for Foreign Affairs, Senator Gareth Evans, engaged in a frenzy of treaty making with scant reference to parliament, the states or the public. Parliament was often not informed before treaties were entered into and became binding on Australia. Treaties were being entered into at the rate of between thirty and fifty per year and tabled in parliament in bulk every six months. Such contempt for parliament drew widespread criticism and a damning report, *Trick or Treaty?* (Parliament of the Commonwealth of Australia 1995), from the Senate Legal and Constitutional References Committee. Its reform recommendations were embraced by the Liberal and National parties Coalition in their electoral platform and announced as government policy in May 1996 by the new Minister for Foreign Affairs, Alexander Downer. The reform measures include tabling of treaties in parliament at least fifteen days before the government takes binding action (except for urgent treaties which require subsequent explanation); including with tabled treaties a National Interest Analysis explaining the need and likely impact; establishing a Parliamentary Joint Committee on Treaties; supporting a Treaties Council as an adjunct to COAG; and establishing a treaty database for easy access by the public. While it is too early to judge the effectiveness of the reforms, the example shows how excessive use of powers which are not constitutionally constrained, in this instance that of the executive to make treaties, can provoke a corrective political reaction and new sub-constitutional arrangements for its control (Galligan and Rimmer forthcoming).

The *Teoh* case (1995) added another wrinkle when the High Court ruled that treaties entered into by the Commonwealth government were not entirely quarantined from domestic law. In that case it was broadly affirmed, as the opinion of Mason and Deane put it, 'that the provisions of an international treaty to which Australia is a party do not form part of Australian law unless those provisions have been validly incorporated into our municipal law by statute' (*Teoh* case 1995: 361). Nevertheless, the court held that ratification of an international treaty was 'an adequate foundation for a legitimate expectation, absent statutory or executive indications to the contrary, that administrative decision-makers will act in conformity with the Convention' (Mason and Deane in *Teoh*: 374). At issue in the case was the failure of Commonwealth officials ordering the deportation of Mr Teoh, who was not an Australian citizen, for drug related charges to take account of the best interests of his children who were to remain in Australia. Since Australia had ratified the international covenant against cruelty to children, the judges ruled that officials should have considered the interests of the children. The Labor government reacted negatively and introduced a bill into parliament in June 1995 asserting that entering into an international treaty was not reason for raising expectations that government decision makers would act in accordance with a treaty if the relevant provisions had not been enacted into domestic law. The Liberal and National parties in opposition were supportive of the government, but civil libertarians and minor parties controlling the Senate were appalled at what they claimed was the government's double standard. However, the bill lapsed in the Senate prior to the March 1996 election.

Implied rights

In the area of rights, the High Court was not satisfied to leave the running to the Commonwealth executive and parliament after it had opened up broad jurisdictional scope via the external affairs power. In one of the most controversial developments in constitutional jurisprudence ever, the court began finding implied rights in the constitution in the 1990s. Earlier, in *Street v Queensland Bar Association* (1989), the High Court had given an expansive interpretation of section 117 of the constitution which prohibits discrimination against citizens of another state. In that case the court struck down state restrictions limiting professional membership of the Brisbane bar to those residing in the proximity. Overruling legislation on the basis of constitutional implications rather than specific clauses of the constitution was a bolder step.

In the *Political Advertising* case (1992), the High Court ruled that the Commonwealth's attempt to ban political advertising on the electronic media during election campaigns was invalid because it violated an implied right to freedom of communication. Such a right was implied by representative democracy which was embodied in the constitution, particularly in the voting provisions for the Senate, section 7, and the House of Representatives, section 24. In a related case, *Nationwide News* (1992), the High Court held that Commonwealth industrial relations legislation protecting members of the Industrial Relations Commission from criticism also breached the same guarantee of freedom of communication. These decisions provoked a storm of protest from politicians on both sides of politics, certain state premiers and others with a conservative notion of the role of the High Court.

This new development in bold judicial creativity in constitutional interpretation was complemented by the controversial *Mabo* decision (1992) which overturned the common law doctrine of *terra nullius* and recognised native title. Although not a constitutional decision, *Mabo* was, if anything, more significant because of its symbolic and practical consequences. Recognition of native title was symbolically important because it entailed acknowledging that Aboriginal peoples had been dispossessed on grounds that were now seen as discriminatory and unjust. Such acknowledgement is a prerequisite for reconciliation. The practical consequences were more limited because the High Court reaffirmed the sovereignty of governments in extinguishing native title. Hence only limited areas of land where title had not been extinguished by governments was involved. The Keating government followed the High Court's lead and passed legislation to set up national procedures for recognising native title, and Western Australia's unilateral attempt to extinguish native title was overruled by the High Court. The High Court's recent decision in the *Wik* case (1996) that Queensland pastoral leases had not extinguished native title has caused further furore and, at the time of writing, the Howard government's response was still awaited.

The scope and implications of the implied rights decisions were much exaggerated by proponents and critics alike, with both sides canvassing the likelihood of possible developments towards a judicially created bill of rights. However, such hopes and anxieties failed to take account of the limited nature of the decisions. The implied freedom found by the High Court was restricted to political discussion and was more a 'representation reinforcing' guarantee or limitation on the exercise of government power rather than a fundamental right *per se*. That was affirmed in the subsequent *Theophanous* case (1994).

After Chief Justice Mason had retired and Justice Deane had become governor general, the Brennan court signalled a more cautious approach in eschewing any implied right to free political speech in the *Langer* case (1996). Albert Langer, a radical activist, had been jailed by a Victorian court for contempt of court because he persisted in handing out leaflets advocating a method of preferential voting in which only minor party candidates were enumerated. Although Langer's method was actually accepted by the Electoral Commission as a valid expression of voter preferences, its advocacy during an election campaign had been banned in an amendment to the Electoral Act supported by the major parties. If ever there was a blatant infringement of the individual's right to free political speech this should have been it, but the High Court upheld the legislation and thereby scotched any prospects for a judicially created bill of rights.

In the subsequent *McGinty* case (1996), the Brennan court reaffirmed the earlier *McKinlay* decision (1975) of the Barwick court denying that 'one vote, one value' was implied in the Australian constitution through the requirement of section 24 that members of the House of Representatives must be 'directly chosen by the people'. McGinty was the Labor opposition leader in Western Australia who had challenged his state's electoral arrangements privileging country voters and favouring the non-Labor parties. The 'one vote, one value' claim has no historical basis in Australian constitutional law or electoral practice, but its proponents were encouraged by the United States example where such an implication had been read into the constitution by judges. Its rejection by the current High Court again signalled the end of a more adventurous decade of judicial review.

Constitutional change through political innovation

Although judicial review is more significant in changing the constitution system than referendum, it is less significant than innovation in actual political practice. This should not be surprising since the written constitution is a skeleton document, specifying only some of the detail of the whole constitutional system, and it is essentially the written text which judges interpret. Moreover, innovative governments can find novel ways of doing things which otherwise might lie outside their jurisdictional domain. Within Australia's federal constitution, much of the High Court's constitutional work has been in resolving jurisdictional disputes between the Commonwealth and the states and interpreting the federal division of powers. Jurisdictional boundaries can be changed and superseded, however, through cooperative agreements so that the court never gets to decide the issue. Such developments in a federal constitution are often the most significant ones, but receive less attention because they are not as easily specified as in referendums or particular cases decided by the High Court.

One enormously important change to legislative and executive relations in the Australian system mentioned earlier was the advent of disciplined party politics which the ALP introduced in its own parliamentary organisation and provoked on the part of others. As we have seen, this innovation enabled the party executive to control parliament, or at least the House of Representatives, rather than parliament controlling the executive as traditional Westminster theory, espoused as late as 1967 by Menzies, would have it. On the other hand, the dominance of minor parties and independents in the Senate because of the electoral system of proportional representation on a state-wide constituency basis has ensured that the Commonwealth government is unlikely to control the Senate. These two developments show how factors that are not strictly constitutional can produce fundamental changes to the way Australia's bicameral legislature works.

Another key area is that of constitutional convention governing the prime minister and cabinet – the 'efficient' executive, to borrow Bagehot's term. These bodies and the rules that govern their operation are not mentioned in the constitutional text at all, except for the stipulation that ministers must be, or become within three months, members of one or the other house of parliament. The executive chapter of the constitution focuses on the formal executive of Queen and vice-regal surrogate, the governor general, and is positively misleading in its archaic language of absolutist monarchic power. While the broad parameters of executive government have not changed in recent times, the executive is a complex and multi-faceted institution where evolving practice may accumulate into effective constitutional change.

Probably the most important factor shaping the development of the federal constitutional system is the ongoing dynamic of intergovernmental relations. If the Commonwealth and states are in conflict, jurisdictional disputes go to the High Court for resolution. But that is a winner-take-all venue that is not well suited to crafting complex intergovernmental arrangements. The obvious alternative is for governments to cooperate in devising mutually acceptable solutions and shared arrangements for handling complex policy areas in which both the Commonwealth and the states have policy interests. The environment is one area where shared arrangements are necessary and where jurisdictional disputes and court decisions have been replaced largely by intergovernmental arrangements (Lynch and Galligan 1996). COAG is an ongoing process of seeking intergovernmental ways of addressing policy areas of joint significance to the Commonwealth and states (Carroll and Painter 1995).

Constitutional challenges

The main constitutional challenges which the Australian system has to meet come from globalisation and the 'new politics'. Globalisation is a broad and disputed concept, and is used here to refer to the increasing internationalisation of decision making and standard setting, together with Australia's greater involvement in, and responsiveness to, such international regulatory regimes and to the world economy. With progressive deregulation of its economy and the dismantling of its traditional 'protective state', combined with a concerted national effort to become export oriented, Australia is being more closely integrated into the international economy. Due to rapid technological change in travel and communications, Australian citizens are directly linked into international networks and forums. The 'new politics' of social movements and groups, that are not geographically based, such as the environmental movement, or are demanding new jurisdictional arrangements, such as the Aboriginal peoples through self determination, are strongly influenced by globalisation. Their concerns are not those of the old politics of class differences between left and right, or Labor versus Liberal in the Australian context, or of federal conflict between the Commonwealth and states.

This has led some to question the suitability of the constitutional system for the twenty-first century. Federalism in particular is criticised as an inappropriate structure for responding to the challenges of globalisation threatening the nation–state. In an earlier era, critics argued that federalism was obsolete because it fragmented political action when its concentration at the national level was required to deal with business corporations which were becoming national and an economy which required macroeconomic management of the sort popularised by Keynes (Greenwood 1946). With the increasing dominance of transnational corporations and the world economy, modern critics argue that we need to concentrate political power nationally in order to deal with increasingly global policy making, international business and world economic markets.

But such a remedy hardly fits the problem. If the nation–state is indeed being undermined by globalisation, then attempting to bolster it to do more of the work of governance seems doomed to failure. As I have argued elsewhere, federalism is more compatible with globalisation than is the traditional sovereign nation state (Galligan 1996). That is, provided federalism is understood not in terms of discrete geographical units defined by regional lines on a map, but as a system of diffuse power centres, multiple government centres, overlapping and shared jurisdiction. In these aspects, federalism within a nation is not dissimilar to the emerging global order of transnational associations, international centres of policy making and rule setting, and overlapping of global and national policy making that both constrains the nation–state and also gives it a stake in larger international regimes of decision making and regulation (MacCormick 1993).

In addition, there are powerful structural and democratic reasons reinforcing the localism which sub-national units of government within a federal system provide. These are: one, popular demand for local governance and the subsidiary principle; two, technological change which favours and interconnects the local and the global, not just information technology but technologies that are changing work and living patterns; and three, the sheer complexity in human affairs which is enhanced, in a democracy, by public decision making at the local level as well as local participation in larger issues involving national government. In other words, democratic aspirations, technological change and institutional complexity are all, potentially at least, working in favour of consolidating sub-national centres of governance.

The need for constitutional change

If we accept the above arguments that the federal constitution is broadly suited to national governance at a time of increasing globalisation, there is not much need for major constitutional change. If anything, democratic imperatives combined with structural changes affecting peoples lives are reinforcing sub-national governments. If it were not for the bicentenary of 1988 and the forthcoming constitutional centenary of 2001, it is doubtful whether there would be much public interest in constitutional change. However, the centenary does encourage review with a view to reform, especially as it coincides with a new century and a new millennium.

Sufficient has been said in earlier sections about the adequacy of the existing constitutional system for dealing with the challenges of new political movements. Multiple governments enhance the opportunities for new movements to gain public voice and representation. Competition between governments for new support groups and coalitions increases the chances of new movements being included and their policy demands addressed. This has been true both for environmentalists and for Aboriginal peoples. If policy responses have been inadequate, politics and policy making rather than the constitution are to blame.

Nevertheless, there are a number of significant issues on the current constitutional agenda that merit attention. These are republicanising the head of state, recognising indigenous peoples in a preamble and possibly their special rights, such as an inherent right to self-determination, entrenching a bill of rights in the constitution, and cementing closer political relations with New Zealand.

Depending on what powers the Australian head of state were to have and whether that office were to be made popularly elected, republicanising the head of state would be either of symbolic or substantive significance. Unless there is agreement between the major political parties, there is not much likelihood of a referendum carrying. Moreover, since the people strongly prefer a popularly elected head of state whereas politicians prefer either nomination or election by parliamentarians, there is not much likelihood of a groundswell popular movement. In any case, with the Howard government opposed to such a move, it is doubtful whether it will get off the ground. Howard's promise to have a constitutional convention of elected and nominated delegates to consider this and other matters was a way of deflecting attention and pressure when he was opposition leader and the issue had been given some momentum by Prime Minister Keating's personal advocacy. So far at least, Prime Minister Howard has made no firm proposals for a constitutional convention and his government provided no funds for that purpose in the 1996–97 budget. Regularising the Australian federal republic through formally republicanising the head of state seems inevitable. But the political and technical difficulties are large, while the benefits are small or symbolic. Without leadership to mobilise popular consensus, the prospects for such change by the turn of the century are not strong.

The recognition of Australia's indigenous peoples in a constitutional preamble is a noble symbolic cause, but not one which so far commands much popular support. Nor is the constitutional entrenchment of an inherent right to self determination likely for the same reason. It would seem more appropriate for Aboriginal peoples and their supporters to concentrate efforts in devising sub-constitutional arrangements for self determination in areas such as the Torres Strait and in the Northern Territory, and to share in redesigning national institutions such as ATSIC to better suit indigenous aspirations.

Claiming Aboriginal sovereignty, either as a historical fact which needs recognition, as Henry Reynolds does in a recent provocative book (Reynolds 1996), or as a continuing right, as some activists such as Michael Mansell do, does not help because sovereignty has overtones of absolute and undivided authority. Such discourse is as unsuited to Australia's federal constitutional system as it is to traditional Aboriginal social organisation and occupation of Australia. Better to abandon overblown sovereignty talk altogether and articulate the limited character of governance of both Aboriginal tribes and colonial settlers. Once the sovereignty baggage is jettisoned, it is easier to see possibilities for designing institutions which allow variations of self rule and shared rule. Indeed, federalism is one form of this, and Aboriginal self government might be another with arrangements tailor-made for particular Aboriginal peoples in particular parts of Australia, such as the Torres Strait Islands and other parts of northern and western Australia.

An entrenched bill of rights would be the most significant of the above changes, but quite unlikely to occur. The Liberal and National parties, now dominant in Commonwealth and state government, are strongly opposed to a bill of rights, and not likely to bring forward a referendum proposal. Despite having a platform plank favouring a bill of rights, Labor parliamentarians are opposed to an entrenched bill because that would entail courts and judges rather than politicians and parliament having the final say on rights matters. Even if the Australian people favour an entrenched bill of rights (the Australian Right Project found from a national survey that some 70 per cent did), there is little prospect of consensus among political elites that would be necessary to mount a successful referendum.

Closer political relations with New Zealand are proceeding in the wake of the agreement on Closer Economic Relations and because of geographic proximity and traditional close links between the two countries. So far at least there has been no apparent need or much inclination for formalising closer political links by constitutional means. New Zealand delegates actually attended the original 1891 constitutional convention but subsequently took no further part in federation, despite 'Australasian' being retained in the name of the 1897–98 convention and the possibility of New Zealand subsequently joining the federation being left open. The evolving closer political relationship with New Zealand in areas of regulatory policy and mutual recognition show how transnational relations can develop without formal constitutional structures provided there is cooperation and trust.

Thus, the prospects for constitutional change through referendum are not strong in the immediate future, nor is the Brennan High Court likely to be as adventurous in developing the constitution as the previous Mason High Court was. But that does not mean that Australia is constitutionally a frozen continent because changes can occur and are occurring in the working of the constitutional system through the ongoing processes of intergovernmental relations and innovative uses of existing powers combined with restructuring of federal arrangements. The main challenges facing

Australia today are not constitutional ones but political economy and public policy ones requiring strong political leadership, constructive partnership between the Commonwealth and the states, sophisticated policy design and the redesign of sub-constitutional institutions and intergovernmental arrangements. The federal constitution, on the analysis presented here, is otherwise sufficiently flexible to allow Australia to meet the challenges of globalisation and domestic governance into the next century.

References

Ackerman, B. (1991), *We the People: Foundations*, Cambridge, MA: Harvard University Press.

Beer, S. H. (1993), *To Make a Nation: The Rediscovery of American Federalism*, Cambridge, MA: Harvard University Press.

Brennan, F. G. (1993), 'A critique of criticism', *Monash University Law Review*, 19: 213–16.

Carroll, P. and Painter, M. (1995) (eds), *Microeconomic Reform and Federalism*, Canberra: Federalism Research Unit, Australian National University.

Chesterman, J. and Galligan, B. (forthcoming), *Citizens Without Rights: Aborigines and Australian Citizenship*, Melbourne: Cambridge University Press.

Galligan, B. (1995a) *A Federal Republic: Australia's Constitutional System of Government*, Melbourne: Cambridge University Press.

Galligan, B. (1995b) 'Constitutionalism and the High Court' in S. Prasser, J. R. Nethercote and J. Warhurst (eds), *The Menzies Era*, Sydney: Hale & Iremonger.

Galligan, B. (1996) 'What is the Future of Federalism?', *Australian Journal of Public Administration*, 55(3):74–82.

Galligan, B. and Rimmer, B. (forthcoming), 'Political Dimensions of International Law in Australia' in B. Opeskin and D. Rothwell (eds), *International Law and Australian Federalism*, Melbourne: Melbourne University Press.

Greenwood, G. (1946), *The Future of Australian Federalism*, London: Cheshire.

Lynch, G. and Galligan, B. (1996), 'Environmental Policymaking in Australia: The Role of the Courts' in K. Holland, F. L. Morton and B. Galligan (eds), *Federalism and the Environment*, Westport, Conn.: Greenwood Press.

MacCormick, N. (1993), 'Beyond the sovereign state', *Modern Law Review*, 56: 1–18.

Mason, A. (1993), 'The role of the courts at the turn of the century', *Journal of Judicial Administration*, 3.

Menzies, R. G. (1967), *Central Power in the Australian Constitution*, London: Cassell.

Parkin, A. (1980), 'Pluralism and Australian political science', *Politics*, 15: 50–3.

Parliament of the Commonwealth of Australia (1995), *Trick or Treaty? Commonwealth Power to Make and Implement Treaties*, Report by the Senate Legal and Constitutional References Committee, Canberra: AGPS.

Reynolds, H. (1996), *Aboriginal Sovereignty: Reflections on race, state and nation*, Sydney: Allen & Unwin.

Sawer, G. (1967), *Australian Federalism in the Courts*, Melbourne: Melbourne University Press.

Whitlam, E. G. (1978), *Reform During Recession: The Way Ahead*, Toowong, Qld: University of Queensland ALP Club.

Cases

Australian Capital Television v Commonwealth (No. 2) 177 CLR 106
Engineers case (1920), *Amalgamated Society of Engineers v Adelaide Steamship Company* 28 CLR 129
Horta v Commonwealth (1996) 123 ALR 1
Langer v Commonwealth (1996) 134 ALR 400
Lemontyne Forest case, *Richardson v Forestry Commission* (1988) 77 ALR 237
Mabo v Queensland (No. 2) (1992) 175 ALR 1
McGinty v Western Australia (1996) 134 ALR 289
McKinlay case (1975), *Attorney-General (Cwlth) ex rel McKinlay v Commonwealth* 135 CLR 1
Minister for Immigration v Teoh (1995) 128 ALR 353
Nationwide News v Wells (1992) 177 CLR 1
Political Advertising case (1992)
Polyukovich v Commonwealth (1991) 172 CLR 501
Queensland Rainforest case, *Queensland v Commonwealth* (1989) 167 CLR 232
Street v Queensland Bar Association (1989) 168 CLR 461
Tasmanian Dams case, *Tasmania v Commonwealth* (1983) 158 CLR 1
Theophanous v Herald and Weekly Times (1994) 182 CLR 104
Wik case, *The Wik Peoples v The State of Queensland and Others* (1996) Unreported, High Court 23 December

3

Politics in the states

Campbell Sharman

For most of the time, politics is state[1] politics. When something needs attention in your neighbourhood, the chances are that an agency of the state government will be expected to look after the problem. The delivery of health, education, welfare, policing, and urban transport services are provided by state agencies, and the supply of water, electricity and gas all come from state owned or regulated bodies. Urban planning, zoning and the multitude of services required by Australia's cities from building codes to garbage collection, and from licensing electricians to shopping hours are all state responsibilities. Roads, ports, agriculture, mining and the ownership and use of land are managed by state governments, as are laws regulating public health, food standards, child welfare, most criminal law and the administration of justice. The sale of books and magazines, the regulation of prostitution, gambling and liquor consumption are state matters. The police are predominantly state police, and prisons are all state prisons.

The high politics of economic management, foreign affairs, international trade and defence, is the preserve of the national government. Its sole access to income and most sales taxes gives Canberra a powerful lever to buy a voice in a multiplicity of domestic policy areas, and there is hardly an area of government activity that does not rely on federal funds to a greater or lesser extent (Galligan, Hughes and Walsh 1991). But this involvement is predominantly in the form of transfer payments to individuals and state agencies, usually with conditions attached. Federal politics is the politics of revenue raising, income tax, tariffs, corporate finance and regulation, and of grants, payments, transfers, redistribution and equalisation. It is the politics of the cheque book, the intergovernmental meeting, and the national plan for some particular policy area.

The result is that Canberra is driven largely by the trade in information, expertise and influence. It is bureaucratic politics and the politics of the once or twice removed. Services may be paid and planned for by the Commonwealth, but they are delivered by the states. The remoteness of Canberra from the cutting edge of practical politics is built into the design of the federal system which preserves control of day to day politics for the six political communities that formed the federation in 1901. In spite of vigorous attempts by Canberra to become involved in grass roots politics, the distance remains. In some respects, the gap between citizens and the central government is being increased by corporatising, privatising, and exposing to competition some of the few Commonwealth agencies that deal directly with citizens — Qantas, Australia Post, the Commonwealth Bank, and Telstra. The result is that only at budget time does the hip-pocket nerve guarantee the immediacy of federal politics to the average person in the street.

In contrast, three themes run through state politics which guarantee the sensitivity of state government action to the bulk of voters. The first is the delivery of services. Above all, the administration of health and education dominate the concerns of the state public sector. In political salience, these are closely followed by the supply of public utilities and transport, welfare services and local government. There are always demands for more and better services, and it is the state government that has to provide them and is blamed for their shortcomings.

The second theme is development. State governments see increasing population, economic activity and wealth as major indicators of political success, but the states bear the practical consequences of economic growth in terms of increasing demand for public services and infrastructure (Head 1986). Because the control of land is predominantly a state responsibility, new economic activity, whether in the shape of agriculture, mining, industrial development or urban housing, is always a contentious matter for state politics. Quite apart from environmental concerns, competing claims for land use are often hotly contested, and drive much of the controversy that frequently surrounds local government.

The third theme is state control of the coercive power of government. State police maintain law and order, and state legislatures decide the ambit of criminal law. While there are many offences specified under Commonwealth laws, they deal with technical and specialist areas or relate to national defence or customs matters. The day to day traffic offence, assault, murder, drug offence, robbery and fraud all fall within the state responsibility for the administration of criminal justice. The politics of law and order is a perennially sensitive issue which has the potential to grab the headlines like no other. Nothing has demonstrated the dominance of the states in all aspects of policing than the issue of uniform gun control laws prompted by the Port Arthur massacre in April 1996. The prime minister may propose and fund a national gun control plan, but it is the legislatures and police services of the states that must cope with the problems of settling the details and putting the plan into effect, with all the political costs that this entails.

Related to this coercive power is the ability of the states to prohibit, restrict and license a wide range of day to day activities. From pest controllers to medical practitioners and from lawyers to hairdressers, the ability to pursue many occupations is dependent on possession of the appropriate licence from the state. All kinds of activities and sports require permits, and shops and many other premises need licensing before they can do business. In addition, the ownership of animals and the trade in agricultural products often require state permits or are controlled by state regulations. All this means that there are a multitude of interest groups clamouring to influence the nature and extent of state licensing powers. While licensing is a significant source of revenue for the states, it is equally important as a lever to influence other policy areas and a powerful source of state patronage.

State politics is community politics. However arbitrary the original decisions to draw state boundaries where they are, the borders now enclose political communities bound together by long established patterns of communication and service provision that are focused on the state capitals. This is so, even where the pre-eminent place of the state capital and its preoccupation with urban politics is resented by outlying regions whose claims for fair treatment by the state government are a common theme in state politics. The state as a political entity is an important point of attachment for Australians, particularly those living outside the urban areas of Canberra, Melbourne and Sydney (note Denmark and Sharman 1994). From the slogans on car licence plates to setting the time (Davison 1993), state government activity has a subtle influence on the way citizens define their identity.

Reinforcing the community basis of state politics, the media are largely state based if for no other reason than the great bulk of the population is clustered in a few large urban areas centred on state capitals. While the *Australian* and the *Australian Financial Review*, with their national circulation, have a growing influence, particularly among commercial and political elites, the state capital dailies dominate their markets and provide the coverage of local happenings that most readers require from the press. Television and radio are largely controlled by national networks, but the coverage of news and current affairs is strongly shaped by local concerns. Where there is dominance of the electronic media, it is the dominance of Sydney with its concentration of media interests, both public and private, rather than Canberra.

Pressures for change

The community basis of state politics and its dependence on a multiplicity of regionally based interests makes state politics conservative, pragmatic and strongly influenced by patronage. Political ideology and the clash of ideas have little place in state politics. The job of a state government is a never ending round of coping with competing claims for state action, expenditure, regulation, and subsidy, punctuated by criticism of state service delivery and the problem of finding the resources to pay for the public sector. Partisan activity in the states provides a shell for accommodating coalitions of interests based around core constituencies. For the Australian Labor Party (ALP) the core is composed of large sections of the trade union movement and welfare organisations, and for the Liberal Party, many of the commercial and industrial employer groups and their affiliated interests. But these core interests are supplemented by a wide and over-lapping range of groups who are dissatisfied with the opposing party's attitudes to particular policies at any given time. The big divide between the major parties is being in office or in opposition: this provides the context for understanding the great bulk of partisan activity at state level.

Change in such a system is to be taken piecemeal and only when it is demonstrated that the benefits will outweigh the costs, and can be accommodated without offending key interests. There may be innovation, but it is more likely to be in areas of service delivery and administration rather than radical shifts into new policy areas (Nelson 1985). But if incremental change has been the experience of state government in normal times, the period since the 1970s has not been normal. Beginning with the buffeting the states experienced from the radical alterations to the federal system attempted by the Whitlam ALP government from 1972 to 1975, state governments have had to cope with an increasingly rapid rate of change. Since the mid 1980s, there have been three interrelated sets of issues generating pressure for radical adaptation of the context, style and institutions of state politics.

The federal context

The first of these have been changes in the federal context of state politics. Much of this can be put down to the limitation of Commonwealth transfers to the states and the consequent budgetary stringencies faced by state governments. Equally important has been the steady change in the mode of transfer payments and the attempts by Canberra to restrict state discretion in the expenditure of Commonwealth funds (see generally Collins 1993; Galligan 1995: ch. 9). Both of these have led to state experimentation in revenue raising and in methods of cutting the costs of administration. As with the Whitlam period, attempts to limit the states have led to a vigorous reaction. This has taken the form of reshaping the state public sector in ways which have increased the resilience of state governments and confirmed their determination to retain broad discretion in the expenditure of funds in areas of political importance to the states (Parkin and Summers 1996).

Another aspect of the changing context has been the reluctant, and then enthusiastic, acceptance since the late 1980s of the virtues of competition in the supply of government services, and free trade across state borders (Carroll 1995; Parkin 1996b). Much of the drive for these changes sprang from the Commonwealth government's deregulatory policies of the mid 1980s, and the push for the removal of barriers to the free flow of goods and services across state borders recommended by the Hilmer Report (Hilmer 1993). This may be one of those few occasions where changing ideas have had a direct impact on state politics: there has been a sea change in the attitude of many senior state public officials and some state politicians who now accept the benefits of corporatising, privatising, and opening the state public sector to greater competition. New forms of service delivery, including the contracting out of services formerly provided by government departments, are transforming the way in which the state public sector operates (note Evatt Foundation 1996; Evatt Research Centre 1989). Many of these policies are only in the early stages of implementation and their effects, both economic and political, are yet to be assessed. But they represent a marked change from the structure and style of state administration in the past.

Failure

The second set of issues spring from economic and commercial failure. Three of the six states incurred massive public sector debt as a consequence of failed commercial speculation by public sector agencies in the 1980s. South Australia, Victoria and Western Australia lost billions of dollars with consequences that have scarred politics in these states. Queensland escaped the financial contagion of the 1980s only to suffer from an equally debilitating revelation of impropriety and corruption that destroyed the National Party government in 1989.

When coupled with changing attitudes to the role and operation of the public sector, the excesses of the 1980s have spurred the current generation of state governments towards an overhaul of the operation of state administration. The commitment to greater administrative responsibility for managers of state agencies has continued from the 1980s, but this has been supplemented by much more awareness of the need to have an effective monitoring system (Davis 1995). The key words now are accountability and openness, and all governments are being urged to enhance the transparency of public sector operation and involve state parliaments in this process (for example WACOG 1995–96).

Many of these administrative changes derive from political prudence and a need to demonstrate to the voting public that the problems of the past will not be repeated. But there has also been a concern with ethics and codes of conduct that expresses a genuine sense that standards of public probity have dropped. Whether the requirement that all government agencies produce codes of ethical conduct, and the proliferation ethics consultants will improve the performance and general image of the public sector remains to be seen. There is some irony in the fact that the embracing of a contract, market driven, user pays model of public service delivery is being matched with government soul searching about the need to instil a sense of public duty, community obligation and ethical conduct in the operation of public sector agencies (note Preston 1995).

Institutional shortcomings

The third element making for change in state politics might be summed up as a questioning of the institutions of government. Since the mid 1980s, various aspects of state government have been found wanting. In its most dramatic form, this has been shown by police corruption in New South Wales and Queensland of a kind that called into question the whole system of the administration of justice (Fitzgerald 1989; Wood 1996). Less dramatic, but of even greater significance for the governmental system, has been the disclosure of improper or reckless conduct by public officials, including ministers, in the use of power and public funds (Chaples and Page 1995; Coaldrake 1989; Hede, Prasser and Neylan 1992; Prasser, Wear and Nethercote 1990). A succession of commissions of inquiry in all states since 1980 has severely dented public trust in many aspects of government. The two best known of these inquiries were the Fitzgerald Commission into police corruption and related matters in Queensland, and the Western Australian Royal Commission which investigated the propriety of commercial activities of the Western Australian government, often referred to as WA Inc. (Stone 1993; 1994). The reports of these commissions (Fitzgerald 1989; WARC 1992) precipitated the electoral defeat of the two governments concerned, and the subsequent state governments established commissions of inquiry to recommend major structural changes to their systems of government, the Electoral and Administrative Review Commission in Queensland, and the Commission on Government in Western Australia.

These disclosures have fuelled a public questioning of the effectiveness of existing institutions for keeping public officials accountable. While there is little criticism of parliamentary government as an ideal, there have been repeated suggestions that state parliaments should work more effectively to scrutinise the operation of the executive, and that there should be a broader repertoire of institutions to keep government open and accountable. Some of this pressure has originated within parliaments themselves, particularly those where independent members of parliament have held the balance of power, or where upper houses have not had majorities controlled by the government of the day (Moon 1995; Smith R. 1995). State governments, however, have been reluctant to relinquish their dominance of the parliamentary process and have been much slower to accept the need for change to political institutions than they have for commercial and administrative ones.

Given this process of institutional questioning, it might be assumed that there would be evidence of major shifts in patterns of partisan voting at state elections. The failures and financial scandals of the 1980s and the major restructuring of the public sector could be seen as prompts for a realignment of the party system. Yet the extent of change in voting patterns since the mid 1980s has not been so dramatic as to point to an unequivocal shift in voting alignments in most states. It is true that the ALP has suffered major losses, but the question is whether these amount to a permanent and significant discontinuity in voting patterns. The same ambiguity extends to other trends which may signal longer term change, chief among them being the small but persistent rise in support for third party, single issue, and independent candidates.

Given the pragmatic nature of state politics, it could be argued that the political process at state level will adjust to these changes. The style may have altered but the game is the same: services must be provided, interests need to be accommodated, and the administration of the state must be paid for and run smoothly. But it may also be that the nature and extent of change in the state political arena is putting real strain on political parties as the agencies that provide some broad coherence to state politics.

Parties: Change and disenchantment

While political parties still play a critical role in shaping electoral contests and in recruiting government office holders, the major parties in the Australian states, in common with parties across western liberal democracies, are in a period of flux. The traditional picture of a mass party as an organisation with intra-party democracy and stress on rank and file participation has never been an accurate description of how large parties operate in practice. Party elites have always had disproportionate influence in the selection of officials and candidates, and the parliamentary representatives of the party, particularly on the conservative side of politics, have always played a dominant role in shaping party policy. But changes to the operation of both Labor and Liberal parties over the last decade have moved the operation of parties ever further from the control of the party membership, and into the hands of professional public relations consultants, policy advisers, polling organisations, and fund raisers.

These developments have been well documented elsewhere (Ward 1989; 1991), and they correspond with, and reinforce, changes to the nature of party membership. People now join parties less out of a sense of long term commitment to a party's broad ideology and more because of an interest in a particular set of policies or personal ambitions. Ward (1989) has shown an increasing turnover of branch membership, and an interest in single issues that can be pursued just as effectively outside a party as within it. Participation in political activity beyond the simple act of voting in elections, is moving away from the major parties and towards single issue groups, minor parties and lobbying (note Richardson 1995; Stewart and Ward 1996: ch. 12). The major parties are left as organisations run by a small group of party functionaries who contract out most of the traditional activities of parties to other agencies.

These changes have contributed to tensions between the branch membership of parties and the newly influential professional elements within party organisations. In several states these differences have been exacerbated by rivalries over policy and personal ambition so that there has been severe disruption of the party organisation. The most common source of these disputes has been the selection of candidates for parliamentary elections, and attempts to discipline members of the parliamentary party. These problems often reflect a clash between the preferences of the central executive and the parliamentary leadership on one side, and local branch members and disaffected members of parliament on the other. This situation can be exacerbated by factional disputes and allegations of branch stacking, the misuse of party procedures, and the betrayal of party policy. Some of these disputes have been bitter and have led to disaffected candidates standing as independents, and members of parliament resigning from the party to sit on the cross benches. This has recently occurred in the ALP in Victoria and New South Wales but most spectacularly in the Western Australian Liberal Party. There had been long standing conflict within the state branch of the Liberal Party over the selection of candidates which had led to the resignation from the party of state Liberal parliamentarians. In the preparations for the 1996 federal election, bitter arguments over the endorsement of candidates in Western Australia led to the expulsion of a senator and the election of two former Liberal MHRs as independents after particularly acrimonious campaigns.

Such events were of particular importance in the early 1990s and, for a time, three states (New South Wales, South Australia and Western Australia) had minority governments dependent for their survival on the support of independent members (Moon 1995; Smith R. 1995). In a fourth state, Tasmania, the government relied on a block of Green parliamentarians who had originally been elected as independents (Haward and Larmour 1993). In the five states retaining powerful upper houses, independents have also played an important role (note Bennet 1992: ch. 6). The continuing small but significant number of independent members in most state parliamentary chambers is an indication of a dissatisfaction with major party politics. While the label independent is used by candidates with very different political histories, a common theme is resignation from a major party and hostility to a dominant central party machine.

TABLE 3.1   *The partisan composition of Australian state legislatures, 1 June 1996*

State and party affiliation of members	Chamber and number of members	
New South Wales	Legislative Assembly	Legislative Council
Australian Democrats		1
Australian Labor Party	51	17
Better Future for our Children		1
Call to Australia		2
Greens		1
Liberal Party	29	12
National Party	16	6
Socialist Party		1
Independents	3	1
	99	42
Victoria	Legislative Assembly	Legislative Council
Australian Labor Party	29	10
Liberal Party	49	28
National Party	9	6
Independent	1	
	88	44
Queensland	Legislative Assembly	
Australian Labor Party	44	
Liberal Party	16	
National Party	28	
Independent	1	
	89	
Western Australia	Legislative Assembly	Legislative Council
Australian Labor Party	23	14
Greens WA		1
Liberal Party	26	15
National Party	6	3
Independents	2	1
	57	34
South Australia	House of Assembly	Legislative Council
Australian Democrats		2
Australian Labor Party	11	9
Liberal Party	35	11
	46	22
Tasmania	House of Assembly	Legislative Council
Australian Labor Party	14	3
Greens Tasmania	4	
Liberal Party	16	1
Independents	1	15
	35	19

These attitudes also characterise two of the smaller parties who have contested state elections, the Australian Democrats and, more recently, the Greens. Both these parties stress the importance of active participation by party members and have post-materialist agendas (Bean and Papadakis 1995), although the Australian Democrats have recently been moving towards the left of the political spectrum. Both have national politics as their prime focus, in large part because the system of proportional representation used for the Senate, the federal upper house, gives a chance to turn their dispersed electoral support (typically in a range up to 10 per cent) into parliamentary representation which may give them the balance of power (Bean and Papadakis 1995). For a similar reason, these parties aim to secure representation in the three state upper houses using proportional representation. In 1996, these parties held seats in the Legislative Councils of New South Wales (Australian Democrats), South Australia (Australian Democrats) and Western Australia (Greens), and have held the balance of power in the South Australian Legislative Council (see Table 3.1). Tasmania is the only state to have proportional representation for the election of lower house members, and a group of Green independents (now Greens) have played a major role in state politics since 1982. For the other states, the Australian Democrats and the Greens have, as yet, only a minor influence on state politics.

To these newer players must be added yet other groups (note Stewart and Ward 1996: ch. 11). Some, such as Grey Power or the Shooters Party, may run candidates in elections as a way of influencing government policy on particular issues. Other groups may not field candidates but use the electoral process as a way of publicising their policies by ranking the candidates of other parties according to their sympathy towards the group's goals. All of these developments have implications for the decline of the major political parties as associations incorporating broad public membership.

Patterns of state partisan support

This being said, parties continue to play a dominant role in the electoral process. Changes in party votes signal broad shifts in popular support for governments and, if there are major changes in the public sector, it might be expected that this would register in the share of the vote gained by competing parties at election time. As has been outlined, the last ten years have seen periods of rapid change and political turmoil in the public sectors of all states. The party system in terms of the pattern of partisan competition can be examined to see whether this turbulence has been reflected in partisan support and to put the results for recent elections in perspective.

The Australian party system has been notoriously stable since it emerged in its present form around 1910 (Jaensch 1994). The only lasting amendment to the competition between the left of centre Labor Party and the right of centre Liberal Party has been the Country Party (now National Party) which has played an important role in non-Labor politics since the 1920s in all states except South Australia and Tasmania. Much of the explanation for the stability of the Australian party system and the national level and in the states can be attributed to the fact that the ALP has usually been the largest party in terms of vote share at all elections in all states since 1920. While there are important variations in the party systems of the states (Sharman 1990), these stem predominantly from the nature of non-Labor politics in each state and the role of minor parties.

The ALP first preference vote thus provides a good measure of the extent of change in a state party system. Variation between 40 and 50 per cent of the vote can elect or defeat ALP governments, but a vote below 40 per cent signals a major decline for the party, and a vote below 30 per cent is a disaster which, if maintained, may signal the rise of an insurgent party and a major realignment. In the charts below (Figures 3.1 to 3.6), the ALP vote is shown for all general elections for state lower houses since 1945, and a two election moving average is provided to give a trend line.[2]

The charts also provide another indicator of change. This is the extent of the popular vote for minor party and independent candidates derived by subtracting the combined vote for the ALP, Liberal and National parties from the total valid vote. This residual can be used to show the extent of disillusionment with existing partisan choices. A figure below 10 per cent can be taken as not significant for the party system, even though it may be

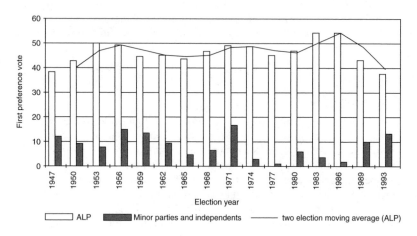

FIGURE 3.1   *Western Australian Legislative Assembly: Vote for ALP and for minor party and independent candidates, general elections, 1945–93*

important for the parliamentary system if these votes are sufficiently concentrated in electoral districts to elect the occasional independent and minor party candidate. As the vote approaches 20 per cent, substantial partisan turbulence is indicated.

Western Australia

Western Australia is in many ways a benchmark state. It has a strongly dichotomised style of politics even though a small National Party has played a critical role in non-Labor politics since 1945 (Sharman, Smith and Moon 1991). The state has had several alternations in government between Labor and non-Labor since 1945, has had an ALP vote exceeding 40 per cent for all but two elections (the first and last in the period) and has no consistent pattern of minor party or independent insurgency over the period. The Burke governments of 1983 and 1986 gained higher voter support for the ALP than ever before in the state, and the fall after 1986 was marked but not catastrophic. The financial scandals of what became known as WA Inc., drove the ALP from government in 1993 but did not change the party system. The only imponderables are whether, in the Legislative Assembly election due in early 1997, ALP support will return to a level above 40 per cent, and whether the problems in the Liberal Party machine will prompt an increase in the number of successful independent candidates. Neither of these developments, however, is likely to prompt major change to the party system, and those displeased with the policies of Premier Court and the Liberal Party (note Evatt Foundation 1996: ch. 14), are likely to move to support the ALP.

Victoria

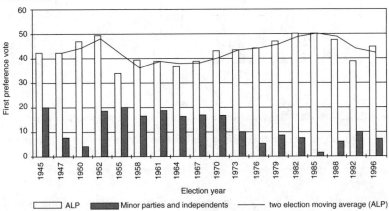

FIGURE 3.2   *Victorian Legislative Assembly: Vote for ALP and for minor party and independent candidates, general elections, 1945–96*

While the shape of the trend line for the Victorian ALP vote is similar to that of Western Australia with highs around 1950 and the mid 1980s, there are more elections (six) where the vote fell below 40 per cent. The effect of the split in the Labor Party and the creation of what became the Democratic Labor Party (DLP) drove the ALP vote down to 33 per cent in 1955. The slow decline of the DLP vote from a high near 20 per cent shows the damage done to the ALP by this party until the 1970s. The ALP did not regain a vote above 40 per cent until 1970 and did not win office until 1982. In 1982, the Cain Labor government began a period of ten years of ALP rule that attempted to resist much of the new style of deregulatory politics espoused by the Labor government in Canberra (Considine and Costar 1992). After a string of financial scandals, the Cain/ Kirner government fell from grace in 1992 with a substantial decline in electoral support, but at 38 per cent, still above that of 1955. By the election in early 1996, the ALP vote had risen above 40 per cent and there was no sign that the long term pattern of Victoria politics is about to change. Again, those dissatisfied with Premier Kennet and the policies of the Liberal Party (Evatt Foundation 1996: ch. 12) are likely to move to the ALP.

South Australia

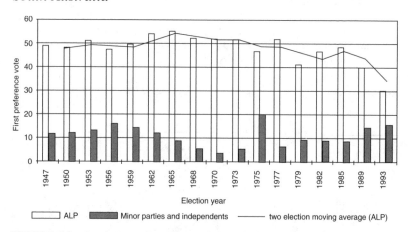

FIGURE 3.3   *South Australian House of Assembly: Vote for ALP and for minor party and independent candidates, general elections, 1945–93*

South Australia is the only state where the highest ALP vote for the period occurred in the 1960s. From a high of 55 per cent in 1965 when the Liberal and Country League Playford government finally lost office, the

ALP vote drifted to less than 50 per cent for all the elections in the 1980s with a minor peak at 48 per cent in 1989 (note Parkin and Patience 1992). By 1993 the vote had dropped dramatically to 30 per cent. At this election, the Bannon/Arnold ALP government was soundly defeated after the failure of a range of policies, including massive debts incurred from speculative activity by the State Bank. The trajectory of the ALP vote has been steeply down for the last two elections to 30 per cent, a level at which major change in the party system becomes possible. It is too early to say that the ALP vote has stabilised at this level or will start to rise, even though the vote has a long way to go before the ALP can reach a level to regain office.

The other element in a realignment requires the rise of new parties. The Democratic Labor Party played a minor role in South Australia after 1956 and disarray in the Liberal Party in the early 1970s led to the emergence of a moderately successful Liberal Movement with a peak vote in association with other minor and independent candidates of 19 per cent in 1975 (note Parkin 1981). After this date, the vote for minor party and independent candidates fell below 10 per cent and has only risen to 15 per cent of the vote in the last two elections. At the election due in 1997 it may be possible to see whether the support for Australian Democrat, Green and independent candidates amounts to a new and enduring element in South Australian elections for the lower house, but the tendency in South Australian politics has been for strong bipartism to reassert itself.

Queensland

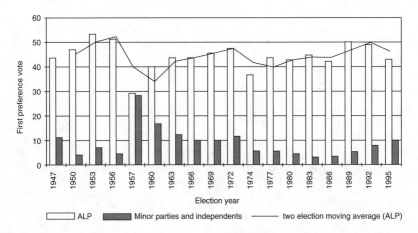

FIGURE 3.4 *Queensland Legislative Assembly: Vote for ALP and for minor party and independent candidates, general elections, 1945–95*

The ALP vote in Queensland is roughly the mirror image of South Australia; the party vote has trended up from the 1960s to a high point at the 1989 and 1992 elections. The 1950s split in the Labor Party was worse in Queensland than in any other state (Murray 1972), throwing the Gair ALP government out of office with a vote of 29 per cent in 1957, a drop of 22 per cent from the previous election. The Queensland, later Democratic, Labor Party gained 28 per cent of the vote in 1957 but this dropped substantially in subsequent elections and the party system was not permanently changed (note Hughes 1969).

The vigorous competition between the Liberal and National parties for the non-Labor vote in Queensland means that showing only the ALP vote masks a major source of variation in party politics in this state. The 1980s were dominated by increasing turmoil on the non-Labor side of politics and the idiosyncratic government of National Party Premier Bjelke-Petersen (Coaldrake 1989). The 9 per cent jump in the ALP vote in 1989 and the election of the Goss Labor government was, in large part, a response to the revelations by the Fitzgerald Commission regarding corruption in the previous National Party regime (Stevens and Wanna 1993). After the 1995 election, the Borbidge National Party/Liberal Party coalition won government by one seat at a by-election ordered by the Court of Disputed Returns. But this was not the result of any long term trend against the Labor Party and, at 42 per cent, Queensland in 1996 had the highest ALP vote in any state.

New South Wales

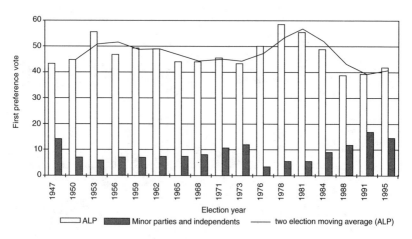

FIGURE 3.5   *New South Wales Legislative Assembly: Vote for ALP and for minor party and independent candidates, general elections, 1945–95*

The pattern in New South Wales is similar to that of Western Australia and Victoria except that the peak ALP vote, a remarkable 58 per cent of the first preference vote, was reached in the late 1970s rather than the mid 1980s. The bottoming of the ALP vote also occurred more than five years before the other states, with a postwar low of 38 per cent marking the defeat of the Wran/Unsworth government in 1988, a point from which the Labor Party has made only small gains.

The decline of the ALP vote since the late 1970s can be attributed, among other factors, to an unwillingness of the Wran Labor government to deal with serious problems in the structure of the public sector in New South Wales, including recurrent allegations of corruption (note Chaples, Nelson and Turner 1985). The reformist Liberal–National Party coalition government of Greiner, elected in 1988, set about changing the state's public sector in ways which have become commonplace in other states (Laffin and Painter 1995), but the fortunes of the Greiner government were to be affected by another aspect of the politics of New South Wales. The state has had a long tradition of electing a few independent candidates to its lower house, often from rural seats but, during the 1980s, from urban seats as well. In 1991 the combined independent and minor party vote reached 16 per cent and gave independent members the balance of power, with major and lasting consequences for the style of parliamentary government in the state (Smith R. 1995). The minority Greiner/Fahey government was defeated in 1995 and the Carr Labor government was elected, but only with 41 per cent of the first preference vote.

The change to the level of the ALP vote since 1988 represents a marked departure from the previous level of postwar electoral support with the last three elections having the lowest ALP vote since 1945. The vote for independent and minor party candidates has been around 15 per cent for the last two elections and the question must be asked if the picture of New South Wales as a solid ALP state should be modified. Has a small but significant portion of the ALP vote permanently shifted its allegiance to non-major party alternatives? The pattern of the last three elections shows that this may well be the case.

A final characteristic of the New South Wales vote is an apparent countercyclical response to the electoral success of the ALP at the national level. Since the 1930s, New South Wales has rarely had governments of the same partisan colour as Canberra, in marked contrast to Victoria (see Sharman 1994: 39–40). Whether this represents a conscious choice on the part of New South Wales voters or simply reflects the fact that they are half a cycle ahead (or behind) of the rest of Australia is a matter for speculation.

Tasmania

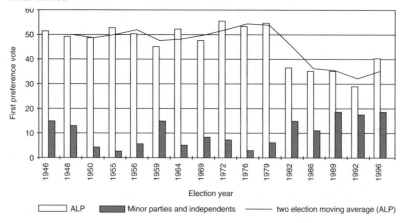

FIGURE 3.6   *Tasmanian House of Assembly: Vote for ALP and for minor party and independent candidates, general elections, 1945–96*

The island state has always had a distinctive style of government in which brokerage politics and strong regional loyalties within the state have been defining characteristics. These attributes of Tasmanian politics have been reinforced by features of the system of proportional representation used to elect the members of the House of Assembly, the lower house of the Tasmanian parliament (Newman 1992). These disparate elements have been accommodated by two large parties, Labor and Liberal, although the nature of these parties differs in several ways from their relatives in other states (Sharman, Smith and Moon 1991). The Labor Party in particular, has played a dominating role in state politics and reached a high point in the 1970s, winning all three elections with a share of first preference votes exceeding 50 per cent.

The clash between hydro-electric power development and environmental concerns split the Labor Party and precipitated a dramatic fall in the ALP vote from 54 per cent in 1979 to 37 per cent in 1982. From 1989 to 1992, a group of Green independent members of the Tasmanian lower house held the balance of power and proposed major changes to the style of Tasmanian government. Although the Liberal Party gained office in 1992 and, as a minority government, in 1996, the electoral support for minor party and independent candidates has remained constant at around 17 per cent for the last three elections, the ALP vote barely reaching 40 per cent in 1996. These developments are similar to those in New South Wales, except that the Tasmanian experience of decline in the ALP vote has been confirmed over a longer period. It appears that a substantial minority of

ALP voters has shifted to support independent and Green candidates. Given the nature of Tasmania's system of proportional representation for its lower house, these changes signal a significant alteration to both the electoral and the parliamentary party systems. Tasmania alone of all the states has clear evidence of a major change to its party system and the dynamics of parliamentary politics in its lower house.

State party systems: Reflecting or absorbing change?

The institutional context of state lower house party systems makes them very resistant to change. The naturally bifurcated character of parliamentary politics divided between government and opposition means that most voters have a dichotomous view of politics. This is reinforced by single member preferential voting in all but one of the state lower houses which fosters the belief that electoral politics, no matter how many candidates are on the ballot, is really about voting for one of two big parties. The rhetoric of the two largest parties strongly advocates a majoritarian views of the political process, where the contest is always between a government and an alternative government. All of these factors create a predisposition for the persistence of a party system dominated by two large parties.

In such a system, the largest party in opposition is always the beneficiary of government failures and incompetence. Throwing the governing rascals out implies throwing the opposition in. The renewal of governing ethos, policies and personnel is a task for existing opposition parties, not for entirely new parties or movements. The defeated governing party retires to opposition and the task of accumulating the support of those in the community who become disgruntled with the new government. The failures that followed from the Bannon, Bjelke-Peterson, Burke and Cain premierships require only that the relevant parties purge themselves and rebuild in a form that can reacquire the confidence of the electorate.

This kind of party system implies that major change to the party system itself occurs only in two circumstances: the emergence of new social groupings that cannot be incorporated within the existing large parties, or a major split in one of the existing large parties. Changes of the first kind have not occurred since the rise of the ALP around the turn of the century and the emergence of the Country Party in the 1920s (McAllister 1992: 110–20; Jaensch 1994: ch. 2). Changes of the latter kind have taken place on several occasions since 1910 but the wounded major party has eventually regrouped and re-emerged as one of the two dominant parties again. The clearest example of this in state politics was the split in the Queensland ALP that demolished the party in the 1957 election but did not displace it as a major party in subsequent elections.

If this description of the party system is accepted, failure in government, no matter how catastrophic, cannot lead by itself to the destruction of a large party. This is borne out by the experience of the ALP in Western Australia and Victoria, and the National Party in Queensland. All three states saw the governing party humbled in electoral defeat after the demonstration of ineptitude or corruption, but remain as the major opposition party and the principal beneficiary of the actions of subsequent governments. Queensland is the furthest through this process with two elections since the defeat of the National Party government in 1989. Victoria has had one election since 1992, and the ALP in Western Australia awaits its first post-defeat election in 1997. In Queensland and Victoria, some of the support for the former governing parties has returned, and only in Western Australia has the minor party and independent vote exceeded 10 per cent. For all these states, major government failure has not been synonymous with the destruction of the governing party.

But the pattern in the lower houses of the remaining states is not so straightforward. Tasmania has clearly experienced a major shift in its party system since the defeat of the ALP in 1982. With a major decline in the ALP vote, and minor party support running above 10 per cent for the last five elections, and above 15 per cent for the last three, there has been a split in ALP support if not in the party organisation itself. The defeat of the ALP government in 1982 corresponded with an inability to accommodate issues now championed by Greens and independents (Smith G. 1982), a constituency which now comprises above 10 per cent of the Tasmanian electorate. A similar if less sudden decline in ALP vote and rise in minor party and independent support has occurred in New South Wales and, in a still more muted form, in South Australia.

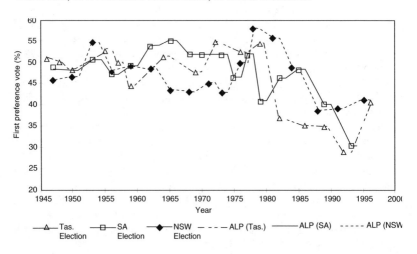

FIGURE 3.7   *Evidence of state party system change: First preference ALP vote, Tasmania, South Australia and New South Wales, 1945–96*

These trends are summarised in Figure 3.7. Perhaps we are seeing the consequences of a shift in social values – those who talk of the importance of post-industrial politics certainly think so (for example Papadakis 1990). But if this is the case, why only in these states? Why have the large parties not been able to absorb these new groups? And how permanent are the changes likely to be?

Some answers to these questions can be found in the institutional structure of both parties and of state governments. If, as Ward (1991) argues, the electoral professional party is to be the form in which large parties are to operate, the only reason to join such a party is as a prospective candidate or party official. This means that anyone who wants to participate in a political organisation which is broadly consultative must consider joining a small party or a single issue group, or the support group for an independent member of parliament. The consequence is that, for a small but significant group of politically concerned people, membership of a large party is no longer a satisfactory form of political participation. The ability of the organisations of the larger parties to accommodate such people has been lost. This tendency and its electoral consequences can be exacerbated by the style of particular party organisations, and this may provide some of the explanation for the problems of the ALP in New South Wales, South Australia and Tasmania, and the Liberal Party in Western Australia.

Where, as in Tasmania, proportional representation for lower house elections reduces the barriers for the representation of small parties and independents, such a shift in attitudes can result in a permanent change. For the other states, the institutional pull towards a simple dichotomy of choice at lower house elections will act to limit, if not reverse, the drift to small parties and independents. The moral seems to be that only when both the major parties operating in a majoritarian system have lost the trust of the electorate, as in the case of New Zealand, will major change to the party system be precipitated (note Mulgan 1995). But state politics operates in a context which works to minimise the chance of such an occurrence. The federal system disperses partisan tension across the two spheres of government, and the remorseless focus of state politics on providing community services acts as an insulation against attempts at rapid and large scale change which can alienate large sections of the community.

The abiding impression of state politics since the 1980s has been the persistence of its nature as the centre of gravity of political life in Australia. No matter how passionately political differences are debated, the pot-holes in the road still need to be fixed. The other impression is the resilience of the state political systems in absorbing radical changes to assumptions about the way government services should be delivered and operated. State public sector activity is now run on very different lines from those of twenty years ago. Most states have also had to cope with major political and budgetary problems brought on by the incompetence or recklessness of their political leaders. Yet these events have been digested, and remedies undertaken, without fanfare and, it must be said, without much credit from either commentators or the electorate. Perhaps this is as it should be: even visionaries and revolutionaries want their bank managers to be conservative, predictable and unobtrusive.

Notes

I would like to thank Imogen Fountain and Richard Miles for their assistance in obtaining some of the information on which this essay is based, and Jeremy Moon for his comments on a draft of this essay. The research on which the chapter is based is part of an Australian Research Council large grant project on politics and government in the Australian states.

1   The six Australian states have now been joined for many purposes by two self-governing territories, the Northern Territory and the Australian Capital Territory. While many of the general comments in this chapter relate to politics in these territories, their short history of self-government and the idiosyncrasies of their political circumstances has meant that they are not dealt with in this study (note Bennet 1992).

2   The data on which these charts are based are taken from Hughes and Graham (1968) and Hughes (1977; 1986), supplemented with figures from the various state electoral commissions. The presentation of such data in electronic form is part of a project funded by the Australian Research Council, the principal investigators being Jeremy Moon and Campbell Sharman, Political Science Department, University of Western Australia. The coding of the data in 1996 was undertaken by Imogen Fountain to whom I am indebted for preparing the electoral information on which these charts are based.

References

Bean, C. and Papadakis, E. (1995), 'Minor Parties and Independents: Electoral Bases and Future Prospects', *Australian Journal of Political Science*, 30: Special Issue: *Party Systems, Representation and Policy Making: Australian Trends in Comparative Perspective*, 111–26.

Bennet, S. (1992), *Affairs of State: Politics in the Australian States and Territories*, Sydney: Allen & Unwin.

Carroll, P. (1995), 'Mutual Recognition: Origins and Implementation', *Australian Journal of Public Administration*, 54(1): 35–45.

Chaples, E., Nelson, H. and Turner, K. (eds) (1985), *The Wran Model: Electoral Politics in New South Wales, 1981 and 1984*, Melbourne: Oxford University Press.

Chaples, E. and Page, B. (1995), 'The New South Wales Independent Commission Against Corruption' in M. Laffin, and M. Painter (eds), *Reform and Reversal: Lessons from the Coalition Government in New South Wales 1988–1995*, Melbourne: Macmillan.

Coaldrake, P. (1989), *Working the System: Government in Queensland*, Brisbane: University of Queensland Press

Considine, M. and Costar, B. (eds) (1992), *Trials in Power: Cain Kirner and Victoria 1982–1992*, Melbourne: Melbourne University Press.

Collins, D. J. (ed.) (1993), *Vertical Fiscal Imbalance and the Allocation of Taxing Powers*, Sydney: Australian Tax Research Foundation (Conference Series No. 13).

Davis, G. (1995), *A Government of Routines: Executive Coordination in an Australian State*, Melbourne: Macmillan.

Davison, G. (1993), *The Unforgiving Minute: How Australia Learned to Tell the Time*, Melbourne: Oxford University Press.

Denemark, D. and Sharman C. (1994), 'Political Efficacy, Involvement and Trust: Testing for Regional Political Culture in Australia', *Australian Journal of Political Science*, 29 Special Issue: *Election '93*, 81–102.

Evatt Foundation (1996), *The State of Australia*, Sydney: Evatt Foundation.

Evatt Research Centre (1989), *State of Siege: Renewal or Privatisation for Australian State Public Services?*, Sydney: Pluto Press.

Fitzgerald, G. E. (1989), *Queensland, Commission of Inquiry Into Possible Illegal Activities and Associated Police Misconduct*, (Fitzgerald Report) Report of a Commission of Inquiry Pursuant to Orders in Council, Brisbane: Queensland Government Printer.

Galligan, B. (1995), *A Federal Republic: Australians Constitutional System of Government*, Melbourne: Cambridge University Press.

Galligan, B., Hughes, O. and Walsh, C. (eds) (1991), *Intergovernmental Relations and Public Policy*, Sydney: Allen & Unwin.

Haward, M. and Larmour, P. (eds) (1993), *The Tasmanian Parliamentary Accord and Public Policy 1989–92: Accommodating the New Politics?*, Canberra: Federalism Research Centre, Australian National University.

Head, B. (1986), 'Economic Development in State and Federal Politics' in B. Head (ed.), *The Politics of Development in Australia*, Sydney: Allen & Unwin.

Hede, A., Prasser, S. and Neylan, M. (eds) (1992), *Keeping them Honest: Democratic Reform in Queensland*, Brisbane: University of Queensland Press.

Hilmer, F. G. (1993), *National Competition Policy: A Report by the Independent Committee of Inquiry*, (Hilmer Report), Independent Committee of Inquiry into Competition Policy in Australia, Canberra: AGPS.

Hughes, C. A. (1969), *Images and Issues: The Queensland State Elections of 1963 and 1966*, Canberra: Australian National University Press.

Hughes, C. A. (1977), *A Handbook of Australian Government & Politics, 1965–1974*, Canberra: Australian National University Press.

Hughes, C. A. (1986) *A Handbook of Australian Government & Politics, 1967–1984*, Canberra: Australian National University Press.

Hughes, C. A. and Graham, B. D. (1968), *A Handbook of Australian Government & Politics, 1890–1964*, Canberra: Australian National University Press.

Jaensch, D. (1994), *Power Politics: Australia's Party System*, 2nd edn, Sydney: Allen & Unwin.

Laffin, M. and Painter, M. (eds) (1995), *Reform and Reversal: Lessons from the Coalition Government in New South Wales 1988–1995*, Melbourne: Macmillan.

McAllister, I. (1992), *Political Behaviour: Citizens, Parties and Elites in Australia*, Melbourne: Longman Cheshire.

Moon, J. (1995), 'Minority Government in the Australian States: From Ersatz Majoritarianism to Minoritarianism?', *Australian journal of Political Science*, 30: Special Issue: *Party Systems, Representation and Policy Making: Australian Trends in Comparative Perspective*, 142–63.

Mulgan, R. (1995), 'The Democratic Failure of Single-Party Government: The New Zealand Experience', *Australian Journal of Political Science*, 30: Special Issue: *Party Systems, Representation and Policy Making: Australian Trends in Comparative Perspective*, 82–95.

Murray, R. (1972), *The Split: Australian Labor in the Fifties*, Melbourne: Cheshire.

Nelson, H. (1985), 'Policy Innovation in the Australian States', *Politics*, 20: 77–88.

Newman, T. (1992), *Hare-Clark in Tasmania: Representation of all Opinions*, Hobart: Joint Library Committee of the Parliament of Tasmania.

Papadakis, E. (1990), 'Minor Parties, the Environment and the New Politics' in C. Bean, I. McAllister and J. Warhurst (eds), *The Greening of Australian Politics: The 1990 Federal Election*, Melbourne: Longman Cheshire.

Parkin, A. (1981), 'The Dunstan Governments: A Political Synopsis' in A. Parkin and A. Patience (eds), *The Dunstan Decade: Social Democracy at the State Level*, Melbourne: Longman Cheshire.

Parkin, A. (ed.) (1996a), *South Australia, Federalism and Public Policy: Essays Exploring the Impact of the Australian Federal System on Government and Public Policy in South Australia*, Canberra: Federalism Research Centre, Australian National University.

Parkin, A. (1996b), 'South Australia, Federalism and the 1990s: From Co-operative to Competitive Reform' in A. Parkin, *South Australia, Federalism and Public Policy: Essays Exploring the Impact of the Australian Federal System on Government and Public Policy in South Australia*, Canberra: Federalism Research Centre, Australian National University.

Parkin, A. and Patience, A. (eds) (1992), *The Bannon Decade: The Politics of Restraint in South Australia*, Sydney: Allen & Unwin.

Parkin, A. and Summers, J. (1996), 'The States, South Australia and the Australian Federal System' in A. Parkin, *South Australia, Federalism and Public Policy: Essays Exploring the Impact of the Australian Federal System on Government and Public Policy in South Australia*, Canberra: Federalism Research Centre, Australian National University.

Prasser, S., Wear, R. and Nethercote, J. R. (eds) (1990), *Corruption and Reform: The Fitzgerald Vision*, Brisbane: University of Queensland Press.

Preston, N. (1995), 'Public Sector Ethics in Australia: A Review', *Australian Journal of Public Administration*, 54: 462–70.

Richardson. J. (1995), 'Interest Groups and Representation', *Australian Journal of Political Science*, 30: Special Issue: *Party Systems, Representation and Policy Making: Australian Trends in Comparative Perspective*, 61–81.

Sharman, C. (1990), 'The Party Systems of the Australian States: Patterns of Partisan Competition 1945–1986', *Publius: The Journal of Federalism*, 20(4) Fall 1990: 85–104.

Sharman, C. (1994) 'Discipline and Disharmony: Party and the Operation of the Australian Federal System' in C. Sharman (ed.), *Parties and Federalism in Australia and Canada*, Canberra: Federalism Research Centre, Australian National University.

Sharman, C., Smith, G. and Moon, J. (1991), 'The Party System and Change of Regime: The Structure of Partisan Choice in Tasmania and Western Australia', *Australian Journal of Political Science*, 26: 409–28.

Smith, G. (1982), 'The Tasmanian House of Assembly Election of 1982', *Politics*, 17(2): 121–7

Smith, R. (1995), 'Parliament' in M. Laffin, and M. Painter (eds), *Reform and Reversal: Lessons from the Coalition Government in New South Wales 1988–1995*, Melbourne: Macmillan.

Stevens, B. and Wanna, J. (eds) (1993), *The Goss Government: Promise and Performance of Labor in Queensland*, Melbourne: Macmillan.

Stewart R. and Ward, I. (1996), *Politics One*, 2nd edn, Melbourne: Macmillan

Stone, B. (1993), 'Accountability Reform in Australia: The WA Inc Royal Commission in Context', *Australian Quarterly*, 65(3): 17–29.

Stone, B. (1994), 'Constitutional Design, Accountability and Western Australian Government: Thinking With and Against the "WA Inc" Royal Commission', *University of Western Australia Law Review*, 24: 51–67.

Ward, I. (1989), 'Two Faces of the ALP in the 1980s', *Australian and New Zealand Journal of Sociology*, 25: 165–86.

Ward, I. (1991), 'The Changing Organisational Nature of Australia's Political Parties', *Journal of Commonwealth and Comparative Politics*, 29: 153–74.

WACOG (Western Australia, Commission on Government) (1995–96), *Report, Nos 1–5*, Perth: Commission on Government.

WARC (Western Australia, Royal Commission into Commercial Activities of Government and Other Matters) (1992), *Report*, Perth: WA Inc. Report.

Wood, J. R. T. (1996), *Interim Report*, (Wood Commission), New South Wales, Royal Commission into the Police Service, Sydney: Government of New South Wales.

4

Parliament

John Uhr

Introduction

This chapter reviews a range of institutional developments in the Australian federal parliament over the last decade. Space does not allow a detailed account of the effect on parliamentary institutions of the Australian constitutional and electoral systems. Although the focus here is on recent parliamentary changes, it is generally true that the power, structure and composition of parliament reflects the formative influence of earlier designs included in both constitution and electoral law (see for example Reid and Forrest 1989: 84–131).

Two brief preliminary comments are in order. First, the constitution establishes the parliament as the formal law-making authority, defines the general scope of the legislative power which parliament may exercise, lays down the basic parliamentary structure which is organised around a bicameral (that is, two house) system with a House of Representatives and a Senate, and specifies the narrow but important set of limitations on the legislative power of the Senate. Second, the electoral system is based on constitutional provisions relating to the distribution of House of Representatives seats among the states according to population, and to the equal representation of each original state in the Senate, the size of which is limited to half that of the lower house. Through such acts as the Electoral Act and the Franchise Act, parliament itself has determined many important details of parliamentary representation, such as compulsory voting. For our purposes, one of the most important of these details is the 1948 establishment of proportional representation as the basis of Senate representation (see Reid and Forrest 1989: 112–14, 122–4).

One effect of this adoption of proportional representation has been to reinforce a basic distinction between the political orientation of the two houses. The lower house is often regarded as 'the house of government' by virtue of the fact that the government of the day is formed from the party or parties holding a majority in that house, and further that the leading minority party forms the official opposition or 'shadow government' (Browning 1989: 39–48, 117–21). The Senate is often regarded as 'the house of review', suggesting that its primary role is one of scrutiny and review of government operations, as distinct from more proactive tasks in which it might collide with the lower house over the conduct and direction of government. This orientation towards 'reviewing government' as distinct from 'doing government' is reinforced by the fact that the balance of power in the Senate is generally held by what are termed 'the minor parties', that is, those smaller parties or independents which have no prospect or even real intention of forming government, but a public commitment to making government more open and accountable (Evans 1995: 11–14, 117–20).

The mention of political parties forces us to acknowledge that 'the parliament' is really not one unified or coherent political institution, but instead a set of overlapping institutions. Some parliamentary institutions are formal constitutional mechanisms, like the House of Representatives and the Senate, and then their various committees. Others are less formal but no less real, like the three political parties and five independents currently represented in the lower house, and the five political parties and one independent represented in the Senate, not to mention the growing network of unofficial but influential set of party working groups and policy committees. Other parliamentary institutions include the specialist parliamentary clerks and other officials who advise members and exercise considerable influence through their management of much of the detail of parliamentary business; or outside public service bodies, like the national audit office, which operate independently of government in generating information and reporting to parliament about the performance of government operations. Parliament is thus something of an umbrella under which are sheltered many competing political bodies (Solomon 1986).

There is bound to be conflict among so many interrelated institutions. The constitution is realistic in anticipating partisan conflict between parliament and the interests of what it openly recognises as 'the government' (see for example Constitution section 53), but it is important to note that its conflict-resolution mechanisms are primarily directed to 'disagreements' between a government and the Senate over government legislation. Although governments have anything up to a third of their ministry drawn from the Senate and, to use the 1993–96 figures, introduce around a third of their legislation in the upper house, the rules of the constitutional game pay particular attention to disagreements by the Senate to government bills passed by 'the house of government' (see Constitution sections 53–57).

Over the last decade, conflict has intensified between governments and the Senate, or at least between parties in government and the non-government parties which dominate the Senate. As the constitutional framers appreciated, 'the parliament' is unlikely to act as one coherent political institution. It should come as no surprise then to find that this untidy set of political institutions which we call 'parliament' has considerable capacity to complicate the life of governments. But it is another question again as to whether parliament has the capacity to move on from this spoilers' role and make positive contributions to Australian government.

Does parliament matter?

There is a risk in examining parliament that one might unduly inflate its role in Australian government, which is a form of representative government often called a 'parliamentary government' or 'parliamentary democracy'. The standard political labels suggest that parliament is a central feature of Australian government, but labels can be misleading. As we shall see, parliament performs many important roles in Australian government – although being *at the centre of* the political process is not the same as being *central to* the political process.

A basic task performed by parliament is acting as an electoral college to determine the party or parties in whose hands is placed the responsibility of selecting the prime minister and other ministers, who exercise the executive power of government. Party practices vary in the power they concede to the governing party to select the ministry, but under the constitution all ministers must be parliamentarians or become one within three months. To a large extent, parliament is an instrument of party government, formally established as a vehicle of popular representation but operating in practice as a platform for the governing party. Many aspects of parliamentary business demonstrate the power of the government of the day to use parliament to promote its own political interests: for example, the basic ordering of business; the special rights of ministers to introduce financial measures; even the rules of debate which, at least in the House of Representatives, allow the government to curtail the time available to the opposition (Browning 1989: 288–97, 353–9, 432–8).

Over recent years, parliamentary resistance to executive domination has had a growing share of success, even to the point of seizing initiatives which have traditionally rested with executive government. Consider three recent instances which dramatise both the prevailing domination of the political executive and also the slow fuse of parliamentary resentment against the weight of government domination. The instances are drawn from each of the three most recent prime ministers, illustrating new tensions in the working relationships between governments and the parliament from which they are drawn – and the emerging limits to any government's control of parliament.

The first example concerns Prime Minister Bob Hawke, who announced Australia's involvement in the 1990–91 Gulf War without any formal consultation with parliament. In January 1991, Hawke authorised the participation of an Australian naval task force in a United Nations operation marshalled in response to Iraq's invasion of Kuwait. Although parliament had been earlier informed by the prime minister that Australia was prepared to participate in such operations, the decision to commit Australian forces to combat was taken by the ministry alone. Having made that decision, Hawke recalled parliament to meet for an unscheduled two day session so that parliament could place on the record its support for the government's action. The risks to the government then emerged: significant opposition among women's groups in the government backbench generated intense public scrutiny on wider dissent within parliament, which included the lone independent in the house and a number of minor party senators who recorded their reservations. Recalling parliament placed the government dissenters under great party pressure, but also forced the government to acknowledge that community opposition to its policy was more widespread than had been admitted (Sawer and Simms 1993: 173; House *Hansard* 21–22 January 1991: 1–269; Senate *Hansard* 21–22 January 1991: 1–269).

Although parliament overwhelmingly supported the government policy, there was far less support for the government's obvious reluctance to consult with parliament. The prime minister defended his late recalling of parliament with the claim that the war power 'constitutionally is the prerogative of the Executive' (House *Hansard* 21 January 1991: 3). Although constitutionally correct and not queried during debate, this view does not preclude parliamentary consultation; and the opposition effectively argued that the government's recall of parliament was not altogether voluntary, given that, according to the Senate opposition leader, the prime minister 'knew that the Senate was out of his control and was likely to be recalled'. The opposition contrasted the government's reluctant recall with the greater parliamentary participation of 'most democracies', such as the United Kingdom and Canada, where their parliaments 'have been meeting and have endorsed the decisions of their respective governments' during the process of government decision-making. The pointed contrast with the proactive role of comparable parliaments reinforced the commitment of non-government parties to the basic line, as put by the Senate opposition leader, that 'it is Parliament to which this Government is accountable' (Senate *Hansard* 21 January 1991: 9). What little opposition there was to the government's military strategy was combined with increasing cynicism that the recall was a form of sham accountability, with an independent Western Australian senator arguing that 'it is a waste of time and money for Parliament to return for set pieces' (Senate *Hansard*, 21 January 1991:

97). Although the government won its sought-after parliamentary approval, that victory came at a price, with increased suspicion of the government's genuine commitment to parliamentary accountability.

The second example concerns Prime Minister Paul Keating, who, in 1993, overhauled the traditional procedures for question time and established a roster system in which different ministers faced oral questioning on selected days, with the prime minister available for questioning on only two days of each sitting week. The suspicion which this aroused among the opposition recalled their earlier protest over Keating's statement that question time 'is a courtesy extended to the House by the Executive branch of Government', and did not reflect any right that parliament might pretend to have to demand an account from the political executive (House *Hansard* 24 November 1988: 3206). Once again, the example also indicates the limits to executive control. The opposition's criticism of the roster system locked the incoming Howard government into reinstating the traditional mode of question time. But even restorative changes can have unexpected consequences: in this case, the incoming speaker went beyond his government's initial intentions in renovating the traditional format by allowing the new opposition to use supplementary questions – modelled on Senate practice which the new government had mastered in its thirteen years of Senate opposition between 1983 and 1996.

The third example concerns the newly-elected Prime Minister John Howard, who, after the 1996 election, made substantial alterations to the machinery of government well before the new parliament had met. Many departments were saddled with new names and responsibilities, and many smaller agencies were transferred across portfolios. Typical was the restructuring of the Department of Prime Minister and Cabinet, which not only saw the appointment of a new secretary from outside the federal public service, but also the establishment of a new cabinet office, the transfer of the Office of Multicultural Affairs to the Department of Immigration, and the shrinking of the Office of the Status of Women. The fact that parliament had authorised the budget for this and every other portfolio was not held to imply any permanency in the machinery of government, or that alterations required either parliamentary consultation or approval. To use the language of United States legislative studies, parliament's passage of the financial *appropriations* for the public service departments is not a formal *authorisation* of any particular organisational arrangement (see for example Oleszek 1984: 44–53). There was certainly no protest from parliament when it finally did convene, which is consistent with the convention that the administrative arrangements of public service departments is a matter of executive convenience and not a matter of public law or public policy requiring parliamentary involvement.

But there are limits, as emerged in anxiety within parliament about the government's unprecedented sacking of half a dozen departmental secretaries, and more pointedly in response to the government's attempts to restructure the Aboriginal and Torres Strait Islander Commission (ATSIC), one aim being to make the ATSIC chair appointed by government rather than elected by the Commission. ATSIC is a good example of a special type of public body known as statutory authority, that is, established under law or statute so that any major alteration requires change to the law as distinct from simply executive action, and therefore risks parliamentary objection or obstruction. The Howard government had made an election issue of ATSIC's lack of accountability: but election promises are cheap when compared to the cost of legislative implementation. The government's proposed changes were introduced by the minister, senator Herron, who had to cope with the decision of the Senate to refer the bill to a legislation committee. Although that committee spent only one day in public hearings, it was a long day for the minister, who repeatedly had to defend many of his proposals against the criticism of not only committee members but many other witnesses (SF&PALC 1996). The committee process was far more taxing for a minister than traditional forums such as question time, and illustrates the considerable cost to governments of managing the legislative process when trying to deliver on election promises. Within days, the Senate overhauled the government's bill, censured the minister, and put the government on notice that it could not treat all areas of public administration as executive conveniences. The government's response was to put aside the amended bill and to reintroduce its original bill, thereby setting the course toward a possible double dissolution if the Senate again rejected the government's legislative proposal (Senate *Hansard* 26 June 1996: 2204–18, 2271–91; 27 June, 2395–429).

These three examples illustrate the emerging tensions between governments and parliaments. Why should governments resist such new pressures for greater parliamentary participation in their decision-making? The following sections examine two reasons: first, that governments presume that their right to rule rests on a special 'mandate' which the community has conferred on them; and second, that while governments acknowledge that parliament has formal authority to make laws, they doubt that parliaments have the policy competence to take legislative initiatives as though they really were 'the legislature'. In recent years parliamentary forces have emerged to test both of these executive presumptions.

Mandate magic

One of the magic words in Australian politics is 'mandate', as used, for example, to refer to the Howard government's massive election victory of 1996 as giving it a mandate to implement its election policies. When used in this sense, 'having a mandate' means having the popular authority, and hence democratic legitimacy, to proceed with a promised course of action in law or policy, even over the objections of non-government parties in parliament. Mandate is a magic word in the sense that it is used just as magicians use special words to conjure up extraordinary effects to reinforce their spellbinding authority. The language of 'mandate' is normally used by political executives to argue that the defeated forces in parliament have no political authority to obstruct the passage of the victor's legislation. But over recent years the traditional magic has begun to wear off, especially as minor parties in the Senate have not accepted that they, unlike the official opposition, are defeated forces. They might be small parties, but to an extent that minority position is by choice, reflecting a deliberate strategy to aim to hold the balance of power between government and opposition parties. The minor parties have developed their own version of 'mandate' theory which holds that they too have been returned to parliament with a 'mandate' from electors endorsing their public commitment to subject government legislation to the closest possible scrutiny short of outright obstruction – to 'keep the bastards honest' to use a slogan frequently employed by the most established of the minor parties, the Australian Democrats.

The aftermath of the federal election of 1996 is a good example of the confusions which now surround the once-magical term of mandate. One would suspect that the Australian electoral system, with its characteristic combination of lower house with half-Senate voting, especially considering the presence of proportional representation in the Senate, makes it difficult for any incoming government to claim a 'mandate' for representing 'the nation'. The claim makes more sense as a sign of a government's frustration with parliamentary impediments to its will. Thus it comes as no surprise that simultaneous or so-called 'double dissolutions' for the whole Senate as well as the whole House of Representatives have taken place on six occasions, when justified by the constitutional provisions regulating the resolution of disagreement between the two houses: 1914, 1951, 1974, 1975, 1983 and 1987 (Evans 1995: 75).

John Howard claimed victory on the night of the election, publicly noting his 'very powerful mandate' arising from his remarkably large forty seat majority. The Coalition's share of the final two-party preferred vote for the house was very large by historical standards: just under 54 per cent. This decisive electoral victory received the bonus which the electoral system always gives to winning parties, when that victory was translated into a commanding majority: around two-thirds of the total number of seats. At the election, representation in the Senate altered less dramatically than in the lower house: the new government won half of the available Senate seats, but still did not secure a Senate majority. Needing thirty-nine seats for control of the Senate, the new Coalition government found itself after the election with thirty-seven seats, the Labor opposition with twenty-nine seats, and the minor parties once again enjoyed the balance of power with ten seats, which was enough to restore their self-confidence and their self-styled mandate. The political makeup of the new Senate pre-figured frequent tied votes between government and opposition, with neither side easily able to garner a working majority. The mandate wars lasted well into the life of the new government, fuelled by the government's determination to see its legislation passed as quickly as possible. The government denounced the Senate's decision to refer a number of the government's most favoured bills to committees for detailed examination involving public hearings, charging that the action met the criteria of a 'failure to pass', which is one of the conditions recognised in the constitution as cocking the double dissolution trigger (see for example Senate *Hansard* 20 May 1996: 744–63). One can identify three different parliamentary responses to the claimed mandate. First, Labor as the official opposition totally disregarded the claim, still struggling to accept that it had lost office but also outraged that the government used its extraordinary majority in the house to 'guillotine' debate on the first of its mandate-bills. Second, the Australian Democrats stuck to their counter-offensive with their claim to their own distinctive mandate – one directly opposed to that claimed by the government. Closely related to this was the response of the other minor party, the Greens, which trumped the Democrats version of mandate by taking the issue back to its popular basics, arguing that the Senate must continually renew its own institutional mandate and 'bring the community into the process' of law-making (Senate *Hansard* 20 May 1996: 758). A third response was given by the crucially-placed independent senator, Brian Harradine, who warned the government's mandate claim 'certainly needs to be placed on the scales, but so do a whole lot of other issues …' (Senate *Hansard* 20 May 1996: 763). Harradine warned the government that it had to balance its case against 'the greater mandate that is in the constitution' which confers legislative power on parliament – and not the government (Senate *Hansard* 21 May 1996: 805; Senate *Hansard* 23 May 1996: 1044).

At the end of the day, the mandate wars are the latest episode in the ongoing dispute over the relevance of 'the Westminster model' as an explanatory or interpretative device for Australia's 'Washminster' government (Thompson 1980). The misleading model of 'mandate' is drawn from the British parliament at Westminster, where the mandate theory developed in the pre-First World War struggle between the House of Commons and the unelected House of Lords. The irony is that it was the Lords which foolishly taunted the Commons with the charge that a range of contentious government bills on social policy lacked a mandate. The Commons successfully curtailed the power of the unelected Lords to obstruct government bills, and adopted the strategy of claiming a mandate for every contentious bill. The Howard government expected the Senate to comply with what in the United Kingdom is known as 'The Salisbury convention', under which the Lords have agreed, since the end of the Second World War, not to obstruct bills which implement a government's election promises. Mandate theories derive from the inter-cameral disputes of Westminster, and seem an inappropriate response to the realities of parliamentary power in Australia, where the two houses are virtually equal in their legislative power: after all, the Senate may 'request' the house to amend those financial bills which the constitution prohibits it from amending in its own name (Evans 1995: 295–304).

The mandate wars reveal the increasingly contentious character of parliamentary representation. Opinions differ on the merits of mandates, depending on the value one is prepared to give to the claims of representation raised by those non-government parties which defend their right to use their share of parliamentary power to modify government policy. We turn next to the second battleground of executive–parliamentary tensions, which concerns the renewed parliamentary interest in taking its legislative responsibilities seriously. The constitution spells out the legislative powers which parliament may competently use, but historically parliament's participation has been quite reactive: either along house lines as a rubber stamp authorising government initiatives or along Senate lines as a road block obstructing government initiatives (Reid and Forrest 1989: 184–206). The following sections examine recent changes to the parliamentary organisation of the legislative process which provide a useful guide to parliament's capacity to enhance a basic feature of Australian government. While many parliamentary observers focus on the changing fortunes of question time and other arenas of executive exposure, it is important to appreciate the less public, but deeper, changes working their way through the legislative process.

House legislative processes

With the consent of government, House of Representatives legislative procedures were overhauled in the early 1990s, opening up new opportunities for members to bring long over due deliberation to bear on the core business of legislation. In the immediate background to this procedural reform was the growing breach between professed norms and prevailing practice. By the late 1980s, the routine practices of the lower house gave a less than attractive picture of a parliamentary institution. Reliance on the 'the guillotine' tells the larger story: the number of bills which the government declared as urgent and therefore requiring time constraints rose from twenty-six in 1985 to 101 in 1991, with 132 out of the 282 bills in 1992, and even 111 in the election year of 1993. The effect of this procedure was that frequently 'government amendments are agreed to without debate ... and opposition amendments cannot even be moved, let alone considered' (HRPC 1993: 4; HR 1995: 169; Lovell 1994: 167–8).

The referral of bills to legislative committees was formally proposed by the lower house procedure committee, at first unsuccessfully in 1986 then again, successfully, in 1993. The committee did not consider the option of extending the number of days in which the house might sit – which had been strongly recommended by the procedure committee in 1986, when it proposed 'a significant increase' of nearly 40 per cent in lower house sitting days from around sixty to eighty per year – which would still bring it below half of the time spent by the national parliaments in the United Kingdom and Canada. The house adopted the committee's recommendation for the formal abolition of the traditional and little used committee stage debate, and for the establishment of 'a second legislative stream' – the so-called 'main committee' – in which routine bills could be considered both in principle and in detail, thereby freeing up the house to concentrate on controversial legislation demanding more extended debate and close consideration (HRPC 1993: 38; compare Lovell 1994: 62–3, 120–1).

Referral of bills to specialist legislative committees for public hearings is a different matter. In some contrast to the main committee initiative, the use of legislative references is justified by its contribution to 'constructive and expert input at the initial stages of a bill's consideration' (HR 1995: 8). During the thirty-seventh parliament from 1993–96, ten advisory reports were completed on some thirteen bills, covering five committees. Few bills emerged over the initial 1994–95 period of referrals without unanimous endorsement for recommendation or ministerial action: ranging from a low of five quite general recommendations for ministerial action by the industry, science and commerce committee in relation to the trade practices amendment bill; to highs of thirty-eight recommendations by the same committee in relation to the legislative instruments bill; and to thirty-nine recommendations by the public accounts committee in relation to the package of bills on financial accountability – which was sufficiently large to sidetrack the bill from the government's legislative priorities.

The evidence of constructive impact of the committee referrals on the legislative process is striking. To begin, dissenting reports are very rare, with only one surfacing: in relation to the corporations and securities report on the first corporate law simplifications bill, and as an 'expression of concern' by an opposition member on the legal and constitutional affairs committee report into the child sex tourism bill. Not surprisingly, government acceptance of the need for amendments to their own bills is high. A good example is the fate of the bills referred to the legal and constitutional affairs committee: both the war crimes bill and the employment services bill were extensively amended, reflecting the government's general acceptance of the thrust of the committee's unanimous views on the probable defects of those bills.

Senate legislative processes

One can distinguish between two general phases of Senate reform since the 1949 introduction of proportional representation. I call the first phase 'the age of majority' to refer to the prevailing ethos which was compatible with the norms of strong party government. This first phase covered the period from 1949 through to the late 1960s, which includes the hey-day of the first minor party, the Democratic Labor Party (DLP) which broke way from Labor and effectively entered an alliance with the Coalition government against Labor, and did comparatively little to transform the ways of the Senate. I call the second phase the 'age of minority' in recognition of the arrival of the second wave of minor parties which were less committed to shoring up the major parties in government. Between the decline of the DLP and the arrival of the second-wave minor parties, there was something of an interregnum, coinciding with the Fraser government's unprecedented command of a majority in both houses of parliament between 1976 and 1980.

Two reservations should be borne in mind when thinking of an age of minority. First, it is rational for minority parties to resist routine reliance on legislative committees as a substitute for chamber consideration because the chamber is the one site in which minor parties, and especially independents, can marshal their legislative power to constrict the flow of legislative business. Thus it comes as no surprise that the age of minority gives rise to more complex rules for chamber treatment of government proposals, equal in importance to the threat of referral of bills to committees (Evans 1990: 18). Second, there is no single cut-off date separating the age of majority from that of minority: the two overlap, with the result that the Senate can still revert to type whenever the minor parties lose the will or interest to hold the line against the combined ambition of the major parties. The major reforms associated with the age of minority occurred at the end of the Keating government, when the Democrats were joined by the Greens. But the tone was set in the mid 1980s when Democrat Senator Macklin successfully moved what became known as the 'Macklin motion' – a resolution declaring that the Senate would defer until the next period of sittings consideration of any bills received after a specified deadline (Evans 1995: 253–5). The purpose was to counteract the trend in which government legislation was forced through in the last few weeks of a ten to twelve week sitting. The budget sittings are typical: in 1972, some 40 per cent of bills were passed in the final fortnight; by 1987, that figure had risen to nearly 68.8 per cent (Evans 1995: 254).

Unfortunately, the effect of this resolution was that the government began to comply with the Senate cut-off date, but at the cost of reducing the initial time available for consideration of the bills in the House of Representatives, with a dramatic increase in the use of the guillotine.

Almost as a symbol of the arrival of the age of minority, the Greens successfully revised the Senate resolution from the budget sittings of 1993 to include a 'double deadline' with an earlier deadline for introduction into the House of Representatives. Although the Senate may waive its deferral of legislation, the onus is on the government to convince the Senate to lift the ban on a case by case basis, which is itself a time-consuming burden. In the initial period of operation from November 1994 through to mid 1996, the Senate exempted 141 government bills, and refused exemptions for only fifteen government bills, or less than 10 per cent of government requests. The proportion might suggest that the Senate tends to cave in to government demands, but one should remember that the legislative process is now so tight that governments only apply for exemption in those cases where they genuinely believe that there is some pressing need for early consideration of nominated legislative proposals.

Characteristic of the age of minority is the procedural revolution of 1994 which broke the government choke-hold on committee power. It had long been observed that although the post-1949 Senate almost never had a government majority, standing orders reflected the interests of the established parties competing for government by requiring that the power of the chair reside in the party in government. Even in the absence of procedural protection, Senate power reflected the interests of the governing party, which is nowhere better illustrated than in the convention that the presidency is a gift to the party in government, regardless of that party's proportion of Senate power. Why not have that power shared to reflect the actual balance of the parties represented in the Senate? That traditional convention held sway until the minor parties brokered a new accord which eventually obtained Senate support (Senate *Hansard* 24 August 1994: 166–92; Evans 1995: 392–3).

The first manifestation of the new committee system was the division of each former committee into two new separate committees: a legislation committee of six members with government chair and majority; and a reference committee of eight members with non-government majorities and chair, shared between the opposition and the Democrats on a 3:1 ratio. Other Senate committees to be granted opposition chairs include the scrutiny of bills committee, the privileges committee, and the senators' interests committee. The original intention was that the references committees under opposition control would target matters of public policy and other matters referred to them. Events are never as neat as the rules intend. Early in the life of the Howard government, the Senate successfully referred a number of important government bills to reference and not legislative committees, on the basis that the former but not the latter had non-government majorities. Thus, despite the initial logic behind the two spheres of responsibility, the Senate adopted the more sustainable logic of using its numbers to take government legislation out of the hands of government majorities, and to incorporate the references committees into the routines of the legislative process.

Legislative score card

What does the overall picture of legislative activity look like? Importantly, it varies between the House of Representatives and the Senate. To start with in the lower house it is clear that the reforms of 1994 have altered the legislative flow, with significant increases in the proportion of bills being sent to either an 'advisory' or the 'main' committee – steadily increasing during the thirty-seventh parliament from 16.35 per cent in 1993 to 38.6 per cent in 1995. The figures on bills amended during passage through the House of Representatives shows another recent rate of increase: although the 1988–95 average of bills amended sits at 17.5 per cent, the percentages for 1994 and 1995 are respectively 19.3 per cent and 27.3 per cent, indicating a strong upward trend. The other side of the coin is that the proportion of bills declared urgent has fallen dramatically from 60.3 per cent in 1993 to 7.1 per cent in 1994 to 0.6 per cent in 1995 – which is truly astonishing, given that the average proportion of urgent bills over the period 1988–95 is 35 per cent. The explanation is that the establishment of the 'main' committee has released the pressure on business in the chamber.

What is the state of play in the Senate? The trend is that 20 per cent of bills passed by the Senate receive prior committee examination, and this process is the source for some 20 per cent of Senate amendments, although 30 per cent of eventual amendments have been aired or considered during committee consideration (Evans 1995: 262). Taking the thirty-seventh parliament as an example, the Senate record shows that the government had 482 bills passed during that 1993–95 period, 140 or 30 per cent of which were referred to Senate committees for examination. Taking amendments to government bills as a good test of the Senate's legislative will, the record shows that 157 or 33 per cent of these 482 bills were amended. It is true that a majority of these amendments are recorded as government amendments, but a high proportion of these indicate a change of legislative mind on the part of a government as it moves to repair provisions which, to judge from the state of Senate opinion, might otherwise not pass.

During the thirty-seventh parliament, 157 bills attracted 1812 successful amendments at an average of eleven per bill. The bills withstood many more proposed amendments which were unsuccessful, including half a dozen of the government's own proposed amendments. The spread of successful non-government amendments is: official opposition 267 or 15 per cent, Australian Democrats 159 or 9 per cent, Greens seventy-six or 4 per cent, and independent two or less than 0.1 per cent. This understates the impact of the Australian Democrats who have had many proposed amendments taken up by the government and formally moved either by the government alone or in co-sponsorship with the Democrats. The statistics on recorded committee and other divisions in the Senate during the thirty-seventh parliament show that in general the Australian Democrats voted with the government more often than not: 53.9 per cent, while voting with the formal opposition only 20.5 per cent. The other minor parties show steadily less support for the government and more for the opposition, suggesting that the smaller the minority party the less support there is for the government: comparable figures for the Greens are 43.5 per cent and 23 per cent, and for independent Harradine are 23.5 per cent and 49.3 per cent. The official opposition voted with the government 28.1 per cent of the time.

Accountable government

Of course, the legislative process is not the only or even the most influential of the processes conducted by parliament. As we have seen, even before the legislative machine is engaged parliament acts as an electoral college to determine who holds government. A corresponding role is as an arena of accountability, with sets of procedures designed to hold ministers and the public service accountable for their share of power in government decision making over law and policy. Question time is typical of the procedures directed at ministers, and much is known about the formality and limitations of this type of accountability mechanism (Reid and Forrest 1989: 316–21; Browning 1989: 507–12; Evans 1995: 498–502). Inquiries by the parliamentary public accounts committee and Senate estimates hearings are typical of the procedures directed at the public service, which have risen in importance as a basic supplement to established mechanisms of ministerial responsibility.

For the purposes of this chapter, it is important to appreciate that whatever vitality is enjoyed by these newer forms of bureaucratic accountability can be explained in terms of their close association with the legislative roles which parliament is redefining. The public accounts committee is responsible for reviewing the forms and substance of public service management of public funds; it is a statutory committee which investigates statutory obligations in relation to financial propriety of public service bodies. Senate estimates hearings are conducted by its set of legislative committees as part of their detailed consideration of the annual appropriations bills. Both the public accounts committee inquiries and the Senate estimates hearings are increasingly important forms of parliamentary accountability in which public servants are directly accountable for their share of responsibility in implementing programs funded by parliament.

The important point is that the most interesting recent development in these forms of parliamentary accountability comes from executive government rather than parliament itself – and this is the development of public service doctrines which, however grudgingly, acknowledge that public servants no less than their ministers have obligations 'to explain and justify' their performance before the appropriate parliamentary committees (MAB 1993; compare Uhr 1990a: 4–9; 1990b: 79–112). By contrast, question time reflects a traditional orientation which is unlikely to be affected by alterations in legislative roles. The Howard government restored the pre-Keating system in which ministers are no longer subject to a rostered system of appearances. Although the new speaker has allowed the opposition to follow Senate practice in the use of supplementary questions, one should not expect great things to flow from such modest rehabilitations of the so-called 'Westminster system'. In terms of greater parliamentary accountability, the more significant changes are occurring off-stage in the rearrangements of the legislative process to involve more regular use of committee inquiries with government and public witnesses.

Conclusion: Multi-party decision making

The changes to the legislative process reflect other changes slowly making themselves felt in parliament. I have stressed that change is not confined to the Senate, but one has to concede that many of the House of Representatives changes are slow adaptations of Senate innovations. It is impossible to predict what other parliamentary changes might be in store, although an essential prerequisite is to record the trend in Senate procedural experiments. The recent history of change has provoked speculation about the future of multi-party decision making in the Australian parliament (see Jackson 1995; Marsh and Uhr 1995). The orthodox model of Australian responsible party government is undergoing considerable change, with significant injections of multi-party decision making and shared responsibility. The trend is towards greater parliamentary accountability of government, with the introduction of a range of measures which primarily meet the needs of the minor parties for greater access to government information, including explanations and justifications of ministerial and bureaucratic decision making. By way of summary, the following list of selected procedural developments illustrates the trends towards multi-party decision making in the Senate.

- The imposition of a requirement that ministers, if they fail to provide answers to written 'questions on notice' within thirty days, must provide 'an explanation satisfactory to that Senator' who asked the question, or run the risk of Senate debate on their ministerial failure to provide either information or explanation to the Senate.
- The reform of 'questions without notice' through the establishment of time limits for both questions and answers, and the establishment of

thirty minute post-question time debate to allow dissatisfied senators 'to take note' of ministerial answers, again with time limitations for each speaker facilitating an even spread of opportunity to participate.

• The use of 'returns to order', by which the Senate formally 'orders' that specified documents be 'returned' or submitted to the Senate by a certain date. The Australian Democrats adapted this procedure to a long overdue legislative purpose when they established a regular, half-yearly 'order' that government provide details, including a statement of reasons, of all legislative provisions, such as parts or sections of Acts, which have been passed by parliament but not yet proclaimed.

• The use of 'orders' directing the Auditor-General to investigate matters on the Senate's behalf, as pioneered by independent Harradine in relation to the integrity of financial statements by Australia Post. This could signal a revolution in parliament's use of so-called 'parliamentary officers' as investigative arms of non-government parties. The non-government parties generally are experimenting with this new power to direct ministers, as was demonstrated in the treatment of Minister Collins in the 1993 'pay TV affair'; and in the latest pursuit of returns of bureaucratic policy advice, a sensitive subject still attracting claims of executive privilege.

Changes in Senate practice need not carry over into practice in the House of Representatives. One implication, however, is that the traditional distinction between an initiating house of government and a reactive house of review is becoming increasingly blurred. The challenge now is to ensure that the community obtains a clear view of which parts of 'the parliament' are responsible for enhancing, and which are responsible for restraining, the prospects of further reform.

References

Browning, A. R. (ed.) 1989, *House of Representative's Practice*, 2nd edn, Canberra: AGPS.

Evans, H. (1990), 'Consideration of Legislation by Committees', *The Table*, Vol. LVIII, 16–23.

Evans, H. (ed.) 1995, *Odger's Senate Practice*, 7th edn, Canberra: the Senate.

HR (Department of House of Representatives) (1995), *Annual Report*, Canberra: AGPS.

HRPC (House of Representative's Procedure Committee) (1993) *About Time*, Canberra: House of Representatives, October.

Jackson, R. J. (1995) 'Foreign Models and Aussie Rules', *Political Theory Newsletter*, 7/1, July, 1–18.

Lovell, D. (1994), *The Sausage Makers? Parliamentarians as Legislators*, Parliamentary Research Service: Political Studies Fellow Monograph No. 1, Canberra: AGPS.

Marsh, I. and Uhr, J. (eds) (1995), 'Party Systems', *Australian Journal of Political Science*, Special Issue: Vol. 30.

MAB (Management Advisory Board) (1993) *Accountability in the Commonwealth Public Sector*, Canberra: AGPS.

Oleszek, W. J. (1984), *Congressional Procedures and the Policy Process*, Washington: CQ Press.

Reid, G. S. and Forrest, M. (1989), *Australia's Commonwealth Parliament*, Melbourne: Melbourne University Press.

Sawer, M. and Simms, M. (1993), *A Women's Place*, Sydney: Allen & Unwin,

SF&PALC (Senate Finance and Public Administration Legislation Committee) (1996), *Hansard* of Hearing, 21 June.

Solomon, D. (1986), *The People's Palace*, Melbourne: Macmillan.

Thompson, E. (1980), 'The "Washminster" Mutation' in P. Weller and D. Jaensch (eds), *Responsible Government in Australia*, Melbourne: Drummond, 32–40.

Uhr, J. (1990a), 'Estimates Committee Scrutiny of Government Appropriations and Expenditure' in *Senate Estimates Scrutiny of Government Finance and Expenditure*, Canberra: the Senate, 4–9.

Uhr, J. (1990b), 'Public Expenditure and Parliamentary Accountability' in *Senate Estimates Scrutiny of Government Finance and Expenditure*, Canberra: the Senate, 79–112.

5

The core executive

Glyn Davis

When John Howard stands at the dispatch box in the Commonwealth parliament, he speaks for the government of Australia. The key players sit behind the prime minister, on the front benches of the House of Representatives, or next door in the Senate. Arrayed behind the ministers, with ambitions of their own, are the parliamentary members of the Liberal and National parties. It is their number, their majority in the lower house, which allows John Howard to command the confidence of parliament, and so the administration of the nation.

Yet it would be a mistake to see the government as just those politicians arranged neatly for the cameras at question time. Watching events on closed circuit monitors within the house are the ministerial advisers who help devise and implement political strategies. They will be busy inventing policy initiatives, spinning stories to the media, meeting with interest groups, anticipating issues and working on responses. Beyond the precincts of parliament, in government buildings across Canberra, numerous senior public servants are preparing cabinet submissions or ministerial briefs, taking up issues debated in the chamber and giving them expression through policy and legislation.

Government, then, is a complex, collective enterprise which extends beyond the parliamentary arena to embrace interlocking networks of advisers and bureaucrats. It requires the skills and energy of many different people, in varied institutional roles. Governing brings together elected representatives, political professionals and an impartial public sector which serves loyally the government of the day, whatever its political makeup. When John Howard speaks of 'the government' he uses a shorthand description for a moment in time when a temporary but powerful configuration of ideas, players and structures known as the core executive is given unity by a shared commitment to a policy program.

The core executive

By convention, the executive comprises the prime minister and cabinet. Their authority is implied rather than detailed in the Australian constitution, which mentions ministers only in passing as officers appointed to 'administer such departments of State of the Commonwealth as the Governor-General in Council may establish' (section 64). Ministers hold office at the pleasure of the Queen's representative. If not in parliament when appointed, a minister must become a senator or a member of the House of Representatives within three months. The constitution makes no reference to a prime minister or a cabinet.

Yet behind these silences are longstanding customs about the executive. Over nearly a century the Australian parliamentary system has developed widely understood – if still sometimes controversial – conventions about the role of the prime minister, the responsibility of ministers to parliament, and the limited role of the governor general (RAC 1993: 27–8). These conventions sustain a set of relationships at the centre of Australian political life designed to give the majority parties in parliament control over government activity.

In traditional terms the executive is a committee drawn from parliament to govern in its name. In return, that committee must answer to parliament for its choices. Ministerial responsibility is the personal obligation to account for actions of the department entrusted to a minister, while collective responsibility requires ministers to defend all decisions taken by cabinet, even those an individual minister opposed in the cabinet room. Should ministers feel unable to support an important cabinet decision in public, they must resign. Such departures are rare in Australian politics, so strong is the sense of solidarity among ministers, so firm the desire to remain among this most important group of people in public life (Healy 1992).

Of course newspaper editorials are still fond of lecturing readers on the allegedly vanishing tradition of ministerial and collective responsibility. Such learned leaders inevitably quote British Prime Minister Lord Melbourne from 1874 ('I do not care whether the price of corn is to go up or down – so long as all Ministers tell the same story') and Prime Minister Lord Salisbury ('For all that passes in Cabinet each member of it who does not resign is absolutely and irretrievably responsible') (usually drawing on Jennings 1969). Yet both forms of ministerial accountability have been relatively weak in Australia. Ministers typically refuse to resign because of mistakes by their departments. Direct impropriety usually brings down a minister, though Special Minister of State Mick Young was reappointed to the ministry in 1984 despite a Royal Commission finding that he breached national security. To criticise a cabinet decision remains an important lapse, which is why most ministers do so through private 'background briefings' to the media.

It is unlikely ministerial responsibility ever flourished in Australia in quite the ideal form suggested by textbooks. Ministerial resignations on principle are few and far between, with most being part of complex power games within a government. When Malcolm Fraser resigned from cabinet in 1971, for example, he did so in order to bring down his leader. Andrew Peacock made the same calculation in 1981, and Paul Keating in 1991. The rise of disciplined political parties has changed irrevocably the logic of ministerial responsibility. The censure of the parliament is no longer at issue, since party loyalty ensures a solid government majority. Parliament becomes only a forum for airing criticism of ministerial performance. Yet if that attack is sufficiently damning, it may well destroy the minister, by threatening the credibility of the government. In such circumstances the prime minister must make a pragmatic judgement: will the government be least damaged by dismissing a minister or allowing them to stay in office?

Collective responsibility has also been changed by new institutions, in this case an expanded ministry. For though the executive comprises ministers drawn from both houses of parliament, not all are members of cabinet. Certainly, when the Commonwealth government began, in 1901, all eight ministers were members of cabinet. Yet as this number grew to twenty-two ministers in the years after the Second World War, cabinet meetings became cumbersome, and prime ministers sought a smaller, more focused forum. In 1956, Prime Minister Robert Menzies divided his ministry between an inner group, all members of cabinet, and an outer ministry, whose members would be called into cabinet only for items related to their portfolio. While Prime Minister Gough Whitlam included all twenty-seven Labor ministers in cabinet, his successors from both sides of politics have followed the lead set by Menzies. One dilemma has been whether to apply collective responsibility to junior ministers absent from the cabinet room when a decision is taken. The *Cabinet Handbook*, prepared by the Department of Prime Minister and Cabinet (PM&C) and published in 1988, contains the solution: junior ministers can oppose cabinet decisions in the party room, but not in public.

The executive, then, is broader than cabinet. In important senses it is also broader than the ministry, for politicians must work closely with the public service. Cabinet decisions by themselves have no legal force, and matter only because government agencies accept such choices as binding. Without a public sector to implement its wishes and to write its legislation, the executive would be of little consequence. To speak of the executive, therefore, is necessarily to consider the wider set of institutions involved in governing.

To address these definitional concerns, Rod Rhodes (1995: 12) has proposed the term 'core executive'. While the prime minister, cabinet and ministry remain the centre of political authority, the core executive refers to 'all those organisations and procedures which coordinate central government policies, and act as final arbiters of conflict between different parts of the government machine'. The idea of a core executive recognises that, at its centre, government is a web of key politicians, institutions, committees, networks and government agencies. There is endless movement across this network, not always involving the same players. Some policy issues, for example, will travel through bureaucratic channels to cabinet but others may be settled by the prime minister alone, or by ministerial staffers.

The core executive is thus defined by its proximity to the centre of power, and by its influence over outcomes. The boundaries of such a system will change according to the goals and manner of the prime minister. An influential Canadian study by Aucoin (1986: 90) observed how prime ministers reshape the machinery of central government, and so the core executive, to match their 'personal philosophies of leadership, management styles, and political objectives'. Some Canadian prime ministers prefer to work through established bureaucratic process, others through political brokerage and deal making. Similar patterns can be observed in Australia, from the relatively 'hands off' management style of Bob Hawke, to the intensely personal interest and involvement in policy development of Malcolm Fraser, Paul Keating and John Howard. Around each a different configuration of core executive players emerges, recognisable in outline as the familiar structures of central government, yet varying in detail about the relative importance of institutions, and the distribution of authority.

What does the core executive do?

Whatever the variations around prime ministers, the task of the core executive remains constant: to govern. Ministers did not seek high office in order to be irrelevant. They want to direct what happens in government, to nudge the activities of the state toward objectives agreed by cabinet. The core executive exists to direct national policy in directions supported by the parliamentary majority.

Governing is inherently political in nature, since the objective is to pursue – and renew – an electoral mandate. Yet political objectives often in turn rely on policy and administrative systems which extend far beyond the core executive into the bureaucracy or out into society. The core executive can be understood as criss-crossing networks and systems designed to address the three constant and interconnected concerns of government:

- *Politics* – the need for government to appear in control and speak with one voice. Ministers must be seen to share common objectives, and the government must appear responsive to community pressures, and to the expectations of those who supported its election. Politics is about achieving and holding power, and about using office to pursue the beliefs and interests of those who govern.

- *Policy* – the need for government to generate and assess objectives, and to prevent contradictory policies in which one choice undermines others. Governments come to office with policy, but they also face new challenges for which they have no ready answer. Governments must therefore be able to develop plausible responses, test consequences, and ensure implementation.
- *Administration* – the need to ensure the public sector is working efficiently and effectively toward goals set by cabinet. Ministers are responsible for the management of government agencies, and can be hurt by accusations of poor administration or of corruption. While in office therefore, ministers must manage and direct the agencies in their care. (Drawn from Davis 1996: 19)

Clearly these categories overlap. Many involve the same players, who must speak as a politician to one audience, and as a minister administering a department to another. Yet ministers, their advisers and agencies, come to understand government in terms of a political, policy and administrative set of functions. Each of these tasks tends to attract its own institutions, players and rules. Some, particularly the networks of ministerial staffers, are overtly political. Others, such as the policy departments, are resolutely non-partisan, serving loyally any duly elected government. All understand they must work together if the core executive is to exercise effective authority in the interests of coherent and effective government. In the following sections, each of these functions is examined, before a conclusion suggests how politics, policy and administration interact around the prime minister to provide the familiar features of Australian governance.

Authority over politics

Government is a political activity, as politicians strive to hold onto office and to impose their preferences on society. Not surprisingly then, politicians pay great attention to political questions, and have developed a network of players to assist. Each minister has a private office, which in turn works closely with the prime minister's often large and powerful private office. This political domain is focused on political strategy, which involves positioning the government on particular issues, working for support from interest groups, and managing media perceptions.

Though the prime minister is also central to policy and administrative decisions, the office looms particularly large in political considerations. Media attention focuses on the leader, and governments carry their name. Though technically 'first among equals', the prime minister has authority over hiring and firing ministers (a power constrained by caucus in the

Labor Party), control over the agenda, structure and process of cabinet, responsibility for the machinery of government, leadership of the governing party or coalition, centralised access to the media, extensive personal patronage and the personal support of a large and professional bureaucratic machine. The prime minister sets the tone for a government, and becomes its chief spokesperson. So dominant has the office become, some now label our political system 'prime ministerial government' (see Weller 1985).

Certainly all recent prime ministers at times have demonstrated their ascendancy over parliament and the national political scene. Yet each knows a party room vote can remove them at any time. Prime ministers are like street gang leaders – they exercise authority only so long as the gang members will tolerate them (Davis 1992). When a prime minister can no longer keep their side of the bargain – a strong prospect of re-election for the government – the party becomes restless and disobedient. As Liberal leader John Gorton discovered in 1971, and Labor Prime Minister Bob Hawke in 1991, parties are unforgiving of a leader who no longer commands confidence. Prime ministers are powerful, the most significant political figure in the nation, but their authority always rests on an exchange between a party room which wants leadership and a leader who needs party support.

Further, patterns of authority within government vary greatly. Dunleavy and Rhodes (1990) report for Britain a spectrum of leadership styles. Some prime ministers exercise power with little reference to colleagues. Others work through 'kitchen cabinets' (small cliques of senior ministers), or through continuous cabinet government. There have been weak prime ministers who allow ministers great latitude, governments driven by powerful outside interests, and executives dominated by the public sector. No one pattern describes most recent Australian prime ministers; all these modes of behaviour can be cited, often from different periods within the term of a single incumbent. Malcolm Fraser, for example, could dominate many of his ministers, yet always placed great store on proper cabinet procedure and accepted a majority vote (Weller 1989). Bob Hawke at times liked to work with an inner group, and also suffered some major defeats in cabinet. Both Paul Keating and his successor, John Howard, leaned to a more commanding and distant stance, with greater control over outcomes.

As John Hart (1992: 184) observes, political scientists have been arguing for decades about the growing dominance of Australian prime ministers, without much compelling evidence of systematic change to the role. While media coverage tends to focus single-mindedly on prime ministers as though they enjoyed the individual mandate and fixed term in office of an American president, 'Australia has not imported American-style presidential government, nor even a watered down version of it' (Hart 1992: 185). Unlike their American counterparts, Australian leaders remain hostage to their party and to parliament. Even in times of triumph, they must rely on the support and goodwill of their colleagues.

For ministers, as for prime ministers, working at politics is only part of their role. Those in the ministry must also represent their departments in cabinet, maintain their position within the party, respond to the media and position themselves for further advancement. They also remain members of the House of Representatives or Senate, who must attend to their local constituencies (Weller and Grattan 1981). Ministers juggle these roles while under intense scrutiny from the parliament and the media, and while carrying a heavy workload of committees, meetings and departmental paperwork. Not all prove up to the task, for while senior ministers are usually among the most talented in their party, others are chosen for coalition, regional, gender or interest balance. Such representative roles have provided a platform for some exceptional individuals, but also for some less impressive performers.

Given their range of responsibilities, time is short for ministers, who come to rely on their staff to carry through many basic political tasks. Since the Whitlam government of 1972–75 (and intermittently before then), ministerial advisers have been important players within the core executive. Despite their significance, ministerial staff occupy an ambiguous position within Australia's responsible government framework. They are more than simple advisers, since many act in the name of their minister by requesting policy information from government agencies, or by directing the activity of public servants also assigned to the minister's office. Yet advisers have no formal authority, and no clear place in the line of accountability that runs from the public service through the minister to parliament. Though their pay and conditions are regulated by the Members of Parliament (Staff) Act, ministerial advisers are not public servants (some may be drawn from the bureaucracy on secondment). Rather, they are partisan political players, committed to the party in power and dependent on continued electoral success for employment.

Ministerial advisers live in a world of deals and patronage, of exciting political drama but also, increasingly, of policy expertise and specialisation. Many will spend a relatively short time in ministerial offices before pursuing a political or public service career. Some, such as John Hewson, a former adviser to Treasurer John Howard in the Fraser years, rise to head their parliamentary political party. Others, such as Dr David Kemp, become ministers themselves in later governments. A few have developed a career as a ministerial staffer, moving between various states and Canberra, depending on the fortunes of their side of politics.

While studies of ministerial staff are still rare (though see Walter 1986; Dunn 1995), it appears advisers are characterised by 'relative youth, middle-class origins, high education, specialist credentials, and the leap from academic or governmental – but rarely political – backgrounds into the inner circle of leadership' (Walter 1986: 115). Advisers will be younger, and usually more highly qualified, than the ministers they serve. Walter's survey of senior Commonwealth ministerial staff under the Hawke government found 80 per cent of advisers to be male, and 65 per cent still in their thirties. Nearly 90 per cent of advisers held at least a bachelor's degree. While political advisers had often previously worked for a minister or shadow minister, press secretaries were likely to be drawn from the media. Indeed there is now a regular circulation of journalists between the press gallery and ministerial offices, raising interesting questions about previous and subsequent objectivity (see Henningham 1995).

Advisers bring a political sensibility to policy proposals drawn up by a minister's department. Sometimes this 'second guessing' creates friction between the ministerial office and the bureaucracy, but the aim is to protect a minister from accepting advice which is 'rational' but electorally unpopular or inconsistent with the government's political strategies. Understanding those strategies requires continuous liaison among ministerial offices. Weekly meetings chaired by the prime minister's chief of staff or principal media adviser help develop and disseminate a consistent theme for the government. Announcements are sequenced so that ministerial press conferences do not crowd each other out, or send contradictory messages to the media. In times of crisis, ministerial staff talk with the prime minister's office to settle an approach for the issue at hand. The daily business of managing political perceptions, of projecting a united, coherent government, is achieved through the unceasing – and usually exhausting – work of these political networks.

Recent prime ministers have relied on their private offices to reinforce the leader's authority over the government's political strategy. Prime Minister Keating, for example, worked closely with his chief of staff, press secretary and speech writer in shaping the directions of his term in office. His successor decided to experiment with a new structure, so changing the shape of the core executive. Among machinery of government arrangements, Prime Minister Howard included a new 'Cabinet Office' within the Department of PM&C. This Cabinet Office, said the prime minister, would be a 'small unit, staffed within and outside the Public Service, which will provide the prime minister with advice on issues before Cabinet as well as strategic policy directions' (quoted in Nethercote 1996). While many Australian states have a similar organisation, these typically belong in the public service. Members of Howard's Cabinet Office, though, are employed on the same terms as ministerial advisers, so creating an institution which straddles the traditional separation between a partisan prime ministerial office and a permanent public service.

The creation of a new institution at the centre of government demonstrates the flexible nature of the core executive, which has shifted once again to accommodate the style of a prime minister. It also emphasises the evolving relations within the core executive. Once ministerial offices and advisers barely rated a mention in discussions of the ministry. Now their role must be acknowledged. Advisers are among the most conspicuous and busy players in the dense network around the cabinet. They are a continuing presence in parliament house, surrounding each minister, providing links to other ministerial offices, to the backbench, to interest groups and the media. Advisers help shape and market government initiatives, provide intelligence and suggestions, and stand in for their ministers in many discussions about political tactics. Though their role is confined still to the political implications of policy, advisers have 'provided a basis for the elected executive to extend their control over the departments' (Dunn 1995: 519). The rise of ministerial offices indicate that institutions within the core executive are always temporary and subject to modification. The Australian polity is famous for its stability, yet at the political heart of government is constant ferment and frequent innovation.

Authority over policy

Policy is the main business of government, the reason for contesting office. Much core executive attention focuses on framing and considering policy proposals. Key institutions of the policy domain include the cabinet and the central public service agencies which support the cabinet process.

Cabinet meets each week to consider submissions made by ministers. Though a committee without formal legal standing, cabinet is recognised as the apex of government, the forum which makes central choices for the nation. Weller (1990) argues that cabinet performs at least six major roles. It is a clearing house for routine government business, an information exchange letting ministers know what is happening in government, an arbiter resolving disputes between agencies and ministers, a political decision maker applying electoral judgements to bureaucratic submissions, a co-ordinator of government activity, and a guardian of the strategy, keeping the 'big picture' in front of the ministry.

Faced with complex choices, cabinet must draw together the threads of electoral survival, policy rationality and administrative feasibility. There is no rational 'calculus' which can weigh up contending economic and political considerations and arrive at the ideal answer, only a group of ministers, fallible and often tired, who must work through a topic and arrive at a definitive judgement. Many such choices are routine; the Fraser Coalition government of 1975–83 made some 19 500 decisions, or about ten decisions every working day (Kelly 1984: 61). Others are difficult and require many meetings to consider all the implications. In 1991, for example, cabinet was sharply divided over whether to allow mining at Coronation Hill in the Northern Territory. Some ministers in economic portfolios strongly favoured the development, given its export potential.

Others were deeply concerned about the electoral consequences of allowing mining in a national park. Cabinet kept revisiting the issue, unable to decide. Finally it became clear ministers had talked out the issue without reaching consensus. They expected the chair of cabinet, Prime Minister Hawke, to settle the issue. He proved unable to do so for some time, and so helped destroy his own leadership (on this period see Gordon 1993).

Not all cabinet business happens in cabinet. Increasingly, ministers rely on an extensive committee system which allows specialised attention to issues. Committees meet after cabinet as business requires, and take responsibility for broad policy envelopes, such as defence and security or economic development (Weller 1992: 11ff). Some are permanent, others exist only for a particular issue. In principle, most cabinet committees are chaired by the prime minister, though in practice they may meet without the leader. Committee decisions are reported to cabinet, but rarely debated (Codd 1990). Some major government responsibilities, such as preparing the annual budget, are now handled by standing cabinet committees, including the powerful Expenditure Review Committee (ERC). Under successive governments for nearly a quarter of a century, ERC ministers have met regularly to reduce departmental spending. On coming to government in 1996, for example, Prime Minister Howard instructed the ERC to find some $8 billion in savings from Commonwealth outlays.

To handle the volume of material through cabinet, detailed procedures are codified in the *Cabinet Handbook*. Cabinet relies on extensive routines, managed by central agencies, to compile, coordinate and offer opinions on the wealth of proposals requiring an authoritative decision. The *Handbook* sets out rules about what issues may come to cabinet, and in what form. It requires extensive consultation within government before the submission reaches cabinet, and sets out a template for cabinet documents (PM&C 1994). Cabinet procedures matter, because they define who makes choices and with what information. By insisting on due process, a prime minister can ensure ministers have before them all relevant data, including costs, social and economic implications, employment issues and likely responses from the media and interest groups. A systematic cabinet process, with circulation of submissions a week before consideration, also allows ministers to be briefed by their department. What makes sense for Immigration and Multicultural Affairs may cause difficulties for Foreign Affairs and Trade. Cabinet provides a forum for such conflicts to be argued out and resolved.

The policy work of cabinet relies in turn on support from the bureaucracy, in particular the Department of PM&C. Founded in 1911 on the instruction of Prime Minister Andrew Fisher, the Department of PM&C manages cabinet documents, records and distributes cabinet decisions, and provides detailed advice to the prime minister on all submissions (Walter 1992). The secretary of the Department of PM&C is also head of the

Australian public service, exercising influence over the appointment of all departmental secretaries and other senior bureaucratic appointments. The secretary is the prime minister's principal adviser on policy issues, and sits in on cabinet meetings. While the exact delineation of roles between the Department of PM&C and the new Cabinet Office is yet to emerge, it seems unlikely the central authority of the Department of PM&C will be much diminished. Rather, the Cabinet Office will probably assume responsibility for policy advice previously provided by the prime minister's private office. This will ensure the prime minister has access to a public service brief, and a political commentary, on each matter before cabinet.

When line departments prepare policy submissions, they recognise the importance of policy advice from central agencies. To meet required standards, and to garner support, cabinet submissions are negotiated across the bureaucracy. The Department of PM&C provides advice over format and levels of data. The Department of Finance advises on budget implications, and on costings provided for the proposal. Legal aspects may be referred to the Attorney-General's Department, and employment relations consequences to the Public Service Commission or the Department of Industrial Relations. Where disagreement occurs, it must be recorded under 'consultation' in cabinet documents. By the time submissions reach cabinet they have been discussed across government, and often rewritten many times to incorporate views from concerned agencies.

The policy domain of the core executive thus begins with the ministry and extends into the public service. Policy making is highly regulated and ritualised, in a process designed to ensure consistency of information and coherence of choice. While the political domain is concerned with political and image management by politicians and their advisers, to create policy, ministers must work as a team with public servants. The core executive must therefore host both cabinet as a collection of politicians and cabinet as a meeting of government agency representatives, supported by key institutions such as the Department of PM&C.

Authority over administration

Ministers contest office to pursue policies, but find themselves responsible for large and complex public sector departments. These organisations matter, both because they are the instrument for delivering policy programs, and because ministers who manage their agencies poorly will be exposed to criticism in parliament. The core executive thus has important political and policy reasons to invest time and thought into administration. To keep control over what happens inside the public sector, the core executive uses three key instruments – design of the structure of government, control over the budget, and personnel policy.

Australian prime ministers have wide powers to structure government in whatever manner suits their program. They can invent new departments to express priorities, and downgrade or abolish those no longer required. Commonwealth Administrative Arrangements Orders do not require consideration by cabinet or endorsement from parliament, only agreement from the governor general to a proposal from the prime minister.

For much of this century the Commonwealth government was characterised by the slow accretion of new functions. During the sixteen year tenure of Prime Minister Menzies, for example, only three new departments were created. The pace of change quickened under his Coalition successors Holt, Gorton and McMahon, and hastened dramatically under Labor Prime Minister Whitlam. Indeed, from 1972 change in administrative structures became a constant, as prime ministers struggled to find an architecture for government which reflected their objectives. Whitlam created new ministries such as the Media, and Urban and Regional Development. His successor, Malcolm Fraser, abolished many of the innovations and then created his own. When Fraser could not get the range of policy options he wanted from Treasury, he split the agency, creating a Department of Finance in 1976.

The most dramatic change, however, occurred under Prime Minister Hawke in July 1987. Hawke considered the continuous restructuring of the public service expensive and inefficient. He sought instead structures which could endure. Fresh from an election victory, Hawke announced the consolidation of the existing twenty-seven Commonwealth departments into just sixteen agencies. Each would be represented in cabinet by a minister, assisted in turn by up to two junior ministers. This amalgamation, argued the prime minister, would free cabinet from dealing with 'more routine administration', allowing instead a focus on major issues (Hawke 1994: 416). By bringing together related areas such as foreign affairs and trade, the government would be able to pursue strategic economic policy goals without being distracted by arguments over competing departmental responsibilities.

The 1987 amalgamations indeed achieved a significant reduction in cabinet workload, and greater stability in structures. The number of submissions considered by cabinet fell from 709 in the first year of the Hawke government to just 366 in 1988, the first full year of the new portfolio structures (Weller 1992: 7). Cabinet committee meetings more than halved, and while there had been an average of eighteen major machinery administrative changes each year since the days of Prime Minister Gorton, from 1987 major changes dropped to less than four per annum (MAB–MIAC 1992: 81–5). The Hawke structures were modified by incoming Coalition Prime Minister Howard in 1996, but the essential logic of a small number of agencies, each with broad and integrated policy responsibilities, endured. Name changes, such as the addition of 'Youth Affairs' to

Employment, Education and Training following the 1996 election, reflect political symbolism rather than a return to the instability of previous decades. The core executive has learned to value stable bureaucratic structures – not least because control over the public sector is now more likely to be exercised through financial instruments.

Governments have always paid close attention to financial management, with the Commonwealth budget an annual statement of priorities and objectives. Key economic departments such as Finance and Treasury have close links into the core executive, and are central players in framing fiscal and expenditure parameters for any government. Detailed supervision of public finances has been augmented by new management techniques. Sometimes broadly characterised as 'managerialism', or an emphasis on results, new financial processes have devolved responsibility to program managers while imposing strict accountability requirements. Initiatives such as the 1983 Financial Management Improvement Program (FMIP) required departments to move from 'line item budgets' setting out expenses, toward program budget statements which list what a program has achieved, and the costs involved in delivering that service (Wanna and others 1992: 92ff). Such budgets rely in turn on sophisticated information systems to track activity, and on corporate plans with performance indicators and evaluation cycles.

As managerialist techniques adopted during the 1980s provided the core executive with greater reach over departmental activity, so older control systems became less relevant. In particular, the very detailed personnel system managed by the Public Service Board (PSB), with its staff ceilings and central approval for all position creation and promotion, was no longer required. Employees, now termed 'human resources', became just one input when managing a program budget. The powers of the PSB were curtailed in 1984, and the organisation abolished altogether in 1987. Though a new Public Service Commission set out general guidelines for management of the public service, authority over many aspects of employment devolved to departmental chief executives. Those chief executives in turn became more clearly identified with the government of the day. In 1996 new Prime Minister John Howard removed six departmental secretaries appointed by his predecessor, substituting people drawn from within the Commonwealth public service or from the state and private sectors.

It is much too early to suggest Australian public administration has crossed an invisible threshold, abandoning a career public service in favour of American-style party appointments to the bureaucracy. Most departmental secretaries in Canberra are still life-long public servants, with impressive professional credentials. Yet as Defence Department Secretary Tony Ayers commented on the 1996 dismissals, 'we have taken a very significant step away from the Westminster system and it will not be reversed'. The emerging pattern of senior appointments sympathetic to the program of the government suggests, once again, an evolving core executive, finding new structures and routines to deal with the ever growing pressures of governance.

Drawing together the core executive

Faced with the challenges of governing, the core executive develops identifiable political, policy and administrative structures and routines. Each domain is designed to ensure coherence and collective purpose; together these domains organise government around the objectives of the elected leadership. The arena where domains overlap and interact is the core executive, a space for networks of politicians, their staff and the public sector.

Figure 5.1 sketches the core executive, identifying key (but by no means all) actors in the drama of governance. The three domains of politics, policy and administration circle the office of the prime minister. This recognises the centrality of the leader to government, but should not give a false sense of solidity and permanence. All prime ministers survive in

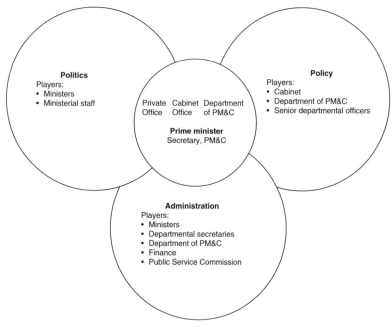

FIGURE 5.1   *Three governing tasks*

Source: Based on Davis 1996: 28

office only so long as their party room will support them. One sign of a leader in decline is a breakdown at the centre, as the prime minister loses authority over cabinet, over ministerial offices and so over policy implementation. There is perhaps a cycle of influence for prime ministers – from acknowledged ascendancy after an election victory, through acquiescence during good times, to unhappiness and plotting across the core executive as the polls turn sour and the government looks unlikely to survive. In such bad moments, as during the final year of prime ministers Gorton or Hawke, ministers distance themselves from the collective enterprise, staff privately criticise the leadership to the press, and the discipline and shared vision of a successful government is lost amid bickering and eventual collapse. Most prime ministers, of course, are defeated or retire before reaching that final nadir, leaving a new leader to begin the cycle afresh.

The core executive is a moveable feast, changing shape and membership with each new prime minister. Relationships between ministers and their staff, between ministerial offices and the public service, are renegotiated endlessly. New techniques, such as recent financial and personal reforms in the public sector, are adopted quickly in the search by the core executive for leverage and control. Bargaining is the norm, as policy plans are traded for political goals or administrative convenience. Deals, the essence of politics, keep ideas moving through the complex matrix of electoral considerations, policy concerns and administrative feasibility which preoccupies the core executive. It is a system not easily captured on paper, since words do little justice to this tumultuous, evolving, three dimensional world.

Yet such complexity is unavoidable. National government is characterised by detailed and intricate arrangements with state and local administration, increasingly international obligations, and the management task of large and sometimes competing bureaucracies. Authority must be shared among players, no matter how dominant the prime minister; as Kooiman observes, 'no single actor, public or private, has all the knowledge and information required to solve complex dynamic problems' (quoted in Rhodes, forthcoming: 26). Effective governance means interdependence among people and structures within the core executive, achieved through continuing interaction and negotiation.

In practice, regular meetings bring together the domains of politics, policy and administration around the prime minister. Such gatherings include pre-cabinet briefings by the head of the Cabinet Office and the secretary of the Department of PM&C. There are also regular scheduled discussions between the prime minister and those reporting to him, which may again include dialogue across the table between political and policy considerations. Initiatives with public sector implications may draw the Public Service Commissioner into discussions. Each person stays within their particular role, but exchange is essential. To plan a political strategy, the prime minister's office must be informed about forthcoming policy issues; to write policy proposals, the public service must understand the government's political objectives. 'Partisan mutual adjustment', a phrase coined by economist Charles Lindblom (1965) to describe how autonomous participants adjust to each other's actions, is the hallmark of the core executive (Rhodes forthcoming: 28).

Yet there may come a point of overload, when the complexity of governance overwhelms even the most sophisticated core executive. Already demands on the prime minister's time and interest are overwhelming, and the rapid ageing of all incumbents demonstrates most graphically the pressures of office. The prime minister standing at the dispatch box must keep together a fragile coalition of party, electorate support and government. The leader needs to worry about political strategy, policy objectives and effective administration. When they address parliament they must speak for themselves, their colleagues and the nation. Their moment at the centre will be brief and probably end unhappily; only one Australian prime minister in nearly a century has retired at a moment entirely of his own choosing. Yet for those few short years each prime minister gives shape, coherence and purpose to the core executive and, through it, can make a difference for the nation.

References

Aucoin, P. (1986), 'Organizational Change in the Canadian Machinery of Government: from rational management to brokerage politics', *Canadian Journal of Political Science*, 19,1, 3–27.

Codd, M. (1990), 'Cabinet Operations of the Australian Government' in B. Galligan, J. R. Nethercote and C. Walsh (eds), *The Cabinet and Budget Process*, Canberra: Centre for Research on Federal Financial Relations, 1–22.

Commonwealth of Australia (1986), *The Constitution of the Commonwealth of Australia*, Canberra: AGPS.

Davis, G. (1992), 'Prime Ministers and Parties' in P. Weller (ed.), *From Menzies to Keating: The development of the Australian prime ministership*, Melbourne University Press, 64–80.

Davis, G. (1996), *A Government of Routines: Executive coordination in an Australian State*, Melbourne: Macmillan.

Dunleavy, P. and Rhodes, R. A. W. (1990) 'Core Executive Studies in Britain', *Public Administration*, 68,1, 3–28.

Dunn, D. D. (1995), 'Ministerial Staff in Australian Commonwealth Government', *Australian Journal of Public Administration*, 54,4, 507–19.

Gordon, M. (1993), *A Question of Leadership: Paul Keating, political fighter*, University of Queensland Press.

Hart, J. (1992), 'An Australian President?' in P. Weller (ed.), *From Menzies to Keating: The development of the Australian prime ministership*, Melbourne University Press, 183–201.

Hawke, R. J. (1994), *The Hawke Memoirs*, Melbourne: William Heinemann.

Healy, M. (1992), *That's It – I'm Leaving and other Kirribili Tales: Ministerial resignations and dismissals 1901–1991*, Canberra: Department of the Parliamentary Library.

Henningham, J. (1995), 'Political Journalists' Political and Professional Values', *Australian Journal of Political Science*, 30, 2, 321–34.

Jennings, I. (1969), *Cabinet Government*, 3rd edn, Cambridge University Press.

Kelly, P. (1984), *The Hawke Ascendancy*, Sydney: Angus & Robertson.

Lindblom, C. E. (1965), *The Intelligence of Democracy*, New York: The Free Press.

MAB–MIAC (1992), *The Australian Public Service Reformed: an evaluation of the decade of management reform*, Taskforce on Management Improvement Prepared for the Commonwealth Government Management Advisory Board with Guidance from the Management Improvement Advisory Committee, Canberra: AGPS.

Nethercote, J. (1996), 'Cabinet Office Move Ill Advised', *Canberra Times*, 3 April.

PM&C, Department of (1994), *Cabinet Handbook*, Canberra: AGPS.

RAC (1993), *An Australian Republic: the options*, Vol. 1, Report of the Republic Advisory Committee, Canberra: AGPS.

Rhodes, R. A. W. (1995), 'From Prime Ministerial Power to Core Executive' in R. Rhodes and P. Dunleavy (eds), *Prime Minister, Cabinet and Core Executive*, London: Macmillan, 11–37.

Rhodes, R. A. W. (forthcoming), 'Shackling the Leader? Coherence, capacity and the hollow crown' in P. Weller, H. Bakvis, H. and R. A. W. Rhodes (eds), *The Hollow Crown? Countervailing trends in core executives*, London: Macmillan.

Walter, J. (1986), *The Ministers' Minders: Personal advisers in national government*, Melbourne: Oxford University Press.

Walter, J. (1992), 'Prime Ministers and their Staff' in P. Weller (ed.), *From Menzies to Keating: The development of the Australian prime ministership*, Melbourne University Press, 28–63.

Wanna, J., O'Faircheallaigh, C. and Weller, P. (1992), *Public Sector Management in Australia*, Melbourne: Macmillan.

Weller, P. (1985), *First Among Equals: Prime ministers in Westminster systems*, Sydney: Allen & Unwin.

Weller, P. (1989), *Malcolm Fraser PM*, Ringwood: Penguin.

Weller, P. (1990), 'Cabinet and the Primer Minister' in J. Summers, D. Woodward and A. Parkin (eds), *Government, Politics and Power in Australia*, 4th edn, Melbourne: Longman Cheshire, 28–42.

Weller, P. (1992), 'Prime Ministers and Cabinets' in P. Weller (ed.), *From Menzies to Keating: The development of the Australian prime ministership*, Melbourne University Press, 5–27.

Weller, P. and Grattan, M. (1981), *Can Ministers Cope? Australian federal ministers at work*, Melbourne: Hutchinson.

6

Parties and elections

Clive Bean

Political parties and representative elections are central features of any modern democracy. The two, of course, are inextricably connected, since parties derive their legitimacy from voter support at regular elections, but at the same time the electoral process would be chaotic without parties. While parties by no means meet with universal approval (Sharman 1994), in practice it is difficult to imagine a modern democracy operating without them. What makes political parties so indispensable is the aggregating and representational functions that they fulfil. As a result, longevity has become a key feature of parties in many western nations: party systems established decades ago have exhibited remarkable durability throughout most of the twentieth century (Lipset and Rokkan 1967).

In a typical western democracy a small number of parties dominate, capturing the bulk of the vote and the vast majority of legislative seats at each election. The formation of viable political parties usually stems from clearly delineated societal cleavages which become politicised and in so doing provide both the impetus and initial support base for new parties. Once established, parties develop and maintain their positions by accumulating a large core of loyal supporters (or party identifiers) within the electorate, the vast majority of whom can be counted on to vote for the party at every election. This ongoing partisan support – in addition to a variety of other advantages entrenched parties enjoy, such as substantial control over the political agenda and the benefits of electoral systems that often favour larger parties – helps to ensure the maintenance of relatively stable political alignments over long periods of time. For these reasons, new political parties find it very difficult to succeed.

Partisan alignments and new challenges

Nowhere is this picture of entrenched political parties and stable electoral alignments better exemplified than in Australia (Aitkin 1982; Jaensch

1983; McAllister 1992). Together, the Australian Labor Party, on the left of the political spectrum, and the Liberal and National parties, on the right, have dominated Australian politics at the national level for over eighty years and, despite the occasional incursion of minor parties, such as the Democratic Labor Party in the 1950s, the Australian Democrats since the late 1970s and, most recently, the Greens, the joint supremacy of the major parties has never seriously been threatened. Australia stands out as exceptional in this respect, as the massive social, economic and political change in the period since the Second World War takes its toll on party systems elsewhere.

In many countries, changing social structures and values have coincided with a decline in partisan alignments based on social class or social position and also with reduced support for mainstream political parties (Dalton, Flanagan and Beck 1984; Franklin, Mackie, Valen and others 1992). The theory behind these developments is that the pace of change in the late twentieth century has meant that the societal foundations upon which democratic political parties formed in the early decades of the century have fundamentally altered, leaving the original *raison d'être* of class-based parties irrelevant in the modern world. The Australian party system, however, has shown much more resistance to change than party systems in many other western democracies. While Australia has certainly experienced class dealignment (Aitkin 1982; Goot 1994; Kemp 1978; McAllister 1992) this development has not led to dealignment from the major political parties as has occurred in other countries.

Part of the reason why the major Australian parties have been able to maintain their dominance in the face of change is linked to institutional factors such as the compulsory voting system which, by compelling all members of the electorate to vote at every election, helps to reinforce the partisan attachments that most voters have to one or other of the major parties (Aitkin 1982; McAllister 1992). Another reason is the parties' ability to adapt to changing times and to adopt new policy agendas to help stave off the challenge that political parties with new perspectives represent. In particular, the factional system within the Australian Labor Party helps in this process and the conservative parties also have somewhat similar, if less formal, mechanisms (McAllister 1991).

The electoral system also plays a crucial role in mediating voters' party choices. The preferential voting system in the House of Representatives and the single transferable vote system of proportional representation in the Senate thus play important roles in the major parties' success (Papadakis and Bean 1995). In the House of Representatives, voters have the opportunity to express support for a minor party in the first instance, but ultimately they must indicate a preference for one of the two major party groups over the other. The Senate system provides greater opportunities for minor parties to achieve success and this is reflected in the lesser dominance of the major parties in that chamber. Yet, this very feature of the Senate system may in some ways help reinforce the supremacy of the major parties in the lower house, since it provides an effective outlet for expressions of voter discontent.

In the 1990s, it is less certain that the major parties retain the same stranglehold on power that they have enjoyed for most of this century. A variety of authors have begun to argue than the Australian party system is increasingly under challenge from new forces and that there are now signs of dealignment from the major parties (for example, Chaples 1993; Hughes 1997; Marsh 1995; Papadakis 1990). If true, this development suggests that the distinctive features of the Australian political system which have hitherto rendered international theories of partisan dealignment inappropriate in this country may merely have delayed the onset of this phenomenon in Australia rather than prevented it altogether. It is also a potentially important development, not only for what it may imply about the future of the party system, but also ultimately for the future of the political system as a whole, given the central role that political parties play in ensuring ongoing political stability. However, when a wide variety of evidence is taken into consideration, support for the proposition of party decline remains mixed: while some indicators do suggest evidence of dealignment, others suggest that the dominant party system remains strong.

This chapter examines three themes relating to the topic of parties and elections in order to address the question of the state of the Australian party system in the 1990s, and in particular whether the major political parties are under greater challenge now than in the past. First, the chapter reviews aggregate evidence on the fortunes of the political parties in federal and state elections. Second, it examines changing levels of party membership and, third, it considers data on party identification within the electorate. In order to set the period since 1990 in context, the chapter adopts a long term perspective in its exploration of party system developments.

Party support and success in federal and state elections

The first set of data we examine is aggregate results from federal and state lower house elections over the forty years from the middle of the 1950s to the middle of the 1990s. The results are grouped into ten year periods and are shown both for the 'elective party system' – party shares of the popular vote – and the 'parliamentary party system' – party shares of seats (Rae 1971). These are the fundamental data for investigating the condition of the party systems throughout the Australian political arena and the extent to which they may be under challenge. Initially, we concentrate on Commonwealth elections. The first section of Table 6.1 contains the period averages described above, showing federal electoral support for the Labor Party, the Liberal–National Coalition parties and for 'others', which include a variety of minor parties as well as independent candidates.

TABLE 6.1   *Changing party vote and seat shares in federal and state lower house elections*

| | Votes | | | Seats | | |
	Labor %	Liberal–National %	Other %	Labor %	Liberal–National %	Other %
Federal						
1956–65 (n=3)	45.4	44.9	9.7	42.3	57.7	0.0
1966–75 (n=5)	45.7	46.7	7.5	42.9	56.9	0.2
1976–85 (n=4)	45.4	45.8	8.8	47.1	52.9	0.0
1986–96 (n=4)	42.2	45.3	12.6	49.6	49.1	1.4
New South Wales						
1956–65 (n=4)	47.2	45.8	7.0	52.7	45.7	1.6
1966–75 (n=3)	43.7	45.9	10.4	44.3	53.3	2.4
1976–85 (n=4)	53.0	41.3	5.7	60.6	37.4	2.0
1986–95 (n=3)	39.6	46.0	14.4	45.3	50.2	4.6
Victoria						
1956–65 (n=3)	37.5	46.1	16.4	26.8	72.7	0.5
1966–75 (n=3)	40.3	45.8	13.9	25.6	73.1	1.4
1976–85 (n=4)	46.9	48.1	5.0	45.0	54.7	0.3
1986–96 (n=3)	44.6	48.4	7.0	38.6	61.0	0.4
Queensland						
1956–65 (n=4)	41.0	43.8	15.3	39.2	51.6	9.2
1966–75 (n=4)	42.9	47.7	9.4	31.6	65.0	3.4
1976–85 (n=3)	42.8	53.6	3.6	32.5	67.1	0.4
1986–95 (n=4)	45.8	48.6	5.6	51.4	48.3	0.3
South Australia						
1956–65 (n=4)	51.4	36.1	12.4	46.2	48.7	5.1
1966–76 (n=4)	50.4	42.1	7.6	52.8	45.0	2.2
1976–85 (n=4)	46.8	45.4	7.9	51.6	44.1	4.3
1986–95 (n=2)	35.3	49.7	15.2	34.0	63.8	2.1
Western Australia						
1956–65 (n=4)	44.9	44.6	10.4	48.5	49.5	2.0
1966–75 (n=3)	47.4	44.7	7.9	46.4	53.6	0.0
1976–85 (n=3)	47.8	48.7	3.6	46.1	50.9	3.0
1986–95 (n=3)	44.2	47.3	8.5	50.8	48.5	0.6
Tasmania						
1956–65 (n=3)	48.7	41.1	10.3	51.0	47.0	2.0
1966–75 (n=2)	51.3	41.2	7.5	54.3	44.3	1.4
1976–85 (n=3)	47.9	44.8	7.3	49.5	48.6	1.9
1986–96 (n=4)	34.8	49.1	16.1	37.1	50.7	12.1

Sources: Mackerras 1994: 182; Australian Electoral Commission; Parliamentary Research Service; Victorian Electoral Commission.

When we look at the data for votes, on the left hand side of the table, one of the most striking features is how even the support for the two major party groups has been throughout the period at the national level. Indeed, both Labor and the Coalition parties have tended to average somewhere around 45 per cent of the first preference vote for the House of Representatives in each ten year grouping. Curiously, the most substantial deviation from this pattern is Labor's vote over the last four elections in the late 1980s and the 1990s, when the party's average vote dropped to 42.2 per cent, despite the fact that Labor won on three of the four occasions. Equally interesting is the fact that Labor averaged a larger share of the first preference vote than the Liberal–National parties in the three elections from 1956 to 1965, even though the Coalition won all three.

These two observations serve as a reminder that the role played by the electoral system in translating voters' expressions of support for their favoured parties into a final distribution of party strength in the legislature sometimes leads to unexpected results. Thus, the Coalition's worst average performance in terms of votes during the period, in the ten years from 1956 to 1965, coincided with its best performance in terms of seats – an average of 44.9 per cent of the votes won the Coalition parties 57.7 per cent of the seats – and the same is true for Labor for the period 1986 to 1996, when 42.2 per cent of the votes translated into 49.6 per cent of the seats. Furthermore, the consistently even balance between the two major parties in terms of votes contrasts with an almost equally consistent imbalance in terms of seats, with the Coalition clearly doing better from the electoral system's translation of votes into seats in all ten year periods except the last.

The influence of the electoral system is also clearly seen in the fortunes of minor parties and independent candidates which, until the last three elections, have virtually been excluded altogether from representation in the federal lower house. Perhaps the most interesting column of figures in the table, however, is the votes for 'other' parties and candidates. The figures suggest something of a cyclical pattern to minor party support. In the late 1950s and early 1960s, when the Democratic Labor Party was in its heyday, minor party support averaged close to 10 per cent. From the mid 1960s to the mid 1980s minor party support first dropped and then rose a little, but in the late 1980s and the 1990s it rose markedly to average 12.6 per cent in the four most recent elections. This rise is due to the presence of the Australian Democrats – although their fortunes have not been uniformly high over this period – as well as to the emergence of the Greens as an organised political force – although the level of their support is sometimes exaggerated. But it is also partly due to the success of a variety of miscellaneous independent candidates in the 1990, 1993 and 1996 federal elections.

When added together, support for 'other' parties and candidates has totalled in excess of 10 per cent of the vote in each of the three elections in the 1990s, a feat that was achieved only very rarely before then. In other words, whereas the combined vote for the major parties regularly totalled well over 90 per cent in the past (Hughes 1997), in the last three elections it has been under 90 per cent on each occasion, something that has not previously happened in any two successive elections since the Second World War. While for each election it would be possible to explain the size of the minor party vote by particular factors specific to the circumstances of that election, it is difficult to deny the proposition that at the federal level the dominance of the major political parties is under greater threat than at any time in the last half century. Furthermore, the recent inroads made by minor parties have occurred in the absence of any 'major shock' to the party system of the kind that happened in the 1950s, for example, when the Labor Party split and the Democratic Labor Party was formed. What we should remember, of course, is that by international standards even at their low point of 82.9 per cent in 1990, the major parties retained a healthy combined share of the vote.

How general is this pattern of greater challenge to the dominant party system in the 1990s compared with earlier periods, across the party systems of the different Australian states? While the party systems of the states have much in common they also diverge from one another (Sharman 1990) and there is no reason to assume that they would all follow the pattern at the federal level. The remainder of Table 6.1 contains data on party fortunes in the different states, grouped and presented in the same way as for federal elections. Several patterns are evident. First, with respect to the major parties, there is a group of three states – New South Wales, South Australia and Tasmania – in which, with certain qualifications, Labor has tended to be dominant over the Coalition parties (in their various manifestations) – until the most recent set of elections. In each of these three states, the Labor vote has fallen dramatically compared with earlier years, to an average of under 40 per cent in elections since the mid 1980s. In two other states – Victoria and Queensland – the Coalition parties have been more or less dominant throughout, while in Western Australia the balance between the major parties has been remarkably even.

When we consider the support for 'other' parties and candidates, again a cyclical pattern is evident in all states. Minor parties performed well in most states in the early part of the period, which coincided with the rise of the Democratic Labor Party, whose greatest strength was in Victoria and Queensland. In those two Coalition-dominant states, minor parties have not fared so well in recent times. In Western Australia, where neither major party has consistently dominated, there is little sign of any trend in the minor party vote. In the remaining three states, however, the vote for minor parties and independent candidates has risen sharply in the last decade to its highest level throughout the forty year period. In Tasmania, and to a lesser extent in New South Wales, the increase in votes has also led to increased success for the minor parties and independents in gaining parliamentary seats, but the same has not occurred in South Australia. The three states also differ in that the principal minor party achieving success in Tasmania has been the Greens, in South Australia it has been the Australian Democrats, while in New South Wales the success has come in the form of a variety of independent candidates and minor parties.

Thus, in addition to the national arena, in three of the six states the dominant political party system appears to be under greater pressure from minor parties in the last decade than in the past. Note that these are the same three states – New South Wales, South Australia and Tasmania – in which the Labor Party vote has slumped in this period. Furthermore, it may or may not be a coincidence that these are also states in which Labor had previously been the more dominant of the major parties. Finally, we may recall that the equivalent rise in the minor party vote at the federal level has also coincided with a decrease in Labor Party support.

Party membership

Membership of a political party is arguably the most fundamental of the various links that tie voters to parties. Without at least some branch members to give it an organisational presence within the electorate, no democratic political party could survive. As a result, changes in party membership numbers are regarded as a key indicator of whether parties are declining in western democracies. The fact that the numbers of party members nowhere constitute more than a small fraction of the potential voters for a party does not diminish the importance of this evidence, since party membership indicates the existence of a core of enthusiastic sup-porters who ensure the ongoing inflow of ideas and who can mobilise the party's vote at election time. The crucial aspect of membership levels is not so much the absolute numbers but whether these numbers rise, fall or remain static. It is now well accepted that the mass membership of mainstream political parties is generally declining in western democracies, particularly in western Europe (Katz, Mair and others 1992; Katz and Mair 1994), although some have noted that this pattern of decline is not universally true (Selle and Svåsand 1991) and others have argued that it need not be irreversible (Hofnung 1996).

What of Australia? Branch membership of political parties is low in Australia by world standards, which is probably in part a consequence of a distinctive structural feature of the Australian political system, compulsory voting. Compulsory voting reduces the motivation for political parties to encourage extensive mass memberships because one of the main roles performed by party activists in political systems with voluntary voting is 'getting out the vote', a function that in Australia is performed by the institution of compulsory voting (Aitkin and Kahan 1974: 440; Hughes 1966: 94–5; Jupp 1982: 188).

As a number of researchers have cautioned, Australian party membership figures tend to be unreliable (Ward 1991: 156; Watson 1973: 362) and this is underlined by the fact that different sources sometimes produce different figures for the same party in the same year (see, for example, Ward 1991: 156). However, these discrepancies are not usually of large magnitude and if we assume that the 'unreliability' could derive from a temptation to exaggerate party membership numbers, there is no particular reason to suppose that the figures will be inconsistent in this respect from one point in time to another. Thus, even though the raw figures may be somewhat dubious and perhaps generally inflated, any trends are likely to be valid. Another consideration is that, as others have pointed out, party membership levels can fluctuate markedly from year to year (Ward 1991: 157; Warhurst 1983: 259). For example, during the 1970s, branch membership of the Liberal Party went from around 88 000 throughout Australia in 1971 to just under 152 000 in 1976 and then fell back to 105 000 in 1979 (communication from the Liberal Party to the author).

None of these qualifications negates the unambiguous trends that emerge from the data on party membership levels. Table 6.2 shows branch membership in the three main Australian political parties at five time points spanning the three decades from the mid 1960s to the mid 1990s. The table shows the raw numbers of party members, in thousands, and also puts these numbers into perspective by converting them to percentages of the total electorate, which, during this period, almost doubled. Let us first consider the absolute numbers. We see that the Labor Party has always had fewer members than either of the two conservative parties throughout this period. Labor's lowest membership level was in 1967, when it had fewer than 43 000 branch members after almost two decades in opposition, but in general its membership numbers have been relatively consistent at around 50 000 or slightly more.

The Liberal Party began the period with three times as many members as Labor and many more than the National Party. However, the story for the Liberal Party, even from these raw figures, is one of declining numbers over the period and even if we had data for every year, the year-to-year fluctuation mentioned above would almost certainly not lead to a different overall picture. The decline appears to have been particularly steep during the 1980s, most of which was spent in opposition, so that in 1996 Liberal Party membership numbers are not markedly greater than Labor's. The National Party has performed better, with its branch membership having grown in absolute terms since the 1960s, and it now has by far the largest membership of the three parties.

TABLE 6.2   *Branch membership of major political parties (numbers in thousands, with percentages of the electorate in parentheses)*

	1967 000s	(%)	1972 000s	(%)	1980 000s	(%)	1990 000s	(%)	1996* 000s	(%)
Labor	42.7	(0.7)	56.5	(0.8)	53.5	(0.6)	51.9	(0.5)	50.0	(0.4)
Liberal	127.0	(2.1)	100.2	(1.4)	108.7	(1.2)	73.4	(0.7)	70.0	(0.6)
Labor + Liberal	169.7	(2.7)	156.7	(2.2)	162.2	(1.8)	125.3	(1.2)	120.0	(1.0)
National	81.0	(1.3)	80.0	(1.1)	–		118.3	(1.1)	115.0	(1.0)
Total	250.7	(4.0)	236.7	(3.3)	–		243.6	(2.3)	235.0	(2.0)

* Figures for 1996 represent the mean point of estimates on a range for both the Liberal Party (range 60 000 to 80 000) and the National Party (range 110 000 to 120 000). Substituting the highest or lowest figures in the range does not alter any of the substantive conclusions.

Sources: Australian Electoral Commission; McAllister and others 1990: 64; Nelson and Watson 1969: 286; Ward 1991: 157–8; Warhurst 1983: 258; Watson 1973: 364, plus communications from political parties to the author.

These absolute numbers mask a significant pattern that emerges when we look at party members as a proportion of the electorate (shown in parentheses in Table 6.2). Since 1967, the Australian electorate has grown from just over six million registered voters to nearly twelve million in 1996 and, as a percentage of the electorate, membership of all three political parties has declined over this period. Even the National Party, whose absolute membership level has increased by approximately 35 000, has suffered a small decrease in relative terms. The decline has been greatest for the Liberal Party (as we would have expected from the raw numbers), whose membership as a percentage of the electorate has fallen by over two-thirds, while Labor's membership has dropped by nearly half in relative terms.

The steep and relentless pattern of relative decline in party membership is depicted graphically in Figure 6.1, which plots one line for Labor plus Liberal and another for all three parties combined. Both lines show substantial decline at each successive year of measurement. For example, in 1967 membership of all three parties together amounted to 4 per cent of the electorate (itself a very low figure in international terms); by 1996 the equivalent proportion had halved. Sample survey evidence from the Australian Political Attitudes surveys of 1967 and 1979 and the Australian Election Study of 1996 trace a similar pattern of decline in party membership (although in each case the proportion of members is higher than for the data shown in Table 6.2 and Figure 6.1), from 6 per cent in 1967, to 5 per cent in 1979, to 3 per cent in 1996. However, as Mair (1994: 4) has noted with respect to several European countries, the decline in membership is almost entirely relative; as the raw figures in the final line of Table 6.2 show, there has been only a small decline in absolute numbers across the three parties combined. Moreover, there is no reason to assume that the trends revealed by these data are irreversible. After thirteen years in opposition, Liberal Party membership numbers may have reached a low point in 1996 and a sustained period in government could well lead to increased membership.

Party membership may be declining, but rank and file members still provide an important link between the mass electorate and the organisational and parliamentary party elites. How distinctive are party members in social and political terms? Are they representative of the wider elec-

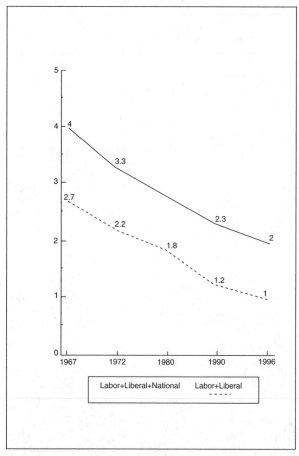

FIGURE 6.1   *Major party membership as a percentage of the electorate, 1967–96*

Sources: Australian Electoral Commission; McAllister and others 1990: 64; Nelson and Watson 1969: 286; Ward 1991: 157–8; Warhurst 1983: 258; Watson 1973: 364, plus communications from political parties to the author.

torate or at least of the larger pool of party supporters? To answer this question, we turn to survey data from the 1996 Australian Election Study. Respondents were asked whether they were currently or had ever been members of a political party. By combining current and past members we increase the numbers for analysis, although even so the total number of past and present members still only amounts to 7 per cent of the sample. Table 6.3 provides a sociopolitical profile of party members, looking separately

TABLE 6.3   *Characteristics of party members compared with non-members and party voters*

	Labor members %	Liberal–National members %	All party members %	Non-members %	Labor voters %	Liberal–National voters %
Sex – women	51	52	52	52	48	52
Age – under 35	24	8	13	29	30	23
– over 55	37	47	46	29	28	35
Education – degree	26	13	18	20	22	18
Occupation – non-manual	63	87	80	70	66	74
Union member	30	12	23	31	44	21
Subjective class – middle	47	72	64	50	43	58
Religion – Catholic	36	18	23	29	32	28
– Protestant	23	67	52	43	35	51
– no religion	38	6	14	16	20	11
Birthplace – overseas English speaking country	5	4	8	11	11	11
– non-English speaking country	13	6	8	12	15	11
Interest in politics – a good deal	59	58	62	29	30	36
Party identification – very strong	46	25	33	14	19	17
(N)	(39)	(67)	(126)	(1611)	(622)	(892)

Source: Australian Election Study, 1996 (n=1797).

at Labor members, Liberal and National members and then members of all political parties combined (including minor parties). For comparison, the table also shows the equivalent figures for non-members and for Labor and Coalition voters.

The first line in Table 6.3 shows that party members and non-members alike are about equally likely to be women rather than men. Only Labor voters – but not Labor Party members – are slightly distinctive in this respect, with women comprising a little under half of Labor voters, compared with slightly more than half of all other groups in the table. Party members, however, have a highly distinctive age profile. Among voters who are not members and never have been – remembering that this amounts to over nine-tenths of the sample – just under 30 per cent are aged less than thirty-five and about the same number are fifty-five or over. Labor voters have a similar age profile, while Liberal–National voters are somewhat more likely to be older and somewhat less likely to be young. But party members, of all persuasions, are far more likely to be in the older age group than the rest of the electorate at large. This imbalance is particularly marked in the case of the Coalition parties, 47 per cent of whose members are in the over fifty-five age group compared with only 8 per cent under the age of thirty-five. A clear imbalance in the same direction, if much less marked, is also observable for Labor Party members.

Turning to indicators of socioeconomic status, we see that members of the Labor Party are disproportionately likely to have a university degree, whereas Liberal–National members are less likely to possess one. On the other hand, fully 87 per cent of Coalition members are from non-manual occupations, but so are 63 per cent of Labor Party members. While this latter evidence reinforces Ward's (1987; 1989) claims about the 'middle class' character of Labor Party members, it is also true that this is the smallest proportion of non-manuals of any group in the table, including Labor voters. In other words, in a world in which over two-thirds of all occupations are non-manual, Labor Party members are slightly more likely than other groups to be from manual occupational backgrounds – but only slightly. The party is certainly no longer a 'working class' haven, an argument reinforced by the data for the next two variables in the table. Although Labor Party members (30 per cent) are much more likely to be trade unionists than Liberal–National Party members (12 per cent), they are slightly less likely to be union members than voters who are not party members and substantially less likely to be than Labor voters. Labor Party members are also more likely to consider themselves to be 'middle class' than Labor voters (47 per cent versus 43 per cent), although they are less likely to do so than members of the electorate in general, while Liberal–National Party members are much more likely to call themselves 'middle class' (72 per cent). For both occupation and subjective social class, the divide between Labor and Coalition members is much sharper than between Labor and Coalition voters.

The same is true of the denominational profiles of the party members compared with the party voters at large. More than one in three Labor members are Catholic, compared to only 18 per cent of Coalition party members. Among party voters, we see only a pale imitation of this division: 32 per cent of Labor voters are Catholic compared with 28 per cent of Liberal–National voters. Likewise, two-thirds of Liberal–National members are members of Protestant churches, compared to under a quarter of Labor members, while the equivalent figures for voters for the two parties are 51 per cent and 35 per cent, respectively. Finally, while only 6 per cent of Liberal–National Party members state that they have no religion, 38 per cent of Labor Party members are secular. Again, although the same pattern is evident when we examine voters for the two parties, the division is of much lesser magnitude (11 per cent for Coalition voters versus 20 per cent for Labor voters).

Ethnic origin, as measured by country of birth, also reveals distinctive patterns for party members. Whereas 11 per cent of the electorate, and also of both parties' voters, were born in the British Isles or other English speaking countries, less than half that proportion of members of each of the two major parties have similar origins. If the parties are alike in that respect, they differ in terms of their proportions of members born in non-English speaking countries, with such people being under-represented among the membership of the Coalition parties but not among Labor members (although the proportion of non-English speaking immigrants among Labor members is not as high as among Labor voters). All in all, to an even greater extent than across the electorate at large, political party members tend to have been born in Australia.

The final two variables in Table 6.3 are attitudinal measures of political involvement, interest in politics and strength of political party identification (as defined in the next section), and these data emphasise that party members have certain characteristics in common with each other, which make them stand apart from the rest of the electorate. Thus, while only about 30 per cent of non-party members report having 'a good deal' of interest in politics (and the figure is similar for Labor voters and not much higher for Coalition voters), by contrast nearly 60 per cent of Labor and Liberal–National members express strong political interest. With respect to party identification, not surprisingly much larger proportions of party members claim a 'very strong' identification with their chosen party than non-members (46 per cent for Labor members and a somewhat lower 25 per cent for Liberal–National members, compared with only 14 per cent for non-members and a few per cent more for Labor and Coalition voters). However, while party members are clearly distinct from other electors in this respect, we may wonder why even more of them do not report a strong affinity with their party.

In assessing the evidence on the profiles of political party members in contemporary Australia, it is important not to forget that the numbers of party members in the sample are small and the data may therefore not be highly reliable. Nonetheless, even with this caveat, party members are distinctive on a variety of social and political dimensions, not only from the rest of the electorate but also from the larger mass of party supporters. And while in some respects Labor and Liberal–National Party members are starkly different from one another, in certain other respects members of the two opposing major parties have much in common.

Party identification

A much more pervasive measure of partisan sentiment within the electorate, and thus a more important indicator for assessing the strength and stability of the party system, is party identification. Party identification is a long-standing psychological attachment to one or other of the political parties which develops through political socialisation and which most voters carry with them throughout their adult lifetime (Campbell, Gurin and Miller 1954; Campbell, Converse and others 1960). It is similar to other kinds of broad identifications, such as ethnic or religious identifications or indeed identification with a sporting team. Party identification, or partisanship, tends to strengthen over time and has a powerful influence on political behaviour. Because large and roughly equal numbers of voters identify with one or other of the major party groups, party identification is a strong force for stability in the party system. Developed in the United States, the concept has been shown to be generally applicable in other Anglo-American democracies, including Australia (Aitkin 1982), although its validity has been questioned in some other settings, such as in countries of continental Europe (Budge, Crewe and Farlie 1976).

As discussed in the introduction, until recently the Australian party system had shown immunity from the international trend towards partisan dealignment, although some evidence has started to emerge that Australia may finally be emulating other countries (see, for example, Bean 1996; Marks 1993; McAllister 1992: 40–1). Here we use data from the 1987–96 Australian Election Studies to investigate recent developments in the level and strength of party identification in Australia. In presenting the data on the level of party identification, the chapter employs the methodological strategy outlined in the Appendix. Briefly, this means that for the 1993 and 1996 surveys, the figures for the total proportion of party identifiers and for the proportion of major party identifiers (that is, people who identify with either the Labor, Liberal or National parties) are the actual percentages produced from the data, whereas the figures for 1987 and

1990 have been deflated by 6 percentage points so as to make them more directly comparable with the later two surveys.

Using these adjusted figures, we see that the line in Figure 6.2 depicting the total proportion of electors who identify with any political party, either major or minor, is almost horizontal from 1987 to 1993, registering a level of party identification of 88 or 89 per cent in each of the three surveys. In other words, only about 12 per cent of the electorate failed to register an identification with some party – a high level of party identification by world standards. Moreover, these figures are consistent with data from prior

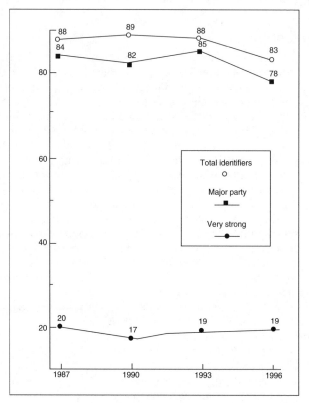

FIGURE 6.2   *Level and strength of party identification, 1987–96* (percentages)*

* Levels of party identification in 1987 and 1990 have been adjusted to compensate for measurement differences. See text for further details.

Sources: Australian Election Studies 1987 (n=1825), 1990 (n=2037), 1993 (weighted n=2388), 1996 (n=1797).

surveys which have shown party identification to be at around the same level in a number of studies since 1967 (Aitkin 1982; Bean and Kelley 1988; Bean 1996). Thus, over many years the Australian electorate has maintained a consistently high degree of partisan alignment despite the widely observed trend elsewhere towards declining levels of party identification.

However, while Figure 6.2 shows that this resistance to partisan de-alignment extended into the 1990s, the data also provide evidence to suggest that the level of party identification may be finally declining. Asked for their party identification in 1996 (using the same question format as in 1993), some 5 per cent fewer respondents in the Australian Election Study nominated a party identification. This decline in the level of identification, from 88 to 83 per cent, is a statistically significant difference (at the p<.05 level), leaving the proportion of voters rejecting a party label now standing at 17 per cent.

A more appropriate measure of partisan alignment may be the level of identification with the Labor and the Liberal–National parties, since it is their collective support that determines the stability of the system and thus a switch towards identification with minor parties could itself be interpreted as a challenge to the dominant party system. When we consider this measure, a broadly similar pattern is revealed. On average, the level of identification with the major parties is about 5 per cent lower than the total proportion of identifiers with all parties, although in 1990, the year in which minor parties and independents recorded their highest ever vote in a federal election, the gap was somewhat greater, as major party identification slipped, before returning to a higher level in 1993. But in 1996, as with total party identification, the proportion of major party identifiers fell, to under four-fifths of the electorate. One sample survey, of course, can never establish a definitive trend and it remains to be seen whether future surveys confirm this pattern, but it is not inconsistent with the other evidence from recent elections concerning the inroads made by minor parties and independents into voter support previously reserved for the major parties.

In addition to providing evidence about the aggregate level of party identification, Figure 6.2 also presents data on the second important dimension of partisanship, its intensity. While the most vital piece of information about partisanship is the party with which an individual identifies (if any), knowing how strongly the person holds that attachment provides further information on the extent to which partisanship will influence the individual's political behaviour and attitudes. Those who have a very strong partisan attachment, for example, are almost certain to vote for the party they identify with, while those whose identification is not very strong are rather less likely to be faithful at the ballot box. Thus, if strength of party identification declined, even when the overall level of identification remained high, this would be an indication in itself of a weakening of the party system. Indeed, this is exactly what appeared to happen in Britain in the 1970s – the level of identification with the major parties fell only slightly, while the strength of identification dropped dramatically (Crewe, Särlvik and Alt 1977; Heath and others 1991: 12–13).

There is some evidence that a modest decline in the strength of identification occurred during the 1980s in Australia, although again there are methodological problems in comparing earlier and later data (Bean 1994; 1996). The line at the bottom of Figure 6.2, however, suggests that there has been little if any further decline in the strength of identification (among those who accept a party label) in the 1990s. Partisans reporting their identification to be 'very strong' numbered 20 per cent in 1987 and, while this figure dipped to 17 per cent in 1990, it returned to 19 per cent in 1993 and remained at that level in 1996. Most notably, there is no hint of a decline in the strength of identification in 1996 to accompany the slump in the total number of party identifiers.

It is always possible that the lack of change in the strength of party identification masks movements that have occurred among supporters of different parties. Table 6.4 addresses this possibility by showing the percentages of 'very strong' identifiers by party. Among Labor identifiers there does appear to have been a small decline in strength of identification between 1987 and 1996. In 1987, 21 per cent of Labor identifiers held that attachment very strongly, compared to 18 per cent in 1996. It would be unwise to infer too much from these data by way of a downwards trend, since there were slightly more very strong Labor identifiers in both 1993 and 1996 than in 1990, but it is reasonable to conclude that in the 1990s the proportion of very strong Labor identifiers dropped below 20 per cent for the first time.

TABLE 6.4   *Strength of identification by party, 1987–96 (percentages of very strong identifiers)*

	1987	1990	1993	1996
Labor	21	17	19	18
Liberal	18	18	20	20
National	24	20	21	20
Liberal–National	19	19	20	20
Democrat	8	9	2	5
Other	39	35	34	23

Sources: Australian Election Studies, 1987 (n=1825), 1990 (n=2037), 1993 (weighted n=2388), 1996 (n=1797).

With respect to Liberal Party identification, and identification with the two Coalition parties combined, we see a reverse pattern, with slightly more strong partisans in 1993 and 1996 than in 1987 and 1990. On its own, however, the National Party shows a similar pattern to that for Labor, with rather fewer strong partisans in 1996 than in 1987 (although the numbers of National Party identifiers are relatively small, making the individual estimates for that party less reliable). Overall, however, the message from the data for the major parties, as for the total proportion of strong identifiers in Figure 6.2, is one of little change in strength of identification over the last decade. The same is largely true for strength of identification among supporters of the Australian Democrats and other minor parties – to the extent that there is an apparent trend, in both cases it suggests a decline in strength, but again the numbers of respondents are very small.

Trends in the level and strength of party identification provide important indicators of the extent to which the established party system is or is not under challenge. Yet it is equally important to consider the influence of partisanship upon political behaviour. Party identification has a strong impact on electoral choice, but this does not mean that everyone who holds a partisan attachment votes for his or her preferred party at every election. At any one election, some partisans may feel disillusioned with their party, they may find the leader of another party particularly appealing, or they may feel drawn to a different party because of some issue of special importance. The extent to which party identification and vote correspond with one another and whether this relationship changes or remains static over time is a further indicator of the persistence or decline of partisan stability – and in some respects a more important one than simple trends in the level and strength of party identification.

Table 6.5 examines the faithfulness of identifiers with the Labor and Liberal–National parties at the four federal elections from 1987 to 1996, following a procedure employed by Crewe, Särlvik and Alt (1977: 144) and Aitkin (1982: 288), in which the proportion of major party identifiers who vote in accordance with their identification (treating the Liberals and Nationals as one party) is compared with the proportion who vote for some other party. In Britain, Crewe and his colleagues found that between the

TABLE 6.5 *Fidelity of vote among major party identifiers, 1987–96*

	1987 %	1990 %	1993 %	1996 %
Vote in accordance with party identification	90	86	92	90
Vote not in accordance with party identification	10	14	8	10
	100	100	100	100
(N)	(1576)	(1703)	(1980)	(1307)

Sources: Australian Election Studies, 1987 (n=1825), 1990 (n=2037), 1993 (weighted n=2388), 1996 (n=1797).

mid 1960s and the mid 1970s, the period when partisan strength began to decline in that country, the proportion of major party identifiers voting in accordance with their partisanship fell from 86 per cent to 77 per cent. Aitkin, by contrast, found no sign of such a decline in partisan fidelity in Australia between 1967 and 1979.

The analysis here differs slightly from these two in that it excludes non-voters, who comprise only very small numbers in the Australian compulsory voting system. Nevertheless, the data in Table 6.5 contain findings similar to those of Aitkin. In each of the surveys from 1987 to 1996, around 90 per cent of major party identifiers voted in agreement with their identification and only about 10 per cent were unfaithful to their chosen party at the ballot box. In 1990, when the vote for minor parties was unusually high, the proportion of faithful major party identifiers dipped to 86 per cent, but rebounded in 1993 to its highest level in the four elections. Notwithstanding the dip in 1990 and the readjustment in 1993, there is no sign of any trend in party fidelity, with exactly the same high proportion of major party identifiers voting in line with their partisanship in 1996 as in 1987.

Conclusion

In addition to reviewing developments in the Australian party system using the most fundamental measure of political party support, aggregate votes for political parties at federal and state elections, this chapter has assessed evidence from trends in one very limited behavioural measure of party support (party membership) and one broadly-based attitudinal measure (party identification) in order to address the question of whether the party system as a whole is under challenge in the 1990s. The evidence remains mixed.

The data on federal and state party support contain some evidence in favour of the 'challenge' thesis, in that the major parties at the federal level and in three states appear to have been in a weaker position in the past decade than at any time over the last forty years. However, in two states the major parties collectively have been in a more dominant position recently than in the past. The most unequivocal evidence is based on party membership, which shows a clear decline. Yet, party membership levels have never been high in Australia and this measure is the least likely of those we have considered to have a major impact on the party system overall. The data on party identification, on the other hand, show a much less definite picture: the overall level of party identification has declined, but only recently, while the strength of party identification has remained relatively stable in the last four elections, although it had probably declined to some extent prior to then. Finally, the relationship between major party identification and the vote remains high and shows no downward trend.

All in all, and especially when we consider the national level, the evidence implies that the major Australian political parties are in a less comfortable position now than they have been in the past. Moreover, ongoing social, economic and attitudinal change is unlikely to reduce the pressures on them in the future. The Australian Democrats appear to be well entrenched as Australia's most successful minor party and the Greens are also likely to be a persistent political force for the foreseeable future. The evidence from the aggregate analysis of state and federal electoral patterns indicates that the Labor Party has suffered more than the Liberal and National parties from the successful invasion of minor parties and independents into the major parties' erstwhile electoral territory.

Exactly why this should be so is a question requiring further research. However, one possible explanation may be that the ideological location of the prominent minor parties tends to be closer to Labor's ideological position than to that of the Coalition. This scenario has potential advantages as well as disadvantages for Labor. While it leaves Labor vulnerable to the vote-pulling power of these minor parties, it also creates a larger pool of potential Labor supporters than exists for the Coalition parties. And indeed, the historical success of the mainstream political parties over many decades serves to remind us of their powers of adaptation and recovery and of their ability to alter their appeals to the electorate so as to maintain their political dominance in the face of ongoing change.

Appendix

Measuring trends in levels of party identification in Australia is hampered by a variety of methodological problems, which impair the comparability of data from earlier and later periods (Bean 1994; Charnock 1992; 1996). Even the figures from the four studies in the same series that are used in this chapter are not all strictly comparable with one another. The basic party identification question itself follows a form used widely elsewhere and is the same in all four surveys: 'Generally speaking, do you usually think of yourself as Liberal, Labor, National or what?' This is followed by a question asking whether the respondents judge their identification to be 'very strong', 'fairly strong' or 'not very strong'.

With regard to the first question, the 1987 and 1990 surveys gave no explicit option among the list of possible responses for participants in the survey to choose 'no party', whereas the 1993 and 1996 surveys did. Other research has shown that in the absence of an explicit 'no party' option, more respondents give a party identification than when it is present (Bean 1994; Charnock 1996). Indeed, it can be argued that when the question is asked without the 'no party' option in a self-completion format, it gives the equivalent overall level of party identification to the two-part question often used in face-to-face interviews, in which those respondents who initially deny a party identification are asked whether they consider themselves to be closer to one of the parties than the others (I am grateful to Roger Jones for this suggestion).

If we accept this argument, we can adjust the party identification figures from 1987 and 1990 in order to make them equivalent to those for 1993 and 1996. In major Australian surveys in which the two-part question has been used, the difference between the more encompassing version of party identification (including those who say they are closer to a party in addition to those who give an identification in answer to the first question) and the more basic version averages 6 per cent (see Aitkin 1982: 287; Bean and Kelley 1988: 85). If we thus assume that the overall level of party identification in the two earlier Australian Election Studies is inflated by this margin relative to the two later surveys, it follows that the level of party identification in 1987 and 1990 needs to be adjusted downwards by 6 per cent in order to arrive at figures which are comparable with those for 1993 and 1996.

Note

The author is grateful for help and advice from Gerard Newman, Statistics Group, Parliamentary Research Service.

References

Aitkin, D. (1982), *Stability and Change in Australian Politics*, 2nd edn, Canberra: Australian National University Press.

Aitkin, D. and Kahan, M. (1974), 'Australia: Class Politics in the New World' in R. Rose (ed.), *Electoral Behavior: A Comparative Handbook*, New York: The Free Press.

Bean, C. (1994), 'Stability or Change? Party Identification in Australia, 1967-93', Paper presented to the Australasian Political Studies Association Conference, Wollongong, October.

Bean, C. (1996), 'Partisanship and Electoral Behaviour in Comparative Perspective' in M. Simms (ed.), *The Paradox of Parties: Australian Political Parties in the 1990s*, Sydney: Allen & Unwin.

Bean, C. and J. Kelley (1988), 'Partisan Stability and Short-term Change in the 1987 Federal Election: Evidence from the NSSS Panel Survey', *Politics*, 23(2): 80–94.

Budge, I., Crewe I. and Farlie, D. (eds) (1976), *Party Identification and Beyond: Representations of Voting and Party Competition*, London: John Wiley & Sons.

Campbell, A., Converse, P. E., Miller, W. E. and Stokes, D. E. (1960), *The American Voter*, New York: John Wiley & Sons.

Campbell, A., Gurin, G. and Miller, W. E. (1954), *The Voter Decides*, Evanston, Illinois: Row, Peterson & Co.

Chaples, E. (1993), 'The Australian Voters' in R. Smith (ed.), *Politics in Australia*, 2nd edn, Sydney: Allen & Unwin.

Charnock, D. (1992), 'Party Identification in Australia, 1967–1990: Implications of Method Effects from Different Survey Procedures', *Australian Journal of Political Science*, 27: 510–16.

Charnock, D. (1996), 'Question-Wording Effects on the Measurement of Non-partisanship: Evidence from Australia', *Electoral Studies*, 15: 263–68.

Crewe, I., Särlvik, B. and Alt, J. (1977), 'Partisan Dealignment in Britain, 1964–1974', *British Journal of Political Science*, 7: 129–90.

Dalton, R. J., Flanagan, S. C. and Beck, P. A. (eds) (1984), *Electoral Change in Advanced Industrial Democracies: Realignment or Dealignment?*, Princeton, NJ: Princeton University Press.

Franklin, M. N., Mackie, T. T. Valen, H. and others (1992), *Electoral Change: Responses to Evolving Social and Attitudinal Structures in Western Countries*, Cambridge: Cambridge University Press.

Goot, M. (1994), 'Class Voting, Issue Voting and Electoral Volatility' in J. Brett, J. Gillespie and M. Goot (eds), *Developments in Australian Politics*, Melbourne: Macmillan.

Heath, A., Jowell, R. Curtice, J. Evans, G. Field, J. and Witherspoon, S. (1991), *Understanding Political Change: The British Voter 1964–1987*, Oxford: Pergamon Press.

Hofnung, M. (1996), 'Public Financing, Party Membership and Internal Party Competition', *European Journal of Political Research*, 29: 73–86.

Hughes, C. A. (1966), 'Compulsory Voting', *Politics*, 1: 81–95.

Hughes, C. A. (1997), 'Individual Electoral Districts' in C. Bean, S. Bennett, M. Simms and J. Warhurst (eds), *The Politics of Retribution: The 1996 Australian Federal Election*, Sydney: Allen & Unwin.

Jaensch, D. (1983), *The Australian Party System*, Sydney: Allen & Unwin.

Jupp, J. (1982), *Party Politics: Australia 1966–1981*, Sydney: Allen & Unwin.

Katz, R. S. and Mair, P. (eds) (1994), *How Parties Organize: Change and Adaptation in Party Organizations in Western Democracies*, London: Sage Publications.

Katz, R. S., Mair, P. and others (1992), 'The Membership of Political Parties in European Democracies, 1960-1990', *European Journal of Political Research*, 22: 329–45.

Kemp, D. A. (1978), *Society and Electoral Behaviour in Australia: A Study of Three Decades*, St Lucia: University of Queensland Press.

Lipset, S. M. and Rokkan, S. (1967), 'Cleavage Structures, Party Systems, and Voter Alignments: An Introduction' in S. M. Lipset and S. Rokkan (eds), *Party Systems and Voter Alignments: Cross-National Perspectives*, New York: Free Press.

Mackerras, M. (1994), 'General Election, 13 March 1993: Statistical Analysis of the Results', *Australian Journal of Political Science*, 29(Special Issue): 158–84.

Mair, P. (1994), 'Party Organizations: From Civil Society to the State' in R. S. Katz and P. Mair (eds), *How Parties Organize: Change and Adaptation in Party Organizations in Western Democracies*, London: Sage Publications.

Marks, G. N. (1993), 'Partisanship and the Vote in Australia: Changes over Time 1967-1990', *Political Behavior*, 15: 137–66.

Marsh, I. (1995), *Beyond the Two Party System: Political Representation, Economic Competitiveness and Australian Politics*, Melbourne: Cambridge University Press.

McAllister, I. (1991), 'Party Adaptation and Factionalism within the Australian Party System', *American Journal of Political Science*, 35: 206–27.

McAllister, I. (1992), *Political Behaviour: Citizens, Parties and Elites in Australia*, Melbourne: Longman Cheshire.

McAllister, I., Mackerras, M. Ascui, A. and Moss, S. (1990), *Australian Political Facts*, Melbourne: Longman Cheshire.

Nelson, H. and Watson, L. (1969), 'Party Organisation' in H. Mayer (ed.), *Australian Politics: A Second Reader*, Melbourne: F. W. Cheshire.

Papadakis, E. (1990), 'Minor Parties, the Environment and the New Politics' in C. Bean, I. McAllister and J. Warhurst (eds), *The Greening of Australian Politics: The 1990 Federal Election*, Melbourne: Longman Cheshire.

Papadakis, E. and Bean, C. (1995), 'Independents and Minor Parties: The Electoral System', *Australian Journal of Political Science*, 30 (Special Issue): 97–110.

Rae, D. W. (1971), *The Political Consequences of Electoral Laws*, rev. edn, New Haven & London: Yale University Press.

Selle, P. and Svåsand, L. (1991), 'Membership in Party Organizations and the Problem of Decline of Parties', *Comparative Political Studies*, 23: 459–77.

Sharman, C. (1990), 'The Party Systems of the Australian States: Patterns of Partisan Competition, 1945–1986', *Publius*, 20(4): 85–104.

Sharman, C. (1994), 'Political Parties' in J. Brett, J. Gillespie and M. Goot (eds), *Developments in Australian Politics*, Melbourne: Macmillan.

Ward, I. (1987), 'Labor's Middle-class Membership: A Profile of the Victorian Branch of the ALP in the Eighties', *Politics*, 22(2): 84–91.

Ward, I. (1989), 'Two Faces of the ALP in the 1980s', *Australian and New Zealand Journal of Sociology*, 25:165–86.

Ward, I. (1991), 'The Changing Organisational Nature of Australia's Political Parties', *Journal of Commonwealth and Comparative Politics*, 29: 153–74.

Warhurst, J. (1983), 'One Party or Eight? The State and Territory Labor Parties?' in A. Parkin and J. Warhurst (eds), *Machine Politics in the Australian Labor Party*, Sydney: Allen & Unwin.

Watson, L. (1973), 'The Party Machines' in H. Mayer and H. Nelson (eds), *Australian Politics: A Third Reader*, Melbourne: Cheshire.

PART II

Contemporary issues

7

Republicanism and citizenship

Helen Irving

Republicanism

Republicanism is a theory of government which, according to most commonly accepted definitions, means (at the very least) the absence of arbitrary power. For the majority of commentators this self-evidently also means a system without hereditary rulers such as kings and queens, although some have suggested that republicanism can co-exist with a monarchy, so long as the monarch has no legal or political power (Gibbs 1994).

Political philosophers describe republicanism as a complex political model of long lineage, involving much more than the absence of hereditary power. Phillip Pettit (1992) discusses republicanism as system of checks and balances on tyranny, and also as a model of 'civic virtue' based on a commitment to 'positive' liberty, rather than liberty defined simply as freedom from interference (Pettit 1993). Brian Galligan (1995) identifies the doctrine of the separation of powers, outlined by the political theorist Baron de Montesquieu in the eighteenth century, as the key feature of early republicanism, with popular sovereignty being the foundation of the modern form of republicanism.

James Warden draws a distinction between classical republicanism based on civic virtue, republicanism of the English and American revolutions of the seventeenth and eighteenth centuries based on the separation of powers, and modern republicanism built in the nineteenth century around theories of representation, demands for the franchise and the growth of class politics. He finds traces of all such traditions in the evolution of Australian political institutions, and argues that 'the republican tradition is not a recently created figment of a political sect ... [nor] a legalistic arrangement of formal and constitutional powers', but a central part of the Anglo-American tradition adopted in Australia in the nineteenth century (Warden 1993: 85).

Graham Maddox, in contrast, distinguishes between Athenian democracy in which all the citizens participated in political discussion and decision making, and what he describes as the essentially undemocratic Roman republican model which 'preserved a form of central executive authority inherited from the monarchy'. From the latter model, via the American federal model, there evolved in Australia, Maddox argues, a 'rigid, written constitution falsely construed as an agreement of the people' (Maddox 1993: 24).

Such scholarly debates have had, however, relatively little impact upon the political republican movement in Australia. In John Hirst's words: 'All around the country professors of politics are indignant. The republican movement has taken off without waiting to listen to their lectures on the true nature of republicanism' (Hirst 1994: 28). For many, in particular outside academic arenas, republicanism is taken to be 'simply a system of government that does not have a hereditary monarch as head of state' (MacMillan, Evans and Storey 1983: 174).

Australians have been debating whether Australia should be a republic since the middle of last century, arguably even earlier (McKenna 1996). Republican organisations and parties have existed over much of this time, gaining significant, if short-lived, public support and political attention at certain historical moments in the nineteenth century, most notably in New South Wales during the Queen's jubilee celebrations of 1887. While, more recently, serious political strain upon the institutions of constitutional monarchy in Australia occurred during the constitutional crisis of 1975 (Archer and Maddox 1985 compare West 1985), the republican goal of replacing the British monarch with an Australian head of state, has never really appeared likely to succeed in Australia until the 1990s. In striking contrast to earlier times, the first half of this decade has proved to be remarkably productive of republican writings and initiatives, and appears more likely than at any other time to lead to the creation of an Australian republic.

In 1991 the Australian Republican Movement (ARM) was established. Writer Tom Keneally has described the expectations of founding members at the time that 'the ferment would soon die' and that the ARM 'would have a job to keep the debate rolling for the next ten years and try to give it a visible face'. But, he records, unlike earlier attempts, it immediately gained official attention: a furore had been created 'which would not diminish' (Keneally 1993: 1).

One reason was the commitment of the Labor government, by then approaching the tenth anniversary of its election, to pursue in practice the policy of republicanism that the Australian Labor Party had adopted in 1981, that is, to seek the alteration of the constitution so that an Australian citizen would replace the Queen as Australia's head of state. While the Labor Party, with its historical origins in the Irish Catholic working-class, had always been inclined to oppose all forms of hereditary English power, this was the first time the party in government had declared its commitment to the formal processes of republicanism.

During earlier periods in government, the Labor Party had achieved a number of very significant changes in constitutional relations between Australia and Britain, including appointing an Australian governor general in 1931, ratifying the Statute of Westminster in 1942, passing a Nationality and Citizenship Act in 1948, changing the Australian title of the Queen in 1973, and ending appeals from Australian Courts to the English Privy Council (Hudson and Sharpe 1988). Such initiatives had effectively exhausted what could be achieved through acts of parliament alone. Removing the English monarch as head of state would require an alteration in the words of the constitution, and this can only be done, as specified in section 128 of the constitution, by a referendum of all the Australian electors. The Labor government under Prime Minister Paul Keating committed itself, thus, to putting a Constitution Alteration Bill through parliament, in order to set in train a referendum. But specifically what alterations would be required to achieve a republic remained to be determined.

In early 1993, Malcolm Turnbull from the ARM, was invited by the prime minister to chair an official Republic Advisory Committee (RAC) which had the task of preparing an options paper describing 'the minimum constitutional changes necessary to achieve a viable Federal Republic of Australia, maintaining the effect of our current conventions and principles of government' (RAC 1993: iv). Following wide consultation and the receipt of several hundred submissions, this committee concluded with a recommendation for what became known as the 'minimalist' position: a republic in which the Australian head of state would be chosen by a vote of two-thirds of a joint sitting of the Commonwealth parliament to replace the current head of state whose position is inherited by birth. In all other respects, under this model, the Australian constitution would remain as far as possible unaltered.

In mid 1995, the prime minister announced his government's response to the RAC report, endorsing the 'minimalist' model and emphasising that this would entail very little change to Australia's political system. The new head of state, the president, would 'perform essentially the same functions as the Governor-General', that is to say, largely symbolic and ceremonial functions, designed primarily to unify the nation, and to provide 'national leadership' (Keating 1995: 7). A referendum to alter the constitution would (if successful) ensure that formal administrative duties performed currently by the governor general as the Queen's representative must in all cases be performed only on the advice of the government. The means for achieving an Australian republic would also be 'minimalist', that is to say, by referendum alone, rather than through any other processes such as a constitutional convention, prior to a referendum.

This position raised three principal questions upon which many republicans remain divided. One concerns the powers of a future republican president. Republicans disagree over whether the 'reserve powers' — those powers able to be employed in emergency situations by a head of state without or contrary to the government's advice — should be 'codified' by being written down in the constitution, or whether they should be left open, remaining unspecified conventions (long standing practices) as is currently the case. The fundamental (and also the most controversial) reserve power is that of dismissing a government during its term of office, that is, in between elections.

Since the events of 1975 when Governor General Sir John Kerr sacked the Labor Prime Minster Gough Whitlam and his government during a deadlock between the two houses of parliament, there has been widespread and deep disagreement over the circumstances which might legitimately lead to the head of state's exercise of this particular reserve power. The RAC recommended that the reserve powers should be codified; on the matter of dismissal it suggested that the president's power of dismissal should be legitimately employed only where a government persisted in breaching the constitution (for example by spending money that had not been lawfully appropriated). Other commentators (their views outlined in the ARC report) have argued that the only justification for invoking the reserve powers is when a government loses the 'confidence' of the house, that is, when it no longer commands majority support in the House of Representatives, but fails to resign. A deadlock between the two houses of parliament, with the Senate refusing to pass supply bills (essential for a government to continue to govern), is another scenario where, some feel, dismissal is justified.

With these controversies in mind, the Keating government declared for non-codification, arguing that 'it is probably impossible to write down or codify these powers in a way that would both find general community acceptance and cover every possible contingency' (Keating 1995: 9). Critics, in return, suggested that a republican constitution which did not codify the reserve powers would simply leave open the possibility of controversial constitutional action on the part of the president, comparable to the events of 1975.

The second unresolved question concerns the manner in which a republican president should be chosen. The current method of selecting a governor general (the Queen's representative in Australia), in practice by choice of the incumbent prime minister, is based on the fiction that this is a nomination only and that the choice is actually made by the Queen. Any alteration of the constitution to achieve a republic will end this fiction, but in anticipating such a change, the question invariably arises whether prime ministerial choice should become *de jure* instead of *de facto*. There have been some suggestions that a republic might do without a head of state altogether, but this position has not attracted significant support. Most debate has assumed the importance of such a role. While both the ARM and the RAC endorsed the government's preference for a parliamentary method of choice, debate had already begun to focus on alternatives.

One alternative, direct popular election of the president, had been and continues to be, overwhelmingly supported by the public in opinion polls. Direct election gained some further support in media commentary and academic publications. Harry Evans has suggested that a directly elected president would indeed be the only really republican method, because republicanism is a system structured to prevent the rule of factions and excessive concentrations of power. Presidential appointment by the parliament, Evans argues, would lead to political deals and trade offs, compromising the independence of the presidency (Evans 1996). The majority of official and expert commentary, however, has concluded that popular choice is fundamentally incompatible with Australia's political system. An elected president, George Winterton argues, would have a separate power base from that of the government and might even claim a mandate from the people to act politically, thereby undermining the role of cabinet and the sovereignty of the parliament, both key components of the Westminster model (Winterton 1994b).

The third question concerns the manner in which the changes necessary to achieve a republic in the first place should proceed. The question remains whether a referendum, although legally necessary, is sufficient. Criticism of the 'minimalist' model has suggested, among other things, that a referendum alone would not provide adequate opportunities for public participation, especially by groups under-represented in the parliaments and in the major political parties. Proposed alternatives include holding a plebiscite prior to a referendum, that is to say, an indicative but not binding national vote, designed to give a clear indication of whether or not Australians want a republic before they vote in a formal referendum on the specific constitutional alterations involved. A plebiscite, it has been argued by Malcolm Mackerras (1996), might also include alternative choices, options for the manner in which a future president is to be selected. A constitutional convention prior to a referendum has also been suggested, as a means of debating whether Australians want a republic, or for 're-writing' the constitution along republican lines, prior to a referendum.

A less controversial issue, but one that is still a significant constitutional challenge, revolves around the status of the individual states as separate monarchies in their own right. The states have their own constitutions, each providing for a monarchical system, including a governor who is appointed in theory (although in practice on the advice of the premier) by the Queen. It is still unclear whether constitutional amendment at the Commonwealth level is able to reach the states so that unilateral change to a republic could be achieved, either by referendum or through the exercise of a Commonwealth power (Carney 1994). But even if it were constitutionally possible for a state on its own to hold out and remain a monarchy, would it be a politically viable arrangement? The majority of commentators conclude that it would not.

Among these issues, the means of achieving a republic has generated the greatest debate in recent times, in large part because of the change of federal government in March 1996. In opposition, the Liberal Party of Australia had made a commitment to holding a 'People's Convention' which would 'give the Australian people their proper voice in any review of our Constitution' (Downer 1994). A proposal to hold a plebiscite if a clear consensus did not emerge from the convention's deliberations was later added. The Liberal Party's plan at the time was for the convention to be made up of delegates, half of whom would be elected in a national ballot and half selected by the government. Its role would not be confined to a discussion of republicanism. Indeed the plan anticipated that the role of the head of state would be no more than one among a number of constitutional issues for review, including the distribution of state and federal powers, new states, the length of term of the parliament, and the use of the external affairs power (section 51 xxix).

With its election in March 1996, the Liberal–National Party Coalition government confirmed its support for this model, although informally raising some concerns soon after about the costs involved in electing convention representatives, and floating the idea that a plebiscite might be held first, or even held instead of a convention, with the process then moving directly to a referendum. Another model, which may well emerge as the government's choice, is a non-elected convention, in which the delegates are appointed by local or state governments. At the time of the Coalition's first federal budget in August 1996, it was still unclear in which direction matters would proceed.

Official initiatives on the part of both the previous and the current government emerged against a background of intense examination of republicanism in publications, both scholarly and popular. An unusual feature of many of these works is the blending of historical and political analysis, sometimes with discussion of philosophical or jurisprudential questions surrounding the concept of republicanism, and at times also with personal testimonial or advocacy (see Hudson and Carter 1993; Headon, Gamage and Warden 1994).

A number of such personal contributions appeared early on in this new phase of republican exploration. *The Coming Republic*, published in 1992, includes a collection of intimate accounts by individuals prominent in Australian sporting, cultural and political life, describing their own path to republicanism. It concludes with a discussion of the history of Australia's 'cultural cringe' (famously named by A. A. Phillips in a literary article in

1950), and a rejection of what is described as the attitude of condescension adopted by the British towards Australians (Horne and others 1992).

In *The Australian Republic*, former Labor immigration minister, Al Grassby, argued for a republic in order to resist global economic hegemony and to end, once and for all, the cultural cringe. Grassby invoked a long tradition of radical republicanism in Australia, including the writings of John Dunmore Lang and Daniel Deniehy, and the rebellions of the Eureka Stockade and Ned Kelly, and he tied this together with both the condition of independence in Aboriginal Australia before the arrival of the British, and with subsequent Aboriginal resistance. Writing in 1993, during a period of Liberal leadership under John Hewson (whose position on the republican question appeared at least potentially favourable) Grassby concluded that the republic was fast approaching, with few opponents left, even in the Liberal Party. The 'long summer and autumn [of 1993] came to a close leaving the supporters of the hereditary monarch located in a foreign country in a rapidly dwindling minority facing the coldest winter' (Grassby 1993: 296).

That same year, Tom Keneally, then chair of the ARM, published *Our Republic*, an optimistic personal account of his observations and travels in Australia and Britain, and of the development of political strategy within the ARM (Keneally 1993). As in Horne's and Grassby's works, Keneally's approach gave interpretive priority to Australia's historical subservience, to the imperial context of the constitution's writing, and to the continuing 'cringe' and colonial character of Australian culture. An Australian republic, these works argue, must be created as a radical break from the past, as a means of striking back against the long shadow of British imperialism. This interpretation was also manifest in the 1992 speech made by the prime minister on the fiftieth anniversary of the fall of Singapore, in which regret was expressed at the British military decision of the time not to deploy adequate forces in the region and it was implied that Australians, having been abandoned to the invading Japanese in 1942, should now feel comfortable with striking out on their own to establish a republic.

Soon after, however, a shift in interpretation can be observed, with historians and republican advocates beginning to emphasise the essentially democratic character of Australia's formation as a nation, and to describe the future republic as an inevitable conclusion to this process, an extension of the sovereignty already embedded in the Australian Commonwealth. The republic is most recently depicted as a positive conclusion to foregoing sovereign processes, rather than a radical break with Australia's history.

In this manner, John Hirst's *Republican Manifesto* presented a 'generous' minimalist case based on the theme of the monarch's irrelevance to Australian politics. Hirst argued that a republic would bring no effective change to Australian life except in generating confidence in the Australian people that they could finally manage on their own. It reiterated his earlier

'Conservative Case for an Australian Republic' which argued that the Queen, having lost the civic status she once importantly held in Australian society, is no longer the source of unity or civic loyalty. Instead of fighting to retain the monarchy, conservatives should accept this change, Hirst concluded, and recognise that 'once nationalism is appeased with a republican Australia it will be easier to acknowledge again that Australia's institutions are British' (Hirst 1991).

In *The Republican Manifesto*, Hirst described a new generation of Australian republicans. For the first time in Australia's history they are 'single-minded', rather than motivated by or committed to political causes (such as Irish independence) outside Australia. The old republicans were radicals, 'on the fringes of society, and of very little influence', where in contrast, the new (effectively the members of the ARM) are mainstream, members of the Australian middle class, even celebrities. They are rapidly becoming the majority, the descendants not of the few radical republicans of the past, but of 'the people who demanded self-government from the British ... who made the Commonwealth out of six colonies ... who adopted our own flag and our own national anthem' (Hirst 1994: 98, 106). Their success, Hirst concluded, was inevitable.

In *The Federal Republic*, Brian Galligan argued that the Australian constitutional system had always been 'republican', because it was originally based on the sovereignty of the Australian people. This sovereignty was exercised through the processes by which the constitution was written and popularly approved in the 1890s. Furthermore, in its adoption of a system of federalism for its institutional framework, Australia's constitution reflects a republican system of checks and balances. Such an argument, Galligan concedes, 'might not be congenial' to either republicans or monarchists, because, if Australia is indeed already a 'federal republic' some of the passionate and exaggerated rhetoric on both sides will be undermined (Galligan 1995: 4).

Debate on the republic has evolved during the decade to include the contribution of historians, political scientists and others, alongside experts in constitutional law. In this respect, the republican movement is importantly serving the process of 'de-mystifying' the constitution, and potentially (depending on one's view of the constitution's purpose) re-defining it as, or restoring it to its original purpose as, a 'people's' document. Part of this process includes a re-examination of history, and an emphasis on the role played by the people in the federation organisations of last century, in the election of delegates to a constitutional convention in 1897 and in the referendums of 1898 and 1899. Although there has been some questioning of the extent to which these were genuinely 'popular' processes (Macintyre 1994), the idea that the constitution is 'owned' by the Australian people has gained wide support, even implicitly in recent High Court judgments.

The change of republican rhetoric on the constitution's history, from rejection to embrace, may have been in part also due to the use first made by constitutional monarchists of the argument that Australia is already sovereign and in no way compromised by its constitutional ties to the monarchy. The current system, monarchists argue, provides stability and avoids the conflict which may arise if the head of state is Australian and therefore not 'above' politics (Kirby 1993). Anti-republicans in addition point to the safeguards now provided against British interference (such as the Statute of Westminster, and the Australia Acts of 1986) through which all the rights that the British parliament (hence the crown) and the Privy Council once held in respect of Australian law are now severed (Hudson and Sharp 1988).

In *The Muddle Headed Republic*, Alan Atkinson (1993), in addition, has attempted to take seriously the republican argument that the Queen should not be Australia's head of state because she is not an Australian citizen. He advocates the establishment of an Australian royal family, through the re-location of one of the minor royals to serve as head of state, and to provide heirs and successors to continue the hereditary office. This alternative, Atkinson concludes, would meet the republicans' main criticism, while maintaining the stability and impartiality sought by monarchists.

While argument about the social and political impact of republicanism proceeds around such issues, in the area of law the question remains how precisely such a transition might be made. The complexities of constitutional law are indeed at the heart of the republican question, but although Malcolm Turnbull (RAC chair) has argued (1993) that the necessary constitutional change is in fact quite straightforward, having been made to appear complex and mysterious by lawyers, it cannot be said that there is a uniform or unambiguous legal agreement on this. On the detail of constitutional alteration required to effect an Australian republic in law, considerable difference of opinion exists. For example, there is still debate over whether section 128 of the constitution (which describes the means of constitutional alteration via popular referendum) can reach the constitution's covering clauses, among which, most significantly, is included the constitution's preamble (Winterton 1994a: ch. 8).

The preamble is one part of the constitution most likely to undergo change in the transition to a republic: its references to an indissoluble Commonwealth 'under the Crown' will require deletion, for both legal and symbolic reasons, if the preamble is to be retained as anything other than a historical curiosity. Other words in the preamble have been targeted for possible change. There appears to be widespread support for the inclusion in a modified (or a new) preamble of recognition of the prior ownership of Australia by the Aboriginal people, although it is likely that strenuous opposition will also come from some quarters if this proposal gains official sanction. Some debate has also centred on whether the expression 'humbly relying on the blessing of Almighty God' should be retained, and suggestions for further inclusions (such as a reference to sharing and protecting the environment, to adherence to democracy, and to respect for basic values) are in abundance.

A draft republican constitution has been written by George Winterton, in which the references to the monarch (as well as a number of extraneous, out of date sections) have been deleted and replaced by appropriate, alternative words or sections. Originally published in the *Independent Monthly*, it has been reprinted on a number of occasions (Winterton 1994b), and serves essentially as the point of departure for the minimalist position. Caricatured by some as the 'tippex' approach to republicanism (Abbott 1994), this form of minimalism is consistent with recent historical analysis which underlines the simple, almost uneventful nature of a transition to a republic.

Minimalism, however, has not been embraced by all republicans. If republicanism is essentially a system without arbitrary power, incompatible with rule from 'above', it requires, some have argued, rule from 'below,' that is, rule by the people. The establishment of an Australian republic, these commentators conclude, must therefore involve a move towards greater popular sovereignty and this means a radically different type of political structure from the present Australian system. The republic would be meaningless, 'maximalists' suggest, without the chance to alter fundamental features of the Australian political system or to invigorate the community with a new sense of responsibility and a new commitment to participation.

This position has been developed by Andrew Fraser, for whom authentic republicanism must entail the transfer of power from the parliaments to the people, through the creation of a constitutional assembly, a charter of rights, elected judiciaries, and democratised corporations, all adding up to a 'multiplicity of little republics within the institutional life of Australian civil society'. In such institutions, Fraser argues, lies the 'classical republican ideal of a free, active and virtuous citizenry' (Fraser 1993: 59, 39).

Other 'maximalist' options were publicly explored early in the republican campaign of the 1990s, including suggestions that republicanism should create opportunities to dismantle the federal system by abolishing the states, or to institute new parliamentary forums, or to move to an American style appointed executive, replacing the Westminster model of 'responsible government' in which the ministry is chosen from members of parliament.

In an address in 1993, former Liberal Minister Ian Macphee argued that a republic was inevitable by the end of the twentieth century, but that 'if we simply substitute a President for the Governor-General, we will accomplish nothing substantial' (Macphee 1993: 2). Macphee's alternative involved the replacement of Australia's federal system with a unitary model, abolishing the states and putting in their place both a strong central government with national powers and regional governments responsible for regional matters only, funded by local ratepayers. Macphee foresaw greater efficiencies in addition to enhanced responsiveness and accountability arising from such restructuring.

While such forms of 'maximalism' have not developed far nor been adopted as party political goals, the line between minimalism and maximalism is not always clear. Some writings in which the 'minimalist' goal is questioned advocate, for example, the inclusion of a bill of rights in the constitution (Emy 1994), but it remains to be seen whether this will remain a 'maximalist' demand, or emerge for serious consideration in whatever constitutional forums are established to determine whether Australia becomes a republic. A range of other constitutional alterations which are not strictly 'republican' in the minimalist sense (that is, concerned with the identity and powers of the head of state alone) have also been suggested from time to time as possible further subjects for debate in such forums. The Liberal Party, for example, although committed in its policy of retaining the constitutional monarchy, seeks a modification to the 'external affairs' power of the constitution to restrict the application of international treaties to areas of state jurisdiction, arguing that this represents more of a threat to national sovereignty than the fact that Australia has a British head of state.

One issue upon which the majority of commentators, both republican and monarchist, seem in agreement, concerns what might appear of symbolic significance only. With the award to Sydney of the year 2000 Olympic Games, the question immediately arose whether the Queen, as Australian head of state, should open the games. The international Olympics Charter specifies that this function should be performed by the head of state of the host country, but even conservatives in Australia appear reluctant to see the Queen play this role. In response, some have argued that the Queen is not in fact Australia's head of state, that it is the governor general who is and that he, therefore, should declare the games open. Others suggest that the charter is flexible, and leaves the national government to decide whom to invite for this task. But the question will not be resolved easily. Although it is not a constitutional matter, or even a matter of law, it demonstrates how powerful symbolism is in political questions, and how much the republicanism issue is bound up with the symbolic representation of Australia's identity as an independent nation, even if, in law, it is already sovereign.

Feminist writers have been particularly aware of the importance of symbolism in the debate and have subjected both republican theory and the republican movement to feminist critique. Recent contributions to this critique can be divided into two approaches, roughly approximating two different stages: the first, which involves an analysis principally of the focus and direction of the formal republican movement, and the second, a critique of the formal processes of constitutional review, in which women's increased participation is targeted.

In the first, debate was stimulated by the simple recognition of the fact that (although four women sat on the RAC) women were relatively under-represented in prominent republican positions. Tied to this was the observation that women, when asked in opinion surveys, tended to support an Australian republic less than men (Lake 1996). The masculine imagery employed in republican rhetoric, the use of military metaphors and references, and the emphasis on independence, alienated women, it was argued, and failed to provide them with an imaginative point of entry into the republican goal (Irving 1993–94; 1994). Marilyn Lake described in addition the anxieties she perceived to be felt by women about the potential loss of security in a republic, in particular the loss of a comforting, prominent female figure, currently found in the person of the Queen (Lake 1993). This theme was developed further in an exploration of women's traditional distrust of the political, and the perception of the Queen 'as a non-political figure motivated solely by the sort of selfless duty that is still required of the majority of women' (Lake 1996: 14).

Responding to the minimalist agenda, some feminist theorists specifically identified a 'maximalist' opportunity for women in constitutional change. They argued both for a women's bill of rights and for change to the electoral system employed for the Commonwealth parliament so that the lower house would be elected by proportional representation (as the Senate is) thus increasing the likelihood of women's election to a seat. The ideas of British feminist, Anne Phillips, whose *Engendering Democracy* (1991) includes an examination of the impact of proportional representation on women's representation and her argument for taking representative democracy beyond issues, into the 'politics of presence', have been very influential in these debates (Phillips 1995).

A women's bill of rights as a republican goal was also raised elsewhere, as a means of recognising 'the context of women's lives' in the law. The absence of specified fundamental rights in the constitution, Vicky Marquis argued, leaves their identification to 'discovery' by a judiciary which is not 'well equipped … to understand, interpret and take into consideration the context of women's lives when making judgements based on as-sumptions and stereotypes about women' (Marquis 1993). While the example of the Canadian Charter of Rights suggests that a bill of rights may in practice create problems for women in the absence of a feminist political strategy specifically designed to affirm and promote women's rights, this should be further explored, 'to encourage women to challenge men's ownership of the Republican debate' (Bacchi and Marquis 1994).

In 1996, following the election of the Howard government, women began to press for special measures to provide a guarantee of women's equal representation in any future constitutional convention in which the character of an Australian republic may be determined. 'Women into Politics', a pressure group consisting of affiliated women's organisations, has argued for a 50 per cent quota for women representatives in a future constitutional convention (Women Into Politics 1996). The case for a constitutional guarantee of equal representation for women in parliaments has also been advanced. Kim Rubenstein and Deborah Cass argue that recent High Court decisions which identified an implied guarantee of freedom of political communication in the Australian system of representative government effectively provide, in the modern democratic context, a guarantee of equal representation for all citizens, male or female (Rubenstein and Cass 1996).

The feminist critique of republican discourse and its argument for using the republican debate to press for institutional change leading to greater representation of women in politics, was a critique essentially aimed at claims for citizenship rights. The issue of constitutional reform leading to an Australian republic began, in this way as in others, to merge with the re-examination of conditions for 'citizenship' in Australian political culture.

Citizenship

In what appeared as part of a 'trilogy' of initiatives from the Keating government (of which the establishment of the RAC was the first and the Centenary of Federation Advisory Committee chaired by former Premier of Victoria, Joan Kirner, the second), a Civics Expert Group was set up in June, 1994. Chaired by Stuart Macintyre, its primary term of reference was 'to provide the Government with a strategic plan for a non-partisan program of public education and information on the Australian system of government, the Australian Constitution, Australian citizenship and other civics issues' (Civics Expert Group 1994). Curriculum development along these lines was under way by early 1996, 'to increase ... understanding of Australian civic life and to promote informed citizenship among our young people' (Curriculum Corporation 1996).

In preparing its report, the Civics Expert Group commissioned a survey of political knowledge among Australians which found that levels of knowledge were low, especially among women and youth. The report advocated a range of school and community programs of civics education built around a national curriculum involving the study of Australian political history, institutions, values and citizenship roles. Although it recognised a high level of citizen participation in voluntary and community organisations, the Civics Expert Group implicitly worked with a model of citizenship based on knowledge, rather than direct experience. In doing so it departed from a long standing critique of citizenship based on social and economic factors.

This latter had emerged from the postwar work of British theorist T. H. Marshall who argued that, while civil rights (freedom of the person, freedom to hold property, freedom of contract, speech and conscience) and formal political rights (the right to vote and stand for election to political office) had been accomplished for all in western nations during the twentieth century, full citizenship was not possible while economic inequalities endured. The state, Marshall argued, should provide for welfare and education, so that each person may be a full citizen, living 'the life of a civilised human being according to the standards prevailing in the society' (Marshall 1965: 78).

This model had been very influential in left-wing and liberal postwar politics, and to an extent Marshall's analysis still provides a point of departure for much discussion of citizenship. In a recent Australian work on citizenship and employment, Jocelyn Pixley (1993) argues that political rights and participation are currently structured in such a way as to rule out those who are not in paid employment from full citizenship. While Pixley criticises Marshall for an inadequate appreciation of the gendered nature of citizenship and for an over-optimistic assessment of the degree to which citizenship rights have been achieved and remain stable, she nonetheless argues in the style of Marshall that there is a nexus primarily between economic status and citizenship opportunities.

A related argument has been developed by those feminist theorists for whom citizenship rights go beyond or are independent of formal representation in parliaments. Neither classical nor modern definitions of citizenship, allow women to be full citizens, Rian Voet (1994) has argued. Women are neither equal members of the polis, nor soldiers, nor bearers of equal civil, social and political rights. Full citizenship for women, Voet concludes, 'will require temporary affirmative action, special reproduction rights ... and the revision of Marshall's citizenship rights from a female perspective'. Some have suggested specifically that women's citizenship is restricted by the status of occupational roles to which they are statistically confined, and by the unwillingness of men to play a full part in the domestic sphere (Cass 1990). The culture of national politics early this century, others argue in addition, was constructed around difference and it constructed a 'gendered citizenship', with men identified as 'citizen-soldiers' and women as 'citizen-mothers'. Both were seen as making a contribution to the nation, but were relegated to a limited, gendered field, which was subject to 'policing' by the state (Pettman 1996).

Carole Pateman has subjected the category of citizenship itself to feminist critique, arguing that the very nature of liberal democratic politics as it historically developed in the west is based in a 'sexual contract'. She suggests that the concept of citizenship, derived from liberal individualist notions of contract and a gender-based division into public and private, fails even to recognise women's activities and contribution. In the west, she argues, the assumption prevails that caring for children, invalids and the elderly is the private concern, 'almost invariably' of individual women; this type of activity is, furthermore, not counted as a public contribution, not recognised as a form of citizenship. Such a recognition would, Pateman (1992) concludes, require a fundamental reconsideration of the concepts of both citizenship and democracy.

Running through such arguments is the recurrent question of whether women have special qualities to contribute to citizenship, or whether they have identical abilities to those of men and will, in time, if given the opportunity, become full citizens alongside men (Lister 1995). Some theorists note the emphasis placed by the suffragists last century on the special qualities of women (a special sensitivity to 'welfare' issues, especially in relation to children, and an avoidance of aggressive, competitive political debate) and on the transformation they believed women could bring to politics as a consequence, if they were given the vote and the right to enter parliament. Something of a modern parallel to this position has been suggested by Ann Millar (1996) in an analysis of the Senate as a 'feminised' house of parliament. Millar notes not only that proportional representation, introduced for Senate elections in 1949, has given rise to a much greater percentage of women Senators than is found in the House of Representatives, but also that the constitutional design and role of the Senate favours women's approach to politics, and that the Senate itself has evolved and adapted to the numbers of female Senators. But the difference versus equality debate is probably further from being resolved now than it was at the high tide of second wave feminism in the late 1960s and 1970s.

If the concept of citizenship has an especially positive status at present, there remain to be resolved specific issues of who belongs to the category of 'citizen'. The tendency for 'citizenship' to be used as a neutral, universal category, presents problems not only in an analysis of gender and citizenship, it also challenges other forms of 'difference', such as ethnicity and Aboriginality. In a discussion of feminism and Aboriginality, Jan Jindy Pettman underlines the problems created by the need to recognise special citizenship claims of minority groups — 'collective political identities' — in a liberal democratic system which is based on the idea of 'individual relation of citizen and state' (Pettman 1996: 8).

While, with the extension of the Commonwealth vote in 1962 and in the remaining states (Queensland and Western Australia) soon after, formal political rights for Australian Aborigines were finally granted throughout Australia three decades ago, the claim that Aborigines now enjoy full citizenship can only be sustained from the most literal, legal perspective on what citizenship means. Even if voting rights were thought sufficient to establish citizenship, Aboriginal people who already had the vote in some states, and thereby in the Commonwealth, were frequently denied it in practice by the exercise of unlawful and arbitrary discretion on the part of officials (Stretton and Finnimore 1993). Other forms of exclusion, in respect of passports, naturalisation rights and welfare rights were also applied at times to Aboriginal people. The overriding principle of 'citizenship' in the period prior to the first Nationality and Citizenship Act of 1949 (and with little change once this was passed) was 'whiteness' (Clarke and Galligan 1995).

Although important constitutional changes have occurred in respect of the Aboriginal people, it is to draw a long bow to see these as tied to the acquisition of citizenship. The successful 1967 referendum through which the Commonwealth gained powers to make laws specifically for the Aboriginal people (and which removed from the constitution the section excluding Aborigines from being counted in the Commonwealth census) is still spoken of by many as a 'citizenship' referendum. This is partly, it seems, because the 1967 referendum is often mistakenly thought of as one which gave voting rights to Aborigines, and partly because it appeared at the time to herald a new era for Aboriginal empowerment. What it did in fact was enable a Commonwealth government for the first time to pursue changes in Aboriginal conditions throughout the nation, rather than simply in the Northern Territory (over which the Commonwealth had jurisdiction since 1911) if, but only if, its policy was framed in this way. Aboriginal policy became a matter of political will as much as formal powers, and thus provided only a flimsy basis for 'citizenship'. The 1967 referendum, it must be noted, did not give the Commonwealth powers over land title. These powers remained with the states.

The Whitlam Labor government began a process of major reforms in Aboriginal living standards in the early 1970s, but it was confined in its land rights policy to the Northern Territory. The Fraser Liberal government followed through the Northern Territory land rights program after defeating the Whitlam government in 1975. In addition, the Racial Discrimination Act was passed by the Labor government in 1975, giving the Commonwealth powers under international treaty obligations to prevent the states from passing discriminatory legislation in respect of Aboriginal people, as well as others. This act was employed in 1982 in the *Koowarta* case (*Koowarta v Bjelke-Petersen*) to override a Queensland government law preventing the purchase of a pastoral lease by Aborigines. It was also the legal ground on which the more famous *Mabo* case was decided in 1992. The Racial Discrimination Act and the broad range of human rights obligations to which the Commonwealth has committed itself via ratification of treaties, have opened up the prospect of asserting and defending, albeit in a negative sense, the rights of Aborigines to equal citizenship with non-indigenous people. But full 'citizenship' in the sense theorised by T. H. Marshall, depending at the least upon an equality in social and economic conditions, was far from achieved.

With the High Court's *Mabo* judgment, in which the long standing doctrine of *terra nullius* was overturned and Aboriginal title to land was now recognised alongside common law title, the opportunity for a new form of 'citizenship' for Aborigines was created. Aboriginal citizenship, it may emerge, will be built around the recognition of a special relationship between indigenous Australians and the land, as well as through the social advantages that are attached to property ownership. Neither theoretical nor jurisprudential work, however, has yet reconceptualised 'citizenship' in such a way, and the political arguments for Aboriginal citizenship have yet to resolve the equality versus difference dilemma.

Claims by some Aboriginal activists for sovereignty and nationhood have challenged the value of 'citizenship' altogether. To accept citizenship, they have argued, as Tim Rowse points out, 'is inconsistent with proclaiming Aborigines' sovereignty over the continent'. Rowse himself concludes that Aborigines are both citizens and 'colonised subjects', and that they face, therefore, 'a strategic choice about which of these statuses to emphasize in the rhetoric, tactics and demands which characterise their political mobilisation'. The history of Australian politics, he concludes, suggests that gaining sovereignty from the Commonwealth need not be ruled out (Rowse 1994: 183, 200–1).

Citizenship in respect of immigrants and people from non-English speaking backgrounds also remains a theoretical and political challenge. After a lengthy process in which the status of Australians changed from British subject to Australian citizen/British subject (in 1949) to Australian citizen alone (in 1973), and during which the rights of British immigrants to automatic citizenship were attenuated, formal citizenship rights were standardised for all immigrants in 1984 when the electoral law was amended to provide uniform qualifying conditions for the franchise, by requiring all new voters including British immigrants to be legal citizens. In addition the official policy of multiculturalism adopted by governments in the 1980s, appeared to create the conditions for acceptance of immigrants with non-British backgrounds as full members of the political and cultural community, and anti-discrimination acts made formal exclusion of immigrants from social rights (such as housing) an offence.

In *Sykes v Cleary*, a key High Court judgment in 1992, however, legal citizens holding dual nationality were ruled to be constitutionally ineligible (through section 44 i) to stand for election to parliament, by virtue of their owing 'allegiance to a foreign power'. This judgment underlined the fact that legal citizenship is not sufficient to acquire full rights of political participation (Irving 1993). More recent argument has revolved around the question of whether 'social citizenship' rights should be available to all, with some suggesting that only legal citizens should be entitled to Austudy, social security or unemployment benefits. A government bill before the parliament in late 1996 aims at extending from six to twenty-four months the period before which newly arrived immigrants to Australia may be entitled to unemployment benefits.

Conclusion

Why 'citizenship' became a prominent, even fashionable, concept across the political spectrum in the 1990s, when the term had long held conservative, even reactionary, connotations for left-wing politics, has not yet been fully analysed. One explanation is likely to be that the challenges to socialist theory and politics wrought by political changes in the former Soviet Union and eastern Europe, have created a void for left wing theory, and cast doubt on the efficacy of seeking equality principally through economic redistribution. Claims for citizenship rights have provided a renewed opportunity for critical debate and self reflection, and importantly, also a tool with which to challenge dominant ideologies from within their own language and principles. The idea that individuals should have opportunities to participate in the political community, and that members of parliament should be the representatives of the interests of 'citizens' are still central to the liberal-democratic model, and are accepted across most political positions.

Stuart Macintyre (1996) points out, in addition, that 'while the Australian concern with citizenship draws on particular issues of urgent national relevance, including multiculturalism, reconciliation and the republic, it is by no means restricted to this country'. Macintyre draws attention to the forces of globalisation and to the international 'convulsions' experienced with the breakdown of the old world order, the creation of mass populations of non-citizens, as well as new, internationalised categories of citizenship, and major challenges for national and citizen autonomy. In Australia's case, specifically, the apprehension of such challenges and awareness of the reactions to them which have at times been violent in other countries has led, Macintyre argues, to a concern with protecting the 'precious resource' of citizenship in Australia.

The question of what defines a citizen is generating a considerable amount of analysis and discussion, and in Australia reaches well into the republicanism debate. For many, including those theorists who have identified an analytical as well as historical lineage between republicanism and classical concepts of citizenship within a framework of civic humanism, there is a natural link between the two debates. Others, including advocates of indigenous rights (Brennan 1994), believe that embracing the goal of a bill of rights in a republican constitution, will be a major step towards achieving full citizenship for socially disadvantaged groups. Donald Horne (1994) has argued that the antipathies of republican versus monarchist politics can be transcended by recognising in Australia a 'civic identity', based on core citizenship values and commitments.

Whether equal citizenship can be reached principally through education, legal processes, constitutional review, or all three remains to be tested. If citizenship means more than formal equality, however, its accomplishment must remain one of the greatest challenges facing any democratic system. The achievement of an Australian republic, constitutionally complex and politically difficult though it might be, would appear to have a greater likelihood of short term success.

References

Abbott, T. (1994), '"Manana" — The Politics of Becoming a Republic' in M. A. Stephenson and C. Turner (eds), *Australia: Republic or Monarchy?* St Lucia: University of Queensland Press.

Archer, J. and Maddox, G. (1985), 'The 1975 Constitutional Crisis in Australia,' in D. Woodward, A. Parkin and J. Summers (eds), *Government, Power and Politics in Australia*, 3rd edn, Melbourne: Longman Cheshire.

Atkinson, A. (1993), *The Muddle Headed Republic*, Melbourne: Oxford University Press.

Bacchi, B. and Marquis, V. (1994), 'Women and the Republic: "Rights" and Wrongs', *Australian Feminist Studies*, No. 19.

Brennan, F. (1994), 'Aborigines and Torres Strait Islanders' in M. A. Stephenson and C. Turner (eds), *Australia: Republic or Monarchy?* St Lucia: University of Queensland Press.

Carney, G. (1994), 'Republicanism and State Constitutions,' in M. A. Stephenson and C. Turner (eds), *Australia: Republic or Monarchy?* St Lucia: University of Queensland Press.

Cass, B. (1990), 'Gender and Social Citizenship', SPA paper, Bath, 1990, cited in R. Voet (1994) 'Women as Citizens: a Feminist Debate', *Australian Feminist Studies*, 19, Autumn.

Civics Expert Group (1994), *Whereas the People ... Civics and Citizenship Education*, Canberra: AGPS.

Clarke, T. and Galligan, B. (1995), '"Aboriginal Native" and the Institutional Construction of the Australian Citizen 1901–1948', *Australian Historical Studies*, 105, October.

Curriculum Corporation (1996), 'Civics and Citizenship Education Broadsheet', February.

Downer, A. (1994), Media release, 17 November.

Emy, H. (1994), 'Republicanism and constitutional reform: Does the minimalist position go far enough?' in G. Winterton, (ed.), *We, the People*, Sydney: Allen & Unwin.

Evans, H. (1996), 'The Australian Head of State: Putting Republicanism into the Republic', *Agenda*, Vol. 3, No. 2.

Fraser, A. (1993), 'Strong Republicanism and a Citizen's Constitution,' in W. Hudson and D. Carter (eds), *The Republicanism Debate*, Kensington: University of NSW Press.

Galligan, B. (1995), *A Federal Republic*, Melbourne: Cambridge University Press.

Gibbs, H. (1994), 'The Australian Constitution and Australian Constitutional Monarchy' in M. A. Stephenson and C. Turner (eds), *Australia: Republic or Monarchy?* St Lucia: University of Queensland Press.

Grassby, A. (1993), *The Australian Republic*, Sydney: Pluto Press.

Headon, D., Gamage, W. and Warden, J. (eds) (1994), *Crown or Country*, Sydney: Allen & Unwin.

Hirst, J. (1991), 'The Conservative Case for an Australian Republic', *Quadrant*, September.

Hirst, J. (1994), *A Republican Manifesto*, Melbourne: Oxford University Press.

Horne, D. and others (1992), *The Coming Republic*, Sun Australia.

Horne, D. (1994), 'A Civic Identity - Not a National Identity' in M. A. Stephenson and C. Turner (eds), *Australia: Republic or Monarchy?* St Lucia: University of Queensland Press.

Hudson, W. and Carter, D. (eds) (1993), *The Republicanism Debate*, Kensington: University of NSW Press.

Hudson, W. J. and Sharp, M. P. (1988), *Australian Independence: Colony to Reluctant Kingdom*, Melbourne University Press.

Irving, H. (1993), 'Citizens and Not-Quite Citizens', *Constitutional Centenary*, August.

Irving, H. (1993–94), 'The Boy's Own Republic', *Arena Magazine*, 8, December/January.

Irving, H. (1994), 'Republicanism, Royalty and Tales of Australian Manhood', *Plural/Communal 2*, Sydney: University of Western, 139–52.

Irving, H. (1995), 'Why shouldn't we choose our head of state?', the *Australian*, 14 March.

Keating, P. (1995), 'An Australian Republic: The Way Forward', Speech, Canberra: AGPS, 7 June.

Keneally, T. (1993), *Our Republic*, Melbourne: William Heinemann.

Kirby, M. (1993), 'Reflections on Constitutional Monarchy,' in W. Hudson and D. Carter (eds), *The Republicanism Debate*, Kensington: University of NSW Press.

Lake, M. (1993), 'Sexing the Republic', the *Age*, 2 December.

Lake, M. (1996), 'The Republic, the Federation and the Intrusion of the Political,' in J. Hoorn and D. Goodman (eds), *Vox Reipublicae: Feminism and the Republic*, Melbourne: La Trobe University Press.

Lister, R. (1995), 'Dilemmas in Engendering Citizenship', *Economy and Society*, Vol. 24, No. 1.

Macintyre, S. (1994), 'Corowa and the voice of the people', *Canberra Historical Journal*, No. 33, March.

Macintyre, S. (1996), 'Diversity, Citizenship and the Curriculum', *Crossings*, 1, 1.

McKenna, M. (1996), *The Captive Republic*, Melbourne: Cambridge University Press.

Mackerras, M. (1996), 'Will ballot scuttle the republic?', the *Australian*, 12 August.

MacMillan J., Evans, G. and Storey, G. (1983), *Australia's Constitution: Time for Change?*, Sydney: Law Foundation/Allen & Unwin.

Macphee, I. (1993), 'Challenges for 21st Century Australia: Politics, Economics and Constitutional Reform', Conference paper, Griffith University, 27 March.

Maddox, G. (1993), 'Republic or Democracy?', *Australian Journal of Political Science*, Special issue: 28.

Marquis, V. (1993), 'A Feminist Republic? A Feminist Constitution? Taking up the Challenge — Lessons from the Past', *Australian Quarterly*, 65, 3.

Marshall, T. H. (1965), *Class, Citizenship and Social Development*, New York: Anchor.

Millar, A. (1996), 'Feminising the Senate' in H. Irving (ed.), *A Woman's Constitution? Gender and History in the Australian Commonwealth*, Sydney: Hale & Iremonger.

Pateman, C. (1992), 'Citizen Male', *Australian Left Review*, 137, March.

Pettit, P. (1992), 'Republican Themes', *Legislative Studies*, 6, 2.

Pettit, P. (1993), 'Liberalism and Republicanism', *Australian Journal of Political Science*, 28 (Special issue).

Pettman, J. J. (1996), 'Second-Class Citizens? Nationalism, Identity and Difference in Australia' in B. Sullivan and G. Whitehouse (eds) *Gender, Politics and Citizenship in the 1990s*, Kensington: University of NSW Press.

Phillips, A. (1991), *Engendering Democracy*, Cambridge: Polity Press.

Phillips, A. (1995), *The Politics of Presence*, Cambridge: Polity Press.

Pixley, J. (1993), *Citizenship and Employment*, Melbourne: Cambridge University Press.

RAC (Republic Advisory Committee) (1993), *An Australian Republic: The Options*, Vol. 1, Commonwealth of Australia.

Rowse, T. (1994), 'Aborigines: Citizens and Colonial Subjects' in J. Brett and others (eds), *Developments in Australian Politics*, Melbourne: Macmillan.

Rubenstein, K. and Cass, D. (1996), 'From Federation Forward' in H. Irving (ed.), *A Woman's Constitution? Gender and History in the Australian Commonwealth*, Sydney: Hale & Iremonger.

Stretton, P. and Finnimore, C. (1993), 'Black Fellow Citizens: Aborigines and the Commonwealth Franchise', *Australian Historical Studies*, 25, October.

Turnbull, M. (1993), *The Reluctant Republic*, Melbourne: William Heinemann.

Voet, R. (1994), 'Women as Citizens: a Feminist Debate', *Australian Feminist Studies*, 19, Autumn.

Warden, J. (1993), 'The Fettered Republic: The Anglo-American Commonwealth and the Traditions of Australian Political Thought', *Australian Journal of Political Science*, Special issue: 28.

West, F. (1985), 'Constitutional Crisis 1975 — An Historian's View' in D. Woodward, A. Parkin and J. Summers (eds), *Government, Power and Politics in Australia*, 3rd edn, Melbourne: Longman Cheshire.

Winterton, G. (1994a), *Monarchy to Republic*, Melbourne: Oxford University Press.

Winterton, G. (ed.) (1994b), *We, the People*, Sydney: Allen & Unwin.

Women Into Politics (1996), 'Political Equity for Women: How and How Soon?', National Symposium, September, Canberra.

8

Reshaping the public sector

Martin Painter

All Australian governments in the mid 1990s, regardless of partisan composition, share a common vision of a public sector that spends parsimo-
niously and taxes lightly, and which is more efficient in its delivery of
services. In pursuit of these ends, the public sector is being transformed. In
this respect Australia is part of a global trend (OECD 1995). The trends in
reform that are now clearly evident owe their origins to steps first taken by
Labor governments in the 1980s, but during the 1990s Coalition governments with more radical programs have taken them further. The public
sector is in the process of being 'marketised'. The principal object of this
wave of public sector reform is not, like earlier waves, the strengthening
of the public sector and hence a more effective polity, but rather the
creation of a more competitive economy. Market efficiency is more and
more the ultimate standard, and what remains of the public sector is being
restructured to substitute or mimic the market wherever possible. This
chapter reviews these developments, ponders why they are occurring and
discusses their implications. It reviews a set of parallel changes in state
and Commonwealth governments and also looks at their evolving, cumu-
lative impacts on the federal system of Australian government as a whole.
It is argued that the agenda of change is not just about the instruments of
government and the details of administration, but brings consequences that
raise fundamental issues of how the political system as a whole is
constituted.

From managerialism to microeconomic reform

The emphasis in the public sector reform agenda has shifted from a
primary concern in the 1980s with efficiency in government to a growing

focus in the 1990s on the efficiency of government. In the process, the goal of efficiency has shifted from a preoccupation with managerial or productive efficiency to a broader concern with allocative efficiency, a notion that makes sense only if all activity is evaluated from within the market. The public sector is being evaluated not only against benchmarks of productivity, but also against its wider role in the economy: is government contributing to or hindering overall economic efficiency, competitiveness and growth? Increasingly, positive answers to this question have only been given if government activities have been demonstrably supportive or reflective of market forces. In many instances, the answer to a problem with government has been to have less of it.

At the Commonwealth level under the Hawke Labor governments in the 1980s the emphasis (at least at first) was not primarily on smaller government or on market substitution. Labor ministers were attracted to a more positive program of efficiency improvements within the public sector – for example the financial management improvement program – to improve the quality of services, tighten political control and corporate direction and make management systems more responsive (Halligan and Power 1992). Commercialisation of public enterprises was consistent with this program, but not privatisation. Only later, and to a large extent under the pressure of fiscal policy, was privatisation embraced in a few cases.

Nevertheless, 'marketisation' in various forms was on the march. Management improvement and the search for business models stimulated the creation of quasi-markets for the provision of common services by one government agency to another, and other market-based mechanisms such as contracting out. These extended slowly to include creating contestable markets for the government funded provision of some human services, such as labour market training programs and case work for the unemployed, in which private providers as well as public agencies were contracted to provide the service. As a consequence, provision of a 'public service', as distinct from its funding and policy direction, was less and less considered inalienably to be part of the 'public sector.'

If these measures could be argued to have put the market to the service of government, rather than subordinating government to the market, nevertheless the thrust of public sector reform from the late 1980s was dominated more by an economic policy agenda than by a vision of public sector improvement. The growing emphasis on 'microeconomic reform' (broadly speaking, measures to improve the efficiency of economic markets) became the dominant theme. This ungainly phrase entered the public realm as part of official policy when Bob Hawke announced it as a top priority following his 1987 election win. Microeconomic reform was a rocky road to follow for a Labor government (Gerritsen 1994). It meant, more often than not, removing publicly provided protections and privileges for influential groups in the community. But it had a progressive ring to it, particularly when the targets of reform were some types of 'vested interest', such as primary producers benefiting from marketing schemes and passing higher prices on to shoppers; large public corporations exercising monopoly power over consumers or calling for huge subsidies from the taxpayer; or barristers and doctors benefiting from restrictive practices in the professions. Among the main targets were the transport and communications industries, including aviation, shipping, the waterfront, broadcasting and telecommunications. The ending of the two-airline policy, and with it the arrival of fare discounting, was one of the first and most popular of the Labor government's microeconomic reforms. The agenda was driven essentially by economic doctrine, and its logic swept the reform movement forward, homing in on more and more cases of 'anti-competitive', 'market distorting' institutions and practices. Microeconomic reform became a crusade against 'government failure'.

The stimulus to these changes lay in seemingly unavoidable international pressures which concentrated the minds of policy makers in both Commonwealth and state governments on economic reform and restructuring. The vulnerability of Australia in the international economy, and the need to do whatever it took to be 'competitive', were the driving forces, and leaner, 'more market-like' government presented itself as the only viable alternative to the *status quo*. Nick Greiner, Premier of New South Wales (1988–92), colourfully described the Commonwealth's conversion to reform in the 1980s as being 'mugged by reality' and added, with reference to his own initiatives: 'there is a new market emerging within the international economy ... a market for smaller, more efficient government ... Good government is at a premium' (Greiner 1992: 1, 3). This depiction of impersonal forces sweeping reform before them has been taken further by Gary Sturgess (1995) and David Kemp (1995), who argue that the current wave of reform is an inevitable product of the dynamics of (respectively) post-industrial society and globalisation.

But the direction of reform was set by economic ideas as well as economic forces. A set of doctrines and policy solutions under the banner of 'economic liberalisation' presented themselves as an alternative to the apparently discredited orthodoxy (Henderson 1995). Economic liberalism promoted 'a range of measures ... making the Australian economy freer, more open, and less subject to government regulation and direction' (Henderson 1995). Impediments to a more open, competitive, market economy would be dismantled. These impediments had been put in place as part of a long-settled policy of 'protection all round' and included high tariffs, centralised wage fixing, a large public enterprise sector and a multitude of 'undesirable' cross-subsidies to 'undeserving' groups; in sum, 'all the restrictive practices known to man' (Butlin and others 1982).

By the end of the 1980s, economic or market liberalism had become the policy orthodoxy. In the pressing economic circumstances of the 1980s, the ascendancy of these ideas was as much driven by necessity as by conviction. Cliff Walsh (1991) has argued that the Labor government stumbled upon market liberal reform ideas rather than actively seeking or embracing them, while David Henderson suggests that the emergence of the new agenda was not so much a bold affirmation of a new economic order as a set of remedies that presented themselves as solutions to the defects of the old one: '... the main single impulse (was) negative or reactive, rather than affirmative' (Henderson 1995: 72). One of the attractions of the new doctrines was that they interpreted the apparent decline and the need for change as well as pointing the way forward. For example, an idea like 'government failure', with its images of capture by vested interests and the sclerosis of accumulated bureaucratic inefficiencies, depicted a scene of decay and obsolescence as well as a vision for the future (Painter 1996a). 'Government failure' turned on its head the slogan 'market failure', often used in the past to justify government growth. Government, it was claimed, had failed to deliver prosperity and efficiency; it had become captured by vested interests eager to appropriate public moneys for private interests; it had lost sight of the public good; it had become bloated and unwieldy and a drag on the economy; it was no longer capable of doing effectively even the bare minimum.

The emergence of the contract state

The coming together of economic restructuring and public sector reform under the broad, legitimating umbrella of economic liberalism affected all governments in Australia. They experienced the same economic pressures, they tuned into the same wave-lengths over which the newly fashionable ideas were being broadcast, and they observed the application of each others' remedies, copying and borrowing where appropriate. Although the Commonwealth was a prime mover in microeconomic reform, in 1988 the New South Wales Greiner government took up much of the running. While thwarted in some of its privatisation endeavours by its lack of control of the parliament (Smith 1995), and slow to move on some areas of deregulation when faced with fierce pressure group opposition, it did embark on a fundamental restructuring of government business enterprises (labelled 'corporatisation') and of the public service proper (Painter 1995; Laffin 1995). There were continuities with earlier management reforms of the preceding Labor government in New South Wales (Halligan and Power 1992), but also some doctrinal and policy departures. For example, the 'new public economics', which drew on public choice theory and, in particular, principal-agent and property rights theory (Boston 1991; Davis 1995), had a very direct and explicit influence on environmental policy (Kellow 1995) and on some aspects of corporatisation. These ideas were filtered and reinforced through the experience of reforms in the United Kingdom and New Zealand. Gary Sturgess, Greiner's chief policy adviser, devised an elaborate restructuring of the New South Wales machinery of government in 1991 based on these principles, although they were only in very small part implemented (Sturgess 1991).

But Greiner was only a harbinger. The Liberal dominated Kennett government, elected in Victoria in 1992, took the reform agenda many steps further. In the process it gained a more coherent and far-reaching expression. Kennett's more radical version was also made possible by the sense of crisis created by financial institution collapses in Victoria and by the fiscal problems inherited from the Cain and Kirner Labor governments. The seriousness of the illness demanded strong medicine, and the whole-sale rejection of the prevailing orthodoxy expressed in Kennett's sweeping victory legitimated more radical departures than had been contemplated in New South Wales. Severe cutbacks were justified by the 'fiscal crisis' of debt and deficit left by the previous government. But smaller government was not just a short term expedient, for Kennett it was a longer term goal.

Kennett's public sector reform program has been dubbed 'the contract state' (Alford and others 1994). Kennett's Victoria is only one, perhaps extreme, case: in the 1990s we find elements of this model in operation in all governments. The Victorian Management Improvement Initiative was guided by five principles: first, a focus on transparent accountability mechanisms for identifiable outputs, for example through explicit contracts; second the empowerment of consumers, for example by allocating them funds and leaving the choice of service provider to them; third the paring back of government itself to a basic core, with service-delivery functions hived off and at arm's length (as in contracting); fourth a preference for market mechanisms wherever possible through privatisation, contracting out and competitive service provision; and finally the adoption of the latest business-like methods for managing public agencies, such as risk manage-ment, performance reporting and improved financial management (Alford and others 1994: 4–5). In applying these principles, 'government by con-tract' is to be found in a number of guises: employment contracts embody-ing performance agreements, for example between a minister and an agency chief; in-house service provision contracts between purchasers and providers within government (for example for provision of legal services); contracts between the government as purchaser and a public or private body as the provider of a service to the public; and contracts between the consumer as purchaser and the provider of a public service. By 1996 the Victorian government was boasting that 87 per cent of outlays on health and community services and 90 per cent of expenditure by the Office of Housing had been 'outsourced', that is, contracted out (Victoria, Autumn Statement 1996).

The vision of the contract state draws on principal-agent theory which, like all models and critiques of the public sector derived from economic theory, is premised on the assumption that all actors involved in the process of government are 'opportunistic egoists.' The only thing they can be trusted with is their own self interest. On this assumption, anyone with access to the public purse, whether a program provider or a service recipient, is bound to seek to appropriate public resources for private ends. The Commission of Audit appointed by the Kennett government, for example, blamed 'excessive' levels of expenditure on human services on producer and consumer groups who had 'captured' state agencies and programs for private benefit. For the modern theorist of market liberal public sector reform this phenomenon is the central problem in seeking to achieve efficiency, but many public servants in the traditional mould have found it to be an objectionable proposition, claiming that their performance of tasks in accordance with 'the public interest' is motivated not by greed but by loyalty, dedication and trust. Professional groups with roles in client service make similar claims.

But according to the new public economics, the modern manager is to be held to account purely by external, impersonally enforceable controls. 'Dedication' and 'loyalty' won't come from within, they can only be guaranteed by providing the right external incentive structures, with cross-cutting constraints to reinforce them, so as to put private self-interest to productive uses. The market, it is argued, is one of the most effective of these impersonal control and monitoring mechanisms, wherever it can be put directly to work or mimicked. Thus, for example, multiple private and public providers are encouraged to bid for contracts, with public sector units 'going out of business' if they do not win the contract. A clear separation is made between the roles of 'purchaser' and 'provider' – principal and agent – in order to prevent the gamekeeper turning poacher. The Victorian Commission of Audit recommended a strict application of the 'purchaser-provider split' in order to distance providers and their clients from the core policy making, 'public interest' functions of policy making. Government proper shrinks to a core of planners, priority setters and regulators, defining and specifying service objectives and writing and monitoring contracts while, at arm's length, public and private providers compete for the funds and for the domains of service provision. In the popularisers' jargon, the 'steering' is separated from the 'rowing' (Osborne and Gaebler 1992).

As well, government activities and public provision are increasingly made subject to pro-competitive regulations that seek to ensure a 'level playing field'. Another expression meaning the same thing is 'competitive neutrality', a principle first implemented systematically in Australia under the Greiner government's corporatisation policies (Painter 1995). It means, for example, that publicly owned business units in a competitive setting are subject to the same taxing and regulatory regimes as the private sector, and lose any special benefits – such as crown protection in law – accruing to them as a result of belonging to the government. There is a paradox here. 'The market' turns out to be something that has to be constructed by government in the first place. In fact, all economic markets are regulated, buttressed and structured by law – they are social artefacts, not natural objects (Muetzelfeld 1994). Particular market rules and their application will benefit some and disadvantage others. Governments in pursuing 'more market' reforms in the public sector must first define the rules of the markets (or quasi-markets), but the new public economics fails to tell us why we should expect this process to be untainted by egoistic opportunism. Who or what is to prevent the capture of the market structuring process?

While the 'contract state' is most clearly evident as an emergent form in Victoria, 'contractualism' as an organising principle for the public sector in Australia is a much more general trend (Weller and others 1996). Yeatman (1995: 287–9) gives an example from the sphere of Commonwealth funding of state welfare programs in the Home and Community Care (HACC) program in 1989. The Commonwealth in funding domiciliary care services insisted on a model of provision that divided assessment of need (case management) from delivery of the service to meet that need. With this split in place, the delivery of service could be contracted to home care service providers in a competitive environment. Such a system, it was argued, would break down the self-serving monopoly of care provision enjoyed by existing publicly employed professional providers, maximise diversity and responsiveness, and provide for choice. Yeatman argues that it also added a new layer of administrative complexity, created tensions with the carers by offending their professional sensibilities and, by institutionalising an 'us-them' split, undermined intergovernmental program cooperation. Typically, these 'reforms' to HACC were also accompanied by claims from the funder (the Commonwealth) of prospective savings due to the 'efficiency dividend' that was to be reaped and, hence, by funding cuts.

It is necessary to enter some notes of caution at this point. The 'contract state' and 'contractualism' are more the constructs of critics than a fully-fleshed out design for reform. It is tempting to read into 'contractualism' a set of ideological and doctrinal principles that give the emergent product more coherence than it may deserve. Some of the most significant initiatives in contracting out came as part of the Commonwealth Labor government's commercialisation measures, beginning in the mid to late 1980s. Perhaps one source of inspiration might be traced back to principal-agent theory, but neither the idea nor the practice of contracting out was particularly new or confined to followers of the new public economics. Much public sector reform 'on the ground' has been the result of a search for techniques of efficiency improvement wherever they may be found and irrespective of their ideological or doctrinal origins. In taking up contracting out as an efficiency measure, many public managers and reformers saw it simply as a tool. It followed on as a logical progression from the management improvement programs of the mid 1980s. These had focused on specifying program objectives, devolving responsibility for program management, and putting in place output measures or performance indicators to enable the managers to be held to account for a program's effectiveness and efficiency. With these techniques and procedures for accountable, arm's length program management in place, many of the essential prerequisites for contracting out were already in existence, and it was simply a next step.

One aspect in particular of the 'more market' reform agenda accounts in large measure for its popularity over recent years. While the urge for smaller government is in some cases clearly part of a doctrinal market liberal package, economies had attractions to all Australian governments for pragmatic, practical reasons. Privatisation (that is the sale of assets) was a central part of the Kennett government's strategy of reducing state debt. By mid 1996, proceeds from the sale of electricity assets alone had totalled $10.7 billion, enabling the state's debt to be cut by one third (Victoria, Autumn Statement 1996). The 'fiscal squeeze' is almost a permanent state of affairs for Australian governments in the 1990s. The Commonwealth has been fiscally conservative mainly for macroeconomic policy reasons. State governments have engaged in repeated economy drives due to cuts in Commonwealth grants and coupled with an inadequate underlying tax base, which has further been eroded by interstate tax competition. Moreover, taxpayers have come to expect falling levels of taxation, and politicians have taken new taxes off the political agenda (the fate of John Hewson in losing the 1993 election because of his proposed Goods and Services Tax being the defining moment in this regard). Thus, any doctrine that justifies declining levels of government expenditure is a welcome one, as is any body of reform proposals that promises to make savings. Contracting out, for example, is claimed to result in savings of anywhere between 10 and 30 per cent (Industry Commission 1996: 11). With claims of this sort to support them, the Howard government's National Commission of Audit (1996) saw no difficulty in recommending across the board savings and budget cuts of up to 30 per cent in all Commonwealth departments.

The potential implications of this process of reform for Australian political life are very wide ranging. Aside from the fears of some about undesirable policy reversals, and the demise of some cherished, publicly funded institutions, these implications spread to the core of the structures of Australian government. In the rest of this chapter, by way of illustration, we turn to the impact of these reforms on the Australian federal system.

Public sector reform, microeconomic reform and the 'costs of federalism'

Any public sector activity of any significance in Australia invariably brings to light interdependencies between the programs and agencies of different governments in the federal system. One reason for this is the federal system of finances, in which the Commonwealth, due to the allocation of taxing powers, collects about 80 per cent of total government revenue. State governments depend for about 40 per cent of their budgets on Commonwealth grants, with more than half of this amount coming in special purpose, 'tied' payments. One consequence of such an extreme 'vertical fiscal imbalance' (VFI) is the lack of control of state governments over their own budgets. This, it has been argued, leads to fiscal irresponsibility and can produce difficulties in holding governments fully to account for their spending (Walsh 1992).

This point of view is consistent with the economic liberals' analysis of government failure, which is attributed in part to such structural defects in public accountability and decision making mechanisms. This critique brings the issues of federal finances and microeconomic reform together. Premier Greiner made the point in a July 1990 speech sub-titled 'Microeconomic Reform of Australian Government': 'Much of what has been perceived as irresponsible behaviour by the States has been the rational response to irrational incentive structures caused by a division of responsibility between Federal and State Governments' (Greiner 1990).

But the extent of VFI is also one measure of the Commonwealth's capacity to get its way in conflicts with the states, and this was not something it was keen to surrender. Despite continuing pressure and a united front by the states since 1990, no significant steps were taken to remedy the situation. The incoming Howard government, having made a commitment before the election to consider reforms to remedy VFI, quickly found the benefits of its fiscal powers, and mercilessly bullied the states into taking substantial cuts in grants at the June 1996 Premiers' Conference.

Another aspect of the problem identified in Greiner's 1990 speech was the 'duplication and overlap' arising from the division of functions. As he put it, what was needed was a 'rationalisation of functions' to achieve a 'clean separation' (Greiner 1990). Prime Minister Bob Hawke, in announcing the first of a series of Special Premiers' Conferences in 1990, highlighted this as one of the main targets for reform. Six years later the problem had not gone away, despite a considerable amount of discussion between governments. The National Commission of Audit in 1996 identified it as a major issue and confidently stated that 'reducing program duplication and overlap simply requires a clear delineation between levels of government as to program responsibility'. It listed sixteen reasons (most of them drawn from a submission by state governments) why duplication and overlap produced 'costs and inefficiencies' (National Commission of Audit 1996: 435). Aside from increased administrative costs and confusion of effort, the Commission highlighted the danger of budget blow-outs due to 'cost shifting'. For example some of the costs of running hospitals (a state responsibility) were being diverted to the Commonwealth Medicare and pharmaceutical benefits schemes, with hospital patients being passed on to general practitioners and sent down the road to the chemist for treatment and drugs.

The microeconomic reform agenda brought to the surface other 'costs of federalism' aside from overlap and duplication. The federal system, in its allocation of powers and functions, had created a number of 'cross-border' and national coordination dilemmas (for example the need to har-monise state regulations for interstate buses and trucks). Hawke's Special Premiers' Conferences were convened with a view to creating a 'new partnership' so as to deal with what he labelled 'economic balkanisation'. Something of a log-jam had built up in attempts to coordinate economic reform, for example, in coordination and rationalisation of electricity and gas supply and the establishment of an integrated interstate rail system. The problem in these cases was to achieve agreement on sharing the costs of restructuring, as each government found itself facing different pressures, demands and burdens in the various sectors of state enterprise and regula-tion. Rather, as in the problem of cost-shifting, the interests of governments lay not only in a coordinated, overall improvement but also in strategic action to achieve particular ends (Painter 1992).

It took time for the agenda of reform identified in the Special Premiers' Conferences, and carried forward after 1992 by the Council of Australian Governments (COAG), to dovetail with contemporary public sector reform doctrines and directions, but gradually the latter came to dominate. The agenda at first contained some contradictory ideas and conflicting interests, of the kind common in a federal arena. The 'problem of duplication and overlap' illustrates this best. State premiers and the prime minister all agreed that this was a 'problem' to be addressed by cooperative action, arguing that there was too much waste, inefficiency, delay and friction as a result of a confusion of roles and responsibilities in the distribution of powers and functions between governments. But discussions quickly bogged down, proving to be one of the more unproductive aspects of the initial Special Premiers' Conference reform agenda. It became clear that the apparent meeting of minds was no such thing. 'Duplication and over-lap' had provided a convenient set of symbols and slogans to set going the process of joint action, but in the end the apparent consensus was illusory.

One aspect of this false consensus was the seemingly neutral termino-logy of efficiency – waste and delay – in the critique of duplication. All governments were keen to improve efficiency, and this led to agreement on the need to rationalise the complex and burgeoning system of special purpose grants and agreements. Cost savings were available, for example, if consolidation of agreements along with new forms of monitoring replaced the plethora of funding agreements which, with their detailed specifications – many of them input focused – required costly oversight and compliance reporting. A number of specific purpose grant programs – road funding for example – were already undergoing such changes (Painter and Dempsey 1992). But Commonwealth departments and ministers were not eager to relinquish control. The aim was a substitution of new controls, based more on performance and output measures in line with 'national policy'. Fletcher and Walsh (1992) accurately characterise the Commonwealth's approach to this as a 'managerialist', top down vision of federalism.

The states were highly critical of the levels of detailed oversight in grant agreements and supervision, but their version of a more efficient system was the removal of controls altogether. They objected to the use of special purpose grants as indirect instruments for controlling state expenditures, such as 'dollar for dollar' or 'maintenance of effort' requirements which channelled state resources to Commonwealth programs. The state position on program overlap was based on the desire to see the Commonwealth stop intruding on traditional state functions. A link was drawn between three elements of duplication: first, removal of detailed program controls; second, Commonwealth withdrawal from whole fields of operational policy; and third, the conversion of specific purpose payments to general purpose revenue assistance. The Commonwealth's agenda also had at least three elements, but they were different ones: to assert its role in achieving national, uniform outcomes in key areas of policy; to ensure the states performed efficiently as agents in the performance of the service delivery function, in line with national objectives; and to overcome states' resistance and obstruction to national policies by diminishing their power and discretion. In sum, when the states called for an end to duplication and overlap, it was code for removing the Commonwealth from areas of activity that state governments wished to control. For the Commonwealth, the meaning was very different: limiting the states to a service provision role under the guidance of agreed (or imposed) uniform policies, guidelines and standards.

Principals, agents, duplication and overlap

It is not surprising, then, that the efforts taken by the Special Premiers' Conferences and COAG to reform intergovernmental program funding and service provision ran into difficulties. Wholesale 'swaps' of functions – for example leaving schools to the states under general purpose funding from the Commonwealth, in return for handing over funding of vocational education and training to the Commonwealth – ran into predictable difficulties, both practical and political. For example, would this not create obstacles to coordination and articulation (not to mention incentives to cost-shifting) between the two education sectors? Attempts to define more precisely in particular sectors what was a national policy matter as distinct from a local service delivery issue were no more successful, with one or two exceptions. One such was a clearer delineation of Commonwealth specific purpose road funding payments to a defined network of 'national roads'. Here, the field could be clearly (albeit somewhat arbitrarily) divided, but in the case of health services (for example) more complex inter-dependencies within the service delivery system would make such a division far more difficult, if not counter-productive. These conceptual and practical difficulties may have thwarted speedy, wholesale reform, but there were nevertheless major changes in some service sectors due to the Special Premiers' Conferences and COAG processes. Some of the most significant of these have come about through calling upon the language and tools of the emergent contract state. Most have also advanced a Commonwealth agenda of more effective control.

In a discussion of the achievements of the Special Premiers' Conferences and COAG, Edwards and Henderson (1995: 27–8) describe how unfruitful attempts at a 'clean lines' division of functional responsibilities gave way to a focus in which the key question became how to allocate roles in a policy making and delivery system in order to improve outcomes for clients. Ready to hand for restructuring a division of roles was the language of principal and agent, the tools of contracting and the disciplines of marketisation:

> The flip side of a greater emphasis on client outcomes is reduced focus on inputs and the concerns of providers. An important element of traditional roles and responsibilities debates has been the extent of conditions applying to specific purpose payments (SPPs) and, in particular, conditions focussed on inputs that constrain the way in which the states provide services ... The distinction between funding and providing a service becomes relevant in this context and opens for consideration the possibility of organisations other than governments being funded to provide services, perhaps in competition with government agencies. This adds a new dimension to the traditional debate over roles and responsibilities. (Edwards and Henderson 1995: 27, 29)

In similar vein, the National Commission of Audit in 1996 proposed that where it was impractical to 'cede responsibility entirely to one level of government' (its much preferred option), the best arrangement was a 'clear purchaser/provider delineation': 'the Commonwealth's responsibility could be confined strictly to standard setting [that is the minimum standard of service that will be delivered] and program monitoring arrangements, the States could have full responsibility for service delivery subject to these standards' (National Commission of Audit 1996: 46).

The Commission also suggested that where there were unavoidable, shared responsibility, funds could be pooled and not earmarked for particular programs (National Commission of Audit 1996: 47–8). Where a 'national body' is set up to provide oversight of such a joint activity, it should not be involved in any service provision. In addition, the provision of services for the purchaser should be opened up to competition. The ideal service funding system would be one which placed funds, in the form of entitlements or vouchers, in the hands of the clients, who would then be able to shop around for the most effective provider.

The implications for these models of service planning, regulation, funding and provision are profound if they are pursued to their limits in the intergovernmental context. One example comes from the field of vocational education and training (VET), where the Commonwealth has become increasingly involved since 1992. In late 1991, the Commonwealth made a 'takeover bid' for the VET sector, traditionally a state function and dominated by large, state managed and owned Technical and Further Education (TAFE) systems. Victoria and New South Wales were prepared to countenance the proposition, but not so the smaller states. The next step was a series of negotiations, dominated by a Commonwealth offer of substantial funding growth so long as a national approach could be ensured and the states 'maintained effort' – that is they did not substitute 'growth funds' for their own. The outcome in mid 1992 was an agreement to establish the Australian National Training Authority (ANTA), overseen by a ministerial council comprising state and Commonwealth training ministers, to disburse the Commonwealth's 'growth funds' in accord with nationally agreed priorities. ANTA was to review and approve detailed, annual state training profiles, which had to demonstrate a 'maintenance of effort'. Much greater industry participation in planning and provision was also highlighted. Under the agreement all funds for the VET sector were to be 'pooled' and then distributed to the states under the agreed 'national priorities'. These national priorities, however, were not simply Commonwealth ones, they were to be arrived at by a ministerial council decision, drawing on advice from ANTA and its board, which was made up largely of people from industry (Finn 1995; Taylor 1996).

As might be expected, the new system produced a good deal of intergovernmental friction. Some aspects of the agreement were not effectively implemented, for example the proposal for funds to be 'pooled'. However, the Commonwealth's funds for each of the states were passed direct from ANTA to the state training authorities, bypassing state treasuries and giving effect to the jointly agreed 'national' allocations and the approved state training profile. The implementation of the 'maintenance of effort' clause proved very troublesome. It was agreed that the measure of 'effort' should go beyond mere inputs – that is, money – to look at efficiency and effectiveness in terms of outputs and outcomes. However, agreed measures could not to be found. States did not have consistent or reliable data on the performance of their TAFE systems, and some were accused of 'cooking the books' in order to claim improved effort. In 1994 the Commonwealth threatened to withhold funds from some states which had reduced TAFE expenditures, but these states' claims that they were maintaining effort by improvements in efficiency were hard to challenge in the absence of agreed, reliable performance measures.

The creation of ANTA and a 'national system' of vocational education and training was more than a vehicle for the injection of Commonwealth funds and influence, it carried forward a major reform agenda already under development. This included various forms of standardisation of the training 'product', such as the creation of uniform national training curricula in consultation with industry and trade groups; agreed, uniform 'competency standards' by which to grade and award qualifications at different levels; and a system of national standards for certifying or licensing training providers. The other main target of reform was the states' TAFE systems, which were identified (in varying degrees) as being inefficient, bureaucratic, provider-dominated and unresponsive, despite past efforts to restructure them and a current awareness among most state governments of the need for further reform. Progress in reform was halted in part because of the distractions of the conflicts over maintenance of effort. One of the most significant achievements, however, was agreement in 1995 on the production of standardised databases and performance measures to monitor TAFE outputs.

The reform program taking shape under the auspices of ANTA had support from major industry groups and the broad backing of the Commonwealth. It drew on the new orthodoxy of public sector reform. In outline, the new model is for a clear set of collaboratively framed national standards and priorities to be implemented through a pooling of public funds sourced from Commonwealth and state budgets, for the purpose of purchasing training services in a competitive market of providers, as and when needed by clients and customers. Standardisation of the end-product of various training requirements and needs, coupled with the adoption of agreed output and performance measures, would make it possible to specify the precise requirements of the purchaser in terms of performance standards that could be monitored in a contract. This is a prerequisite for the creation of a more open, competitive market for the provision of training services:

> Exposing the training market to greater competition and contestability of provision is an important means to achieve greater choice for clients, responsiveness from providers and incentives for further systematic efficiencies … [T]he States and Territories should be encouraged to undertake a clear separation of their VET sector advisory, funding [including purchaser and provider splits] and regula-

tory structures ... The Commonwealth expects that competitive processes will encourage the VET system to deliver efficiency gains which do not reduce levels of activity or quality ... (Commonwealth of Australia 1995: 25–6)

In this model, state training authorities are responsible for implementing and monitoring standards and regulations and for purchasing training services to meet the needs of end users, who have a strong say through various consultative mechanisms in service plans and profiles and, along with the trainees themselves, a major voice in the choice of products through their 'purchasing power'. State owned TAFE colleges are to be put on a basis of competitive neutrality with outsider providers. Training providers who attract customers through the appropriateness and quality of their product, and win contracts through the efficiency of their provision, will win the business, resulting in a more responsive, efficient and user-friendly system. The model is far from being implemented in full, but elements of it are beginning to come to fruition. Most of the states are still to confront the most contested and difficult part of this agenda, that is opening up their state TAFE systems to competition. Fierce resistance is to be expected from TAFE teachers, unions and colleges. The National Competition Policy, which was agreed to by all states and the Commonwealth in 1995, may speed things along by possibly giving an enforceable right of access to outside providers to some of the 'monopoly-owned' essential facilities in the state-owned TAFE colleges.

The case of ANTA is only one of a number of similar developments in the restructuring of intergovernmental relations and service provision (Painter 1996b). National bodies (a ministerial council and a national advisory body) arrive collaboratively at a joint set of agreed priorities, guidelines, standards and regulatory arrangements, along with a common set of principles and structures for implementing them in the service delivery process. The Commonwealth is involved primarily at this level and not in aspects of provision. It exerts a strong influence over the delivery systems as one of the joint purchasers, but the actual purchase of services and the monitoring of provision according to agreed standards is undertaken by the states. The national bodies monitor overall outcomes but do not control the processes. Each state will be driven to adopt current 'best practice' models of competitive service delivery, opening up their delivery systems to outside providers. This might come about by joint agreement (possibly even on pain of financial sanctions if the Commonwealth so chooses), or just as importantly could be driven by competitive pressures between the states. Part of the states' regulatory responsibilities will be to ensure that there is a 'level playing field' in the tendering and contracting process so that the most efficient and effective providers – whether public or private – win the business. The trend will be towards system-wide uniformity, with diversity in delivery modes at the local level.

The collaborative arrangements, then, that underpin such restructuring of service delivery systems across jurisdictional boundaries have arisen because the parcelling out of jurisdiction has not been possible. The Commonwealth's National Commission of Audit much preferred a 'clean lines' allocation of functions to one government or another – for example, it proposed a Commonwealth takeover of all funding for VET, with the states left with the role of possible providers in a competitive training market (National Commission of Audit 1996: 56–60). The states, on the other hand, recommended that the Commonwealth should vacate the field. They advocated a model of 'competitive federalism' in which state governments with enhanced autonomy, freed from Commonwealth funding constraints and program controls, developed separate and distinctive approaches to public policy. The claim is that they will innovate and become more efficient through competition in the global marketplace to win economic development for their regions (Nahan 1995). But history is against them in realising this vision. The obstacle is not only the Commonwealth's reluctance to surrender power but also the strong support for a national training system from major business and industry groups. The trend towards a nationally coordinated system is probably irreversible in this, as in many other fields of policy (Nelson 1992). The remnants of states' autonomy and discretion, albeit not insignificant, will by and large be exercised within overarching systems of national regulation and standard-setting (Painter 1996b; Harman and Harman 1996).

Conclusion

What do the sorts of changes we have just described mean for Australia's system of parliamentary federalism? The initial losers are the states. A state government's means of political, financial and administrative control over its own affairs are significantly diminished by either being pooled or by-passed in these new chains of principal-agent relations. In the policy and planning system, the states become part of a joint process of national standard setting and forward planning; as regulators they implement uniform, national standards and models rather than autonomous state ones; as purchasers they meet national performance goals as to levels and types of service, and then purchase services to perform to those broader criteria, with limited discretion to vary them to meet local conditions; and as providers their agencies must be responsive only to the marketplace, and enjoy no standing over and above private providers. As a result, large parts of the states' public sectors are probably doomed to wither away.

The age-old federal problem of 'duplication and overlap' between the sovereign 'owners' of different segments of sectors of public policy is dissolved. A chain of principal-agent relations is constructed in which the boundaries between roles and powers are re-drawn. To achieve this, collaborative planning, funding and regulatory arrangements are set up. The boundaries of the roles and functions of Commonwealth, state and intergovernmental public bodies are defined not by general constitutional provisions but by the nature of the market for a particular service, and the requirements for various levels of uniformity of regulatory and other structures, or diversity in local delivery options. Each public service delivery system is structured not by the variously divided and collected governing powers of whole governments, but by the roles given to new networks of public and private bodies that regulate and operate in a specific product market. In place of the traditional arrangements for political accountability, the model of the market is drawn on to legitimise a new conception of public service responsiveness to the customer. The nature of the product, the need for innovation and flexibility, and the requirements of customers are what will drive policy and administration. Looking beyond any particular policy sector, these developments are perhaps part of a wider set of changes in a 'post-industrial' society in which nation states, sovereign powers and other inherited political arrangements are being transformed by new productive forces and economic interdependencies (Sturgess 1995). Marketisation, in other words, is part of a wider phenomenon that implies a fundamental transformation in political as well as administrative arrangements.

References

Alford, J. and O'Neill, D. (eds) (1994), *The Contract State: Public Management and the Kennett Government*, Geelong: Centre for Applied Social Research, Deakin University.

Butlin, N. G., Barnard, A. and Pincus, J. J. (1982), *Government and Capitalism: Public and Private Choice in Twentieth Century Australia*, Sydney: Allen & Unwin.

Boston, J. (1991), 'The Theoretical Underpinnings of the Public Sector Restructuring in New Zealand' in J. Boston, J. Martin, J. Pallott and P. Walsh (eds), *Reshaping the State: New Zealand's Bureaucratic Revolution*, Auckland: Oxford University Press.

Commonwealth of Australia (1995), 'Submission to the Review of the ANTA Agreement', Canberra.

Davis, G. (1995), 'Making Sense of Difference? Public Choice, Politicians and Bureaucratic Change in America and Australia' in P. Weller and G. Davis (eds), *New Ideas, Better Government*, Sydney: Allen & Unwin.

Edwards, M. and Henderson, A. (1995), 'COAG: A Vehicle for Reform' in P. Carroll and M. Painter (eds), *Microeconomic Reform and Federalism*, Canberra: Federalism Research Centre.

Finn, B. (1995), 'The Australian National Training Authority' in P. Carroll and M. Painter (eds), *Microeconomic Reform and Federalism*, Canberra: Federalism Research Centre.

Fletcher, C. and Walsh, C. (1992), 'Reform of intergovernmental relations in Australia: the politics of federalism and the non-politics of managerialism', *Public Administration*, 70 (Winter), 591–616.

Gerritsen, R. (1994), 'Microeconomic Reform' in S. Bell and B. Head (eds), *State, Economy and Public Policy in Australia,* Melbourne: Oxford University Press

Greiner, N. (1990), 'Physician Heal Thyself: Microeconomic Reform of Australian Government', Address to the National Press Club, 25 July.

Greiner, N. (1992), 'That "Obstructive Spirit of Provincialism" has been Curbed', Discussion Paper No. 11, Canberra: Federalism Research Centre, Australian National University.

Halligan, J. and Power, J. (1992), *Political Management in the 1990s*, Melbourne: Oxford University Press.

Henderson, D. (1995), 'The Revival of Economic Liberalism: Australia in an International Perspective', *The Australian Economic Review*, 58 (1st Quarter), 59–85

Harman, E. and Harman, F. (1996), 'The Potential for Local Diversity in Implementation of National Competition Policy', *Australian Journal of Public Administration*, 55(2), 12–25

Industry Commission (1996), *Competitive Tendering and Contracting By Public Sector Agencies*, Melbourne: AGPS.

Kellow, A. (1995), 'The Environment' in M. Laffin and M. Painter (eds), *Reform and Reversal: Lessons from the Coalition Government in New South Wales 1988–1995*, Melbourne: Macmillan.

Kemp, D. (1995), 'Problems and Prospects' in P. Weller and G. Davis (eds), *New Ideas, Better Government*, Sydney: Allen & Unwin.

Laffin, M. (1995), 'The Public Service' in M. Laffin and M. Painter (eds), *Reform and Reversal: Lessons from the Coalition Government in New South Wales 1988–1995*, Melbourne: Macmillan.

Muetzelfeld, M. (1994), 'Contracts, Politics and Society' in J. Alford and D. O'Neill (eds), *The Contract State: Public Management and the Kennett Government*, Geelong: Centre for Applied Social Research, Deakin University.

Nahan, M. (1995), 'Competitive and uncompetitive approaches to competition policy and microeconomic reform' in P. Carroll and M. Painter (eds), *Microeconomic Reform and Federalism*, Canberra: Federalism Research Centre.

National Commission of Audit (1996), *Report to the Commonwealth Government*, Canberra: AGPS.

Nelson, H. (1992), 'Recipes for uniformity: the case of food standards', *Australian Journal of Political Science*, 27 (Special Issue), 78–90.

OECD (Organisation for Economic Co-operation and Development) (1995), *Governance in Transition. Public Management Reforms in OECD Countries*, Paris: OECD.

Osborne, D. and Gaebler, T. (1992), *Reinventing Government*, New York: Addison-Wesley.

Painter, M. (1991), 'Policy diversity and policy learning in a federation: the case of Australian state betting laws', *Publius: The Journal of Federalism*, 21(1), 143–58.

Painter, M. (1992), '"New Federalism" and Road Transport Regulation', *Australian Journal of Political Science*, 27 (Special Issue), 63–77.

Painter, M. (1995), 'Microeconomic Reform and the Public Sector' in M. Laffin and M. Painter (eds), *Reform and Reversal: Lessons from the Coalition Government in New South Wales 1988–1995*, Melbourne: Macmillan.

Painter, M. (1996a), 'Economic Policy, Market Liberalism and "The End of Australian Politics"', *Australian Journal of Political Science*, 31(3).

166   *Reshaping the public sector*

Painter, M. (1996b), 'The Council of Australian Governments and Intergovernmental relations: A Case of Cooperative Federalism', *Publius: The Journal of
Federalism*, 26(4).

Painter, M. and Dempsey, K. (1992), 'Road grants, intergovernmental competition
and the benefits of duplication', *Australian Journal of Public Administration*,
52(1), 54–65.

Smith, R. (1995), 'Parliament' in M. Laffin and M. Painter (eds), *Reform and
Reversal: Lessons from the Coalition Government in New South Wales 1988–
1995*, Melbourne: Macmillan.

Sturgess, G. L. (1991), 'Why do good fences make good neighbours? — trends in
public sector management', Address to the NSW Division, Royal Institute of
Public Administration Australia, 3 July.

Sturgess, G. L. (1995), 'The Decline and Fall of the Industrial State' in P. Weller
and G. Davis (eds), *New Ideas, Better Government*, Sydney: Allen & Unwin.

Taylor, R. M. (1996), *Report of the Review of the ANTA Agreement*, Canberra:
AGPS.

Walsh, C. (1991), 'The National Economy and Management Strategies' in B.
Galligan and G. Singleton (eds), *Business and Government Under Labor*,
Melbourne: Longman Cheshire.

Walsh, C. (1992), 'Federal reform and the politics of vertical fiscal imbalance',
Australian Journal of Political Science, 27 (Special Issue), 19–38.

Weller, P. and others (eds) (1996), *Contractualism in the Public Sector*, Melbourne:
Macmillan.

Yeatman, A. (1995), 'The new Contractualism: Management Reform or a New
Approach to Governance?' in P. Weller and G. Davis (eds), *New Ideas, Better
Government*, Sydney: Allen & Unwin.

9

Cultural rights in Australia

Chandran Kukathas

Australia is often described as an attractive model of a modern multi-cultural society. Of its eighteen million people, a significant number are overseas born; and, particularly since the ending of the 'White Australia' policy in 1973, its migrants have come from all parts of the world to contribute to a population marked by ethnic, linguistic, religious and cultural diversity. Yet while this variety is no less substantial than that found in other multicultural societies such as the United States – and is more considerable than that found in others such as Malaysia or Germany or France – it prevails in circumstances which are far more peaceful, and politically and socially stable, than those in any of these other countries. This does not mean that there have been no conflicts over cultural issues in Australia, or that there are no divisions within the society about how ethnicity and culture should be handled by the legal and political institutions. The size and the composition of the immigration intake has always been a contentious issue ever since federation. And Aboriginal affairs have, from time to time, assumed centre stage in national as well as state politics. Yet at no stage have the cultural conflicts over such issues endangered the political stability of the society, or even threatened to become a dominant feature of the political landscape. It is in this context that the politics of cultural rights in Australia should be understood.

Nevertheless, there have been important developments in cultural politics over the past decade which reflect significant changes in the nature of the society. As a social system built upon traditions of liberal egalitarianism, Australia's legal institutions have historically been colour or culture blind. Although the constitution gives the Commonwealth parliament power to make laws with respect to 'The people of any race, for whom it is deemed necessary to make special laws' (section 51 xxvi), the federal government has generally declined to do so, and has been reluctant to grant special rights to cultural groups – or to deny them to others. However, the more explicit recognition of cultural diversity in political debate and in government policy has brought this very issue into focus. The principal divide on cultural issues in Australian politics is between those who want to see a greater emphasis on special rights or provisions for cultural groups (Castles and others 1988) and those who reject such measures as an unwarranted politicisation of culture (Bullivant 1989; Kukathas 1991). Interestingly, this division parallels the central philosophical dispute within contemporary liberal democratic theory over the proper liberal response to cultural diversity. Thinkers such as the Canadian philosopher, Will Kymlicka, have argued that liberal principles need to be rethought in order to give more explicit recognition to cultural minorities, and indigenous people in particular, through the establishing of group rights (Kymlicka 1989; Kymlicka 1995). Others, however, have stressed the need to stick to the original liberal idea of individual rather than group rights (Glazer 1983; Kukathas 1992a; Kukathas 1992b; Kukathas 1993).

Politics and policy, however, have been driven less by philosophy than by history and circumstances. In Australia in the 1990s, cultural politics have been shaped by two developments. In Aboriginal affairs they have been shaped by the decision handed down by the High Court in the case of *Mabo v Queensland*. In multicultural affairs, it has been shaped primarily by the ongoing debate about immigration, as well as by the experience of multiculturalism over the 1970s and 1980s. But it is the *Mabo* judgment which has exerted the most profound influence on cultural politics in the 1990s, since it has not only dominated Aboriginal politics but has also raised contentious questions about the most critical institutions of Australian politics. Most important of these questions is that of the nature of sovereignty, and of where it must – or can – reside within the Australian polity. The response of the government, and of political elites more generally, to *Mabo* is testimony to its significance not only for Aboriginal policy but also for multicultural policy more generally. For that reason, this chapter begins with a detailed investigation of the politics of *Mabo*, before turning to examine the more general developments in recent cultural politics.

The *Mabo* judgment

Background

By most measures of well being, Aborigines have long been the poorest members of Australian society. They compare badly with other Australians in terms of life expectancy and general health, as well as employment, income and wealth. Yet it has been the political condition of Aborigines as a dispossessed people which has dominated public affairs over the past thirty years. For the first half of the century government policy had as its primary objective the assimilation of Aborigines. The policy of assimilation officially declared in 1937 reflected a concern for the fate of the growing numbers of Aborigines of mixed descent; yet the implicit understanding of policy makers was that even fully tribalised Aborigines, who were to be given 'inviolable reserves', would eventually be fully assimilated (Hasluck 1988: 69). By the 1960s, however, the consensus of opinion among anthropologists, historians and others who had documented the condition of Aborigines was that assimilation was destructive in its effects upon Aboriginal society (Rowley 1970). And there were growing calls for a change of policy to give Aborigines greater control over their own lives (Stanner 1969). These calls coincided with the growth of Aboriginal demands for change. The 'Freedom Riders' of 1965, inspired by the civil rights movement in the United States, challenged the practices of Aboriginal exclusion from public facilities in New South Wales towns, and used the publicity generated by these activities to raise the profile of a newly emerging protest movement. By the end of the decade assimilation had been repudiated and in its stead Aborigines placed the demand for self determination. This demand was presented most dramatically in 1972 with the erection on the lawns of parliament house of an Aboriginal tent 'Embassy' to symbolise the estrangement of Aborigines from their own lands (Rowley 1978: ch. 1). Here, but also through a number of emerging national organisations, such as the Federal Council for the Advancement of Aborigines and Torres Straits Islanders and the National Tribal Council, they demanded recognition of their dispossession of a continent, compensation for that loss, and, most importantly, land rights. These demands received a sympathetic hearing from the Labor Party which was to win office later in 1972, and which went to election promising Aborigines land rights.

It was not in the political arena alone, however, that Aborigines had sought land rights. In 1970 traditional owners of lands in Yirrkala in the Arnhem Land Reserve on the Gove Peninsula in the Northern Territory, led by Mawalan Milirrpum, sued the Commonwealth and a consortium of mining companies in the Supreme Court of the Northern Territory in an effort to prevent bauxite mining on traditional lands. This was the first effort by Aborigines anywhere to establish the existence of native title to land in Australia. The judgment of Sir Richard Blackburn in the *Gove Land Rights* case (delivered in 1971), was that the plaintiffs were unable to establish that they were the descendants of traditional owners of the country. But it also concluded that the law recognised only individual title to land, and not group interests in land held by indigenous people before colonisation, and ruled that the crown, in asserting sovereignty, had extinguished all Aboriginal rights and interests, whether individual or communal. Blackburn's judgment relied for support of these propositions on the 1970 Canadian case of *Calder v The Attorney General* – a case which was decided differently on appeal in 1973 to the Supreme Court of Canada, which ruled that both the original decision in Calder, as well as Justice Blackburn, were wholly wrong. Nonetheless, in the *Gove* land rights case, Blackburn's judgment stood; and Aborigines thereafter pursued their interest in land rights politically rather than through the courts.

Despite good intentions, very little came of governmental attempts to satisfy Aboriginal demands in the following two decades. The Commonwealth's response was first to create, and then expand, the advisory structures thought necessary to identify and serve the Aboriginal interest. The Office of Aboriginal Affairs, originally established in 1967, was expanded into a ministerial department. In 1973 the National Aboriginal Consultative Committee was created, and this was later replaced by the National Aboriginal Conference in 1977. But conflicts emerged between these different organisations, dashing the government's hopes of finding a representative body which might reveal to it the Aboriginal interest, while at the same time dampening Aboriginal hopes that their interests might indeed be served. These divisions also made it easier for unsympathetic governments (usually in the states) to ignore their claims as unrepresentative of Aboriginal wishes (Bennett 1989: 17).

In the field of land rights, too, aspirations were not matched by results. The Liberal government of Malcolm Fraser passed the Northern Territory Land Rights Act in 1976, but was unable to persuade Liberal and National state governments to give whole hearted support to the idea of Aboriginal land rights. Labor, in opposition, promised to take stronger action against the states in order to secure inalienable freehold Aboriginal title, veto rights over mining, and the protection of sacred sites. Yet once in power in 1983 it too came up against opposition from Labor states (Western Australia in particular) which it was unable to overcome. By 1985 the Labor government under Bob Hawke had abandoned its undertaking to enact national legislation granting inalienable title to lands, rather than merely 'secure title' to reserves. The rest of the decade was thus given over to the politics of symbolism. Earlier talk of a treaty, or makaratta, between Aboriginal and non-Aboriginal Australia was revived, the Prime Minister suggesting that such a document might provide direction to all areas of policy, including land rights (Hawke 1988: 4). Little came of all this, largely because these sentiments betrayed a deeper failure to overcome the institutional obstacles to meeting the demands of Aborigines for land rights and self-determination.

Mabo *v Queensland*

Aborigines had not, however, altogether abandoned legal avenues in the pursuit of land claims. In May 1982, Eddie Mabo, David Passi, Sam Passi, Celia Salee and James Rice of the Meriam people of the Murray Islands claimed lawful ownership of lands on the island annexed by Queensland in 1879. In an action against the state of Queensland brought in the High Court, they claimed that the crown's sovereignty over the Murray Islands was subject to the Murray Islanders' land rights, which were based on local custom and traditional title, and still recognised under law in Australia. In their petition the Islanders asked the court to declare, first, that the Meriam people are entitled to the Murray Islands (a) as owners; (b) as possessors; (c) as occupiers; or (d) as persons entitled to use and enjoy the islands; and, second, that the state of Queensland had no power to extinguish the Meriam people's title. (The action had originally been taken against the Commonwealth as well as Queensland as it had included a claim of rights to sea areas and reefs; but the sea and reef claims were withdrawn, and the Commonwealth then withdrew from proceedings.) When the case was concluded ten years later, after a number of different attempts to resolve or to eliminate the dispute, the High Court ruled, on 3 June 1992, first, that the Meriam people were entitled to possession, occupation, use and enjoyment of the Murray Islands; and, second, that the Queensland parliament and the Queensland governor have the power to extinguish the Meriam people's title, as long as they exercise that power validly, and consistently with the laws of the Commonwealth.

Eddie Mabo had died in 1991; Celia Salee had also passed away, and two others had withdrawn from the proceedings; so only two remaining litigants benefited directly from the judgment: David Passi and James Rice. But in upholding the claims of the plaintiffs in the case of *Mabo v Queensland* the High Court asserted that annexation did not turn the Murray Islands into crown land as that term was understood under the Land Act 1962 (Queensland). It thus effectively rejected the doctrine that Australia had been *terra nullius* upon European settlement. Native title existed, and could continue to exist wherever Aboriginal and Torres Straits Islanders have maintained their connection with the land, and where their title had not been extinguished by valid acts of imperial, state, territory or Commonwealth governments.

The immediate effect of the High Court judgment was to put in doubt the validity of the title of some lands to which people, notably miners and pastoralists, had been granted an interest. This was because the High Court decision, while making clear that native title could be extinguished by valid grants of freehold (and probably leasehold) title by government, also raised the possibility that some grants of interest in land since 1975 may be invalid because they were made in contravention of the Racial Discrimination Act 1975. Earlier in the proceedings, when the case was first brought before the High Court, the Queensland government had sought to get around the Islanders' claims by passing the Queensland Coastal Islands Declaratory Act 1985, whose effect would have been to wipe out any traditional native title rights as of 1879 without compensation. This act was struck down by the High Court in 1988 as inconsistent with the Racial Discrimination Act 1975, which required that governments not discriminate against citizens on the basis of race. After the judgment in favour of *Mabo*, however, the significance of that act lay in its implications for other government grants made without compensation since 1975.

This judgment by the High Court was not unanimous. Chief Justice Mason, and Justices McHugh, Deane, Gaudron and Toohey agreed (with Justice Dawson dissenting) that Australian common law recognises a form of native title; that where it has not been extinguished, native title reflects the rights that the laws or customs of the indigenous inhabitants give them to their traditional lands; and that subject to the effect of some particular crown leases, Queensland law preserves the native title of the Murray Islanders as defined by their laws or customs. Furthermore, four Justices (Mason, McHugh, Brennan and Dawson) also agreed that the crown may extinguish native title without compensation (subject, however, to the Racial Discrimination Act), but three (Deane, Gaudron and Toohey) considered that the crown must compensate for any extinguishment of native title. But this did not detract from the significance of the decisions.

The far reaching effect of the decision was in part a consequence of the court's refusal, in this case brought by the Meriam people alone, to make any distinction between Torres Straits Islanders and Aboriginal people of the mainland – despite the fact that they belonged to different traditions. (Crucially, the Islanders, unlike the mainland Aborigines, were market gardeners who had developed systems of private property.) Justice Brennan indicated that to make such a distinction would have offended against justice, human rights and equality before the law. This opened up the possibility of mainland Aborigines asserting title to lands, even though their traditions were very different.

Interestingly then, the *Mabo* decision has its roots both in the common law, and its traditions of legal equality, and in more recent statutory provisions outlawing racial discrimination. Without those traditions, or without the Racial Discrimination Act which was a product of the emergence of multiculturalism in Australia, the *Mabo* decision might never have been rendered.

Political consequences of Mabo

Mabo has been described as nothing less than a judicial revolution (Stephenson and Ratnapala 1993), largely because it seemed to many to mark a high point in judicial activism in Australia. How far its implications for the Australian polity are revolutionary is another question altogether. Immediate reactions to the judgment, from the Commonwealth and state governments, as well as from Aborigines and from interested groups such as the mining industry, suggested that fears, as well as expectations, were quickly raised. Concern among the states was strongest in Western Australia, where the potential for large land claims by Aborigines was greatest. Among miners and pastoralists the concern was that mining and other titles granted over native title lands since 1975 could now be invalid. Thus the most immediate effect of the *Mabo* decision was to create uncertainty.

The consequence of this was the Commonwealth Native Title Act 1993, which came into effect on New Year's Day 1994. Under it, native title can be extinguished only in accordance with the act, which defined native title as: the communal, group or individual rights and interests of Aboriginal peoples or Torres Strait Islanders in relation to land or waters, where:

a   the rights and interests are possessed under the traditional laws acknowledged, and the traditional customs observed, by the Aboriginal people or Torres Straits Islanders; and

b   the Aboriginal peoples of Torres Strait Islanders, by those laws and customs, have a connection with the land or waters; and

c   the rights and interests recognised by the common law of Australia.

At the same time, the act made provision for the validation of grants of land, and for dealing with invalidly granted leases or interests, in some cases, for example, suspending native title for the duration of mining leases. (The act has, however, created certain difficulties to the extent that it is inconsistent with the Aboriginal Land Rights (Northern Territory) Act, which had since 1977 provided Aborigines in the Northern Territory with a veto over use of traditional lands.) Although the Western Australian parliament passed its own Land (Titles and Traditional Usage) Act 1993, the Commonwealth legislation, whose validity was unquestioned, since consistency with the Racial Discrimination Act was essential, the Western Australian legislation was struck down by the High Court in March 1995.

But the *Mabo* decision has had important implications not only for the operation of laws affecting the economic use of land, even if this was the primary concern of the states and various business interests. The recognition of native title was also in fact a recognition of Aboriginal customary law (Brennan 1995: 136–60). Customary law deals not only with questions of ownership, but also with issues of justice, and punishment, often according to traditions which are considerably at variance with the standards set by the European system of justice. One effect of *Mabo* has been to lend weight to already existing pressures to grant greater autonomy to Aboriginal communities, and also to see customary law remedies recognised under common law. Another effect has been to raise a larger question about the prospects of Aboriginal self determination, and Aboriginal sovereignty. Such aspirations have drawn strength from the *Mabo* judgment under the favourable circumstances created by an international climate sympathetic to the claims of indigenous peoples. For some Aborigines the search for self determination meant seeking autonomy in terms of self management and self government, but not secession. Though what this ultimately amounts to in concrete terms remains unclear (Reynolds 1996). What is clear, however, is that the *Mabo* judgment and its consequences represent a significant stage in the development of Australia as a multicultural society. For the most immediate conclusion of the judgment was to recognise the coexistence within the polity of radically different legal traditions. The judgment had taken the course it did partly because of legislation which was designed as a response to the growing cultural diversity of Australian society – the Racial Discrimination Act. Now that judgment looked to be giving further recognition to the principle of cultural coexistence which had become a cornerstone of social policy.

Multiculturalism

Background

Just as Aboriginal policy in the first half of the century was dominated by the idea of assimilation, the settlement policies of the postwar years were also based uncontroversially on the idea of assimilation of immigrants. The growing numbers on non-British migrants (primarily European) were expected to learn English and adopt the values and ways of Australian society. The period from the end of the war until the 1990s saw a substantial change in the composition of the immigration intake as the proportion of British migrants fell from half the total intake in the 1960s to a little less than 20 per cent in 1990. The beginning of this period also saw the ending of the 'White Australia' policy, and the 1970s saw a rapid rise in the proportion of immigrants coming from non-European (primarily South-east Asian) countries. It was in this context that the policy of assimilation came under criticism, initially from Professor Jerzy Zubryzcki, who argued for 'a modest commitment to cultural diversity through the maintenance of immigrant languages and the development of studies of European culture' (Martin 1978: 55). With this criticism came a shift in policy when, in 1973, Labor Minister, Al Grassby, issued a comprehensive statement anticipating 'A Multicultural Society for the Future'.

While its origins lay in the initiatives of the Whitlam government, multiculturalism was established as a fundamental feature of social policy in the Fraser years. In 1979, in response to the Ethnic Affairs Council's call for a multicultural society, and for measures to establish equality of access for migrants to labour markets as well as to government resources, the government created the Australian Institute of Multicultural Affairs (Graetz and McAllister 1988: 80). This was later replaced by two separate agencies: the Office of Multicultural Affairs (in the prime minister's department), and (in 1989) the Bureau of Immigration Research. In 1989 the Hawke government announced its National Agenda for a Multicultural Australia. Multiculturalism was now defined as a policy recognising the rights of all Australians to express and share their individual cultural heritage; and to enjoy equality of treatment regardless of race, ethnicity, culture, religion, gender, or place of birth (Office of Multicultural Affairs 1989: 3).

Yet, while the 1970s and 1980s saw multiculturalism embraced by governments of both parties, this is not to say that the development of multiculturalism was uncontentious. The early 1980s saw much vigorous debate about immigration policy, which brought with it some persistent criticisms of the ethnic character, as well as of the volume, of immigration. Remarks by Professor Geoffrey Blainey in 1984 about the dangers posed by rapid increases in Asian immigration sparked furious debates about the feasibility of multicultural societies (Blainey 1984; Markus and Ricklefs 1985). By the end of the 1980s, however, other, different, complaints had also been voiced. Not only had the Liberal leader of the opposition, John Howard, and National Senator, John Stone, voiced concerns about the levels of Asian immigration, but others had begun to criticise the growth and influence of the ethnic lobby (Rimmer 1988; Bullivant 1989; Betts 1993; Freeman and Betts 1992). Throughout this period, public debate focused on the question of social cohesion, since this, more than anything else, was the concern of the critics of multiculturalism. Yet despite the vigour of the public discussions, the impact on policy was small. Cuts in immigration numbers in the early 1990s (from a high of 145 320 in 1988–89) were more a reflection of recessionary economic circumstances than anything else. And while the major parties differed in their rhetorical stances, neither resiled from a broad acceptance of multiculturalism. Indeed, what divisions there were within the Australian community over the issues surrounding multiculturalism did not, to any significant extent, reflect party political loyalties.

Multiculturalism and the basis of Australian political institutions

That multiculturalism will not simply endure but prevail is not a matter of contention. Whatever the issues debated in the 1980s, it was, and still is, generally accepted that Australia will remain a society characterised by cultural diversity. The debate now is not so much about whether or not cultural diversity should be accepted but how multiculturalism should be understood, and how it might be seen as consistent with Australia's moral and political traditions.

There are three major views dominating discussion among Australian policy makers and intellectuals generally. The first maintains that, while immigrants might come from different traditions, it is important that they be assimilated in the interests of social cohesion and political stability (Knopfelmacher 1982). The second view maintains that, while migrants may well assimilate if and when they choose, they should also have the freedom and the opportunity to maintain their own languages, customs and traditions in Australia if they so prefer – though this is essentially a private matter (Ten 1993; Kukathas 1993). The third view goes further still, to suggest that multiculturalism requires not simply toleration of the differences exhibited by the various cultural groups in Australia but a more active program to restructure political and legal institutions, and reshape social attitudes in order to accommodate diversity (Castles and others 1988; Theophanous 1995). These views do not correspond to the standard party divisions in Australia, or to ideological divisions among elites. Within the ranks of conservative intellectuals there are disagreements over how multiculturalism is to be understood, or how far it is to be embraced (Frankel 1992: 160–3); just as there are divisions among those on the left.

As the assimilationist idea has receded in influence, it is the third view which has proved most significant in public discussion and in the development of policy. What this view emphasises is the importance of tying multiculturalism to more general objectives of social policy: to secure social justice and attack prevailing forms of inequality (of class and gender as well as of race). It amounts to a rejection of the 'neo-conservative project of multiculturalism' associated with Malcolm Fraser and Jerzy Zubryzcki, which is held to accept existing ethnic chauvinism and sexism, and to trade on such 'regressive elements as aspects of a divide-and-rule strategy for social control in a multi-ethnic society' (Castles and others 1988: 153). The influence of this view is reflected in the passage of the Racial Hatred Act 1995, intended to outlaw racial vilification. Although passed without the support of the opposition, and minus the provisions for criminal sanctions, which were opposed by Green Senators Christabel Chamarette and Dee Margetts, it was the product of a conviction that sterner measures were necessary to combat racial discrimination and the growth of racist violence.

Laws against racial hatred, however, were not the only measures considered appropriate or necessary. Multicultural education to reinforce norms of tolerance and to work to eliminate racism was also promoted. The report of the National Multicultural Advisory Council (1995) recommended a variety of measures to promote education about multiculturalism, including education about the different cultures which are to be found in Australia, in schools and tertiary institutions. According to the proponents of multicultural education, the purpose of such measures is to counter the prejudice which stands in the way of the development of a multicultural society. 'The philosophy underlying multicultural education … assumes that the force of the logic behind the argument for cultural tolerance and acceptance is irresistible – if people are presented with the facts about multiculturalism and cultural diversity, they will be unable to sustain their discriminatory attitudes' (Theophanous 1995: 399).

Generally, the development of multiculturalism has seen a move from the principles of acceptance and assimilation, to the embracing of the integration of diverse cultures, to the promotion of the value of diversity. What began as a call for cultural assimilation has developed into the emphasising of cultural rights. The question which remains to be asked, however, is whether this new emphasis is, ultimately, feasible given the nature of Australian society, or will require other more fundamental changes to society and political institutions.

The contradictions of cultural rights

The development of multiculturalism has seen a growing emphasis on the importance and the value of cultural diversity, and on the need for policy to protect, and even to subsidise, that diversity. At the same time, however, the promotion of cultural diversity has been accompanied by the growth of a preoccupation with questions about Australian identity. The most obvious manifestation of this preoccupation has been in the push, given impetus by the enthusiasm of former Prime Minister Paul Keating, for Australia to become a republic.

At first glance, increase in republican support appears to be consistent with the growing commitment to multiculturalism, and the promotion of cultural diversity. Republicanism represents, above all, a repudiation of the ties that bind Australia to Great Britain. The choosing of a new head of state to replace the Queen would symbolise the breaking away of an independent nation; but it would also be consistent with the changing ethnic face of Australia, which was no longer a country of British immigrants. Indeed, one of the arguments of the Australian Republican Movement was that for most new Australians the traditions of the British monarchy held little relevance.

Equally, moves by some governments and by intellectual elites to embrace Aboriginal traditions as a part of Australia's inheritance also reflected a wish to put greater distance between Australia and Britain, and to assert an identity which reflected the land's earlier origins. For some, *Mabo* was to be considered a revolutionary episode in Australian history 'because, inasmuch as it questions a long established and once dominant history, it threatens many Australians with the loss of their customary narrative and thus the loss of identity and nationhood' (Attwood 1996: 100). One reaction to this was to embrace the *Mabo* judgment and to regard it not as a threat but as an opportunity to chart a new course.

The interest in, and support for, multiculturalism and in Aboriginal self determination is striking for the extent to which the debate about these issues turn out to be debates about national identity. What is less often remarked upon, however, is the extent to which the pursuit of a national identity and the promotion of cultural diversity sit uneasily together as compatible goals. The pursuit of a national identity requires an emphasis on the features of an Australian 'narrative' which identify a heritage, as well as institutions, held in common. Yet the promotion of diversity, which is willing to tolerate a variety of cultural jurisdictions to meet the needs of Aboriginal communities, as well as a variety of immigrant cultural traditions, makes the idea of a single national identity implausible – unless the notion of identity is emptied of any substantive content.

In the end, this is what presents the dilemma for the makers of social policy, as well as for Australian intellectual elites. The resolution of the dilemma may come in the development of a public philosophy which reconciles the idea of a national identity with the promotion of cultural diversity. But if no such public philosophy is forthcoming – or is feasible – either identity or certain cultural rights will have to be abandoned.

References

Attwood, B. (1996), 'Mabo, Australian and the End of History' in B. Attwood (ed.), *In the Age of Mabo. History, Aborigines and Australia*, Sydney: Allen & Unwin, 100–16.

Bennett, S. (1989), *Aborigines and Political Power*, Sydney: Allen & Unwin.

Betts, K. (1993), 'Public discourse, immigration and the new class' in J. Jupp and M. Kabala (eds), *The Politics of Australian Immigration*, Canberra: AGPS.

Blainey, G. (1984), *All for Australia*, North Ryde: Methuen Haynes.

Brennan, F. (1995), *One Land, One Nation. Mabo Towards 2000*, St. Lucia: University of Queensland Press.

Bullivant, B. (1989), 'The pluralist crisis facing Australia', *The Australian Quarterly*, 69:2, 212–28.

Castles, S., Kalantzis, M., Cope, W. and Morrissey, M. (1988), *Mistaken Identity. Multiculturalism and the Demise of Nationalism in Australia*, Sydney: Pluto Press.

Frankel, B. (1992), *From the Prophets Deserts Come. The Struggle to Reshape Australian Political Culture*, Melbourne: Arena.

Freeman, G. and Betts, K. (1992), 'The Politics of Interests in Immigration Policymaking in Australia and the United States' in G. Freeman and J. Jupp (eds), *Nations of Immigrants. Australia, the United States and International Migration*, Melbourne: Oxford University Press.

Glazer, N. (1983), *Ethnic Dilemmas: 1964–1982*, Cambridge: Harvard University Press.

Graetz, B. and McAllister, I. (1988), *Dimensions of Australian Society*, Melbourne: Macmillan.

Hasluck, P. (1988), *Shades of Darkness. Aboriginal Policy 1925–65*, Melbourne: Melbourne University Press.

Knopfelmacher, F. (1982), 'The Case Against Multiculturalism' in R. Manne (ed.), *The New Conservatism in Australia*, Melbourne: Oxford University Press, 40–64.

Kukathas, C. (1991), *The Fraternal Conceit. Individualist versus Collectivist Ideas of Community*, St Leonards: Centre for Independent Studies.

Kukathas, C. (1992a), 'Are there any cultural rights?', *Political Theory*, 20:1, 105–39.

Kukathas, C. (1992b), 'Cultural rights again: A rejoinder to Kymlicka', *Political Theory*, 20:4, 674–80.

Kukathas, C. (1993), 'Multiculturalism and the Idea of an Australian Identity' in C. Kukathas (ed.), *Multicultural Citizens: The Philosophy and Politics of Identity*, St Leonards: Centre for Independent Studies, 145–57.

Kymlicka, W. (1989), *Liberalism, Community and Culture*, Oxford: Clarendon Press.

Kymlicka, W. (1995), *Multicultural Citizenship. A Liberal Theory of Minority Rights*, Oxford: Clarendon Press.

Martin, D. (1978), *The Migrant Presence*, Sydney: Allen & Unwin.

Markus, A. and Ricklefs, M. C. (eds) (1985), *Surrender Australia? Essays in the Study and Uses of History: Geoffrey Blainey and Asian Immigration*, Sydney: Allen & Unwin.

Office of Multicultural Affairs (1989), *Multicultural Policies and Programs*, Canberra: AGPS.

Reynolds, H. (1996), *Aboriginal Sovereignty*, Sydney: Allen & Unwin.

Rimmer, S. (1988), *Fiscal Anarchy: The Public Funding of Multiculturalism*, Perth: Australian Institute of Public Policy.

Rowley, C. (1970), *The Destruction of Aboriginal Society*, Ringwood: Penguin.

Rowley, C. (1978), *A Matter of Justice*, Canberra: ANU Press.

Stanner, W. E. H. (1969), *After the Dreaming. Black and White Australians – An Anthropologist's View*, Sydney: Australian Broadcasting Commission.

Stephenson, M. A. and Ratnapala, S. (eds) (1993), *Mabo: A Judicial Revolution. The Aboriginal Land Rights Decision and Its Impact on Australian Law*, St Lucia: University of Queensland Press.

Ten, C. L. (1993), 'Multiculturalism and the Value of Diversity' in C. Kukathas (ed.), *Multicultural Citizens: The Philosophy and Politics of Identity*, St Leonards: Centre for Independent Studies, 5–16.

Theophanous, A. (1995), *Understanding Multiculturalism and Australian Identity*, Melbourne: Elikia Books.

10

Family policy

Deborah Mitchell

Over the course of the 1990s government policies designed to meet the needs of families represented the fastest growing area of social policy in Australia. Whether measured in terms of the number of programs, the types of services or payments provided, or beneficiary numbers, the growth in family policy programs outstripped all other social policy areas including those for the aged and the unemployed. Departing from what had been a fairly static pattern of provision since the mid 1970s – one major cash transfer program, rudimentary community service programs and the establishment of child care provision – developments since 1985 have produced a significant diversification in family policies and programs. The major developments were: the introduction of a range of child care payments; a hefty expansion in child care places; increases in the real value of social security payments for children; the introduction of a maternity payment; and the proliferation of community service programs to meet a range of family needs.

The growth of these policies may be traced to a range of social, economic and political pressures on successive ALP administrations throughout the 1980s. These pressures included the social wage bargains struck under the accord process as well as the culmination of programs implemented to fulfil the Hawke government's 'no child in poverty' promise made during the 1987 election campaign, the increase in women's labour force participation, and the emergence of a political agenda to address the needs of working women. Related to the latter change, there was also a shift in public policy attitudes towards women away from the traditional policy concept of 'dependent spouse' towards an approach regarding women as independent carers/wage earners.

At the same time as these pressures were effectively expanding and redefining the family policy arena, a number of contractionary pressures were also in evidence. The most notable were: a continuation of policies from the early 1980s which emphasised targeting and means testing; 'managerialist' administrative changes designed to reduce federal outlays and direct public provision of services; and the redefinition of policy responsibilities between various levels of government. These pressures tended to cut at the margins of existing programs and to promote cost shifting between the Commonwealth and the states, between the public and community (voluntary) sectors, and between government and families. An assessment of the net outcome of these conflicting pressures on family policy is not clear cut. If one focuses on the areas of growth, the result would be the view that family policy has now become a much more diverse and complex policy arena. Alternatively, a focus on the marginal cost cutting and cost shifting which has occurred would lead to an assessment that these forces have resulted in program fragmentation, lack of policy coherence and uneven policy development.

Part of the explanation for this lack of cohesive development can be attributed to the absence of clear differences in the policy platforms of the major parties and the relatively minor status which has been attached to family policy in the past. During the 1996 election, however, the family policy arena was targeted by the major parties for active campaigning. Both the ALP and the Coalition parties presented extensive family policy platforms, the underlying directions of which were strongly opposed: the ALP favouring a more modernist approach to support working women, while the Coalition promoted a conservative agenda to reorient policies to support 'women at home'.

This chapter starts with an overview of the policies and programs encompassed by the term family policy and examines the growth in programs in this area from the federal perspective. This is followed by a discussion of the expansionary and contractionary pressures which shaped policy development over the 1990s and the apparent outcomes of these opposing forces. The chapter concludes with a discussion of future policy trends as signalled by the Coalition in the 1996 budget and the policy recommendations of the Coalition-appointed National Audit Commission.

The scope of family policy

Until the mid 1980s family policy in Australia was a relatively minor aspect of social policy, especially when compared with most other OECD nations. Apart from one universal child benefits program and social service programs funded by federal grants and delivered by the states and community organisations, family policy at the federal level remained relatively under-developed. To a large extent this situation arose from the overarching character of the Australian welfare state which developed from the standpoint of the male breadwinner family, where the breadwinner was responsible for the maintenance and care of non-working dependants, whether young or old (Castles 1985). Changes in women's social and labour market expectations in the post-Whitlam era placed this broader welfare framework under increasing pressure, resulting in a continuous shift in the content and relative importance of family policy over the past two decades. The three most critical sources of structural change to the welfare state are briefly described below.

First, under the male breadwinner policy model, the care carried out within families, whether of children or aged parents, has traditionally fallen to women. The rapid growth in married women's labour force participation during the 1980s called into question this basic assumption about the functioning of the Australian welfare state. The conversion of what was formerly unpaid care for dependants to government or privately provided care has increased government outlays on direct cash transfers, subsidies and services (Bryson 1992; Cass 1994; Shaver 1995).

Second, the falling real wages of men and their rising unemployment throughout the 1980s was accompanied by a growing perception that the male breadwinner unit was no longer capable of delivering the standard of living which Australian families expect. Increasingly it was believed that a two-earner family was required to maintain living standards (Carter 1993). This further reinforced the pressure on government to provide social services and other supports which allow women to enter the labour market. Where this was not possible, there was increased demand from the unions and the electorate for transfer policies to supplement wages of low income (typically one-earner) families.

Third, following the introduction of no fault divorce laws under the Whitlam government, the rise of the sole parent family added another dimension to income support policies and programs (Shaver 1995). While most of the growth in this area occurred between 1975 and 1985, these programs remain a significant proportion of federal government expenditure on family assistance programs.

In summary, family policy had previously been concerned with direct income support for children and dependent spouses. As a result of recent changes, the scope of family policy expanded to include the needs of women, especially working mothers. In addition, the delivery of family services was extended to all three levels of government plus the community sector. In order to place reasonable bounds around this extensive and growing policy area, this chapter will be confined to discussing federal programs and funding patterns and, within the federal orbit of programs, will focus on the major programs which deal with direct family responsibilities in relation to the care and financial support of dependent children.

Federal programs and outlays

In the ten year period to 1995, federal outlays in the social security and welfare area grew at an average annual rate of 4.5 per cent. Of the total growth in this period, the major growth areas were assistance to families with children (27 per cent) and assistance to the aged (24 per cent). Figure 10.1 shows the breakdown of outlays in the social security and welfare area since 1986 to the present and projections till the end of the century under current policy arrangements. As Figure 10.1 shows, the growth in outlays for family assistance measures was expected to peak around 1996 and remain stable until the end of the decade. In 1986, expenditure in 1990 prices amounted to just under $0.4 billion rising to around $1.4 billion in 1996.

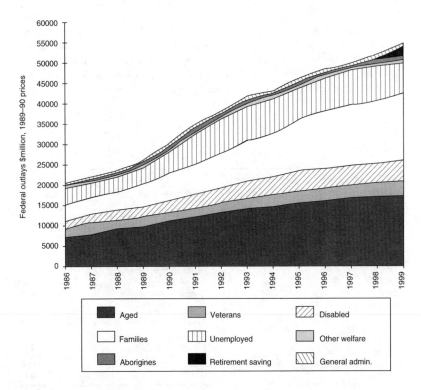

FIGURE 10.1   *Current and projected outlays on social welfare, 1986–99*

While some of the growth in outlays over this period does reflect new areas of expenditure, expansion of existing programs and real increases in transfer payments for children, around half of the apparent increase is a result of a shift of existing program expenditures from elsewhere in the federal budget. In Table 10.1 the chart of accounts for the Assistance to Families with Children component of the social welfare function is shown for 1985–86 and 1995–96. On the left hand side of the table, the 1985 expenditures are shown in 1995 dollars, in order to directly compare where significant changes have taken place. On the right hand side of the table, the 1995–96 chart roughly corresponds with the programs in existence in 1985–86.

The main budget item in 1985–86 was the Family Allowance program which provided cash transfers to families with children, irrespective of family income. In the 1986–87 budget, this program was subjected to an income and assets test which immediately decreased expenditure on this program by around 11 per cent through the exclusion of 3 per cent of existing recipients and a further 7 per cent of potential beneficiaries in the following year. In 1992, the Family Allowance program was subject to further tightening of income tests and renamed the Basic Family Payment. By the 1995–96 budget year the effect of continued targeting measures had reduced outlays on this program by 17.5 per cent in real terms.

TABLE 10.1　*Assistance to families with children: federal outlays 1985 and 1995*

1985–86 budget year		1995–96 budget year	
Program	Outlays (1995 $m)	Program	Outlays est. ($m)
Family Allowances	2563.2	Basic Family Payment	2118.1
Family Income Supplement	82.3	Additional Family Payment	3679.7
Children's Services	244.2	Child Care Services	1107.5
Orphans Pension	6.5	Other Cash Payments	218.7
Other	19.2	Other	487.1
Total	**2915.4**	**Total**	**7611.1**
Supporting Parent Payments	2063.7	Supporting Parent Payments	2685.6
		Home Child Care Allowances	3.0
		Parenting Allowance	2235.0
		Child Care Rebate	14.0
		Maternity Allowance	78.1
Total	**4979.1**	**Total**	**12626.8**

Sources: Budget Paper No. 1; Australian Treasury (1985,1995).

The Family Income Supplement (FIS) program was introduced in 1982 as a measure to overcome 'poverty trap' problems for low income families with children. At the time, the government was concerned that social security entitlements – especially for families with three or more children – often provided a better income alternative than low wages from the market. Thus the FIS program was designed to maintain work incentives by providing direct cash supplements to low wage earners with children. Over the period since its introduction, the FIS program (later renamed Family Allowance Supplement and now Additional Family Payment (AFP)) has experienced considerable growth in beneficiary numbers. In 1985 there were approximately 30 000 families in receipt of FIS, by 1995 nearly 180 000 families received the equivalent AFP. Like the Family Allowance Program, FIS was renamed in 1992 and the expenditures shown in Table 10.1 now include approximately $1200 million of child-related payments transferred from other parts of the social security budget. Even allowing for these shifted expenditures, this supplemental program is now the dominant element of federal assistance for families with children. The reasons for the growth of this particular program are discussed in detail below.

Expenditure under the Children's Services Program covers three forms of support: income-tested fee relief to eligible families using approved services whether provided by non-profit organisation, private or employer sponsored services. In addition to these fee subsidies, the program also provides capital grants and operational subsidies for a wide range of child care services. The dominant element of the program is direct child care fee relief to families with two earners, with the growth in expenditure largely driven by the increase in working mothers.

After a decade of rapid growth in the numbers of sole parents, the number of claimants has remained fairly stable since 1985. In recent years there has been a slight decline in the number of sole parent claimants due to the introduction of labour market programs specifically designed to encourage sole parents into the labour market rather than remain in receipt of pensions. The expenditures on Supporting Parent Payments shown in Table 10.1 reflects this change, with the growth in expenditure primarily due to real increases in benefit levels, rather than reflecting increased numbers of beneficiaries.

The bottom of the chart shows four 'new' programs that were introduced during the 1990s. Two of these programs – the Child Care Rebate and Maternity Allowance – were a direct response to the movement of married women into the labour market. The Child Care Rebate was introduced to assist working parents with the costs of child care. This non-means tested rebate is generally taken up by those families whose incomes preclude them from the two major child benefits programs and child care fee relief. The Maternity Allowance was introduced in 1996 to provide a one-off payment to families following the birth of a child. Although income tested, the income eligibility threshold is quite high, excluding around 10 per cent of potential recipients.

The Home Child Care Allowance (HCCA) was introduced in 1994 to provide a direct cash transfer for those parents who care for their children at home. The expenditure on the HCCA was funded by the cashing out of a tax rebate previously available to the working partner (generally the husband) who supported a non-working spouse. As such, the program represented a shift of funds from the tax system to the social security system, rather than new outlays. Parenting Allowance was introduced in the 1995–96 budget and like the HCCA represents a shift in funds from other parts of the federal budget. This allowance is paid directly to the spouses of pensioners and beneficiaries, rather than the pensioner/beneficiary receiving an additional allowance in respect of the partner. At the same time as this change was made, the program was expanded to incorporate the HCCA.

Because of the number of changes that have occurred over the past decade it is difficult to give an accurate estimate of how much real growth has occurred in the family program budget. An approximate assessment is that gains were made in the FIS (later AFP), Children's Services, other cash payments and programs, Supporting Parent Pension, Child Care Rebates and Maternity Allowances, totalling $4654 million. Payments shifted from other parts of the federal budget include approximately $1200 million of additional pension and benefit for children from unemployment and other transfer programs (now part of the AFP program) and a shift of $2238 million from the redirection of tax rebates and partner allowances into the HCCA/Parenting Allowance, making a total of $3438 million. From the original Family Allowance program there was a loss of $445 million in real terms. In total, the net addition to the budget was $4209 million in real terms over the decade. So rather than an apparent growth rate of 15.3 per cent per annum according to a literal reading of the budget documents, real growth over the last decade is probably closer to 8.4 per cent per annum. The following sections seek to explain the forces which lie behind these apparent gains, losses and shifts in family assistance measures.

Expansion: Working women and the accord

The growth in family policy under the Labor government was directed at two major goals: first, improvements to programs which directly addressed the costs of raising children; and second, the introduction of new programs which recognised the social consequences of the movement of women out of unpaid labour in the household and into the paid labour force. The former goal may be seen as an extension of the policy frameworks of the 1970s and early 1980s, while the latter represents a shift onto new policy terrain. In other countries the supports provided to working women are generally regarded as part of labour market policy. In Australia, however, the legacy of the male breadwinner construction of social policy has pushed changes in these areas into the orbit of family policy. A major implication of this choice of policy framework is that measures designed to reflect the changing role of women have been grafted onto older policy structures which supported the male breadwinner–dependent spouse policy model, creating potential conflict between working women and those at home.

The Labor government dealt with this conflict by creating parallel sets of entitlements for these two groups of women, whereas the Coalition chose to emphasise these differences by campaigning for a return to state support for traditional 'home makers'. While the discussion in this section separates out developments into these two broad areas, it is important to stress that there was considerable overlap in the implementation and timing of these changes. In particular, negotiations under the Prices and Income Accords throughout the 1980s provided a focus for coordinating policy direction on both these fronts.

Direct child support

The increased value of child related payments observed in the 1990s can be traced to two interrelated pressures which developed as a result of policy measures taken in the late 1980s. Within a year of the introduction of income tests for family allowances, a long standing debate over the level of child poverty in Australia was given new vigour by community organisations which were experiencing an increased demand on their resources, primarily from the unemployed and low wage families (Carter 1993). These organisations argued that the savings made from the introduction of income testing arrangements should be ploughed back into improved child benefit levels. Turning the government's social justice rhetoric to their own purpose, the community sector obtained a commitment from the Hawke government, during the 1987 election campaign, to increase the real level of payments made under the Family Allowance and the then Family Allowance Supplement (FAS) programs.

Second, as real wages were restrained by agreements reached under the accord processes, the size of the population eligible for the FAS program increased considerably. As part of the negotiations to improve the social wage of low income earners, the FAS program received considerable attention from the unions and government. This trade-off of wages for benefits had a number of advantages for the government: holding down real wage growth while at the same time using the existing framework of the social security system to target improvements in the social wage to low income families. The combined effect of these changes can be seen from Table 10.1 where expenditures on the Family Allowance program fell in real terms over the decade while expenditures on the FAS program increased in real terms by a factor of thirty over the same period – a massive reversal of the relative importance of the two transfer programs.

Supports for working women

While the provision of child care places had been the main expression of government support for working women throughout the 1980s, a range of new measures were added to this element of government support over the course of the 1990s. Under the accord processes, parental leave provisions were introduced and improved; part time work opportunities were expanded; and maternity allowances were introduced as part of the Accord Mark VII, although heavily prompted by Australia's ratification of International Labour Organisation Conventions 103 and 156. For working women, however, the major gain over the decade was undoubtedly the continued expansion in child care places. As Table 10.2 shows, child care places increased from around 50 000 in 1983 to 234 000 by 1995, nearly a five-fold increase.

TABLE 10.2   *Numbers of child care places by type*

Year	Children's Services Program	Family Day Care	Commercial/ Employer	Outside School Hours	Occasional/ Other Care	Total
1983	20 008*	20 100	na	9 870	*	49 978
1990	39 185	40 424	na	36 416	4 648	120 673
1993	44 347	47 079	42 400	58 386	6 704	198 916
1995	48 247	50 979	55 300	72 186	6 704	233 416

* Includes occasional/other in 1983.

Source: Budget Paper No. 1, 1995.

The changing labour force participation of women also required a reconceptualisation of their role *vis-à-vis* public policy, and the support needed to make this transition possible. The redefinition of women from dependants to independent carers/wage earners is reflected in policy changes which have taken various forms. The most notable is the redirection of family support payments away from men as the primary breadwinners and towards women as the primary carers. Often referred to as a transfer 'from the wallet to the purse', this policy shift was made explicit in the 1994 budget when the Labor government removed a tax rebate for men and created a new direct cash transfer for women (the Home Child Care Allowance). As the budget papers put it: 'The Dependent Spouse Rebate for couples with children will be removed simultaneously with the introduction of the Home Child Care Allowance as part of the Government's *continued commitment to the transfer of payments from the wage-earner to the primary carer*' [emphasis added]. This change of approach under the Labor government may turn out to be short lived, since one of the major election commitments of the Coalition was to reinstitute tax rebates for working men with a partner caring for children in the home.

Cutting at the margins: The bureaucratic agenda

During its term in office, the Labor government was confronted by a bureaucratic policy agenda shaped by neo-conservative economic doctrine, described by Pusey (1991) as 'economic rationalism'. While not explicitly opposed to the changes taking place in the family policy arena, this approach nevertheless under cut many of the policy innovations brought about under the accord and political pressure by working women. Carter's assessment of these countervailing policy forces was that:

> while conservative economic rationalism provided the "bottom line" of social policy, social corporatism was the antidote which encouraged the modest extension of the provision of economic benefits to families to offset the impact of fiscal and wages policies which reduced real incomes and permitted tax inequality. (Carter 1993: 258)

This section focuses on the way in which the economic rationalist agenda promoted marginal cost cutting and cost shifting in search of an improved budgetary bottom line, to the detriment of a cohesive family policy.

Targeting and means testing

The income tested nature of transfer payments in the Australian social security system has generally enjoyed widespread public support (Mitchell, Harding and Gruen 1994). This support has been engendered by the avoidance of severe applications of income tests and the pursuit of a fairly balanced approach to eligibility which in the past sought to exclude only the top 10 or 20 per cent of income earners from measures such as Family Allowances. Over the course of the past decade, however, the dominance of the economic rationalist agenda in the federal bureaucracy has seen a relentless pursuit of ever increasing targeting of benefits for families. This policy approach has excluded a much larger proportion of families from benefits than was perhaps originally envisaged by the Labor government in 1986. In each year subsequent to the introduction of income tests for family payments, incremental changes to the income and assets tests and/or other eligibility criteria have been implemented.

The primary effect of this continuous targeting was to switch the emphasis in child support away from the basic child benefit toward the supplementary income program. Table 10.3 shows the ratio of the basic child benefit payment (universal in 1985–86, means tested by the following year) to the supplemental program for very low income earners. In 1985, the ratio of expenditure was around 30:1 in favour of the basic payment. By 1988, this was down to 3:1 and by the early 1990s the ratio was about even. In 1992–93 the consolidation of other child related payments into the supplemental program (described in the previous section) makes it difficult to estimate the exact size of the supplemental program, the bracketed figures being approximations. Suffice to say that what was once a minor supplemental program of assistance is now the core form of assistance to families with children and addresses a far narrower range of families than the Family Allowance program of a decade ago.

TABLE 10.3   *Relationship between FA and FAS*

Year	Family Allowance ($m)	Family Allowance Supplement ($m)	Ratio FA:FAS
1985–86	1537.6	49.4	31
1986–87	1381.0	60.6	23
1987–88	1353.6	187.7	7
1988–89	1315.0	400.0	3
1989–90	1810.3	513.3	3.5
1990–91	1894.0	572.2	3
1991–92	2329.0	723.8	3
	Basic Family Payment	Additional Family Payment*	BFP:AFP
1992–93	2074.7	2124.1 (1724)	1.0 (1.2)
1993–94	2056.5	3420.4 (2550)	0.6 (0.8)
1994–95	2046.5	3530.8	0.6
1995–96	2118.1	3679.7	0.6

* Figures in brackets are the net expenditure after the exclusion of APB.

Source: Calculated from Budget Papers No. 1, various years.

It is not surprising then that these changes led to a political 'backlash' and the formation of various coalitions of interest to recoup this loss of entitlement via other means. In particular, working women as tax payers sought to have their child care costs recognised and partially offset by government. There is some irony in the fact that the removal of universal entitlement to a single benefit has resulted in the proliferation of a range of new payments as substitutes for families who were income tested out of the family allowance system. In turn, the creation of many overlapping programs has led to considerable complexity in the income transfer system, with low income families in particular often being eligible for several payments, as opposed to the one allowance.

The managerialist agenda

Prior to Pusey's exposure of economic rationalism, scholars of public administration had identified a related trend in public policy making, referred to as 'managerialism' (Yeatman 1987). The managerialist agenda looked to the private sector to provide new models of public service provision. The resulting policy changes are now a familiar part of the policy landscape: user-charging, the contracting out of services to the private sector, and the public subsidy of privately provided services. In the family policy arena, the main effect of this agenda has been the entry of private (for profit) providers of child care into the fee relief system and the payment of child care rebates to families using private care services. While it could be claimed that this change has effectively expanded child care places (see Table 10.2), critics have argued that funds going to the private sector may crowd out future public provision. There is also a concern that quality standards in privately provided services are below those of public or community based services which have had to meet quality targets (Cahir 1996).

Cost shifting

A third feature of the search for reducing the budget bottom line at the federal level was the retreat from direct provision of services by federal departments. The federal government retreat from direct service provision since the late 1980s has seen services such as the Family Support program transferred to the states and the shifting of costs for emergency family relief and other forms of family related care onto the community sector (Carter 1993). With the tightening of fee relief arrangements for long day child care and a reduction in real levels of the Child Care Rebate, child care costs have increasingly been shifted back onto families or absorbed by community organisations.

Outcomes: The Labor legacy

The previous sections have concentrated on recent developments in the family policy arena. To appreciate the full complexity of the current configuration of family policy we need to consider taxation and other income supports that developed prior to the last decade. Table 10.4 lists the range of programs currently in operation and highlights the extent of overlap which has developed.

TABLE 10.4   *Family related payments in the social security and taxation systems, 1995*

Program/payment	Eligibility
1 Dependent spouse payments	
Dependent Spouse Rebate (tax)	Taxpayer with a dependent spouse
Partner Allowance	Partners of pensioners/beneficiaries without children, over 40 and with no recent labour market experience
Wife Pension	No new grants from July 1995. Existing wife pensioners continue to be eligible
2 Caring related payments	
Sole Parent Rebate (tax)	Sole parent caring for at least one child
Sole Parent Pension	Sole parent caring for at least one child
Home Child Care Allowance	Parent at home with at least one child
Parenting Allowance	Primary carer at home of child/ren under 16
Carer Pension	Carer of a disabled/elderly pensioner/ beneficiary
3 Child related payments	
Basic Family Payment	Parent/guardian caring for child under 16 (income test threshold $64 000)
Additional Family Payment	Parent/guardian caring for child under 16 (income test threshold $22 000)
Child Care Rebate	Parent of child under 13 in formal or informal care
Long Day Care	Carer of child in approved care centres or family day care schemes (income test threshold $25 000)
Outside School Hours Care	Carer of child in before/after school care

The programs in the first panel of the table are the remnants of provisions made for non-working wives under the male breadwinner policy model. The Dependent Spouse Rebate (DSR) is now a minor tax relief for wage earners with a partner at home. The value of this rebate has been eroded through non-indexation of the rebate since the early 1980s. As discussed earlier, in 1994 the DSR for tax payers with children was cashed out to provide a direct payment (Home Child Care Allowance) to the mother. The age restrictions placed on the Partner Allowance and the cut-out of new entrants to the Wife Pension are a further indication of the shift away from treating women as 'dependants'. These restrictions also reflect an implicit policy view that women are now primarily wage earners or temporarily out of the workforce due to care commitments. It is precisely on this point that Coalition policies strongly differ from those of the previous Labor government, as indicated by the introduction of the family tax rebate in the recent budget – a rebate paid to the primary breadwinner (usually the husband).

The second panel of programs include long standing tax rebates and pensions for sole parents and three new programs which reflect the new policy attitude to women as carers. The Home Child Care and Parenting Allowances are paid to women in lieu of payments/rebates previously received by the breadwinner. The Carer Pension was introduced partly in response to the shift away from expensive forms of institutional care for the elderly and disabled toward 'community' care but also in recognition of the severe effect which care responsibilities may have on the carer's (usually a woman's) ability to participate in, or re-enter, the labour force. The child related payments in part three of the table either directly boost the incomes of families with children (Basic and Additional Family Payments) or seek to defray the costs of child care for working women.

The complexity of these arrangements is partly a reflection of the major transition in women's lives from being home makers and full time carers in the 1960s and 1970s to breadwinners/working mothers in the 1990s. Some complexity in family policy arrangements is inevitable given the fact that at present there are essentially three generations of women, with varying labour force participation patterns, who make different claims on the state. Moreover, these generational differences are accentuated by women's changing needs across their life cycle and an ambivalent public policy attitude toward 'mothers at home' versus 'working mothers'.

These structural complexities, due to generational change, were further exacerbated by the introduction of a range of programs in response to a backlash against the loss of entitlement to child benefit by a significant proportion of working families. The overlapping entitlement criteria shown in Table 10.4 indicates that there has been a breakdown in the coherence of family policy over the 1990s. This is not just apparent from an administrative viewpoint, but also from the standpoint of claimants on the system (Cass 1994). The uneven nature of family policy development under Labor was a product of, on the one hand, a series of gains being made under the accord processes and the political pressure applied by women seeking improved outcomes from the welfare state. On the other hand, there were the losses through policy interventions dominated by economic rationalist and managerialist aims which picked away at the margins of these programs, fragmenting this policy arena to an ever increasing extent.

Future directions: The Coalition agenda

With the election of the Howard government, many social policy commentators take the view that the future for family policy is one of significant cuts to income transfer and social service programs. This view is partly borne out by the changes announced in the first budget of the Coalition. A series of marginal cuts and restrictions on current programs will result in a decrease of around $36 million to family program expenditures. For example, operational subsidies to support community based long day care centres will cease after 1997, and the Child Care Rebate program will be subject to an income test. These changes, plus cost cutting at the margins of other programs, will have the effect of reducing outlays by $207 million (in current prices) by the end of the decade. However, the family tax rebate, foreshadowed during the election campaign, was introduced in the 1996 budget at a first year cost of $147 million, rising to $600 million by 1999.

The net impact of these changes in monetary terms is probably far less important than the policy attitudes demonstrated by the nature of the changes. The main budgetary cuts to family programs were to measures which assist working women and the redirection of expenditure to breadwinners with non-working partners. Despite the Howard government's rather low key reception of the National Commission of Audit (NCA) Report delivered in June 1996, the policy directions presaged in that report – a continuation of cost shifting, especially to the states; the extension of means testing to programs which are currently universal; and direct cuts to some cash transfer programs in lieu of the tax rebate – were given expression in the 1996–97 budget and thus the NCA document is likely to be a fairly good guide to future change. Taken together, the 1996–97 budget and the NCA recommendations firmly indicate that the Coalition intends to reinstitute a male breadwinner approach to family policy.

References

Bryson, L. (1992), *Welfare and the State: Who Benefits?*, London: Macmillan.
Cahir, P. (1996), 'Child care: Policy issues in the 1990s', Women as Policy Shapers and Policy Takers, Seminar series in Public Policy, Canberra: ANU.
Carter, J. (1993), 'Dealing with Policy Failure: A Social Policy Perspective' in I. Marsh (ed.), *Governing in the 1990s: An Agenda for the Decade*, Melbourne: Longman Cheshire
Cass, B. (1994), *Creating the Links: Families and Social Responsibility*, Final Report of the National Council for the International Year of the Family, Canberra: AGPS.
Castles, F. (1985), *The Working Class and Welfare: Reflections on the Political Development of the Welfare State in Australia and New Zealand, 1890-1980*, Wellington: Allen & Unwin.
Department of the Treasury (1985–95), *Budget Paper No: 1*, Canberra: AGPS.
Mitchell, D., Harding, A. and Gruen, F. (1994), 'Targeting Welfare', *Economic Record*, 70, 210: 310–35.

National Commission of Audit (1996), *Report to the Commonwealth Government*, Canberra: AGPS.

Pusey, M. (1991), *Economic Rationalism in Canberra*, Cambridge: Cambridge University Press.

Shaver, S. (1995), 'Women, Employment and Social Security' in A. Edwards and S. Magarey (eds), *Women in a Restructuring Australia*, Sydney: Allen & Unwin.

Yeatman, A. (1987), 'The Concept of Public Management and the Australian State in the 1980s', *Australian Journal of Public Administration*, 46: 339–53.

11

The environment

Elim Papadakis

After being in the political spotlight for almost a decade, the environment appeared to have diminished as an issue of importance in the 1993 federal election campaign. That campaign was dominated by economic issues, such as the proposed introduction of a goods and services tax by the Liberal Party. Still, the environment, though not foremost in people's minds when it came to casting their vote, remained salient as an issue in many different ways (see Papadakis 1994). In 1996 the environment emerged again as an important issue in the election campaign.

Apart from the standard undertakings to protect and conserve the environment, the 1996 election produced two surprises. The first was the degree of competition over this issue between the major political parties. The second was the innovative manner in which the Liberal Party attempted to outbid the ALP as the party with the policies that would do most to protect the environment. For over a decade the ALP had remained virtually unchallenged (at least as regards perceptions of the major parties) as the more progressive on environmental issues. Furthermore, this had been to its advantage in the 1983, 1987 and 1990 federal elections. In 1996, the Liberal and National Coalition parties offered to spend $1.15 billion on environmental protection. The funding was to come from the partial sale or privatisation of the national telephone company, Telstra. By selling one-third of Telstra, the Coalition proposed to establish a $1 billion National Heritage Trust of Australia. Over a period of between four and five years, the Coalition undertook to spend:

- $318 million on a national vegetation plan
- $163 million on the rehabilitation of the Murray–Darling Basin
- $32 million on a national land and water resources audit

- $80 million on a national reserve system
- $100 million on tackling pollution of the coast and seas.

This would still leave $300 million in the trust fund at the end of five years, and the interest earned on this would be used to support other initiatives.

The reaction to this proposal was mixed. Dr Bob Brown, one of the leading figures in the Green movement who was later elected to the Senate as a representative of the Australian Greens, described the environment statement as a 'quantum leap forward by the Liberal Party – the best environment policy the conservatives have come up with'. Environmental groups like the Australian Conservation Foundation (ACF) and The Wilderness Society (TWS) also welcomed the policies. However, divisions emerged between the two organisations. Whereas the ACF felt that the measures should be enacted whether or not the Coalition was able to sell part of Telstra, TWS appeared to be less concerned about this issue. TWS also declared that, in some seats, it would campaign actively against the ALP, and that it would not advise voters to direct their preferences to the ALP in other seats. TWS wanted to 'punish' the ALP for some of its policies on forests in the previous three years. The challenge by the Coalition to the dominance by the ALP in environmental questions was further reinforced through a policy statement that covered issues such as the protection of endangered species, maintaining biodiversity, a detailed assessment of the costs of environmental damage in drawing up national accounts and policies on soil erosion, salinity, and the pollution of rivers.

The main opposition to the proposal for linking environmental protection to the sale of Telstra came from the ALP and from the Australian Democrats. Both parties accused the Coalition of coercing the electorate into supporting the sale of Telstra. The ALP ran a fierce campaign about the effects of the privatisation of Telstra on phone charges, particularly on voters living in rural areas. Yet, this did not appear to have a significant impact on the campaign. The Coalition maintained its stance, and suggested that Telstra may already have had plans to sell off part of the organisation.

The initiative on the sale of Telstra will require the support of the Australian Democrats in the Senate. Although the Democrats vowed to oppose the sale of Telstra, they face a number of difficulties including the claim by the victors that they have a mandate for this proposal and the threat of a double dissolution to parliament which could undermine their position in the Senate. At any rate, the proposal by the Coalition was both timely in undermining the efforts by the ALP to attract Green preferences and shrewd in reflecting a growing interest in tackling environmental problems in innovative ways. Furthermore, the proposal to link the sale of Telstra with the funding of environmental protection is part of a trend which views the environment and economic development as complementary rather than opposed. To understand key developments in environmental politics in the 1990s we must therefore take into account attempts by political organisations to adapt to the new emphasis on environmental issues on the contemporary political agenda.

Concern about the environment

The regular measurement of trends in public opinion on environmental protection only began in the early 1970s. This itself is indicative of a perception by certain elites, notably politicians and the mass media, that the environment either was or could become a significant factor in Australian politics. As noted elsewhere (Papadakis 1996), it was only around 1972 that the major parties (for instance, Whitlam in his election policy speech) made a significant effort to place the environment on the political agenda. It was not until 1983 that the environment first featured as a significant issue in a national electoral contest, due to the conflict over the proposed construction of a dam on the Franklin River in Tasmania.

From the mid 1970s a substantial proportion of respondents to opinion polls indicated that they paid attention to environmental problems and a small number indicated that this was an issue of great concern to them (see Papadakis 1996: Table 16.1). Figure 11.1 presents trend data on views about

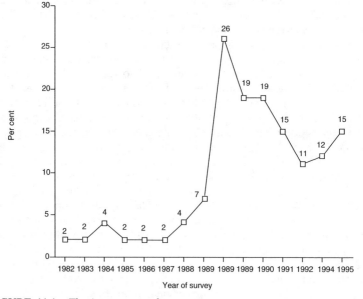

FIGURE 11.1   *The importance of government action on conservation and the environment, 1982–95*

government action on the environment. For most people this issue does not head their list of priorities for government action. Although the percentages are generally small, the data are especially useful as a measure of public concern since respondents were not offered any prompts about all the possible issues that the federal government might be addressing. As Dunlap (1989) has pointed out, this methodology represents a stringent measure of salience.

Of particular interest is the change in trends that took place between February and June 1989, in the level of importance of conservation and the environment from 7 to 26 per cent. Until 1989, the Green movement had campaigned principally for the preservation of forests and wilderness areas and the ALP had become increasingly aware of the strategic importance of attracting the preferences of green voters by taking certain decisive measures (like World Heritage Listing) to protect and preserve forests and wilderness areas (Papadakis 1993; 1996). The shift in opinion in 1989 marked a new phase in environmental politics. It meant that the level of concern about environmental protection compelled established political organisations to make a concerted effort to resolve the tension between environment and development. In the 1990s environmental politics in Australia is being shaped by this effort.

There appear to be two principal reasons for the decisive shift in popular opinion that occurred between February and June 1989. First, there was unprecedented attention in the mass media to the potential impact of the emission of greenhouse gases. By the mid 1980s, scientists had become increasingly aware of the possibility of the earth's atmosphere warming as a result of carbon dioxide emissions. At a conference held in Toronto in 1988 more than 300 scientists and policy makers from around fifty countries noted that a 50 per cent reduction in carbon dioxide emissions would have to be achieved in order to stabilise the atmospheric concentration of greenhouse gases. They suggested, as an initial target, a 20 per cent reduction in carbon dioxide emissions by the year 2000. Coincidentally, in 1988 and 1989, many countries experienced exceptionally warm weather. Though there was no necessary connection between these experiences and the greenhouse effect, some scientists and the media speculated on the connection between the two. Fears about the greenhouse effect also coincided with speculation about the impact of CFCs on the depletion of ozone at high altitudes and the catastrophe that could arise from this.

The second principal reason for a shift in public awareness was the rise of environmental groups in political contests, notably the capture by Green independents of five out of thirty-five seats in the Tasmanian elections on 13 May 1989. The ALP was therefore obliged to share power with the Green independents in order to form a government. At the federal level, the ALP reacted swiftly to what it regarded as a serious electoral challenge. The federal environment minister, Graham Richardson, argued that the states should transfer their powers over environmental policy to the federal government since they had failed to deal with what was now a national problem. He also promised an exceptional publicity campaign for national standards in water quality (*Bulletin*, 6 June 1989). A similar commitment to placing the environment on the national agenda was expressed in July 1989 when the prime minister, Bob Hawke, launched a statement on the environment which included a program for planting one billion trees by the year 2000.

Although the data on trends in public opinion show a gradual decline in concern about the environment as the most important issue after June 1989, there is no sign of a complete reversal of the trends reported in the 1970s through to the late 1980s. Like most political issues, concern about the environment is subject to 'cycles of attention' (Downs 1972). However, the trend over the past two or three decades has been towards a rise in concern.

Another way of assessing the significance of shifts in opinion about the environment is to place it in the context of electoral contests. Table 11.1 examines data from the Australian Election Study surveys which show that in 1987 the environment was very important to 31 per cent of respondents but only ranked ninth in importance on a list of ten issues. In 1990 it rated as important for 52 per cent of respondents and ranked fifth out of ten issues. In 1993, in the midst of a major recession, the environment still rated as extremely important to 41 per cent of respondents. However, its ranking among all issues dropped to ninth position. In 1996 the environment rated as extremely important with about the same proportion of the AES sample – 42 per cent. However, the ranking of the environment as an issue of concern rose to seventh position out of thirteen issues.

TABLE 11.1   *The electoral salience of the environment, 1987–96*

	1987	1990	1993	1996
Importance (%)[a]	31	52	41	42
Rank (number)[b]	9	5	9	7
Of concern to self and family (%)[c]	–	11	4	5

[a] '... When you were deciding about how to vote, how important was each of these issues to you personally?' In 1987 respondents had a choice of 10 issues, in 1990, 9 issues, in 1993 14 issues and in 1996, 13 issues. The percentage refers to responses coded as 'most important' (in 1987) or 'extremely important' (in 1990, 1993 and 1996) on a three-point scale (which also included codes for 'quite important' or 'not very important').

[b] The rank is based on the total percentage scores for the question on the importance of the environment compared to the total percentage scores for all other issues. For example, in 1987 the environment ranked ninth out of 10.

[c] The percentage is based on the follow-up question: 'Which of these issues has worried you and your family most in the last 12 months?' Estimates are for those who coded the environment as the issue of most concern.

Source: Australian Election Study surveys 1987–96.

For the majority of respondents economic issues remain at the top of the agenda. However, two trends are worth noting. The first, which I shall address later, arises from the concept of sustainable development and the willingness by many people to accept that the goals of economic development and environmental protection may not always necessarily be in conflict. The second trend is the emergence of the environment as a permanent feature on the political agenda, even if there is occasionally a decline in public attention. Another way of testing this argument about future trends is to ask respondents what issues are likely to worry them and their families most in ten years from now. The 1993 AES confirmed that the environment had been demoted as a current political issue. However, when asked about the future, respondents ranked the environment much higher: 11 per cent ranked this as the issue likely to be of greatest concern, a figure surpassed only by concerns about unemployment (28 per cent) and health (14 per cent).

In 1991 respondents were asked to select from a list of thirteen issues which would be the most important in ten years' time. The environment, ranked first (with 24 per cent) followed by unemployment (19 per cent) and pensions and care for the aged (10 per cent) (ANOP 1991: 16). In the 1993 ANOP survey respondents were asked whether they believed unemployment and the environment would become more or less important issues in Australia in ten years' time. Again, the environment ranked higher than unemployment by a significant margin. Whereas 56 per cent agreed that unemployment would become a more important issue in ten years' time, 77 per cent agreed that the environment would become a more important issue. Following Yankelovich (1991), it would appear that people are not only aware of the environment as an important issue but that they are now 'working through' the implications of this new awareness. In other words, they are giving serious consideration to how one might strike a new balance between environmental protection and economic development.

Economic development and environmental protection

Despite the focus by many political actors and by the mass media on the conflict between economic development and environmental protection, there is evidence to support the claim that both government and non-government organisations have been able to adapt to changing perceptions. Moreover, they can play a role in influencing perceptions. This influence is reflected in the changes of wording in survey questions and in the framing of questions. None of this is to say that public opinion reflects the uncritical acceptance of the frameworks advanced by those who attempt to influence opinions. Political parties, social movements and the media all contribute to the formation of public opinion. In the 1970s, all these organisations latched onto the notion of 'the limits to growth' and articulated the hypothesised conflict between economic growth and environmental protection. This conflict had become so acute in the 1990s that the federal government created mechanisms like the Resource Assessment Commission and the Ecologically Sustainable Development working groups in order to move from an adversarial to a more cooperative framework for dealing with environmental issues (Papadakis 1993).

Political organisations, established institutions and the media have adopted an adversarial approach to dealing with new challenges. The media have often seized on the character of the relationship between the proponents of economic growth and of environmentalism. It is therefore hardly surprising that since the 1970s opinion polls both in Australia and elsewhere have framed questions to reflect this potential conflict rather than any compatibility of development and environment. The following examples distinguish between an approach that focuses on the potential for conflict (option 1) and an approach that offers the possibility of a resolution (option 2):

- **Option 1:** 'Do you think Australians should concentrate on economic growth even if it means some damage to the environment, or concentrate on protecting the environment even if means some reduction in economic growth?' (Saulwick (Telephone) Poll *Sydney Morning Herald*, 12 April 1994)
- **Option 2:** '*A* – Australians will increasingly have to make hard choices between economic growth and protection of the environment. *B* – It is quite possible to have both a prosperous economy and a healthy environment.' (Respondents are then asked if they 'agree strongly with *A*, agree more with *A* than *B*, (find it) hard to say, agree more with *B* than *A*, agree strongly with *B*) (Keys Young 1994)

Neither of these questions is 'correct' or 'incorrect'. The answers to both can be useful in examining patterns of opinion, though option 1 excludes the choices available in option 2.

In answer to option 1, the majority appear to support environmental protection over economic growth. In 1990 the survey found that 62 per cent supported environmental protection and 26 per cent economic growth. In 1994 the figures were 57 per cent and 33 per cent, respectively (*Sydney Morning Herald*, 12 April 1994). The data, despite any arguments about how the question has been framed, show that there was a slight decline in support for environmental protection relative to concerns about economic growth. Nonetheless, they further support the argument that in the midst of a major recession support for environmental protection remained very high (Papadakis 1994).

When respondents are provided with the opportunity to consider whether or not development and the environment are compatible, as in option 2, we find that more than half the sample (55 per cent) agree that they are compatible. Only 37 per cent think that they are not and 7 per cent are unsure (Keys Young 1994: 50, Table 5.10). Qualitative research shows that how economic and environmental goals are defined in structured surveys is problematic on two counts: it gives the impression that the two goals are necessarily in conflict; and the data suggest that, overall, people are in favour of environmental protection rather than development. The ANOP study shows that respondents tended to be in favour of a 'balance between achieving economic recovery, increasing employment opportunities and protecting the environment' (ANOP 1991: 53).

Unlike many standard opinion polls, the ANOP qualitative study found that there was not a simple preference for environmental protection rather than economic growth among the majority. Rather, the qualitative research supported the view that most people took the short term perspective that 'the balance between environment and economy requires more emphasis on the economy and on unemployment at the present time than on the environment'. Only a minority took the longer term view which emphasised the interdependence of the economy and the environment in the future and saw 'a healthy environment as a necessary precondition to a healthy economy' (ANOP 1991: 55). Still, in a subsequent study, ANOP concluded that people no longer thought in terms of 'jobs versus the environment': 'While some job losses are considered inevitable, protecting the environment is also perceived to result in a creation of jobs' (ANOP 1993: 6–7).

There is a correspondence between these findings from September 1993 and the approach by established political parties and environmental organisations like the ACF during the 1993 and 1996 election campaigns. Another indicator of the weakening of old ways of thinking about environment and development has been the approach by the federal government to reconciling potential conflicts, for instance, through the establishment of ESD (ecologically sustainable development) working groups. Respondents to the ANOP survey in 1991 and 1993 were asked whether they were aware of the notion of ESD. In 1991 one in five were aware of ESD and able to define it, 5 per cent were aware but unable to define it and the remainder were either not aware of ESD or unsure. The figures for 1993 were almost identical. Though only a minority understood ESD, this still represents a substantial proportion of respondents. Among certain groups a high proportion were aware of the concept: 53 per cent of those with tertiary education, 45 per cent of members of environmental groups (ANOP 1991: 99, Table 9.2) and 33 per cent of white collar workers (ANOP 1993: 102, Table 7.1). By the end of 1995 a growing number of people appeared to be aware of the ESD.

The AES surveys conducted in 1990, 1993 and 1996 show that around 80 per cent of respondents felt that 'industry should be prevented from causing damage to the environment, even if this sometimes leads to higher prices'. This finding is significant. However, it does not mean that voters will immediately support a political party that forces industry to raise its prices in order to protect the environment. The question reflects a climate of opinion. It suggests that 'in public' most people are willing to say that they are for the environment and are prepared to make financial sacrifices. Whether or not or how far this is reflected in their actual behaviour is a different matter. Yet, the data show that there is widespread moral support for consideration of the environment to an extent that was perhaps difficult to contemplate two or three decades ago. On this and related issues public opinion does appear to be moving towards the resolution that there is a price to be paid for development and that everyone will have to share the cost.

Party policies on the environment

Over the past five decades political parties have gradually responded to growing public concern about environmental protection. This can be gauged by examining the party platforms and policy speeches of the established parties, including the Australian Democrats (Papadakis 1996). Although the Democrats have provided a significant impetus for change since their formation in 1977, the major parties had all demonstrated, prior to 1977, that they were capable of responding to situations perceived as crises. For instance, the topic of soil conservation was taken up by the Nationals (then the Country Party) in the 1920s, by the Liberals in the 1940s and by the ALP in the 1950s. Both the ALP and the Nationals referred to the National Soil Conservation Program in 1980, followed by the Liberals in 1983. In 1987 and 1988 the Democrats directed attention to the concept of sustainable agriculture and to the notion of tree farming for wind breaks. In 1987 the Nationals called for assistance to farmers for conservation and in 1990 all the major parties drew attention to the Landcare program. In other words, all of the parties have a history of putting forward environmental policies.

A major early concern among the parties was the protection for forests and national parks. The Liberals and Nationals both called for the preservation of forests in the 1940s and 1950s and in 1966 the ALP and the Nationals called for the enlargement of national parks. However, in 1965 the ALP went a step further by advocating a national system of parks and reserves. In 1974 the ALP called for the protection of Northern Australia and the National Parks and Wildlife Conservation Bill and, in 1977, for a ban on the clearing of native forests for softwood plantations and the development of a self sustaining forestry industry.

The advent of the Democrats led to novel proposals on parks, including the creation of a major national park in south-west Tasmania, an end to the issuing of woodchip licences except for sawmill waste, the protection of forests in Pacific Basin countries, and tax incentives for landowners to retain forests. Although the Liberals and Nationals came up with some constructive proposals (in 1979, on protecting the Alligator Rivers Region and nominating Kakadu National Park for world heritage listing and, in 1983, for a youth project in reforestation), most of the new proposals in the 1980s were made by the ALP and by the Democrats, notably on protecting rainforests both in Australia and in other countries. The ALP was especially successful in responding to proposals by environmental groups and by the Democrats on forest protection, as demonstrated by their successful appeals to environmentalists at the 1983, 1987 and 1990 federal elections.

As regards nuclear power, in 1984 the Democrats were the only party to call for a worldwide nuclear freeze and for the closure of the Lucas Heights nuclear reactor. Though the ALP has experienced serious divisions over uranium mining, since 1977 it has been opposed to the mining and export of uranium. In 1984 it also opposed the dumping of nuclear waste in oceans. The Democrats have always resisted the mining and export of uranium. By contrast, the Liberals and Nationals have been in favour of exploiting uranium and only once, in 1984, did the Liberals sound a note of caution by calling for an inquiry on environmental protection with reference to the Ranger Uranium Mine. In the 1996 election campaign, and once installed in government, the Coalition parties continued to favour the development of uranium mines. As regards the testing of nuclear weapons, the ALP and the Democrats were, until recently, the only parties to oppose it. In 1995 the Coalition parties joined in the widespread condemnation of the resumption of nuclear testing in the Pacific by the French government.

The issue of waste management first emerged among the parties in the early 1970s. In 1973 the ALP wanted to promote recycling and the control of hazardous chemicals and wastes. The Liberals drew attention to recycling in 1974 and the Nationals in 1979. The Democrats advanced the agenda in 1979 by advocating 'non-polluting' methods of sewage disposal. Above all, in 1989, they concentrated on controls over crop spraying and pest control machines and over herbicides and pesticides, on the resiting of chemical industries and on the cessation of burning or high temperature incineration of intractable wastes. In 1982 the ALP had taken the lead on informing the public about contaminants and, in 1984, on developing a system for identifying dangerous chemicals. In 1994 the ALP proposed a 50 per cent reduction of wastes to landfill, the creation of national facilities for the storage of hazardous waste and a national inventory of pollutants.

On many issues, institutional inertia, like the established pattern of concern about economic development, has represented a formidable barrier to change. This applied especially to the Liberal and National parties for whom, in the 1950s and 1960s, the logic of economic development combined with short term electoral considerations appeared to prevail over any strategy to deal with environmental problems. The ALP, notwithstanding its strong attachment to materialism and economic growth, was less encumbered by the institutional inertia. Labor managed to maintain a close connection with the social movements and opposition groups that emerged in the 1950s to campaign against the testing of nuclear weapons, and again in the 1970s against uranium mining and other forms of economic development.

The analysis of data over a long time period can be used to demonstrate how political organisations are both capable of adapting to social forces and of how they can operate independently of social forces in order to reshape the political agenda. The recent billion dollar package proposed by the Coalition parties demonstrates the significant shifts that have taken place in the role of environmental issues on the political agenda. Much of this change can be attributed to the dominance by the ALP in government through most of the 1980s and through to the middle of the 1990s, and the influence on the ALP of new social and political movements and parties. The environmental movement has, in effect, become part of, as well as an influence on, the social networks and the norms that constitute contemporary institutional practices.

Media coverage of environmental issues

Political parties play a crucial role in providing the media with cues and frameworks for discussing new issues. These cues and frameworks are crucial for raising public awareness about issues, though not necessarily for resolving conflicts over them. The media receives cues from expert communities and social movements. It also contributes in a distinctive way to setting the agenda for political debates and for attempts to change institutional practices. The media represent a powerful force and have been used to great effect by social movements in trying to reshape norms and social values. The best example of this was the campaign to prevent the construction of the Franklin Dam in Tasmania, although the media have also played a key role in other more recent environmental campaigns (see Burgmann 1993; Papadakis 1993; Sylow 1994). Perhaps more than any other organisations, the established political parties depend on the media for their survival and influence.

The following data capture the intensity and the direction of coverage of environmental issues in the mass media. The analysis makes no claims about representing how all of the mass media frame and articulate concerns about the environment. Rather, it focuses on one source, over a period of thirty-five years, to illustrate how the mass media may influence and reflect public opinion as well as the aspirations of political parties and social movements. The source used in this case study is the popular weekly magazine the *Bulletin*. Although the *Bulletin* is not meant to represent all of the mass media, it provides a good indication of trends. In March 1981 the readership was estimated at 706 000. Since then, there has been a decline – to 507 000 in March 1991 and 450 000 in March 1994. Readers of the *Bulletin* are more likely to be tertiary educated, to be from higher rather than lower socioeconomic groups, and to have professional occupations.

Table 11.2 shows that the intensity of coverage of environmental issues increased steadily from 1960 onwards. Whereas in the 1960s there were only two stories featuring environmental issues, the number had increased to sixteen for the period 1970 to 1974 and to eighteen between 1975 and 1979. In the late 1980s (1985–89) the number of stories rose to forty and in the early 1990s (1990–94) to sixty-one. The intensity of coverage also

TABLE 11.2 *The number and direction of stories on environmental issues in the* Bulletin, *1965–94*

Year	Number of stories	Number of pages	Direction of stories		
			Pro-environment	Neutral	Pro-development
1965	1	2.3	1	–	–
1969	1	2.3	1	–	–
1970	2	5.5	2	–	–
1971	5	9.3	4	1	–
1972	3	6.5	1	2	–
1973	4	11.3	3	1	–
1974	2	7.0	–	2	–
1975	–	–	–	–	–
1976	2	8.0	–	2	–
1977	11	69.8	10	–	1
1978	3	17.5	1	2	–
1979	2	8.0	2	–	–
1980	1	0.5	1	–	–
1981	3	7.5	2	1	–
1982	5	23.0	3	2	–
1983	7	15.5	3	4	–
1984	9	26.3	3	5	1
1985	2	2.3	1	1	–
1986	3	3.0	1	1	1
1987	10	18.0	3	7	–
1988	7	18.5	6	1	–
1989	18	44.0	14	3	1
1990	4	21.0	4	–	–
1991	7	20.5	6	–	1
1992	6	9.5	3	1	2
1993	13	15.3	10	3	–
1994	31	60.0	25	5	1
Total	162	432.0	110	43	8

Source: Analysis of the *Bulletin*.

increased steadily if we gauge this by the number of pages devoted to environmental issues. The exceptionally high figure for 1977 is largely accounted for by a series of stories featuring all the major national parks in Australia. More importantly, inasmuch as we can speculate about the impact of news coverage, we find that most of the stories (68 per cent) were 'pro-environmentalist', with the remainder mostly 'neutral' (28 per cent). In the 1970s, twenty-three out of thirty-four stories (68 per cent) were pro-environmentalist, the remainder being either neutral or pro-development. In the 1980s, 58 per cent (thirty-seven out of sixty-four) were pro-environmentalist – a figure which rose to 78 per cent in the early 1990s (see Papadakis 1996 for details). Overall the number of pro-development stories was very small.

The patterns of reporting on the various topics provide a useful basis for comparisons with agendas set by political parties and with patterns of public opinion. Until 1977 there had been no reporting on forests. Apart from the exceptional series of stories in 1977, it was only between 1982 and 1987 that forests were consistently taken up as an issue in the *Bulletin*. Reflecting issues addressed by social movements and political parties, there was a cluster of stories on uranium mining and nuclear power between 1976 and 1978. Pollution has been an important issue ever since the early 1970s, and appears to follow a pattern of different 'cycles of attention', from 1969 to 1973, from 1981 to 1984, and from 1988 to the present. Similarly, one can identify cycles of attention to other topics such as sustainable development (cycles of attention from 1987 to 1989 and 1991 to 1994). To a degree, the data support Downs' (1972) theory about the 'issue-attention cycle', whereby interest in issues, including concern about the environment, moves through various stages, culminating in their displacement from the political agenda. In practice, the notion of an 'issue-attention cycle' offers only a partial account of interest in environmental issues, since environmental issues have remained on the political agenda over a long period of time.

The mass media have focused with increasing intensity on environmental issues and the reports have usually favoured the views of environmentalists. The sources used by the media have tended to be diverse and suggest a high level of pluralism (see also Sylow 1994), although it is evident that expert communities have been a significant source in this respect. So far, the detailed analyses of news stories suggest a strong correspondence between the content of news stories in terms of the issues that are featured and the policy speeches and electoral platforms of established parties. There are some indications that the media have been taking their cues from political organisations, as far as placing issues on the agenda is concerned. Yet, the media also impose their own logic on events and tend to simplify complex issues in order to articulate a particular point of view – in this case a pro-environment one.

Future challenges

This chapter has shown that despite some variation in the attention paid to environmental issues, particularly as a result of the economic recession in 1994, the overall trend has been for public opinion, the media, policy makers and political parties to focus increasingly on the resolution of the tension between the environment and development. Green organisations have acknowledged the need to link employment with environmental protection. The established political parties have for decades been slow to take up the challenge of environmental protection, but they have now adapted to the growing consensus over the need to address issues such as coastal pollution, the rehabilitation of rivers, protection of endangered species and the proper accounting of the costs of environmental damage. Organisations like the National Farmers Federation and the Australian Council of Trade Unions have supported initiatives like planting trees along the Murray River, controlling feral animals and plants, and improving the water supply. Some of this is due to the dialogue initiated by the ALP government with both farmers and environmentalists, for instance in the development of a National Soil Conservation Strategy. Overall, one also needs to consider the pressure applied by social and political movements over the past fifteen years.

The principal challenge will be how to convert much of the rhetoric into public policy, how to meet targets for reducing greenhouse gas emissions, and how to develop mechanisms to achieve the trade-offs that will be required between environmental protection and economic growth. There are likely to be further opportunities for the development of the industry that has grown up around environmental protection, and of the markets for treating and recycling waste, for reducing air pollution and for cleaning water. Still, sustainable development will often present itself as an elusive objective and will require better coordination among government agencies as well as a genuine dialogue between developers and environmentalists as well as other political actors.

The pronouncements by the major parties during the 1996 federal election campaign and the results from public opinion polls all serve to illustrate the consolidation and widespread acceptance of ideas about the complementarity of economic development and the preservation and protection of the environment. In trying to convert these ideas into effective policies there is a need to question established institutional practices, and to explore possibilities for innovation, both in the presentation and implementation of policies. With regard to the politics of the environment, there is the continuing challenge of achieving bipartisan agreement on many issues and of collaboration between green groups and the new government and the agencies that serve it.

References

ANOP Research Services (1991), *The Environment and the ESD Process: An Attitude Research Analysis*, Vol 1. Sydney: ANOP.

ANOP Research Services (1993), *Community Attitudes to Environmental Issues*, Prepared for the Department of the Environment, Sport and Territories.

Burgmann, V. (1993), *Power and Protest*, Sydney: Allen & Unwin.

Downs, A. (1972), 'Up and Down with Ecology – the "Issue-Attention Cycle"', *Public Interest*, 28, 38–50.

Dunlap, R. E. (1989) 'Public Opinion and Environmental Policy' in J. P. Lester (ed.), *Environmental Politics and Policy*, Durham, NC: Duke University Press.

Keys Young (1994), *Benchmark Study on Environmental Knowledge, Attitudes, Skills and Behaviour in New South Wales*, Vols 1 and 2, NSW: Prepared for the Environment Protection Authority.

Papadakis, E. (1993), *Politics and the Environment. The Australian Experience*, Sydney: Allen & Unwin.

Papadakis, E. (1994), 'Development and the Environment', *The 1993 Federal Election. Australian Journal of Political Science*, 29(Special issue), 66–80.

Papadakis, E. (1996) *Environmental Politics and Institutional Change*, Cambridge: Cambridge University Press.

Sylow, K. (1994), 'The Tasmanian Conservation Movement and the Press', *Australian and New Zealand Journal of Sociology*, 30: 203–10.

Yankelovich, D. (1991), *Coming to Public Judgement*, Syracuse: Syracuse University Press.

PART III

The international dimension

12

Australia and Asia

Russell Trood

Since the end of the Second World War, Australia's efforts to build closer relations with the countries of Asia have been an enduring theme in the evolution of its foreign policy (Millar 1978; Renouf 1979). Forced by war to seek new foundations for the conduct of its foreign relations, Australia began to accept and confront the realities of its geography and to build a fresh identity as a Pacific state. Initially this was an uncomfortable accommodation. With a legacy of racism, hostility and fear to be overcome, progress towards the development of a more constructive set of relationships with the countries of the region was slow and ineluctably shaped by Cold War politics. Through the 1950s and 1960s Australia began to find a place for itself in regional affairs, but it was defined by the imperatives of global security and the mindset of a western developed state highly resistant to the idea that it was a natural or organic part of a region overwhelmingly composed of under-developed states with histories and cultures very different to its own. Even as relations with Asia began to deepen during the 1970s, notions of Australia belonging to 'the region' were largely absent from the rhetoric of contact: by geography and conviction Australia was a state on the periphery of Asia and likely to remain so.

In the early to mid 1980s Australia's relations with the countries of Asia began to undergo profound re-evaluation. Driven by the demands of domestic economic restructuring, the opportunities presented by the Asia-Pacific's economic dynamism, and later by the 'peace dividend' created by the end of the Cold War, first the Hawke and later the Keating governments adopted a single minded policy to enmesh and engage Australia more fully with Asia. In the decade since this agenda was first established, Australia has made considerable progress towards this goal. But perhaps the single most notable achievement of the policy to date has been not so much to draw Australia into Asia, as to draw Asia into Australia. In a relatively short space of time, the Australian mindset towards its region has been changed forever: Asia is now institutionalised in the Australian consciousness and the impact extends well beyond the conduct of Australian foreign policy. Belatedly, perhaps, Australia is in the process of coming to terms with its geography and is acquiring a functional level of 'Asia literacy' that is a necessary precursor to effective integration into its affairs.

This chapter analyses the evolution of Australia's recent relations with Asia with particular emphasis on the developments in the first half of the 1990s. The first part explores the foundations of enmeshment, seeking in particular to draw out the economic imperatives that underpin it. The second part focuses on the evolution of Australian attitudes towards Asia over the last five years, paying particular attention to the policies of the Keating government. Finally, the emphasis shifts to an examination of the changing character of Australia's identity as its embraces its future with Asia and the reaction this has evoked around the region.

Embracing Asia: Hawke and the Asia agenda

When the Hawke government was elected in March 1983 there was little indication that it would adopt what was to become such a radical agenda towards Asia. The themes of the election were largely economic (Mills 1993: Kelly 1994) with Labor emphasising that in government its priorities would be national reconciliation, recovery and reconstruction. Hawke campaigned with some innovative ideas for change, such as his proposal for a national economic summit, but there were few signs that a Hawke administration might adopt anything other than a traditional (Labor) approach to government.

Several factors were to challenge pre-election expectations of the new government's approach to economic management. The most important were the assumptions and attitudes towards the economy which Hawke and his senior economic ministers, particularly the new Treasurer, Paul Keating, brought to government. Their emphasis was on moving the Australian economy to greater international competitiveness through domestic structural economic change and greater integration into the world economy. This not only provided the foundations for reform of the Australian economy, it animated many of the Hawke government's perceptions of Australia's place in the world, particularly its relations with the countries of Asia. In this respect, the Hawke government's foreign policy was often an extension of domestic economic policy and the drive to improve Australia's economic performance.

With the emergence of their own distinctive style of state based capitalism (Stubbs 1995) Asian countries were not necessarily a natural partner in the implementation of Australia's economic reforms. Their models of economic management were interesting, but to many in the Hawke government they remained far removed from the Australian experience and not to be emulated. There could be no gainsaying, however, the dynamic nature of these economies or the regional interdependencies they were beginning to create (Drysdale 1988). Throughout the 1980s the Japanese and 'tiger' economies of Asia grew at rates far ahead of anything Australia, or any other developed economy, could seriously contemplate and the wealth was spreading throughout the region. Following China's economic reforms of the late 1970s and the rapid opening up of its economy, the perception that East Asia was becoming the powerhouse of the global economy was irresistible and all economic indicators testified to the fact. The ASEAN APEC economies now account for around 5 per cent of global GNP compared to the mean 10 per cent thirty years ago (Harris 1995).

As the Australian economy moved into recession and remained depressed throughout the second half of the 1980s, enmeshment with Asia acquired increasing urgency. The amalgamation of the Departments of Trade and of Foreign Affairs into a single Department of Foreign Affairs and Trade in 1987 was not motivated solely by this agenda, but it was certainly a reflection of the government's international economic priorities (Harris 1988). In 1989, two events of considerable significance were to further underscore the importance now being attached to closer economic relations with Asia. Early in the year, during a visit to South Korea, Hawke launched his initiative for the creation of an Asia Pacific Economic Cooperation (APEC) forum and in November Canberra played host to an international conference of twelve Asia-Pacific economies which served to launch the new grouping (Woolcott 1990). In the same year the landmark Garnaut Report on Australia and the Northeast Asian Ascendancy argued that Australia was well placed to take advantage of the opportunities presented by its geographical propinquity to Asia. It made a raft of recommendations how these could be secured (McKay and others 1990).

The speed and intensity with which Australia was embracing its economic future in the Asia-Pacific in the late 1980s might reasonably have been expected to generate a measure of community opposition and dissent. That this was not the case was a reflection of the fact that on the whole Australians appeared to accept both the government's analysis of Australia's economic plight and its prescription of an Asia future as a partial solution. As Bruce Grant commented about the Garnaut Report, it was 'another signpost pointing in the direction of Asia' of which there had been many over the last twenty years (Grant 1990: 3).

By the end of the 1980s these accumulated signs extended well beyond economics. The ethnic composition of the Australian population had already begun to undergo considerable change. With the ending of the White Australia policy and the steady influx of migrants and refugees from the countries of Asia in the years that followed, the 1991 census was to show that 4.9 per cent of the population was born in Asia. Australia had become a multicultural society – although the Blainey and Howard controversies of 1984 and 1988 respectively, suggested that there were some deep veins of community resentment against Asian immigration (Mackie and McNamara 1996).

With Australia's relations with several important Asian neighbours, among them China, Indonesia and Malaysia confronting a succession of problems during the 1980s, the need for Australians to develop a deeper knowledge and understanding of cultures and societies to the north was constantly in evidence. It was in this context that the federal government had formed the Asian Studies Council in 1986 and in 1988 accepted its report proposing a national strategy for the development of Asia literacy in Australia. A year beforehand, a national policy on languages had been established in response to the findings of a Senate report that encouraged the priority teaching of several Asian languages in Australian schools (Kamada 1994). At around the same time, the impact of Asia on the Australian education system was also about to be felt through the tertiary education reforms of John Dawkins whose new policies were, among other things, to open the Australian tertiary sector to increasing numbers of full fee paying students from Asia (Broinowski 1994).

Finally, Australia's growing involvement in Asia was to be reflected in the evolution of Australian security policy. Since 1945 this had been one area where Australia had experienced a very direct engagement with the region, but within the context of the Cold War and on the assumption that the region harboured a range of threats to Australia's interests. The 1987 Defence White Paper began to move Australian defence policy away from its traditional 'threat from Asia' foundations towards a much more self confident posture of self reliance that envisaged the possibility of greater defence cooperation with Asia. Two years later, Gareth Evans, as foreign minister, produced a ministerial statement on Australia's regional security (Fry 1991) that made comprehensive engagement with the countries of South-east Asia the centrepiece of its posture for Australia's regional integration. Both can be seen as markers leading up to Bob Hawke's remark of early 1991 that 'instead of seeking security from Asia ... [Australia] ... should seek security in and with Asia' (Wiseman 1992: 108).

Australia as an Asia–Pacific actor

By early 1990, Evans felt sufficiently confident of the progress Australia had made towards greater enmeshment to declare that:

> It is no exaggeration to say that today Australia cuts a quite a significant and respected figure on the international, and especially the Asia-Pacific regional

stage ... The days when Australia looked out on the region with the eyes of a cultural exile are fast fading. We are more comfortable with the diversity of those around us. We worry less about our distance from our cultural roots. And within the region, we are seen today as a natural participant in regional discussions; a country with a legitimate interest in regional developments; and a nation which seeks to play a constructive role in regional affairs. (Evans 1990)

While the rhetoric was somewhat exaggerated, Australia had certainly attempted to reposition itself within the region. With his passion for intellectual constructs, Evans had begun to conceptualise Australia's new role in the region within a short time of becoming foreign minister in September 1988. Over time his ideas were to become more clearly defined but already by the early 1990s the combination of the Hawke and Keating economic pragmatism and the Evans intellectualism had laid the foundations for a framework approach to regional enmeshment.

The framework drew on the liberal internationalist agenda. In this respect it contrasted markedly with the sombre realism that had shaped Australian external policy for much of the Cold War. Seeking to take advantage of the transformations taking place in the international system through such events as the end of the Cold War and the advent of the global economy, the policy reflected the new salience of economics on the international agenda and the changes that greater economic prosperity had brought to the Asia-Pacific region. Australia would seek to enmesh itself in the region confident that its future lay there in an environment which, although full of strategic ambiguity, offered largely untrammelled opportunities for Australia to advance its interests.

Australian foreign policy may have been liberated in the 1980s, but enmeshment nevertheless faced a formidable array of challenges. Differences and sometimes tensions in Australia's bilateral relations with the countries of the region, including China over human rights, Indonesia over Timor, among many others, all served to highlight the obstacles. Few in government had any illusions about the problems, and the speeches of Hawke, Evans and others of the period were frequently peppered with allusions to the challenges. These flowed not only from the absence of shared political and cultural values between Australia and many of the countries of the region, but also from Asia's natural political, economic and social diversity. Australians persisted in using the term 'Asia' as a collective noun to describe the communities to its north and in doing so obscured the fractured, fissured and fragmented history of their past and the equally complex, multi-layered and highly textured relationships of the present.

Yet, despite the many challenges, Australia's regional diplomacy began to show encouraging signs of maturity in the late 1980s and early 1990s. Its success in launching APEC, in creating the Cairns group (although it

was not restricted to Asian states), in pulling together the basis of a settlement in Cambodia and in helping to launch the ASEAN Regional Forum
(ARF) all served to highlight the new role Australia had begun to create
for itself.

Guided by middle power activism, Australia was a very involved player
in regional affairs. Indeed with Evans as foreign minister the pace was
often frenetic as he demanded as much from the region as from his own
long-suffering, if generally devoted, departmental servants. Patience may
not have been a particular virtue of the Evans personality, but by the early
1990s Australian diplomacy was displaying a functional adaptability in
response to the demands of operating in such a complex environment. A
willingness to consult regularly and often, a desire to build consensus, care
not to press ideas and issues beyond their likely acceptability, greater
deference towards the local cultural traditions that impinged on behaviour,
an avoidance of preaching and a commitment to the shared search for
common problems, all marked this progress. Australia, it seemed, was
beginning to learn the 'Asian way', the challenge in doing so was to ensure
that in the process, it did not sacrifice substance for form or lose sight of
the unique Australian interests that were Canberra's responsibilities to
advance.

From enmeshment to engagement: Themes of the 1990s

The Hawke governments of the 1980s laid the foundation for Australia's
contemporary push into Asia. Their policies built on Australia's earlier
engagements with the countries of the region, including those that
stemmed from the initiatives of its more conservative predecessors – the
Coalition administrations of the Liberal and National parties. As always
with history, the saga of Australia's coming to terms with Asia is infinitely
interesting and complex. This said, however, the Hawke era certainly
marked a distinctive and important era in the evolution of Australia's
relations with the region. The themes were more clearly spelled out, the
urgency of the task more palpable and it was the precursor to further
intensification of relations with the change of the prime ministership in
December 1991.

The Keating government placed its own mark on Australia's relations
with the countries of Asia. Again, more popular commentaries to the contrary, Keating did not fundamentally alter the thrust of his predecessor's
policies. The emphasis on regional economic engagement, the commitment
to institutionalism, the search for the foundations of stable regional order,
among other imperatives, all remained central to Australia's approach. The
differences emerged in the emphasis given to two extant themes: Australia's
relations with Indonesia, and the expansion of the APEC process, and in
the emergence of a new theme, that Australia's identity as a nation state

was bound up with its future as an independent republican state fully integrated into a stable and prosperous Asia-Pacific community. But while these high profile issues attracted much of the public attention, the process of enmeshment, unsubtly altered to engagement, went ahead at a steady pace on a wide range of different fronts which highlighted the increasing diversity of relations.

Economic integration

By the early 1990s the federal government's efforts to forge closer economic linkages with Asia were producing rather mixed results. Australia's overall trade with the region had improved, but perhaps not as much as might have been hoped. In 1985, 42.8 per cent of Australia's international trade was with East Asia, by 1990 the figure had only risen to 43.8 per cent, but by 1995 there had been a shaper increase to 48.3 per cent. By 1990 the region accounted for 52.5 per cent of Australia's exports and 35.1 per cent of imports. By 1995 the figures had risen to 60.5 per cent and 37.0 per cent respectively. The encouraging trend in relation to exports was further reflected in the fact that by mid decade seven of Australia's top ten export markets were in East Asia with annual rates of growth in some markets being quite spectacular. In 1994 for instance, South Korea became the country's second most important market (after Japan) displacing the United States from a position it had held for several decades (Dept of Foreign Affairs and Trade 1986; 1991; 1995). Another encouraging dimension of this growth was the increasing share of manufactures in exports to Asia, up from 22.6 per cent in 1989–90 to 27.4 per cent in 1995 (Dept of Foreign Affairs and Trade 1994a; 1995a). Levels of investment between Australia and the region were not as impressive, but there were signs of some expansion. In the five years to June 1995, Australian investment in Asian APEC countries rose 39.8 per cent to $74 987 million while Asian APEC investment in Australia reached $21 862 million, a rise of 124.5 per cent over the five years (Dept of Foreign Affairs and Trade 1995b)

Hawke and Keating government officials were naturally keen to broadcast this progress and to draw the best possible conclusions for the future. Australia, Keating argued in 1993, had 'been able to take advantage of the economic growth in Asia ... A dramatic change has taken place in the level of our trade, its composition and the places we export to ... There is now every reason to believe that we can significantly increase our market share' (Keating 1993). The reality, however, was that in some markets in East Asia while Australia may have been improving the quantum of its exports, its market share was actually declining. Between 1989 and 1994, for example, Australia's share of overall Asian APEC markets slipped from 3.1 per cent to 2.8 per cent, only holding steady in South Korea at 3.7 per cent (Dept of Foreign Affairs and Trade 1995b). All the evidence appeared to point to the disappointing reality that Australia had not greatly improved its international competitiveness.

Conscious of the disappointing results in some areas, the government intensified its program of economic enmeshment with Asia. This strategy had three principal components. The first involved a complex array of government sponsored and funded initiatives to facilitate greater Australian business success in Asia. Many of these programs were administered through Austrade, the government's main trade promotion agency, which in 1991 had been brought from Industry into the Foreign Affairs and Trade portfolio to emphasise its export mission. In March 1993 the government announced a major expansion of these programs in a package of measures entitled, *Australia in Asia: Economies Growing Together* (ALP 1993). The total package was expected to cost $61.01 million over three years and included initiatives to: increase business information about Asia; expand business frameworks and networks; broaden Australia's image in Asia; and foster better understanding of Asia in Australia. In 1991 inside the Department of Foreign Affairs and Trade, Evans created the East Asia Analytic Unit to undertake economic oriented analysis with a view to expanding Australia's understanding of the challenges of the East Asian environment. These initiatives were further reinforced through the creation in 1993 of the Asia Economic Centre with a mandate to provide business with sharply focused business oriented analyses of specific export and investment opportunities in Asian countries. Also in 1993, the government sponsored the first of what were to become annual National Trade and Investment Outlook conferences with a program specifically oriented towards economic prospects in the region (Evans 1993). The intent behind most of these initiatives was to provide incentives for Australian exporters to take the internationalisation of the economy seriously and exploit the advantages Australia enjoyed by being close to the booming East Asia region. That this sponsored approach to the encouragement of an Australian export culture ran counter to the government's free market rhetoric was largely ignored in the few debates that there were of the policy.

The second element of its strategy was to force open markets through concerted multilateral trade diplomacy centred on APEC. While APEC had been an initiative of the Hawke government, Keating was quick to seize on its potential as a means to advance his regional free trade agenda of economic liberalisation and harmonisation (Trood 1994). After 1991, much of Australia's regional economic diplomacy was focused on APEC with the prime minister himself leading the charge. Partly as a consequence of his efforts, the organisation has achieved some remarkable milestones over the last few years. The leaders' summits, begun in Seattle in 1993 and for which Keating can properly claim a degree of credit, are now a regular feature of the APEC calendar; at Bogor in 1994, the commitment was made to the opening up of markets for the developed states by 2010 and the developing economies by 2020, and in 1995, some progress was achieved in deciding how the 1994 targets would be met (Bonnor and Jennings 1996). Beyond the immediate economic implications of its decisions, APEC's growing status makes a tangible contribution to regional political stability as one of only a very few credible forums for region-wide dialogue.

Despite its supposed advantages, the prime minister's and thus Australia's unswerving commitment to APEC had its critics. The economist, Helen Hughes (1991) was outspoken in her belief that the diplomatic effort being invested in APEC was not worth the economic rewards. As a free market economist she had a predictable point, namely that all the diplomatic maneouvrings in the world would not correct the shortcomings of Australia's economy and the best way to do that was put at least a comparable effort into domestic reform (including the labour market reforms that the Labor Party was conspicuously reluctant to undertake) as was being taken diplomatically. Nor did it escape the government's critics that East Asia's impressive economic growth had been achieved without the benefit of APEC and was likely to continue, APEC or not. To the extent APEC was a factor in encouraging regional economic growth and integration, it was likely to be at the margins. That these hard headed critiques of the government's policy had no discernible impact on the Keating commitment, underscored the prime minister's political ascendancy and the investment he had made in the policy. But it also underscored the widespread belief among attentive members of the Australian community that APEC may have a value to Australia beyond that which was strictly quantifiable. For as much as anything its importance to Australia is that it serves as an institutional mechanism for integrating Australia into a region from which historically it has been alienated and with which it now seeks its future.

Of all the three elements of the government's regional economic strategy, the third – bilateral trade diplomacy, was the least developed. Even so, it was not as neglected as the government's critics sometimes suggested. Over the last five years and well before hand, Australian officials and political leaders have been fanning out across the region in an effort to promote Australia's bilateral trade relations. As prime minister, Hawke's overseas travel was rarely without a trade dimension (Mills 1993) and it was invariably part of the responsibility of all ministers travelling overseas in both the Hawke and the Keating governments to have the issue near the top of their agenda (Trood and McNamara 1994; 1995). And increasingly state governments became actively involved in their own trade promotion in Asia (McNamara 1994; 1996). With the amalgamation of the Departments of Trade and Foreign Affairs in 1987, trade promotion has become an integral part of the culture of Australian diplomacy. Reflecting this emphasis Austrade underwent a comprehensive restructuring in the early 1990s and redirected its efforts overseas to concentrate on East Asia. New trade offices were opened in China, Indonesia, Japan and elsewhere and trade missions were a regular activity. For its part, Department of Foreign Affairs and Trade organised several large Australian promotions – in Korea (1990), Japan (1994), Indonesia (1995), and later in 1996 a similar event was planned for India. At the same time, in 1994 Department of Foreign Affairs and Trade published *Australian Trade and Investment Development*, which offered a close analysis of market opportunities around the region and suggested a set of priorities for achieving them (Dept of Foreign Affairs and Trade 1994a).

Political cooperation

One of the axioms of both the Hawke and the Keating governments was that economic integration with Asia was unlikely to progress very far in the absence of closer political and security relations. In both areas Australia's ties to several regional governments go back a long way, though not in all cases is the history a particularly constructive one, as the examples of Indonesia and China among others, serve to highlight. Canberra was thus forced to build on a sometimes unpropitious legacy. In no small measure the end of the Cold War, the region's own growing political stability and increasing self confidence helped to overcome some of these difficulties, though with almost rhythmic predictability other problems have emerged, including anxiety over the direction of Chinese strategic policy, uncertainty over the future of the United States' military presence, disputes over territorial seas, and the unsettling implications of the regional arms modernisation programs around the region (Millar and Walter 1992).

Australia's political agenda with the countries of Asia has been and remains a very long one. Over the past decade all of the following have been an issue in one or more of Australia's bilateral relationships with regional governments: refugees, drug trafficking, labour relations, tax arrangements, the activities of the media, human rights, the abduction of Australian citizens, resource development, environmental management, health concerns including AIDS, education and tourism, among others. On occasions an issue has the capacity to cause considerable disruption in a relationship, such as the Tiananmen massacre in China 1989, the repression of democratic government in Burma in 1990, and Keating's careless 'recalcitrant' remark about Malaysia's Dr Mahathir in 1993. Yet it is a mark of the growing interconnectedness and maturity of Australia's relations with the governments of the region that Canberra has developed an increasingly sophisticated network of bilateral and multilateral mechanisms to deal with the ever more complex and crowded agenda.

Australia's relations with regional governments are no longer a matter of somewhat serendipitous official contacts between political leaders and irregular and unpredictably timed meetings of officials. Increasingly, they are being managed as a natural and organic part of the business of government. On any one day it is likely that numerous officials from one or more municipal or state governments or the federal government will be visiting the region for meetings with counterparts, or officials from Asian governments will be visiting Australia. In some cases these contacts are facilitated through regularly scheduled forums, such as the Australia-Japan Ministerial Committee meetings, but even in their absence, the range of meetings and the length of their agendas is impressive, as a glance at the accounts of bilateral contacts in *The Asia-Australia Survey* persistently testify. In these circumstances it is not surprising that much of Australia's diplomatic representational effort is now focused on the region and several missions there, notably Tokyo, Jakarta and Bangkok, are among the largest in the world. None of this necessarily precludes the periodic breakdown or crisis in some relationship, nor is it to suggest that the processes of dialogue do not need considerable expansion and improvement, but not only do crises and tensions now occur less often than in the past, the means to manage them are now considerably more advanced allowing earlier and more effective responses.

Of all the issues that Australia confronts in the region, however, one remains persistently difficult to manage and that is the constant need to blend its cultural and political Eurocentrism with the differences it encounters throughout much of Asia. The problem finds its most obvious focus in the subject of human rights. In 1989, Evans argued that 'for a country like Australia, human rights policy involves an extension into our foreign policy of the basic values of the Australian community: values which are the core of our senses of self and which a democratic community expects its government to pursue' (Evans 1989). For Evans, the issue was one of many that reflected Australia's determination to act as a 'good international citizen'. So acting, he had contended in 1988, was not merely a matter of acquiring a 'warm inner glow', the ends were 'inherently valuable' and in relation to human rights, 'just and tolerant societies' bring their own international rewards (Evans 1988). Not all countries in Asia accept the imperatives behind the elegant good international citizen construct and often view the Australian attitude to human rights as akin to that of the United States – in both cases providing a convenient excuse for western moralising and intervention in their domestic affairs. Although the problem does not intrude on every relationship in the region, with political authoritarianism a part of the political culture of many South-east Asian countries and several in North-east Asia, it is a recurring challenge for Australian diplomacy. Over the last decade Australia's relations with Thailand, Vietnam, Indonesia, China, Burma, Cambodia and Malaysia have all been seriously disrupted by it.

The philosophical gulf that divides Australia from the region over the issue was very evident in 1994 ahead of the World Human Rights conference in Vienna. Australia was excluded from participating in the pre-conference preparatory meeting of Asian states and at the conference found itself at odds with the position being pressed by the majority of Asian governments. Where Canberra pressed a comprehensive and universal definition of rights, most Asian states argued the developmental line, namely the need for developing countries to give primacy to economic and cultural rights over political and social entitlements while the economic needs of their people are so great (Trood 1994). The universality principle precludes Australia from conceding this point, though the distinction is one that Canberra has long recognised and on occasions been willing to act on (Hassall and Woodard 1995).

For the most part, developing a formula for the management of human rights has not been easy. Canberra long ago stopped its patronising lecturing of Asian governments on the matter, but with a raft of human rights lobby groups monitoring the issue in Asia and ready to pounce on, and expose, any instances of abuse, it has been unable to ignore the issue. The Hawke and Keating governments found the solution in an inclination to recognise the force of the development argument, but more importantly in private diplomacy: avoiding direct public criticism of countries or governments that commit abuses, except where they are of a demonstrably egregious nature, such as at the time of Tiananmen, or the Dili massacre. Instead, both governments undertook to press the matter privately with officials and political leaders as opportunities presented themselves. As an adjunct to this approach two human rights missions were sent overseas to China and Vietnam, but these constitute the exceptions to the preference for a low key approach. This has not been a particularly courageous approach in the opinion of the most committed activists, but it has the virtues of allowing Australia a continuing voice on human rights, allows a dialogue to take place, preserves stable relations and, in the end, acknowledges the reality that Australia is inherently limited in its ability to shift the offending governments from the intransigent position they have taken up.

Security and defence relations

By way of contrast, the progress in the evolution of Australia's security posture towards Asia has been impressive. As the Hawke government pressed its enmeshment agenda with Asia, during the 1980s, Australia's defence planners came under increasing pressure to re-evaluate the foundations of their security outlook on the region. With rising economic prosperity and growing political stability already challenging Australia's historic perceptions of the region as a source of threat to its security, the end of the Cold War offered a further rationale for a rethink. The pressures have produced incremental changes in Australia's defence policy which have emphasised three broad themes: greater self reliance, expanding defence cooperation with the countries of Asia and support for new strategic architectures for the region. Together these have brought about a fundamental reorientation of Australian security policy in Asia. Within the context of the strategic assessment that Australia is no immediate threat to its security, defence spending as a proportion of the GDP has fallen from around 3.0 per cent in 1990 to 1.9 per cent in 1996.

In arguing the case for self reliance, the Hawke and Keating governments, were anxious to distinguish it from self defence. Australia sought self reliance within the framework of alliance, that is to say, as far as possible to provide for its own security, but maintain its traditional alliance relationships with, for example, the United States and New Zealand. In this respect the 1987 and 1994 White Papers both reaffirmed the tangible benefits of the United States alliance in relation to intelligence cooperation, logistics support, training and the maintenance of joint defence facilities. But they also emphasised a further, more contemporary, theme in alliance relations – Australia, United States security cooperation in the Asia-Pacific (Dibb 1993). The emergence of this theme in alliance relations shifts the focus of the relationship away from the preoccupation with the defence of Australia from threats in Asia which characterised it in the 1950s, 1960s and to an extent the 1970s, to a much broader rationale: a mechanism for ensuring America's continuing engagement in the Asia-Pacific and thus enhancing strategic stability in the region. Underscoring the bipartisan support that exists for this process of modernisation, the Howard government has given considerable attention to this aspiration during its early months in office.

Australia's continuing strategic partnership with the United States serves to highlight the second theme in the recent evolution of Australian defence thinking in the region, namely the development of cooperative defence relations with the countries of the region. While this theme emerged in the early 1980s it has become increasingly important over the last few years. The government's 1990 strategic planning document, *Australia's Strategic Planning in the 1990s* (Dept of Defence 1992), for instance, argued that 'Australia should undertake defence co-operation with Asian countries as a means of enhancing' its ability to 'contribute constructively to the development of regional security' (Dept of Defence 1992: 43), while the 1994 White Paper noted that 'engagement with regional countries as a partner in determining the strategic affairs of the region will be increasingly important element in ensuring our security.' (Dept of Defence 1987: 25)

At one level these statements of policy are an affirmation of the continuing importance of cooperative relationships with countries such as New Zealand, Papua New Guinea, Singapore and Malaysia, which have long been a key part of Australian defence policy. At another, however, they are indicative of the increasing interest Canberra has shown in the development of cooperative security as a foundation for regional stability.

From shortly after he took office (in September 1988) until he left in March 1996, Gareth Evans took a particular interest in the concept (Evans 1993) and increasingly, it found a way into his policy statements and those of his ministerial counterpart in the Defence portfolio.

Unlike traditional threat oriented foundations of security, cooperative security emphasises an expanding and deepening range of collaborative activities that reduce perceptions of threat and encourage higher levels of confidence in the strategic environment. Over the last five years Australia's Defence and Foreign Affairs' officials have put a great deal of energy into encouraging closer contacts with their counterparts in South-east Asia. The results, which have been evident in a rapidly expanding range of collaborative activities in relation to surveillance, military exercises, training activities and more regular high level defence contacts, draw Australia and the countries of South-east Asia into a level of defence cooperation beyond anything they have enjoyed in the past. The Agreement for the Maintenance of Security between Australia and Indonesia (Dupont 1996), concluded in December 1995, arguably has much wider implications for the two governments than merely the underwriting of defence cooperation, but it is a tangible reflection of Canberra's recent determination to expand its defence relationships in the region.

The third important theme in the evolution of recent Australian security planing has been the desire to encourage the development of new security architectures for the Asia-Pacific. One tangible manifestation has been Canberra's contribution to the creation of ARF and its support for the 'second track' process reflected in the Council for Security Cooperation in the Asia-Pacific.

The creation of ARF was the product of agreement between ASEAN and its dialogue partners in Singapore in 1993 and was the culmination, at least in part, of a considerable amount of regional diplomatic activity on the part of Senator Evans and Australian security officials over several years (Trood 1994). As the one organisation that draws key Asia-Pacific countries together into a region-wide forum for dialogue over security issues, ARF has the potential to play an important role in maintaining the regional stability. In the short term, however, the disparate security interests of its members are certain to greatly inhibit the evolution of its role (Jennings 1996). But for a middle power such as Australia, with a natural inclination for multilateral diplomacy, the ARF serves as a useful mechanism for encouraging a collective dialogue over issues of common interest to their security. As such it is yet another means of more deeply engaging Australia with the region.

Australia's identity in Asia

For generations of white Australians it has been the reality of their country's geography that defined their role and place in the world. If white colonial

Australia had a mission it is probably most aptly described as the responsibility to ensure the survival and prosperity of European civilisation in the southern hemisphere under hostile conditions. Even after federation in 1901, Asia was perceived as a brooding and threatening presence that might easily bring about the collapse of the project. Australians defined themselves against Asia: its mysterious and unattractive ways a counterpoint to the 'civilised' Anglo-Celtic society their forebears had brought forth on the continent. Nothing more visibly underscored these differences than the White Australia Policy, the means by which post-federation Australia attempted to preserve the homogeneity and European civility of their society.

Australia's relations with the countries of Asia are today a stark contrast with this distant history. In particular, contacts have intensified appreciably over the last decade. Economic enmeshment, political challenges and the changing focus of Australia's security posture have been the most visible facets of the transformation, but there are few parts of Australian society that have not been touched by the change: the changing ethnic composition of Australian society, the installation of Asian languages and studies on school and university curricula around the country, increasing tourism to and from Asia, expanded scientific cooperation, and the increasing penetration of Asian culture through the media, exchanges in the arts and promotions are all less visible, but mark no less significant signs of change (Trood and McNamara 1996). The monumental nature of the transformation means that the theme of identity through difference is no longer a useful guide to the nature of the Australian character. To be sure, this strain in the Australian character has been under increasing threat since the end of the Second World War, particularly since the opening up of Australian society to mass immigration from Asia in the late 1970s, but the changes of the last decade have been the most critical in stimulating Australians to rethink their identity (Gurry 1995: 26)

One theme in this process is the quest for a geographic sense of place. The notion of Australia as a country being increasingly integrated into the Asia-Pacific region remains a common and reassuring conceptualisation of Australia's place in world affairs. But it is perhaps a reflection of the identity crisis that now afflicts some parts of the Australian body politic, and thus its sense of itself, that ideas of Australia's international personality are frequently being reworked.

In 1995, for example, Senator Evans took the annual ASEAN post-ministerial consultations somewhat by surprise when he argued that Australia was now part of the East Asian hemisphere, a point that could be demonstrated by a glance at the map he had prepared showing Australia centrally positioned between far east Russia and the Antarctic (Bonnor and Jennings 1996). To many in the press in Australia, and no doubt to some at the meeting, Evans' creative cartography displayed an unusually acute lack of self confidence in Australia's identity and an equally alarming lack of sensitivity to his colleagues' ideas of the meaning of being Asian. One participant at the meeting noted afterwards that '[i]f I look at a map, I will immediately say that Australia is not part of Asia' (Bonnor and Jennings 1996).

Evans was undoubtedly capable of displaying a higher degree of subtlety and sensitivity on these issues (Evans 1995), but the incident served to underscore the challenge Australia confronts in seeking to relate itself to the region. By almost every measure it is a fundamentally different country to all others in the Asian region. To some regional leaders, such as Lee Kwan Yew of Singapore and Mohammed Mahathir of Malaysia, this is a gulf that may never be bridged. Other leaders and their governments, including some of Singapore's and Malaysia's partners in ASEAN, the Philippines, and Thailand, display a more equable attitude. Equally, Japan and South Korea have often shown support for Australia's claims to be a natural partner in regional affairs. To date this is a debate that neither Australia nor its regional supporters have been able to win as was evident last year when, despite strong representations, Canberra was precluded from being a party to the first Asia-Europe meeting of leaders of government – ASOM.

Over the last decade Australia has seemingly been obsessed with Asia. Arguably this has been to the exclusion, if not on occasions to the neglect, of other important relationships in the international arena. But it is difficult to argue that the reorientation in Australian foreign policy that has been achieved is not long overdue, whatever the reasons for the neglect may have been. Australia has become more closely engaged with Asia as a result of the policies pursued over the last decade, but it has not come as far as the most ardent enthusiasts of this progress of change would wish and with the change in government in March 1996, it is conceivable that some re-evaluation of the basis of engagement will take place. There is now, however, a consensus on all sides of Australian politics that the process of greater engagement should continue. In the end, Australia may not become part of Asia, but it will find a place for itself in the increasingly complex webs of political, economic and social interdependencies that are shaping its future. For a country on the periphery for so long, this will be no mean feat and is an appropriately grand aspiration for a new century.

References

ALP (Australian Labor Party) (1993) *Australia in Asia: Economies Growing Together*, March.

Bonnor, J. and Jennings, P. (1996), 'Australia's Regional Diplomacy' in R. Trood and D. McNamara (eds), *The Asia–Australia Survey, 1996–97*, Melbourne: Macmillan.

Broinowski, A. (1994), 'Asia Literacy' in R. Trood and D. McNamara (eds), *The Asia–Australia Survey, 1994*, Melbourne: Macmillan.

Deeley, M. (1993), 'Marketing Opportunities for Australia in Asia' in R. Trood (ed.), *The Future Pacific Economic Order: Australia's Role*, Brisbane: CSAAR.

Dept of Defence (1992), *Australia's Strategic Planning in the 1990s*, Canberra: AGPS.

Dept of Foreign Affairs and Trade (1994a), *Australian Trade and Investment Development*, Canberra: AGPS.

Dept of Foreign Affairs and Trade (1986), *Composition of Trade*, Canberra: AGPS.

Dept of Foreign Affairs and Trade (1991), *Composition of Trade*, Canberra: AGPS.

Dept of Foreign Affairs and Trade (1995a), *Composition of Trade*, Canberra: AGPS.

Dept of Foreign Affairs and Trade (1994b), *The APEC Region Trade and Development*, Australian Supplement, November.

Dept of Foreign Affairs and Trade (1995b), *The APEC Region Trade and Development*, Australian Supplement, November.

Dept of Foreign Affairs and Trade (1995c), *The APEC Region Trade and Investment*, Australian Supplement, November.

Dibb, P. (1993), *The Future of the Defence Relationship with the United States*, Sydney: Australian Centre for American Studies.

Drysdale, P. (1988), *International Economic Pluralism: Economic Policy in East Asia and the Pacific*, Sydney: Allen & Unwin.

Dupont, A. (1996), 'The Australia–Indonesia Security Agreement', *Australian Quarterly*, 68:2, 49–62.

Evans, G. (1988), 'Australia's Place in the World', Address to Bicentennial Conference of Strategic and Defence Studies Centre, ANU, December, *Australian Foreign Affairs Record*, 59:12, 526–30.

Evans, G. (1989), 'Human Rights and Foreign Policy', Address to Amnesty International, May, *Australian Foreign Affairs Record*, 60:5, 193–7.

Evans, G. (1990), 'Australia, Indo-China and the Cambodian Peace Plan', Address to Sydney Institute, 13 March, *The Monthly Record*, Department of Foreign Affairs and Trade, 61:3, 142–8.

Evans, G. (1993), *Cooperating for Peace*, Sydney: Allen & Unwin.

Evans, G. (1995), 'Australia in East Asia and the Asia–Pacific: Beyond the Looking Glass', *Australian Journal of International Affairs*, 49:1, pp. 99–114.

Fry, G. (ed.) (1991), *Australia's Regional Security*, Sydney: Allen & Unwin.

Garnaut, R. (1989), *Australia and the Northeast Asian Ascendancy*, Canberra: AGPS.

Grant, B. (1990), 'The Global Context of Australia–Northeast Asian Relations: Some Comments on the Garnaut Report', *Australian Journal of International Affairs*, 44:1, 3–8.

Gurry, M. (1995), 'Identifying Australia's Region: From Evatt to Evans', *Australian Journal of International Affairs*, 49:1, 17–32.

Harris, S. (1988), 'The Amalgamation of the Department of Foreign Affairs and Trade', *Australian Foreign Affairs Record*, March, 59:3, 71–4.

Harris, S. (1995), 'The Economic Aspects of Security in the Asia/Pacific Region', *Frank Cass Journals*, September, 18:3, 32–51.

Hassall, G. and Woodard, G. (1995) 'Australia's Human Rights Policy in Asia' in R. Trood and D. McNamara (eds), *The Asia–Australia Survey, 1995–96*, Melbourne: Macmillan.

Hughes, H. (1991), 'Does APEC Make Sense?' *ASEAN Economic Bulletin*, 8: 2, 125–60.

Jennings, P. and Bonnor, J. (1995), 'Australian Regional Diplomacy' in R. Trood and D. McNamara (eds), *The Asia–Australia Survey, 1995–96*, Melbourne: Macmillan.

Jennings, P. (1996), 'Regional Security Cooperation and the Future Development of the ASEAN Regional Forum' in H. Soesastro and A. Bergin (eds), *The Role of Security and Economic Cooperation Structures in the Asia–Pacific Region*, Jakarta: CSIS.

Kamada, M. (1994), 'Australian Studies in Australia: Approaches Through Education', *Australian Journal of International Affairs*, 48:1, 1–24.

Keating, P. (1993), Address on the Inaugural, Sir Edward 'Weary' Dunlop, Asia Centre Lecture, December, Melbourne.

Kelly, P. (1994), *The End of Centricity, Power, Politics and Business in Australia*, 2nd edn, Sydney: Allen & Unwin.

Mackie, J. and McNamara, D. (1996), 'The Politics of Asian Immigration' in J. Coughlan and D. McNamara (eds), *Asians in Australia: Patterns of Migration and Settlement*, Brisbane: CSAAR.

McKay, J. and others (1990), 'Australia and Northeast Asia: The Garnaut Report', *The Australian Journal of International Affairs*, 44:1, April.

McNamara, D. (1994), State Government Activity in Asia' in R. Trood and D. McNamara (eds), *The Asia–Australia Survey 1994*, Melbourne: Macmillan.

McNamara, D. (1996), 'State Government Activity in Asia' in R. Trood and D. McNamara (eds), *The Asia–Australia Survey, 1996–97*, Melbourne: Macmillan.

Millar, T. B. (1978), *Australia in Peace and War*, Canberra: Australian National University Press.

Millar, T. B. and Walter, J. (eds) (1992), *Asian–Pacific Security After the Cold War*, Sydney: Allen & Unwin.

Mills, S. (1993), *The Hawke Years, the Story from the Inside*, Ringwood: Viking Press.

Renouf, A. (1979), *The Frightened Country*, Melbourne: Macmillan.

Stubbs, R. (1995), 'Asia–Pacific Regionalization of the Global Economy: A Third Form of Capitalism', *Asian Survey*, xxxv: 9, 785–97.

Trood, R. (1994), 'Australia's Regional Diplomacy' in R. Trood and D. McNamara (eds), *The Asia–Australia Survey, 1994*, Melbourne: Macmillan.

Trood, R. and McNamara, D. (eds) (1994), *The Asia–Australia Survey, 1994*, Melbourne: Macmillan.

Trood, R. and McNamara, D. (eds) (1995), *The Asia–Australia Survey, 1995–96,* Melbourne: Macmillan.

Trood, R. and McNamara, D. (eds) (1996), *The Asia–Australia Survey, 1996–97*, Melbourne: Macmillan Education.

Wiseman, G. (1992), 'Australia and New Zealand: a Review of Their Contributions to Asian–Pacific Security' in T. B. Millar and J. Walter (eds), *Asian–Pacific Security After the Cold War*, Sydney: Allen & Unwin.

Woolcott, R. (1990), 'APEC "the Wave of the 1990s"', *The Monthly Record*, 61:2, 62–9.

13

Foreign economic policies

John Ravenhill

The first half of the 1990s was a period of consolidation in Australia's foreign economic policies, years in which benefits began to be realised from the initiatives that the Hawke governments had launched in the 1980s. These initiatives had attempted to address four principal problems in Australia's relations with the global economy: the high levels of protectionism accorded to domestic manufacturing and the consequent failure of much of this sector to compete in world markets; the relative closure of the Australian economy at a time when the share of trade in the economies of most industrialised countries was expanding rapidly; the growth of agricultural protectionism in the world economy; and, finally, a fear that the world economy would fragment into rival regional trading blocs. To a considerable extent, the government increasingly looked towards Asia as providing a solution to both internal and external dimensions of its economic difficulties.

Economic closure and an inefficient manufacturing sector

Several of the problems listed above are closely related, especially economic closure and the emergence of a heavily protected manufacturing sector. Australia at one stage had one of the most open (that is, trade-oriented) economies in the world. In the last part of the nineteenth century, exports plus imports constituted close to 60 per cent of Australia's gross domestic product. This was a time when Australians were widely reckoned to enjoy the world's highest per capita income (Maddison 1977). After federation, however, governments took a conscious decision to attempt to insulate

Australian workers, farmers and manufacturers from the vicissitudes of the world economy. A policy of 'Protection all Around', initiated in the first decade of this century but more fully developed in the interwar years, drove a wedge between domestic and international prices (for details of the unique form that the 'historic compromise' between capital and labour took in Australia see Castles 1988). Australian governments of the day, reflecting widespread fears about national security, had a 'populate or perish' mentality; they viewed protection as necessary to support a larger population essential for the country's long term survival.

Moreover, Australian governments were reluctant to join the postwar trend towards tariff cuts because the principal international body responsible for regulating trade, the General Agreement on Tariffs and Trade (GATT), ignored agricultural products, which at that time constituted the bulk of the country's exports. In the 1950s and 1960s, Australian governments largely abstained from successive rounds of GATT negotiations, arguing that the country's dependence on the export of commodities gave it a 'mid-way' status between less developed and industrialised countries, a position that justified continued protection of domestic manufacturing. In this postwar period of rapid global economic growth, the Australian economy prospered; protection of manufacturing undoubtedly was successful in raising that sector's share of overall employment and output (a point acknowledged even by many critics of protectionism, see Anderson and Garnaut 1987). By the late 1960s, however, as the costs of protection became more obvious and conditions for agricultural exports became more difficult, a marked change occurred in the intellectual climate in favour of liberalisation.

In 1970, the tariff rates on manufactured imports averaged 23 per cent. This figure was nearly four times the level prevailing in the (then six) member states of the European Union,[1] and substantially above that of other members of the OECD, the grouping of industrialised countries. The one exception was New Zealand, which maintained tariffs at levels equivalent to those in Australia. Canada, an economy with which Australia is often compared, on the other hand, had reduced its rates to an average of 14 per cent. The inefficient domestic manufacturing sector that had been fostered by protectionism was unable to compete in world markets. The consequence was that Australia failed to participate in the area of world trade that had expanded most rapidly in the postwar period: the exchange of manufactured goods among industrialised economies. The relatively slow rate of growth in world trade in primary products, a product of greater food self sufficiency in many countries (resulting both from agricultural protectionism and the application of technology to agricultural production, most notably, the 'Green Revolution' in rice production in South and South-east Asia), and of a declining intensity in manufacturing industry's use of raw materials, underlay a decline in the terms of trade of countries specialising in the export of primary products.[2] As Figure 13.1

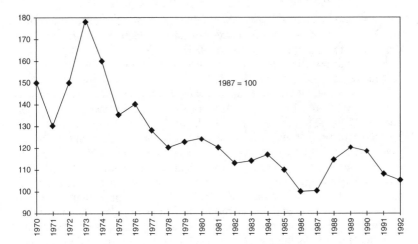

FIGURE 13.1 *Australia's terms of trade, 1970–92*

Source: World Bank.

shows, Australia was no exception – despite the rapid growth in the contribution of fuels, minerals and metals to Australia's exports (up from
8 per cent in 1960 to constitute over a third of export earnings by the start
of the 1980s). Not only did countries specialising in primary product
exports (with the temporary exception of oil exporters in the 1970s) suffer
an overall decline in their terms of trade, but their export earnings also
tended to be particularly volatile, a consequence of periodic booms and
busts in commodity prices.

The declining ratio of exports and imports to GDP reflects Australia's
failure to participate in booming world trade. In the postwar period, this
ratio was dramatically lower than at the turn of the century. By the early
1970s it was little more than 20 per cent, substantially below the levels of
other small industrialised economies (in Canada, for instance, the ratio
was 40 per cent). Protective policies pursued by governments since federation not only insulated but also marginalised the Australian economy.

The initial redirection of Australian policy came in 1973 when the Whitlam
government cut tariffs on manufactured goods by an average of 25 per cent.
This reduction, however, coincided with the world economic recession
that followed the first round of OPEC-induced oil price rises; the tariff
cuts were widely blamed in the community for the country's subsequent
economic problems. In the Fraser years (1975–83) the government courted
electoral popularity by resisting the recommendations of the Industry
Assistance Commission (IAC) for further rapid cuts; in some heavily pro-

tected sectors, such as textiles and automobiles, it raised levels of protection still further. A revival of the process of tariff reduction was to await the election of the Labor government in 1983.

Somewhat reticently at first, the government resumed dismantling the protective cocoon that had sheltered Australian industry for over half a century. The overall effective rate of protection for manufacturing industry was reduced from 21 per cent in 1983 to 19 per cent in 1988 and to 15 per cent in 1991. This average figure is distorted upwards by the continued heavy protection of two major sectors: textiles, clothing and footwear (supported in 1991 by tariffs of 68 per cent for textiles, and 176 per cent for clothing and footwear); and motor vehicles and parts (protected by a tariff of 60 per cent). The protection for many other sectors had been reduced to under 10 per cent by the start of the 1990s. An important milestone came in March 1991 with the government's industry policy statement: this reaffirmed the government's commitment to a policy of tariff reduction, with the aim of reducing the average level of tariffs to 5 per cent by the year 2000. Tariffs on clothing and footwear are projected to fall to 50 per cent by the turn of the century; those on automobiles to 20 per cent.

Besides cutting tariffs, the Hawke governments in the 1980s introduced a number of sectorally-specific measures aimed at industrial restructuring and the promotion of exports. One of the most notable was the scheme for the car industry, named the 'Button Plan' after Senator John Button, the Minister for Industry at the time of its introduction. A major thrust of the Button Plan was to rationalise Australian production to achieve economies of scale by reducing both the number of producers and the number of models they manufactured. The plan also introduced an export facilitation scheme that enabled manufacturers to offset the value of exports against the requirement for local content. By the first half of the 1990s, the automobile industry had become the largest source of earnings from manufactured exports.

Debate continues as to whether the reduction in protection or industry specific measures have been the most important reason for the surge in Australia's manufacturing exports since the mid 1980s. Many economists and the government's IAC have been critical of the industry specific measures, viewing them as a second best solution to distortions created by other government policy measures. Others see the correlation between industry specific measures and the source of rapidly expanding exports as vindicating the interventionist approach (Sheehan, Pappas and Cheng 1994). The lack of an activist approach in the March 1991 Industry Policy Statement disappointed advocates of industry specific measures. It is in fact impossible to determine whether the force of competition or government assistance has made the greater contribution to the improved performance of manufactured exports; it is almost certainly a combination of both factors.

What was clear by the mid 1990s, however, was that a dramatic change in the composition of Australian exports had been effected within a short period of time. The share of elaborately transformed manufactures in Australian exports rose by 50 per cent from the beginning of the decade to constitute 20 per cent of all export earnings from goods by 1995 (Table 13.1). Services contributed another 20 per cent of total export earnings (the largest single source being tourism). By the mid 1990s, the export earnings from manufactures and services combined were more than 50 per cent above those from agriculture (albeit at a time when agricultural earnings reflected prolonged drought and generally low world prices). Australia finally appeared to be laying the foundations for an advanced industrialised economy.

TABLE 13.1   *Composition of Australian exports (% share)*

	Unprocessed primary	Processed primary	Simply transformed manufactures	Elaborately transformed manufactures	Gold
1985	59.3	21.6	8.1	8.9	2.1
1986	57.4	21.6	8.3	9.8	3.0
1987	52.8	21.3	9.9	11.2	4.8
1988	49.5	20.7	11.6	11.5	6.7
1989	47.8	22.7	12.0	11.6	5.9
1990	45.4	23.5	11.0	12.9	7.2
1991	44.6	23.3	10.6	14.4	7.1
1992	43.1	22.7	10.3	15.7	8.2
1993	40.8	23.5	10.1	17.6	8.0
1994	38.9	23.4	10.8	19.1	7.8
1995	35.6	21.7	11.1	24.2	7.5

Source: Trade Analysis Branch, Dept of Foreign Affairs and Trade.

Coalition building in support of global trade liberalisation

Australian complaints about the protection of agricultural sectors in other industrialised countries had suffered a credibility problem when Australia maintained extremely high tariffs on imports of manufactures. One advantage of the moves towards liberalisation of the Australian economy in the 1980s was that it provided a new consistency to Australia's arguments. A push for global trade liberalisation was a natural complement to domestic economic reform.

Yet, at a time when Australia was making a concerted effort at domestic economic liberalisation, the world economy appeared to be headed in the opposite direction. The major industrialised countries had responded to the world recessions that followed the two rounds of oil price rises in 1973–74 and 1979–80 by increasing the protection given to some domestic manufacturing sectors – particularly against the rapid increase in exports from the newly industrialising countries of Hong Kong, Korea, and Taiwan. To circumvent GATT rules, this 'new' protectionism often took the form of non-tariff barriers such as 'voluntary' export restraints (where trading partners agreed to limit the value or volume of their exports of specified products). By the mid 1980s, trade tensions had also increased between the major industrialised traders – the United States, the European Union, and Japan. Relations between the United States and Japan had soured over Washington's complaints that the Japanese market remained closed to many of its exporters because of the existence of 'structural impediments', such as the close links among Japanese corporations, and these corporations' control of retail outlets. Disputes over agricultural trade dominated relations between the European Union and the United States. Washington was upset at the high levels of protection afforded European farmers by the Union's Common Agricultural Policy, and by the Union's use of subsidies to promote its agricultural exports.

It was in this unfavourable context that a new round of GATT negotiations was launched in 1986 (termed the 'Uruguay Round' because the opening talks were held in Punta del Este, Uruguay). Australia had two principal objectives to pursue in the Uruguay Round. The first was to ensure that agriculture be brought under GATT auspices. When GATT was first established, the United States Senate, bowing to the domestic agricultural lobby, was unwilling to allow agriculture to be placed under GATT auspices. Subsequently, the Europeans kept agriculture off the agenda of international trade talks while they constructed a high price support system for their often inefficient farmers. The increasing conflict between Washington and Brussels on agricultural issues hurt Australia in several ways. Australian products were excluded from these economies' domestic markets (recall the importance of the loss of the British market for Australian agriculture when Britain joined the European Union in 1973). As the Europeans became self sufficient in many agricultural products, so world market prices for these products declined. Furthermore, in the late 1970s and 1980s, the Europeans increasingly used subsidies to export surplus production, thereby further depressing world prices. Washington retaliated with its own subsidy scheme, the Export Enhancement Program. Although this program was aimed primarily at the European Union, it also displaced Australian exports from some markets where they had traditionally been dominant.

Australia's second objective was to prevent a fragmentation of the global economy into rival regional trading blocs. The European Union had already expanded to twelve members; plans were in train both to broaden the scope of cooperation (with a further expansion to include several members of the European Free Trade Area), and to deepen it by consolidating the internal movement of goods and people. The latter took the form of the proposed completion of the Single Internal Market in 1992. For outsiders, the fear was that these moves would turn the Union into 'Fortress Europe', an exclusionary trading bloc. After years of being the primary advocate of multilateralism, the United States was also showing more interest in promoting regional arrangements. Frustrations with Japan and the European Union were a major reason for this new interest. For many observers in the United States, the conflict with Japan over market access demonstrated the limitations of GATT rules – in particular, their failure to deal with unofficial non-tariff barriers to trade. Moreover, as the European Union expanded its membership, Washington sought its own regional arrangement to provide it with expanded bargaining leverage. In relations with its regional neighbours, the asymmetry in power assured Washington that it would be able to dictate the terms of any trade agreement. The first step was the conclusion of a free trade agreement with Canada in 1989, which covered the single largest bilateral trading relationship in the world. When plans were announced to turn the United States–Canada agreement into the North American Free Trade Area with the addition of Mexico, and eventually to construct a hemispheric trading zone, observers became increasingly alarmed about a possible breakdown of the global trading system.

The Australian government had much to fear from a world of regional trading blocs. For a small economy, Australia's trade is unusually diversified. Even though Asia (if considered as a single entity) has become by far the most important trading partner (see discussion below), trade and investment links with the European Union and the United States remain of considerable significance. If North America and the European Union became increasingly protectionist, not only would trading opportunities for Australia with these groupings be jeopardised but also the fear was that regional developments elsewhere would provoke the creation of an Asian trading bloc revolving around Japan. And there was no certainty that Australia would be welcomed in such a bloc.

The response of the Australian government to these challenges in the second half of the 1980s was to engage in creative initiatives in intergovernmental coalition building. In an attempt to ensure that agriculture figured prominently on the agenda of the Uruguay Round, Australia played the major role in founding the Cairns Group of agricultural exporters (for detailed discussion of the role of the group in the early years of the Uruguay Round see Higgott and Cooper 1990). The grouping brought together fourteen countries that relied significantly on export earnings from agriculture. The members are Argentina, Australia, Brazil, Canada, Chile, Colombia, Fiji, Hungary, Indonesia, Malaysia, New Zealand, the Philippines, Thailand, and Uruguay. Diverse in their size and level of economic development, the countries were united in demanding that the Uruguay Round promote significant reform of world trade in agricultural products (although maintaining the unity of the group demanded significant diplomatic skills on the part of Australia).

Progress in the early years of the Uruguay Round was very slow, particularly on agricultural issues. This lack of progress, occurring within the context of the expansion of the European Union, and the signature of the United States–Canada Free Trade Agreement, fuelled fears of a collapse of the GATT system. The prospects for the Uruguay Round looked particularly bleak in 1988 when the mid term review of the talks ended with no tangible progress on significant issues. At this point, the Australian government launched the second of its major diplomatic initiatives in the trade field when, in a speech in Seoul in January 1989, Prime Minister Hawke proposed that a ministerial meeting be held to promote economic cooperation in the Asia-Pacific region. In November of the same year, the proposal came to fruition with the founding meeting, in Canberra, of the Asia-Pacific Economic Cooperation (APEC) grouping.[3] The initial list of proposed members of the grouping announced by Hawke consisted solely of East Asian countries and Australasia; it excluded the United States and Canada, a reflection of Australia's frustration with American agricultural subsidies. It soon became clear, however, that apart from Malaysia, little support existed in East Asia for a grouping that excluded the United States. Although APEC did not play a significant role in the Uruguay Round (not surprisingly since two of the principal combatants in the round, Japan and the United States, were both APEC members), its existence did provide a source of bargaining leverage against the European Union – which feared that a breakdown of the round would help consolidate an anti-European alliance between East Asia and the United States.

Cairns and the Uruguay Round

The Cairns Group played a useful, albeit modest, role in keeping agricultural issues high on the Uruguay Round agenda. Its determination was shown in its disruption of the GATT ministerial meeting in December 1990 when its representatives walked out of the talks in protest at the lack of progress on agricultural issues. But its ability to influence the agenda owed much to the American desire that agricultural reform be achieved in these negotiations. Washington was insistent that measures be agreed that would reduce the European Union's subsidies of agricultural production and exports. The Cairns Group was able to push effectively for further reform on agricultural issues only for as long as it had the support of Washington.

Following the breakdown of the Brussels meeting, it took a further twelve months before the drafting of a comprehensive agreement by the GATT Director General, Arthur Dunkel, which included proposals for a sweeping reform of agricultural subsidies, broke the impasse. Initially, the European Union, under pressure from the French government, refused to accept the Dunkel draft. But faced with possible United States withdrawal from the round, and somewhat alarmed by the rapid progress achieved in institutionalising APEC, the Europeans returned to the bargaining table and negotiated a compromise agreement (the Blair House Accord) with the United States in November 1992. The cost of this agreement was a significant dilution of key components of the agricultural proposals of the Dunkel draft. United States deficiency payments and European Union compensation payments were now to be exempted from the requirement that farm subsidies be reduced by 20 per cent over six years (from a 1986–88 base, itself a period of high subsidies). Rather than being applied on a product-by-product basis, the cuts could now be spread across all domestic subsidy programs. And, as important for Australia, the proposed cut in the volume of agricultural exports supported by subsidies was reduced from 24 to 21 per cent. The revised proposals were, however, still unacceptable to the French government; to secure its approval, a further modification of the Blair House Accord was agreed in December 1993 when the timetable for reductions in export subsidies was extended. Faced with this *fait accompli* negotiated by the two big players, the Cairns Group had little option (especially in the context of the expiration that month of the 'fast-track' negotiating authority granted to the United States President by the Congress) but to give a somewhat grudging assent to the pact.

Outside the agricultural sector the achievements of the Uruguay Round were generally more impressive. Overall, tariffs will be cut by a trade-weighted average of about 40 per cent, a larger percentage reduction than those negotiated under the Kennedy and Tokyo Rounds of GATT talks. The Multi-Fiber Arrangement, under which industrialised countries have imposed quotas on imports of textiles and clothing from less developed countries, will be phased out. (Although the 'rear-end loading' of the accord, whereby the industrialised countries will undertake most of the liberalisation in the last few years of a ten year period, increases the likelihood that governments will introduce new protective devices in response to pressure from affected domestic sectors.) A new agreement on government procurement greatly extends the range of government contracts (both from national and sub-national bodies) for goods and services that will be open to bidding from foreign firms. A new General Agreement on Trade in Services establishes a framework for this rapidly growing area of international trade, but further bilateral negotiations will be required to secure sectoral agreements. Intellectual property rights are brought under GATT/ WTO auspices for the first time through the TRIPs (trade related aspects of intellectual property rights) agreement, although less developed countries were granted a long grace period before being required to implement the measure. Trade related investment measures (TRIMs) will also be subject to new rules; perhaps the most significant relate to local content and trade balancing (usually export requirements), which are required to be eliminated within a short period. One of the most significant achievements of the round (albeit one whose value will only be demonstrated if countries in practice respect the new procedures) was to establish new dispute settlement mechanisms intended to expedite decisions and to enhance compliance with dispute panel rulings (for further details of the results of the Uruguay Round see Schott 1994).

From the Australian perspective, the actual details of the Uruguay Round agreement are perhaps less important than that the talks were brought to a successful conclusion. The agreement quickly assuaged fears that the world economy was headed towards a breakdown into rival regional trading blocs. Moreover, the successful outcome appeared to vindicate the emphasis that the government had given to the pursuit of Australian interests in multilateral forums, and enabled it to claim that the round's successful outcome would provide Australians with reciprocal benefits from the country's trading partners to offset some of the domestic economic pain caused by the government's unilateral reduction of tariffs in the previous decade.

However, the direct benefits to Australia from the Uruguay Round's implementation are likely to be modest – largely because of the dilution of the reforms proposed for the agricultural sector. Earlier projections by the Australian Bureau of Agricultural Economics and the IAC of multibillion dollar annual gains to Australian producers from the Uruguay Round agreements appeared to be extremely optimistic. One major econometric study suggested that whereas the total gains from the Uruguay Round for Australia and New Zealand would have been $3.2 billion annually (or 1.6 per cent of GDP) had the Dunkel draft been fully implemented, the limited agricultural reform in the final outcome of the round will reduce benefits to less than one-fifth of the earlier projection – a mere 0.3 per cent of GDP (Nguyen, Perroni and Wigle 1995: 28, Table 1). Such a figure pales in comparison with the 5.5 per cent increase in GDP that the IAC estimates the implementation of the Hilmer reforms of competition policy will generate. Even if the Commission's estimates are as over-optimistic as sceptics have suggested, the benefits from the Uruguay Round are likely to be only a fraction of those achieved through domestic economic reform.

The results of the Uruguay Round demonstrated again the extent to which the big three players – the European Union, Japan, and the United States – determine the outcome of global trade negotiations. Even when acting in conjunction with other agricultural producers in the Cairns Group, Australia's leverage in the Uruguay Round not surprisingly proved to be very limited. Members of the Cairns Group decided, however, that the group's achievements warranted its continuation beyond the Uruguay Round; it will continue to make its voice heard in persevering with its attempts to bring a greater element of economic rationality to world agricultural trade.

APEC

Of all the foreign policy initiatives taken by the Labor governments from 1983 to 1996, the foundation of APEC may well prove to be the most significant. From its initiation as a meeting of ministers from twelve countries, APEC has blossomed into a grouping with a current membership of eighteen, which holds annual summit meetings, which has a permanent secretariat (albeit very small) in Singapore, and numerous working parties charged with promoting cooperation in areas that include human resource development, transportation, tourism, fisheries, telecommunications, as well as trade promotion and facilitation through harmonisation of standards, and the compilation of trade and investment data.[4]

APEC is the most prominent of the institutional linkages that Australia has built with East Asia. It is, however, not merely a bridge to Asia but can also play an important role in maintaining United States interest in the region. And its utility as a potential bargaining chip against the Europeans in world trade negotiations was demonstrated in the Uruguay Round. As a forum for bringing governments together, APEC thus has multiple uses – some symbolic, some functional – that go beyond its contribution to freeing of trade among its member states.

Indeed, these other purposes that APEC serves in providing a forum for its member states may be as important as what it does in the trade field. In Prime Minister Hawke's original proposal for APEC, the intention was to establish an equivalent for the Asia-Pacific region of the OECD, the Paris-based organisation that plays a coordinating and monitoring role for various economic policies of the industrialised countries. In its first few years, however, the APEC agenda became more ambitious as the North Americans, supported by the Australasians, argued that priority should be given to trade liberalisation. Other members of the grouping endorsed this agenda at the APEC meeting in Bogor in 1994. Leaders committed themselves to the realisation of free trade within the region by 2010 for the industrialised countries, and by 2020 for the less developed.

It soon became clear, however, that considerable disagreement existed among the members over their interpretations of the obligations undertaken at Bogor. For instance, what does free trade mean – zero tariffs or lower tariffs? The exact nature of the Bogor commitment to 'free' trade was not spelt out. And many of the Asian participants stressed that the commitments that they made at Bogor were non-binding. Divisions within the grouping were carried over to the next leaders' meeting, at Osaka in 1995. Although a split within the grouping was avoided over the question of whether there should be exceptions to the program of trade liberalisation (the North-east Asian countries had wanted to exclude agriculture), it was apparent that some member states saw the provision in the Osaka 'Action Agenda' for flexibility in implementation as offering them the escape clause that they had sought.

Because APEC allows member states to interpret for themselves the obligations that they have undertaken, political scientists regard it as a weak regime for governing relations among its participants (Aggarwal 1995). APEC itself offers few carrots or sticks in support of the process of trade liberalisation. Reduction in trade barriers occurs on a non-discriminatory basis; consequently the benefits of market opening are available to all countries regardless of whether they are members of the organisation. And because the organisation is so weak, and the obligations of members so poorly defined, no provision exists for retaliation against members that are failing to pursue effective policies of trade liberalisation (Fane 1995; Ravenhill 1995). Moreover, the commitment to free trade within APEC is concerned overwhelmingly with border barriers to trade (tariffs and non-tariff barriers); it does little to address the structural features of East Asian economies that have frustrated western exporters in the last three decades. Whether APEC working groups will succeed in effectively addressing this difficult issue (which lies primarily in the realm of competition policy) remains to be seen.

Supporters of APEC, on the other hand, argue that it plays an important role in socialising member states into a better appreciation of the benefits of unilateral trade liberalisation, building on the processes of information sharing established in PECC and PBEC. They believe that the periodic meetings of the organisation will exert pressure on governments who will not wish to be embarrassed by being seen as recalcitrants on trade liber-alisation issues. Elek (1995) is representative of the now substantial literature by APEC proponents in Australia.

By the mid 1990s, it was unclear how effective an organisation APEC will be. Its prospects are likely to be determined by whether or not pro-gress is made in resolving the major bilateral trade disputes involving member states – principally between the United States and Japan over market access questions, and between the United States and China over intellectual property rights. Absent such progress, it is quite possible that Washington will lose patience with APEC and resort to unilateral approaches in an attempt to maximise its considerable potential economic leverage against Asian countries. The American government has already opposed the establishment of a disputes resolution mechanism within APEC, perceiving such a body as limiting its freedom of action.

Australia and the booming East Asian economies

For many observers, intergovernmental organisations such as APEC were largely irrelevant to the processes of economic integration that were occurring in the East Asian region. These have been driven by the development of various corporate linkages including, but not limited to, foreign direct investment (Bernard and Ravenhill 1995). Corporations have proved to be extremely skilful in circumventing the barriers that governments have placed in their way.

East Asia has been the most rapidly growing area of the world economy for more than a decade. Even though the Japanese economy has performed poorly in the 1990s, rapid economic growth has spread beyond North-east Asia to most of the seven member states of ASEAN (Brunei, Indonesia, Malaysia, the Philippines, Singapore, Thailand, and Vietnam) and, most spectacularly, to China. A principal objective of Australian foreign economic policy in the last decade has been to engage more closely with the booming economies of the Asian region. A major report to the government at the end of the 1980s by a former Australian ambassador to China and Australian National University academic, Ross Garnaut (1989), had emphasised the rapidity of economic growth in North-east Asia and the reforms required in the Australian economy to position it to take advantage of Asian growth. Further investigation of opportunities for Australia in Asia was undertaken in reports published in 1992 from the Department of Foreign Affairs and Trade's East Asia Analytical Unit. These dealt with Korea, South China, South-east Asia, and an updating of the Garnaut Report. The unit published additional reports on Overseas Chinese Business Networks and the Indian economy in 1995. The Australian government's interest in the rapidly expanding Asian economy had spread, following economic liberalisation in the region, from North-east to South-east and most recently to include the south of the continent.

To help Australian companies trying to gain footholds in the rapidly expanding markets, the government directed Austrade, Australia's overseas trade promotion agency, to give new emphasis to Asia. Resources were switched from the United States and Europe to enable Austrade to open new Asian branches. Asian economies were also the primary beneficiaries of assistance given under the Development Import Finance Facility (DIFF). This program combined an aid grant from Australia's aid agency (renamed AusAid in 1995) with export credits provided by the Export Finance Insurance Corporation to enable Australian industry to compete in foreign markets. DIFF support was primarily for large infrastructure projects; close to half of the assistance went to Indonesia with a further one-third to China.

Although it is impossible to estimate how important government reports and assistance for exporters have been in helping Australian companies to gain access to Asian markets, a marked increase in the share of exports going to the East Asian market did occur in the first half of the 1990s. By 1995, East Asian markets together accounted for more than 60 per cent of Australian exports, up from 50 per cent at the start of the decade. The most rapidly growing market was the six (from mid 1995, with the addition of Vietnam, seven) ASEAN countries whose share of Australian exports increased by more than 50 per cent in the first half of the 1990s. East

Asia's increasing share of Australian exports came primarily at the expense of western Europe and North America. Although the European Union, if considered as a single market, was the second most important destination of exports after Japan, its share continued to decline, reaching 11 per cent at the end of the period. The most notable change in the share of individual countries in Australian exports in this period was the displacement of the United States by Korea as the second most important country market. Taiwan continued throughout the period to be a more important market than mainland China, although the relative positions will be reversed when China re-absorbs Hong Kong in 1997 (indeed, barring significant economic and political strife, it is likely that the augmented People's Republic of China will supplant Korea as Australia's second largest export market). Korea, Taiwan, and the ASEAN countries provided the major sources of growth in demand for Australian exports of elaborately transformed manufactured goods (ETMs). Japan, however, continued to be a disappointing market for Australian manufacturers. ETMs constituted under 5 per cent of Australian exports to Japan; for Korea, the share was over 10 per cent, and for the United States fully one-third of total exports.

Asia figured far less prominently in Australia's imports. By the mid 1990s, North-east and South-east Asia combined accounted for 39 per cent of Australia's total imports, a share that had changed little over the previous decade. One consequence of this imbalance between the direction of exports and imports was growing trade tensions with some Asian countries that protested about the increasing trade deficits they ran with Australia. The European Union and NAFTA remained Australia's principal sources of imports; each of these trading giants supplied just under a quarter of Australia's imports in the mid 1990s. The United States was the single most important source of imports – close to 22 per cent of the total. Japan was the second most important supplier with 18 per cent; a large gap existed between these two countries and the next most significant country suppliers, Germany and the United Kingdom, which each accounted for about 6 per cent.

Nor did East Asia figure more prominently in investments flows to and from Australia. Government reports were quick to criticise Australian business for its reluctance to invest in Asia. But in concentrating on the United States and Western Europe, Australian investors were no different from those from Japan. The reason is straightforward: the United States and the European Union remain far larger markets than any in Asia – reinforcing the 'natural' advantages that these locations have for Australian investors in their use of the English language and the structures of their business systems, with which Australian companies are familiar. Moreover, mining companies, the location of whose operations is of course determined by the availability of mineral deposits, would be expected to figure prominently in Australia's foreign direct investment, since it is

usually the largest domestic corporations that undertake foreign investment. Not surprisingly, few of their investments are in Asia.

If the record on closer economic relations with Asia is mixed, that of
public attitudes towards Asia is unequivocal. Public opinion was at best
sceptical and on some issues clearly opposed to the government's push for
closer economic relations with Asia. Although two-thirds of the respondents
to the 1996 electoral survey agreed with the statement that 'Australia's
trading future lies in Asia', close to 60 per cent believed that Australia
should use tariffs to protect its industries. Contrary to Prime Minister
Keating's stance on the Japan–United States trade dispute (on a visit to
Tokyo he expressed support for the Japanese position when Japan was
being criticised by Washington for its closed market), only 14 per cent of
respondents agreed that Australia should side with Japan; 35 per cent either
disagreed or strongly disagreed with Australia supporting the Japanese
position. Moreover, even in a period when the share of Japanese investment in total flows to Australia fell precipitously (owing to the recession
in Japan), 55 per cent of respondents agreed with the statement that 'Japanese
economic influence is too great in Australia'. Clearly the public continued
to have reservations about Australia's economic integration with its Asian
neighbours.

Continuity in foreign economic policies

Foreign policy issues seldom rank highly as determinants of how people
vote. It was curious, therefore, that Prime Minister Keating should choose
to launch both the 1993 and the 1996 election campaigns with statements
on foreign policy. Keating's obvious pride in the foreign policy achievements of his government failed to generate any enthusiasm among voters;
attempts in the 1996 campaign to score political points by suggesting that
the opposition would not enjoy the same close relationship with Asian
neighbours as that established by the ALP government similarly failed to
impress the public.

The 1996 election campaign and the initial statements by the incoming
Coalition government demonstrated the extent to which a consensus among
the major parties had been established on most foreign policy issues in the
last fifteen years. The incoming foreign minister in 1996, Alexander Downer,
wasted no time in repeating the view that 'closer engagement with Asia is
the Australian Government's highest foreign policy priority' (Downer
1996). The Coalition endorsed the emphasis that the previous government
had placed on APEC; indeed, it went even further by appointing an
ambassador to APEC as one of its first foreign policy initiatives. The Coalition
also endorsed the continuation of the Cairns Group. The one major criticism
of the ALP governments' foreign economic policies made in the Coalition's
trade policy statement for the 1996 election was to suggest that the Hawke

and Keating governments had placed excessive emphasis on multilateralism and on Australia's playing the role of good international citizen. At a time when bureaucratic resources were scarce, the Coalition paper asserted, such an emphasis came at the expense of the promotion of Australian interests through bilateral relations (Liberal and National Parties 1996).

Yet it was unclear how the Coalition would introduce a greater element of bilateralism into Australian foreign economic policies. As a relatively small economy, still heavily dependent on the export of a relatively small range of commodities, Australia seldom enjoys significant leverage in international trade negotiations. In any trade dispute with Asian neighbours, the question of who needs whom most would soon come to the fore – and would seldom be answered in Australia's favour. This is not to suggest that Australia completely lacks leverage; the Coalition, however, seems ideologically opposed to the types of government intervention that would be necessary to mobilise leverage in some areas where Australia potentially enjoys some market power, for example in coal trade talks (for further discussion see Ravenhill 1996). Moreover, as part of its cost-cutting efforts, the Coalition announced that it would be reducing assistance to Australian exporters by reducing funding to both the exports development scheme and DIFF. These cutbacks in government assistance to industry were seen as weakening Australia's hand in bilateral economic relations with the region. Not surprisingly, only three months into the new administration, the government announced that it was toning down its pre-election commitment to 'aggressive bilateralism' and would now be promoting policies of 'practical bilateralism' (the *Australian Financial Review*, 5 July 1996: 5). How such a policy will evolve in practice remains to be seen.

The advent of a Coalition government in 1996 did not seem to herald any marked departures in Australia's foreign economic relations from the pattern established by the Labor governments in the previous thirteen years. The most radical new developments in policy were implemented in the 1980s; the 1990s was a period of consolidation. The first half of the 1990s had demonstrated that creative responses to the constraints under which any Australian government has to operate in its foreign relations could bring dividends. But the experience in these years, especially in the Uruguay Round, was another powerful reminder that Australia inevitably enjoys only limited leverage in the global economy.

Notes

1 Until 1993 the European Union had been known as, variously, the European Economic Community and the European Community. The conversion of the Community into the European Union, with what became the Maastricht Treaty, took place in 1992–93.

2 The barter terms of trade is the ratio of the index of export prices to the index of import prices.

3 Controversy erupted in 1995 over claims by a Japanese journalist (Funabashi 1995) that APEC was a Japanese rather than an Australian initiative. APEC certainly grew out of collaborative bodies that reflected previous instances of cooperation between Australia and Japan – the Pacific Trade and Development Conference (PAFTAD) and the Pacific Economic Cooperation Council (PECC) (for discussion of the roles of these bodies see Woods 1993). And several proposals for regional economic collaboration had previously been put forward – by both the Japanese and the US governments. But the actual initiative on this occasion appears to have been that of the Australian prime minister himself – neither his foreign minister nor the secretary of the Department of Foreign Affairs and Trade were aware of the proposal before it was announced.

4 The eighteen members of APEC are Australia, Brunei, Canada, Chile, China, Hong Kong, Indonesia, Japan, South Korea, Malaysia, Mexico, New Zealand, Papua New Guinea, the Philippines, Singapore, Taiwan, Thailand, and the United States. For details of the working groups see Rudner 1994.

References

Aggarwal, V. K. (1995), 'Comparing Regional Cooperation Efforts in the Asia-Pacific and North America' in A. Mack and J. Ravenhill (eds), *Pacific Cooperation: Building Economic and Security Regimes in the Asia-Pacific Region*, Boulder, Co: Westview Press.

Anderson, K. and Garnaut, R. (1987), *Australian Protectionism: Extent, Causes and Effects*, Sydney: Allen & Unwin.

Bernard, M. and Ravenhill, J. (1995), 'Beyond Product Cycles and Flying Geese: Regionalization, Hierarchy, and the Industrialization of East Asia', *World Politics*, 45 (2), 179–210.

Castles, F. G. (1988), *Australian Public Policy and Economic Vulnerability*, Sydney: Allen & Unwin.

Downer, A. (1996), 'Australia and Asia: Taking the Longer View', Speech at University of Adelaide Centre for Asian Studies, 20 April, 1.

Elek, A. (1995), 'APEC Beyond Bogor: An Open Economic Association in the Asian-Pacific Region', *Asia-Pacific Economic Literature*, 9 (1), 1–16.

Fane, G. (1995), 'APEC: Regionalism, Gobalism, or Obfuscation?', *Agenda*, 2 (4), 399–409.

Funabashi, Y. (1995), *Asia Pacific Fusion: Japan's Role in APEC*, Washington, DC: Institute for International Economics.

Garnaut, R. (1989), *Australia and the Northeast Asian Ascendancy*, Canberra: AGPS.

Higgott, R. and Cooper, A. F. (1990), 'Middle Power Leadership and Coalition Building: Australia, the Cairns Group and the Uruguay Round of Trade Negotiations', *International Organization*, 44 (4), 589–632.

Liberal and National Parties (1996), *Meeting the Challenges: The New Global Economy: Liberal and National Party Trade Strategies for the Future*, Canberra: Liberal and National Parties.

Maddison, A. (1977), 'Phases of Capitalist Development', *Banca Nazionale del Lavoro Quarterly Review*, 30 (121), 103–37.

Nguyen, T., Perroni, C. and Wigle, R. (1995), 'A Uruguay Round Success?', *The World Economy*, 18 (1), 25–30.

Ravenhill, J. (1995), 'Bringing Politics Back In: The Political Economy of APEC', Conference on the Future of APEC, Seoul: Institute of East and West Studies, Yonsei University.

Ravenhill, J. (1996), 'Trade Policy Options Beyond APEC', *Australian Quarterly*, 68 (2), 1–15.

Rudner, M. (1994), 'Institutional Approaches to Regional Trade and Cooperation in the Asia Pacific Area', *Transnational Law and Contemporary Problems*, 4 (1), 159–86.

Schott, J. J. (1994) (assisted by J. W. Buurman), *The Uruguay Round: An Assessment*, Washington, DC: Institute for International Economics.

Sheehan, P. J., Pappas, N. and Cheng, E. (1994), *The Rebirth of Australian Industry: Australian Trade in Elaborately Transformed Manufactures 1979–93*, Melbourne: Centre for Strategic Economic Studies, Victoria University of Technology.

Woods, L. T. (1993), *Asia-Pacific Diplomacy: Nongovernmental Organizations and International Relations*, Vancouver: University of British Columbia Press.

14

Defence and security policy

Graeme Cheeseman

The period 1990 to 1995 witnessed a broadening of Australia's 'declared' defence and security policies beyond Labor's earlier concerns with 'defence self reliance' to embrace both regional and international security. A strong self defence capacity buttressed by continuing links with our traditional allies remained important but was no longer sufficient. Following the end of the Cold War, it was considered prudent to begin to cooperate with our neighbours to increase the resilience and security of at least our 'nearer region' as well, and to be prepared to contribute to United Nations and other multinational security operations. This changing focus was reflected in the apparent downgrading of Australia's alliance relationship with the United States in favour of increased 'regional engagement', by increasing levels of cooperation between the Australian Defence Force and its regional counterparts, and by the signing, in late 1995, of a 'historic' security co-operation agreement between Indonesia and Australia.

Most commentaries on these and earlier positional shifts assume that they flow from broader developments in Australia's circumstances (Dibb 1996; Horner 1992; Young 1991a). Our policy makers and their advisers have viewed the changes taking place 'out there' and have developed reasoned and appropriate strategic and force structure responses. While circumstantial change over this period cannot be denied, the assumption that changes to Australia's policies can be explained and justified as a necessary reaction to external strategic developments has been questioned on a number of grounds (George 1992; Cheeseman and Bruce 1996). However much they aspire to objectivity, Australia's policy makers inevitably view their surrounds from particular bureaucratic, cultural or intellectual perspectives where, all too often, the theoretical assumptions underlying these per-spectives – and criticisms of them contained in the broader literature – are either not recognised or acknowledged. Changes in policy, therefore, can reflect the predispositions and values of the policy makers themselves. Policy can be centrifugally as much as centripetally informed. More importantly perhaps, the policy prescriptions themselves are neither mirror-like renditions of Australia's circumstances nor necessarily neutral texts. They can be used by policy makers and their supporters to construct and present 'reality' in ways which maintain or extend their power and interests either within the state or beyond its shores. Seemingly matter-of-fact descriptions of policy and context advanced in defence white papers and other official and semi-official documents can have broader political and ideological purposes.

One of these purposes is to 'defend' and advance particular social and political orders. Robert Cox suggests that hegemonic world orders can be 'founded not only on the regulation of inter-state conflict but also on a globally-conceived civil society' which is 'an outward expansion of the internal hegemony' established within the state (Cox 1982: 171). Bradley Klein similarly argues that strategy can be seen as much as 'cultural practice' as 'military style', and that national strategic cultures are means of legiti-mising, both at home and abroad, the military activities of the state and its institutions (Klein 1988: 136). Within this context, formal and semi-formal (academic) prescriptions comprise a strategic discourse which is less a way of 'describing something "out there" in the real world' as 'a way of producing that something as real, identifiable, classifiable, knowable and, therefore, meaningful. Discourse [in short] creates the possibility, the con-ditions, of knowledge' (Klein 1987: 4). With this knowledge, Klein continues, comes a form of power: 'the power to define, to act upon, to subjugate and to frame the self interpretation of those who are the objects of disciplinary policy' (Klein 1987: 5; see also Said 1995: 3). Klein uses the notion of discourse to expose and comment on the hegemonic status of strategic studies and America's doctrine of nuclear deterrence (Klein 1988; 1994). But as David Sullivan describes, his ideas are also relevant to the Australian experience:

> Klein's discursive analysis of Strategic Studies unsettles the dominant narrative style of literature on Australian security, establishes a firm basis to critique mainstream accounts of what Australian post-war security has been about, and provides theoretical tools to de/reconstruct orthodox interpretations of the theory and practice of Australian security. (Sullivan 1996: 81)

This chapter uses these insights to review and reflect upon the recent changes in Australia's defence and security discourse. It begins with a brief survey of the period leading up to the end of the Cold War and how the accumulating interests (and power base) of our security community were publicly defended and justified. It then examines Australia's subsequent experience from three vantage points: perceived threats to Australia, our changing regional security concerns and practices, and international peacekeeping. In each case, I am less interested in describing what has taken place beyond Australia's shores, although this is not ignored, as with the changing interpretation and representation of these events in Australia's strategic discourse. I argue that over this time, Australia's defence and security community has been less concerned with seeking to understand and respond to external changes as with reconstituting its representation of these in ways that continue to protect or advance, in the case of Australia's regional security discourse, its interests and power.

The emergence of the militarised state in Australia

Up until the Second World War, Australia maintained only small permanent military forces in peacetime and relied on mobilising its citizenry in times of war. These wars were fought almost exclusively in support of British interests rather than in the direct defence of Australia itself. Between the mid 1800s and the end of the Second World War, Australian volunteers fought and died in various imperial conflicts across the globe. These overseas deployments, and the considerable losses in human life that were sustained, were made acceptable to the public by arguing that Australia was surrounded by threats, that it could not defend itself against these threats without British support, and that the prospects of such support would be improved by demonstrating loyalty to Britain and its imperial causes (Renouf 1979; Millar 1991). What was essentially an out-reach of British imperialism was justified by a nationalist discourse which eulogised the exploits of Australia's expeditionary forces and reinforced a popular culture that emphasised loyalty, national unity and military preparedness (McQueen 1970; White 1981; Horne 1989).

The postwar period witnessed the extension and institutionalisation of these early experiences. The small and largely citizen-based structures that had operated prior to the Second World War were developed into a permanent, increasingly professionalised and secretive defence and security apparatus centred around the bureaucratic dynasties currently located in Canberra and incorporating a growing array of actors and institutions. These included, in addition to a full-time defence force, various military and civilian staffs, intelligence agencies, research and development establishments, the so-called 'joint' United States–Australian defence facilities, and a number of academic institutions concerned with carrying out policy and policy related research into defence and state based security (see Ball 1980; Richelson and Ball 1985; Young 1991b).

During the 1950s and 1960s, this emerging security complex was used to help repress troublesome nationalist and post-colonial movements in Australia's region of interest, as well as support the United States and its western allies in establishing and maintaining global supremacy. These developments and activities continued to be justified by a public discourse which exploited the view that Australia was surrounded by threats, and that it was militarily indefensible and so in need of great power protection. Over the period of the 'first' Cold War, Australians were continually warned in parliamentary speeches, in various official and semi-official reports, and at public meetings and conferences of the dangers of Soviet and later Chinese-inspired communist aggression undermining regional stability and threatening to come tumbling, like falling dominoes, towards Australia (Dupont 1991; Murphy 1993; Strahan 1996). That this strategy was largely successful is evidenced by public opinion polls taken during this period which consistently showed a significant proportion of respondents believing Australia to be under threat. Similar numbers felt that Australia could not defend itself and favoured some form of conscription, the continuation of the existing military alliance with the United States, and ever more to be spent on defence (Mathews and Ravenhill 1987; Campbell 1989; MacAllister and Makkai 1991).

In the late 1970s and early 1980s, Australia's defence planners were forced to adjust their strategic rhetoric and doctrines to take account of the defeat of western counter-revolutionary forces in Indo-China, the subsequent shift in American strategic preoccupations away from Asia – first signalled in the so-called Nixon or Guam doctrine – and growing public concern over Australia's continuing involvement in an increasingly nuclearised, and potentially dangerous, United States' world order. This adjustment took some time to occur but was made easier by the election, in 1983, of the Hawke Labor government which had argued in opposition that Australia needed to become more independent and self reliant in defence (Cheeseman 1993a). Following the lead of a 1981 report by the Joint Committee on Foreign Affairs and Defence on *Threats to Australia's Security* (Joint Committee on Foreign Affairs and Defence 1981) and Paul Dibb's later *Review of Australia's defence capabilities* (Dibb 1986), Labor ruled out the possibility of an invasion by Soviet or other forces and argued instead that Australia was likely now only to be faced with so-called 'low level' and 'escalated low level' military pressures coming 'from or through' the islands to our north and north-west (it did not identify the possible sources of these threat contingencies nor explain the likely specific intent of such attacks).

Since this level of threat could generally be handled by Australia's existing forces, Australia was now, by definition, defensible, although, in order to cover the prospect of an escalation in military hostilities, the defence establishment was encouraged to continue to modernise its forces and retain or add to its equipment inventory certain items – such as F-111 strike aircraft and ocean going submarines – that could be used to control conflict escalation or deter a major attack (Babbage 1990: 93–6). Labor also extended Australia's existing security infrastructure to include an invigorated defence industrial sector based around newly developed and largely privatised shipbuilding and aerospace industries (Cheeseman 1993b; 1994).

The Soviet 'threat' was not at this time entirely discounted of course. According to the government's 1987 defence white paper, our national security continued fundamentally to depend on preserving a stable global balance between the two superpowers. While Australia was to focus its future defence efforts on self defence, therefore, it would also, 'as a member of the western strategic community', continue to support the United States in its efforts to contain Soviet expansionism largely, but not exclusively, through its hosting of the 'joint facilities'. As Richard Leaver has argued, Labor was thus able to quell anxieties within the party and the broader Australian community by linking the alliance relationship with declared concepts of Australian sovereignty and independence (Leaver 1991: 238–9).

By the mid 1980s, then, the size and status of Australia's security establishment, or 'armament complex' to use Robin Luckham's apt phrase (Luckham 1984), had grown considerably from its prewar base. Australia's defence budget had stabilised at around 3 per cent of the nation's GDP, and Labor had embarked on an ambitious military modernisation program, involving the expenditure of more than $25 billion on new or replacement capital equipment and facilities (Cheeseman 1990). The government had also instituted a new and, in the view of some commentators, revolutionary strategy for the defence of Australia itself (Mack 1988; Young 1989; Dibb 1992). Yet Labor's rhetoric on 'defence self reliance' notwithstanding, the basic identity and perceived roles of Australia's defence establishment had changed little from those of earlier times (Cheeseman 1991). Our thinking on defence and security remained anchored around an image of Australia as a white, Anglo-American enclave and defender of western cultural and philosophical values against largely non-western, military threats. Australia was firmly part of the postwar order, ever-ready to dispatch its forces to help maintain or advance western interests in the South Pacific or beyond if necessary (Cheeseman and Kettle 1990). Labor's 'new' defence posture and its associated geopolitical identity were celebrated (and reinforced) by an academic and popular strategic discourse which, in spite of the efforts of various 'dissident authors', continued to view issues of defence and security in essentially positivist terms, with priority accorded to the central balance between the superpowers (Dalby 1995).

Australian defence and security after the Cold War

The end of the Cold War and the subsequent collapse of the Soviet Union required a further adjustment in Australia's strategic and defence discourse although, like the response to the allied defeat in Vietnam, this took some time to be affected (Brown 1994: 13–19). The government's strategic basis document, *Australia's Strategic Planning in the 1990s* (ASP 90), prepared in November 1989, continued to talk of the 'Soviet challenge' and the need to continue to support the United States in 'working for a reduction in the level of tension between the superpowers and limiting the spread of influences in our region inimical to Western interests' (Department of Defence 1992: 3). The Foreign Minister's 1989 statement on regional security noted the changes that were occurring within the Soviet Union at the time but argued that it would nonetheless 'remain a great power' and so would continue to seek to play a role in both South-east Asia and the Asia Pacific (Evans 1989a: 5).

The Defence Department's 1991 *Force Structure Review*, which had been commissioned by Defence Minister Robert Ray to 'ensure that Defence planning for the 1990s goes forward in a balanced way', and included a chapter on 'Restructuring the ADF for the Next Century', made no mention of the end of the Cold War let alone the systemic changes taking place within Australia's region of interest. Yet it advanced a series of force structure 'adjustments' which were said 'to better meet strategic priorities' (Department of Defence 1991: 1). In his preface to a declassified version of ASP 90, released in September 1992, Ray acknowledged that Australia and its surrounding region were 'not entirely immune from global developments', but insisted nonetheless that the precipitous events of 1989 and 1990 had no significant impact on either Australia's 'immediate security environment' or its basic approach to defence and security (Department of Defence 1992: iii).

There was no such reticence within Australia's broader academic community. In line with overseas experience, there soon emerged a host of publications on the end of the Cold War and its implications (see for example, Millar and Walter 1993; Leaver and Richardson 1993). A key theme in some of the early writings at least, was the idea that we were entering a new and potentially more peaceful era, one in which traditional political-military concerns were being downgraded in favour of geo-economics and at least the prospects of sizeable 'peace dividends' were being mooted. Possibly spurred on by these developments, Australia's policy makers and their advisers began to change their tune with the response appearing, on the surface, to be in two contrasting directions (Nossal 1995). The first, centred around Australia's foreign minister, sought to locate Australia's defence considerations within a broader security framework. The second approach, typified by the works of Paul Dibb, sought to reconstitute Australia's post-Cold War experience back into a traditional, Cold War framework. As we will see, while the rhetoric of the two groups was certainly different, their basic purpose – to protect and advance the *status quo* – is very similar. What was happening was not necessarily, as some have suggested, a debate over ends and means taking place in the wake of the end of the Cold War, but the emergence of a new and more ambitious strategic discourse aimed at securing continuing support at home while, simultaneously, extending Australia's and its allies' interests abroad.

Securing Australia's insecurity

The disappearance of the Soviet Union presented Australia's defence planners with a dilemma. While they had never specifically planned for a Soviet invasion, both the logic of their strategic discourse and its continuing popular appeal depended largely on being able to point to some form of external entity onto which our traditional apprehensions and obsessions could be projected. The initial response to this dilemma was to seek to create, in the public mind at least, a series of new (and not so new) potential adversaries. This process began in the late 1980s with the then Minister for Defence, Kim Beazley, warning that Australia's changing strategic circumstances now had 'more in common with the political map of nineteenth century Europe, with its shifting alliances and multi-polarity', and that '[t]here is now a range of major powers [China, India, Japan as well as the Soviet Union] on the periphery of the region with the potential to intervene in regional affairs should they consider their interests threatened' (Beazley 1990: 336). Evans' 1989 statement on *Australia's Regional Security* added to this sense of unease by suggesting that there were a number of existing and emerging 'great powers' which could be expected to be interested in and, in some cases, may threaten Australia's region of interest. These included, in addition to the Soviet Union and China, a nuclear-armed India whose:

> … already significant military capabilities, which made it the predominant power in South Asia, will be followed by increasing strategic reach, including into South East Asia. It sees itself as a great power and a major actor on the global scene. It will show greater interest in South East Asia and even the South Pacific (witness its active position on Fiji), and will increasingly claim a voice there. (Evans 1989: 7)

The invasion of Kuwait by Iraqi forces in 1990 was used by members of the Hawke government to underscore these earlier threat projections. In justifying his government's decision to deploy Australian naval forces in support of a then United States-led naval blockade of Iraq and well beyond our declared 'area of direct military interest', Hawke claimed that the Iraqi occupation of Kuwait represented 'one of the gravest international crises since the Second World War' which, if not dealt with immediately, would serve to undermine global and Australia's own security. This was because, first, 'any nation which controlled the oil industries of Iraq, Kuwait and Saudi Arabia would be able to dictate oil prices'. 'There can be no doubt what Iraq's pricing policy would be', insisted the prime minister, and 'no doubt what that would mean for the world's economy and for Australia's' (House of Representatives, *Hansard*, 21 August 1991: 1121–2). Beyond this immediate threat, was the challenge that Iraq's actions were said to pose to the international rule of law on which '[t]he security and prosperity of the world and the security and prosperity of Australia will depend in the years ahead'. In this latter regard, Hawke argued that:

> Iraq's invasion of Kuwait is, tragically, clear proof of the new dangers which exist, ... and could emerge in the Asia Pacific region in the coming years. We need, therefore, to work out how to manage these dangers wherever they may arise. In so doing ... [w]e find ourselves looking again to the United Nations to uphold the rule of law as the principle of international relations over the rule of force. (House of Representatives, Hansard, 21 August 1991: 1121, 1123)

While couched in 'internationalist' terminology, Hawke's defence of his decision neatly invoked many of Australia's traditional concerns: the existence of external threats to the western way of life which, if not dealt with there and then, would spread to our own region and undermine our own security; our need for a powerful benefactor to protect us against such future threats; and military down payments to ensure that we will receive this support when and if it is needed. These basic propositions were repeated without reservation or reflection over and over again in parliamentary speeches and other public statements by government members. The Minister for Trade Negotiations, Dr Blewett, argued, for example, that '[w]hat has happened in the Gulf is a clear indication of the down side of a more multipolar world where some middle powers might see scope to extend their influence, freed from the constraints of a bipolar system'. 'In this more uncertain world order', continued the minister and former professor of politics, 'the role of the United Nations becomes even more important for Australia and the rest of the international community' (House of Representatives, *Hansard*, 21 August 1991: 1129).

The government, of course, could not depend on the regular appearance of 'regional Saddam Husseins' and, in the absence of such events, the identification of specific sources of threat could well be seen to be too crudely self serving, even by Australian standards. Such scare mongering was also increasingly complicated by Labor's broader political and economic agenda of seeking to engage with, rather than resile from, its Asian neighbours. A more sophisticated approach was needed, one which took into account Australia's changing strategic circumstances but continued to exploit the key elements of our popular consciousness. The approach adopted by Australia's defence planners was to focus on the idea of uncertainty which, as Michael Sullivan (1996) and Richard Leaver (1996) both argue, is the *leitmotiv* of the government's 1994 defence white paper. This argues that Cold War constraints had 'produced a measure of stability throughout the region'. With the ending of the Cold War, however, these constraints are being 'loosened', introducing a measure of fluidity and complexity into the region which is likely to 'produce an unstable and potentially dangerous strategic situation in the Asia and the Pacific over the next fifteen years' (Department of Defence 1994: 7–8). In view of this development, the white paper continues, we must continue to be on our guard, for while the region may be presently benign, we can never be sure that something won't happen in the future to change this and put Australia and Australians at risk.

Such a view is based on a highly selective and contentious reading of the 'Asian Cold War'. As Russell Trood argues, while:

> the nuclear stand-off between the United States and the Soviet Union produced stability in the global balance ... this did little to guarantee the peace (or stability) of Asia ... [or] to impede the relentless pattern of violent (and invariably unpredictable) change that was a persistent feature of this region's postwar politics. (Trood 1996: 30)

But the validity or otherwise of the white paper's assertions are not as important as the broader exercise of creating a sense of uncertainty and danger in the minds of the reader. While the white paper acknowledges some of the potential positive developments in Australia's strategic circumstances, these are overwhelmed by a litany of qualifications, apprehensions and forebodings. On page four, for example, we are told that Australia has 'no disputes with other countries which might be expected to give rise to the use of force, and no reason at present to expect that disputes of that sort will develop'. The very next paragraph, however, invokes all of Australia's traditional concerns when it goes on to assert that:

> the next fifteen years will see great change in our strategic environment. With the end of the Cold War, important new uncertainties have emerged about the future strategic situation in Asia. Economic growth will increase the power of nations in our region, and political change may make their policies less predictable. Because of these uncertainties, we acknowledge the possibility that our security environment could deteriorate, perhaps quite seriously in the future. We recognise that at some time in the future armed force could be used against us and that we need to be prepared to meet it. (Department of Defence 1994: 4)

This basic pattern is repeated throughout the white paper's survey of Australia's 'changing strategic outlook' and its 'international defence interests'. We are provided with an ambivalent assessment of the future role of the United States in the region; told that the growth of economic interdependence and cooperation may be offset by 'ethnic and national tensions, economic rivalry, disappointed aspirations for prosperity, religious or racial conflict' and other 'threats without enemies'; informed of the possible military consequences of continuing economic growth; and warned of the potential hegemonic aspirations of Japan, India and China (but not the United States or Indonesia). In this last regard, neither the white paper nor the 1993 *Strategic Review* seek to explore the complex economic and strategic dynamics confronting China, in particular, preferring simply to assert, in the second case, that 'China's strategic influence will grow during the 1990s, as its economic strength gives it the means to become a more powerful factor in the Asia-Pacific', that 'it has signalled its intention to develop a capability to project significant military force beyond its own territory', and that it 'already has the capability to match the forces that South-East Asian nations could deploy in the South China Sea' (Department of Defence 1993a: 9–10; Department of Defence 1994: 9).

As Trood (1996: 31) suggests, the government's revisionist approach to the Cold War and generally alarmist rendering of Australia's evolving strategic circumstances demands close scrutiny. While there is no doubt that the region is complex and there are potentially destabilising forces at work, the all too brief and simplistic account of these offered in both the 1993 *Strategic Review* and the 1994 defence white paper, together with the tendency to focus on the threatening dimensions of political and economic change, raise questions about what is being presented and why. These kinds of concerns have not prevented media analysts and members of the defence academic community from publicly reiterating the central themes of the white paper. In a series of journal and newspaper articles, Paul Dibb, for example, acknowledges the potentially positive developments occurring within Australia's region of interest, but argues that growing interdependence will not lessen the prospects of conflict and warns that economic growth may well facilitate continuing arms build-ups especially by the 'great powers' – China, Japan and India – who will seek to extend their influence where ever opportunities present themselves (Dibb 1994; 1995).

Dibb goes on to (re)present the emerging situation in the Asia-Pacific in simplified and essentially Cold War terms – the earlier bipolar balance is being replaced by a multipolar one – and then uses this framework to advocate stronger defences and regional alliances as part of an intricate power-balancing strategy. Such an approach conveniently ignores the contested and problematic nature of the terminology that is used, as well as the broader theoretical debates taking place over the realist assumptions that underpin his analysis. But this is unlikely significantly to worry Dibb and his ilk since their work is directed less at engaging with academe as 'policing' both the policy community and the Australian public. An important theme in this emerging strategic discourse is that Australia may need to depend more, not less, on the United States in the future, not only as a countervailing power in the region, but also, and more importantly, as a source of supply for the weapons and logistics support that are now 'necessary' for Australia's defence establishment to carry out its post-Cold War role (Gelber 1992; Dibb 1993; Young 1994). This theme was taken up in 1996 by the incoming Howard Liberal–National government which, while generally supportive of regional engagement, felt that Australia's defence relationship with the United States needed to be 'revitalised' and sought, virtually immediately (but unsuccessfully), to encourage an increased American military presence in Australia itself.

Securing Australia's region

Although Australia's security concerns have broadened, they remain focused on our surrounding region. 'Australia's future security', the 1994 defence white paper asserts, 'is linked inextricably to the security and prosperity of Asia and the Pacific' (Department of Defence 1994: 3). This theme – Australia can only be secure in a secure region – is not new. What has changed has been how regional security is to be achieved in practice and how these practices are to be justified. As we have seen, until the 1970s, Australia simply encouraged its imperial benefactors to use their global military reach to secure our approaches and justified this policy by arguing that the containment of (sometimes revolutionary) nationalist movements in South-east Asia provided for the defence of Australia. The end of the colonial era and the prospective withdrawal of American military power from the region following the end of the Cold War, required some further adjustments to both Australia's regional security practices and its support-ing discourse.

This process began in earnest in 1989 with the release of Evans' minis-terial statement on *Australia's Regional Security*. This placed Australia's regional defence policies and the continued expansion of its military capabilities within a framework that extended beyond self defence – still seen as the 'the prime interest of any country' – to include the maintenance of 'a positive security and strategic environment' (Evans 1989a: 1). This latter objective was said to require policy instruments that 'go well beyond those administered by the Minister for Defence, or for that matter the Minister for Foreign Affairs and Trade' to include: 'economic links, dev-elopment assistance, "non-military threat" assistance, and the exchange of people and ideas' (Evans 1989a: 15). In the last case, Evans was par-ticularly concerned that more be done to correct what he described as Australia's 'image problem' in South-east Asia and the South Pacific:

> As regional societies become more complex and their decision-making elites more diverse, we need to influence this wider range of people, and traditional lines of government-to-government communication are insufficient. Greater consideration should be given to what has been described as "second-track" diplomacy: seeking to get our message across and exercise leverage through

various semi-governmental and non-governmental organisations and personnel. (Evans 1989a: 36)

As Greg Fry has argued, in this last regard in particular, the Evans document can be thought of more as a security doctrine, reminiscent of the earlier 'Monroe Doctrine' on the South Pacific, than a policy statement. While it invokes a broader understanding of the nature of security and incorporates themes of 'partnership' and 'community', the document's aspiration remains essentially hegemonic: 'to determine the structures and agenda of regional security and ... forge a regional security community around values, interests and agendas over which [Australia] would have the greatest interest' (Fry 1991: 129–30).

The initial attempts, by Evans himself, to translate these broad organising principles into practice were rather clumsy, involving a proposal, which echoed an earlier Canadian suggestion, to establish an Asian equivalent of the successful Conference on Security Cooperation in Europe (CSCE). As Andrew Mack and Pauline Kerr (1995: 124–6) have described, the suggestion was criticised by both Australia's ASEAN neighbours and the existing regional hegemon, the United States, which insisted that the security challenges confronting the region did not lend themselves to region wide solutions. Confronted by this opposition, Evans backed off, agreeing that it 'made no sense to transplant CSCE institutions from Europe to Asia', and arguing that emphasis now needed to be placed on dialogue rather than institution building. During the ensuing lull, Australia's efforts switched to Evans' so-called 'second-track'.

During the early 1990s there had been, in Desmond Ball's words, 'a burgeoning of non-governmental activities' in the field of regional security, including annual Asia-Pacific Roundtables, organised by the ASEAN Institutes of Strategic and International Studies (ASEAN ISIS), and a series of meetings as part of a project on Security Cooperation in the Asia Pacific (SCAP) (Ball 1994: 168–9). At a meeting of this latter group, in Seoul in November 1992, it was agreed to establish a standing Council for Security Cooperation in the Asia Pacific (CSCAP) in order to provide 'a more structured regional process of a non-governmental nature ... to contribute to the efforts towards regional confidence building and enhancing regional security through dialogue, consultation and cooperation' (Ball 1994: 169). Australia, through the Strategic and Defence Studies Centre at the Australian National University, is a founding member of CSCAP and, according to Desmond Ball and Pauline Kerr, 'one of the most active participants and sponsors of these processes within the region and at home'. The establishment of CSCAP itself was seen by these same authors (one of whom is Australia's principal representative on the council) as 'one of the most important milestones in the development of institutionalised dialogue, consultation and cooperation concerning security matters in the

Asia-Pacific region since the end of the Cold War' (Ball and Kerr 1996: 31).

The importance of the organisation is said to stem from its regional membership – it currently embraces strategic and international studies research institutes from across the region – and its close connections with the ASEAN Regional Forum (ARF) which filled the institutional void left vacant by Gareth Evans and his Canadian colleagues. While initiated by the ASEAN states, Australia and its former foreign minister still sought to play a key role in the forum and its supporting Senior Officials Meetings (SOMs), providing background and discussion papers, organising seminars and inter-sessional meetings, and helping frame ARF procedures, protocols and agendas (see Evans and Dibb 1995; Ball and Kerr 1996: 23–30). The region's 'security agenda' was agreed at the second meeting of the ARF held in August 1995 and involves, in order of precedence: the promotion of confidence building measures, the development of preventive diplomacy, and the development of conflict resolution mechanisms. According to Ball and Kerr:

> The types of confidence-building measures in Stage I are to include: dialogue on security perceptions, including voluntary statements of defence policy positions; greater transparency via defence publications such as Defence White Papers; encouragement of participation in the United Nations Conventional Arms Register; and an annual seminar for defence officials and military officers. Stage II will focus on preventive diplomacy and will be guided by three existing sets of preventive diplomacy principals contained within the UN Charter, the Treaty of Amity and Cooperation, and (with respect to the Spratley Islands) the ASEAN Declaration on the South China Sea. (Ball and Kerr 1996: 29)

These various developments and initiatives (which, in the case of the Stage I proposals at least, closely resembled Australia's own regional security objectives) are seen as particularly important by Australia's defence establishment and its advisers. The 1993 *Strategic Review*, for example, argues that in order 'to help promote stability at a time of considerable strategic change in our region, it is important for Australia to be closely involved in regional affairs' (Department of Defence 1993a: 21). The 1994 defence white paper similarly notes, on page 11, that as Australia's strategic environment becomes more complex, its 'ability to help shape that environment will [also] become more important'. On the following page, the document states that one of the government's 'major objectives' is to establish Australia's place in the 'new patterns of relationships' that are forming within the region in the wake of the end of the Cold War, and 'to shape them to meet Australia's interests'. In line with this view, the Defence Department and the Australian Defence Force have increased dramatically the range and scope of their cooperative activities with their regional counterparts (Ball 1991; Ball and Kerr 1996: 58–72).

For their part, Ball and Kerr (1996: 51–3) argue that 'it is now generally accepted throughout the Asia-Pacific region that increased security co-operation is imperative for many important reasons'. The authors list ten of these which can be grouped into three categories. Broadly-based security mechanisms are said to be needed: first, to manage or counter the increasing uncertainties and 'centrifugal possibilities' that can be found in the region; second, to 'develop common perspectives and policies for addressing the increasing capabilities of the major Asian powers' and to increase 'regional resilience' against these powers; and third, and in line with the views of the defence establishment, to 'provide Australia with a significant role in the region'. In this last case, Ball and Kerr go on to claim that:

> there is an unabashed recognition within the region that Australia is the principal repository of the experience and skills necessary to convert the various notions into viable operational regimes. Australia has not been diffident about capitalising on this important opportunity for regional involvement. (Ball and Kerr 1996: 53)

Apart from its ethnocentric and self-congratulatory timbre, Australia's official and academic discourse on regional security is interesting, and revealing, on a number of counts. Like Australia's defence discourse, it emphasises uncertainty and danger which, in this case, are located beyond Australia's 'nearer region' and need to be addressed through traditional, realist means. As evidenced by this example, the discourse makes extensive use of the language and images found in the field of strategic studies. This is not surprising given the predominance of strategic analysts and strategic studies institutions within the 'second track' process in particular. Indeed, when reading Australian accounts of regional security, one is struck by its similarities with earlier representations of nuclear strategy with their positivist assumptions and endless acronyms.

This is not a trivial point, for, as Michael Sullivan writes, just as nuclear strategists used specialised language and images to exert authority over their field, so Australia's regional security discourse seeks to constitute or 'discipline knowledge of post-Cold War security in the Asian-Pacific region ... to ensure that the Asian-Pacific region which comes into being resembles Australia's truth statements about the region' (Sullivan 1996: 209). It does this in a number of ways, but especially through the use of: authorising concepts, language and acronyms which 'become real objects with a purpose and meaning of their own'; maps which define in advance the territory or imagined community being secured; and discursive practices which, as evidenced by Ball and Kerr's work, equates regional security with continuing dialogue about the importance of cooperation, confidence-building and transparency. As long as there are talks about these issues, the message seems to be, security will ensue. Such a concentration on the means rather than the ends of security-building is not only self-serving –

providing for endless conferences and workshops of officials and sanctioned academics in comfortable hotels around the region – it enables those involved in the process to avoid considering important, and potentially disempowering, questions such as what exactly do we mean by security and whose security are we talking about?

UN peacekeeping: Change and resistance

A similar privileging process underlies Australia's evolving discourse on United Nations peacekeeping and international security. These issues were dealt with only perfunctorily if at all in ministerial statements and key defence policy documents issued before the end of the Cold War. Labor's 1987 defence white paper, for example, devoted only one paragraph to peacekeeping which stated simply that it could be a useful adjunct to the Australian Defence Force's primary role of defending Australia since it allows us to 'contribute to wider Western interests'. But '[i]t is not necessary', the white paper continued, 'to develop forces especially for peacekeeping. Like contributions to allied efforts, such contributions can be mounted from the force-in-being' (Department of Defence 1987: 9). The 1989 strategic basis paper made no mention of peacekeeping or the United Nations, although in his introduction to the public version of the classified document, released in late 1992, Defence Minister Ray acknowledged that 'UN peacekeeping tasks are now increasingly prominent defence activities' (Department of Defence 1992: iv).

Indeed, the period between 1988 and 1994 had seen the Australian Defence Force participate in the Gulf War and ten UN operations with three of the latter involving deployments of 300 or more service personnel (Joint Standing Committee on Foreign Affairs, Defence and Trade 1994: Appendix 5). In the face of these actual operations, which received extensive coverage in the Australian media, the Defence Department had little option than to begin publicly to acknowledge the Australian Defence Force's peacekeeping functions, although it continued resolutely to resist structuring its forces for such a role. Thus the 1993 *Strategic Review* noted that 'with the end of the Cold War, new opportunities have opened for the international community to play a more active role in peacekeeping and peace enforcement', but still described peacekeeping as a 'supplementary activity'. This view was reiterated in a Defence Department document on *Peacekeeping Policy*, released the same year, which added that it was also inappropriate to 'maintain units on standby specifically for peacekeeping operations' or to 'signify units as being available for peacekeeping' (Department of Defence 1993b: 7).[1] The 1994 defence white paper stated Australia would now 'seek every opportunity' to participate in UN and other multilateral operations, but ruled out either earmarking existing forces or establishing special units for such roles. As long as the Australian Defence Force was structured for defending Australia, the document argued, 'the versatility inherent in such a force ensures it can contribute to peace operations. The demands of these peace operations therefore need not, and will not, influence the force development process other than at the margins' (Department of Defence 1994: 108).

The Department's position, to the extent it has been debated at all, has been either supported or meekly accepted by the other key actors in Australia's defence and security community. In its 1991 inquiry into peacekeeping, the Senate Standing Committee on Foreign Affairs, Defence and Trade noted 'there are unresolved tensions in the [Defence Department's] present position' on the issue, but concluded that, 'as a general proposition ... peacekeeping should play no role as a force structure determinant – with one proviso. Provision should be made for an Australian contribution to the development of a regional peacekeeping capability' (Senate Standing Committee on Foreign Affairs, Defence and Trade 1991: 124). A 1994 report by the Joint Standing Committee on Foreign Affairs, Defence and Trade did suggest that the Defence Department include 'international, and in particular United Nations, arrangements in [its] force structure deliberations' since such a role was now likely to be a significant long term responsibility for the Australian Defence Force (Joint Standing Committee on Foreign Affairs, Defence and Trade 1994: 62–3). The committee's recommendation was rejected by the government which would have taken solace in the view of its key adviser, Paul Dibb, on the subject.

In evidence to the Joint Standing Committee Dibb acknowledged 'that there will be increasing and legitimate demands for UN peacekeeping', but insisted that true security can only be achieved through the development and maintenance of strong defences and strong alliances. 'While new international security mechanisms are undoubtedly emerging', the former defence bureaucrat, and now Head of the Strategic and Defence Studies Centre, argued, 'they do not replace the security we gain from a strong independent defence posture focused on the defence of Australia, our strategic commitments to our region and our continuing strong alliance with the United States'. This was especially so in Australia's case, Dibb continued, since:

> ... we have only recently, that is, as recently as 1986, got the Australian Defence Force to focus on agreed force structure priorities for the defence of Australia. That ... was neither an easy or quick resolution of a long outstanding debate in this country. We now have the defence force agreed, in the main, on the priorities for force structuring in the coming decade. I think it is important that we hew to those priorities and that we are not disrupted by the fashion of the moment. (Joint Committee on Foreign Affairs, Defence and Trade, Evidence, 9 October 1993: 240)

The then Foreign Minister, Gareth Evans, and his department appeared, initially, to support the idea of structuring the Australian Defence Force for peacekeeping operations. In a speech to the UN General Assembly in October 1989, Evans argued that states should designate military units and observers 'that could be called upon at short notice and undergo appropriate training in advance. To the same end', Evans continued, 'we would support the establishment of a stockpile of essential supplies, such as transport and communication equipment, which would also be readily available at short notice for new and urgent tasks to which the UN becomes committed' (Evans 1989b). By the early 1990s, however, while the minister and his department continued to stress the importance of Australian participation in UN operations, they had begun to back away from the force structure issue. In his opening address to a conference entitled 'UN Peacekeeping at the Crossroads', held in Canberra in March 1993, Evans stated that even though 'national earmarking or identification of forces would appear to be a practicable way of assisting the UN to improve planning', it was no longer necessary 'to nominate specific units for peacekeeping duties, let alone place specific forces on standby: we believe we can respond quickly and professionally to new situations as they arise without going this far' (Evans 1994: 20).

As we have seen, the Defence Department's case for not structuring the Australian Defence Force for peacekeeping and other international security operations is based, primarily, on the view that the military's principal role is the defence of Australia and that this alone should determine its force structure. Structuring or earmarking elements of the Australian Defence Force for peacekeeping duties would detract from our self defence capacity either directly, by reducing the Australian Defence Force's flexibility and the number and quality of forces available for dealing with threats to Australia itself, or indirectly by cutting into training time and other essential support activities. The department also maintains that the Australian Defence Force's current structure provides a sufficiently flexible and appropriate basis for meeting the country's peacekeeping needs. As I argue elsewhere, neither of these supporting arguments is entirely convincing, often contradicting Australia's own peacekeeping experiences and its criticisms of, and suggested reforms to, UN structures and procedures (Cheeseman 1995). It is also the case that the department's primary rationale has been stated (over and over again) rather than argued. By recourse to language and asserting realist principles and doctrines as self evident truths, defence and its key supporters have been able to exercise control over, or discipline, the discourse on peacekeeping in Australia to suit their own ends. Within this framework, alternative approaches for achieving peace and security are painted as 'fashions of the moment', 'international whims', or the products of 'idealistic' outlooks and perceptions which cannot be allowed to get in the way of the 'serious and long term endeavour' of planning for the defence of the state, although they can, of course, be given some rhetorical recognition, especially where it is politically or bureaucratically expedient to do so.

Conclusion

The period since the end of the Cold War saw Australia's policy makers and their advisers invoke a 'discourse of danger' to maintain popular support for an existing, and in the view of some, outmoded Cold War defence establishment and militarised policy agenda (Smith and Kettle 1992; Cheeseman 1993a; Brown 1994). That they were successful in this enterprise may be seen from both public opinion polls and media and other popular accounts of Australia's post Cold War environment which uncritically accepted the realist tenets of the 1994 white paper and other official statements on defence and security. Further evidence of the hegemonic power of Australia's strategic discourse may be found in the lead up to the Howard government's first budget. In order to fund an alleged $8 billion deficit left over by its Labor predecessors, the new government slashed public spending and jobs and willingly countenanced breaking its election promises in all areas of public policy except one – defence. While other ministers repeatedly argued that their respective departments had to share the burden of the government's cost-cutting frenzy, both the minister for defence and the prime minister simply stated that the Coalition's pre-election promise of holding defence expenditure at existing levels would be honoured: end of story. This decision, not surprisingly, had the unqualified support of Australia's defence academic community. Significantly, it was virtually completely ignored by the media's economic rationalist commentators, in spite of the amounts of money involved – around $10 billion a year.

In addition to 'disciplining' the domestic debate over defence and security, Australia's decision makers also set about 'policing' the emerging discourse on both regional and international security in ways that enabled them to justify continuing levels of expenditure on defence, to provide additional legitimacy for Australia's expanding regional defence presence and activities, to limit force structure planning to sovereignty defence, and, not unimportantly, to allow Australian officials and members of the local strategic studies community to continue to legitimise particular representations of the region, champion realist concepts such as 'order' and 'stability', and marginalise various non-state, non-military and non-elite perspectives and priorities.

Note
1   The document did provide an indicative list of types of units and sub-units that 'could in principle be made available for peacekeeping duties'. The list, which had been forwarded to the UN in August 1990, included an infantry battalion

group, APC squadron, signals squadron, medical unit, field supply company, transport squadron, field workshop, light and medium helicopter flight, military police platoon and movement control unit.

References

Babbage, R. (1990), A *Coast Too Long: Defending Australia Beyond the 1990s*, St Leonards: Allen & Unwin.

Ball, D. (1980), *A suitable piece of real estate: American installations in Australia*, Sydney: Hale & Iremonger.

Ball, D. (1991), 'Building Blocks for Regional Security: An Australian Perspective on Confidence and Security Building Measures (CSBMs) in the Asia/Pacific Region', Canberra Papers on Strategy and Defence No. 83, Strategic and Defence Studies Centre, Canberra: Australian National University.

Ball, D. (1994), 'A New Era in Confidence-Building: The Second-track Process in the Asia-Pacific Region', *Security Dialogue*, 25 (2), 157–76.

Ball, D. and Kerr, P. (1996), *Presumptive Engagement: Australia's Asia-Pacific Security Policy in the 1990s*, St Leonards: Allen & Unwin.

Beazley, K. (1990), 'Australian Defence Policy' in D. Ball (ed.), *Australia and the World: Prologue and Prospects*, Canberra Papers on Strategy and Defence No. 69, Strategic and Defence Studies Centre, Canberra: Australian National University.

Brown, G. (1994), *Australia's Security: Issues for the New Century*, Canberra: Australian Defence Studies Centre, Australian Defence Force Academy.

Campbell, D. (1989), *The Social Basis of Australian and New Zealand Security Policy*, Canberra: Peace Research Centre, Australian National University.

Cheeseman, G. (1990), 'Australia's Defence: White Paper in the Red', *Australian Journal of International Affairs*, 44(2), 101–18.

Cheeseman, G. (1991) 'From Forward Defence to Self-Reliance: Changes and Continuities in Australian Defence Policy 1965-90', *Australian Journal of Political Science*, 26, 429–45.

Cheeseman, G. (1993a) *The Search for Self-Reliance: Australian Defence Since Vietnam*, Melbourne: Longman Cheshire.

Cheeseman, G. (1993b) 'Australia: an emerging arms supplier?' in H. Wulf (ed.) *Arms Industry Limited*, Oxford: Oxford University Press.

Cheeseman, G. (ed.) (1994), *Fostering an Indigenous Defence Industry? Defence Industry Policy after the 'Price Review'*, Canberra: Australian Defence Studies Centre, Australian Defence Force Academy.

Cheeseman, G. (1995) 'Structuring the ADF for UN Operations: Change and Resistance', Working Paper No. 34, Canberra: Australian Defence Studies Centre, Australian Defence Force Academy.

Cheeseman, G. and Kettle, S. (1990), *The New Australian Militarism: Undermining Our Future Security*, Sydney: Pluto Press.

Cheeseman, G. and Bruce, R. (eds) (1996), *Discourses of Danger and Dread Frontiers: Australian Defence and Security Thinking After the Cold War*, St Leonards: Allen & Unwin.

Cox, R. (1982), 'Gramsci, Hegemony and International Relations: An Essay in Method', *Millenium: Journal of International Relations*, 12(2), 162–75.

Dalby, S. (1995), 'Continent Adrift: The Changing Geostrategic Parameters of Australian Discourse', Working Paper No. 35, Canberra: Australian Defence Studies Centre, Australian Defence Force Academy.

Department of Defence (1987), *The Defence of Australia 1987*, Canberra: AGPS.

Department of Defence (1991), *Force Structure Review 1991*, Canberra: AGPS.

Department of Defence (1992), *Australia's Strategic Planning in the 1990s*, Canberra: AGPS.

Department of Defence (1993a), *Strategic Review 1993*, Canberra: DPUBS: 8009/93.

Department of Defence (1993b), *Peacekeeping Policy: The Future Australian Defence Force Role*, Canberra: DPUBS 2092/93.

Department of Defence (1994), *Defending Australia Defence White Paper 1994*, Canberra: AGPS.

Dibb, P. (1986), *Review of Australia's defence capabilities*, Canberra: AGPS.

Dibb, P. (1992), 'The Conceptual Basis of Australia's Defence Planning and Force Structure Development', Canberra Papers on Strategy and Defence No. 88, Canberra: Strategic and Defence Studies Centre, Australian National University.

Dibb, P. (1993), *The Future of Australia's Defence Relationship with the United States*, Sydney: Australian Centre for American Studies.

Dibb, P. (1994), 'The Political and Strategic Outlook, 1994–2003: Global, Regional and Australian Perspectives', Working Paper No. 282, Canberra: Strategic and Defence Studies Centre, Australian National University.

Dibb, P. (1995), *Towards a New Balance of Power in Asia*, Oxford: Adelphi Paper No. 295, International Institute for Strategic Studies.

Dibb, P. (1996), 'Australia's Defence Policies in the Post-Cold War Era' in J. Cotton and J. Ravenhill (eds), *Australian Foreign Policy in the Post-Cold War Era: Australia in World Affairs 1991-95*, Canberra: AIIA/Oxford University Press.

Dupont, A. (1991), 'Australia's Threat Perceptions: A Search for Security', Canberra Papers on Strategy and Defence No. 82, Canberra: Strategic and Defence Studies Centre, Australian National University.

Evans, G. (1989a), *Australia's Regional Security*, Canberra: Commonwealth of Australia.

Evans, G. (1989b), Address to the 44th General Assembly of the United Nations, New York, 5 October.

Evans, G. (1994), 'Opening Address' in K. Clements and C. Wilson (eds), *UN Peacekeeping at the Crossroads*, Canberra: Peace Research Centre, Australian National University.

Evans, G. and Dibb, P. (1995), 'Australian paper on practical proposals for security cooperation in the Asia Pacific region', Canberra: Department of Foreign Affairs and Trade/Strategic and Defence Studies Centre, Australian National University.

Fry, G. (1991), '"Constructive Commitment" with the South Pacific: Monroe Doctrine or "New Partnership"?' in G. Fry (ed.), *Australia's Regional Security*, Sydney: Allen & Unwin.

Gelber, H. (1992), 'Advance Australia – Where?', *Australian Journal of International Affairs*, 46(2), 221–47.

George, J. (1992), 'Some Thoughts on the "Givenness of Everyday Life" in Australian International Relations: Theory and Practice', *Australian Journal of Political Science*, 27(1), 31–54.

Horne, D. (1989), *Ideas for a Nation*, Sydney: Pan Books.

Horner, D. (1992), 'The Security Dimensions of Australian Foreign Policy' in F. A. Mediansky (ed.), *Australia in a Changing World: New Foreign Policy Directions*, Botany: Maxwell Macmillan.

Joint Committee on Foreign Affairs and Defence (1981), *Threats to Australia's Security: Their nature and probability*, Canberra: AGPS.

Joint Standing Committee on Foreign Affairs, Defence and Trade (1994), *Australia's Participation in Peacekeeping*, Canberra: AGPS.

Klein, B. (1987), 'Strategic Discourse and its Alternatives', Occasional Paper No. 3, Center on Violence and Human Survival.

Klein, B. (1988), 'Hegemony and Strategic Culture: American Power Projection and Alliance Defense Politics', *Review of International Studies*, 14(2), 133–48.

Klein, B. (1994), *Strategic Studies and World Order: The Global Politics of Deterrence*, Cambridge: Cambridge University Press.

Leaver, R. (1991), 'Australia's Gulf Commitment: The End of Self-Reliance?', *The Pacific Review*, 4(3), 233–40.

Leaver, R. (1996), 'Becoming Certain About Uncertainty: Political Processes and Strategic Consequences' in G. Cheeseman and R. Bruce (eds), *Discourses of Danger and Dread Frontiers: Australian Defence and Security Thinking After the Cold War*, St Leonards: Allen & Unwin.

Leaver, R. and Richardson, J. (eds) (1993), *The Post-Cold War Order: Diagnoses and Prognoses*, St Leonards: Allen & Unwin.

Luckham, R. (1984), 'Armament Culture', *Alternatives*, X, 1–44.

McQueen, H. (1970), *A New Britannia: An Argument Concerning the Social Origins of Australian Radicalism and Nationalism*, Harmondsworth: Penguin Books.

MacAllister, I. and Makkai, T. (1991), 'Changing Australian Opinion on Defence: Trends, Patterns and Explanations', *Small Wars and Insurgencies*, 2(3), 195–235.

Mack, A. (1988), 'Australia's Defence Revolution', Working Paper No. 150, Canberra: Strategic and Defence Studies Centre, Australian National University.

Mack, A. and Kerr, P. (1995), 'The Evolving Security Discourse in the Asia-Pacific', *The Washington Quarterly*, 18(1), 123–40.

Mathews, T. and Ravenhill, J. (1987), 'Anzus, the American alliance and external threats: Australian elite attitudes', *Australian Outlook*, 41(3), 161–73.

Millar, T. B. (1991), *Australia in Peace and War*, 2nd edn, Canberra: Australian National University Press.

Millar, T. B. and Walter, J. (1993), *Asian-Pacific Security After the Cold War*, 2nd edn, St Leonards: Allen & Unwin.

Murphy, J. (1993), *Harvest of Fear: A History of Australia's Vietnam War*, St. Leonards: Allen & Unwin.

Nossal, K. (1995), 'Seeing Things? The Adornment of "Security" in Australia and Canada', *Australian Journal of International Affairs*, 49(1), 33–47.

Renouf, A. (1979), *The Frightened Country*, Melbourne: Macmillan.

Richelson, J. T. and Ball, D. (1985), *The Ties that Bind: Intelligence Cooperation between the UKUSA Countries – the United Kingdom, the United States of America, Canada, Australia and New Zealand*, Boston: Allen & Unwin.

Said, E. W. (1995), *Orientalism: Western Conceptions of the Orient*, London: Penguin Books.

Senate Standing Committee on Foreign Affairs, Defence and Trade (1991), *United Nations Peacekeeping and Australia*, Canberra: AGPS.

Smith, G. and Kettle, S. (1992), *Threats Without Enemies: Rethinking Australia's Security*, Sydney: Pluto Press.

Strahan, L. (1996), 'The Dread Frontier in Australia's Defence Thinking' in G. Cheeseman and R. Bruce (eds), *Discourses of Danger and Dread Frontiers: Australian Defence and Security Thinking After the Cold War*, St Leonards: Allen & Unwin.

Sullivan, D. (1996), 'Sipping a Thin Gruel: Academic and Policy Closure in Australia's Defence and Security Discourse' in G. Cheeseman and R. Bruce (eds), *Discourses of Danger and Dread Frontiers: Australian Defence and Security Thinking After the Cold War*, St Leonards: Allen & Unwin.

Sullivan, M. (1996), 'Australia's Regional Peacekeeping Discourse: Policing the Asia-Pacific' in G. Cheeseman and R. Bruce (eds), *Discourses of Danger and Dread Frontiers: Australian Defence and Security Thinking After the Cold War*, St Leonards: Allen & Unwin.

Trood, R. (1996), 'Strategic Assessment in the White Paper' in J. Bonnor and G. Brown (eds), S*ecurity for the Twenty-First Century?*, Canberra: Australian Defence Studies Centre, Australian Defence Force Academy.

White, R. (1981), *Inventing Australia: Images and Identity 1688–1980*, Sydney: Allen & Unwin.

Young, T. (1989), 'Problems in Australia's "Defence Revolution", *Contemporary Southeast Asia*, 11(3), 237–56.

Young, T. (1991a), 'Australia's Defence Planning after the Cold War', *The Pacific Review,* 4(3), 222–32.

Young, T. (1991b), *Australian, New Zealand, and United States Security Relations, 1951–1986*, Boulder Co: Westview Press.

Young, T. (1994), 'Prospects for Future Australia-United States Defence Cooperation', *The Pacific Review*, 7(2), 195–204.

15

Australia and international institutions

Shirley V. Scott

A notable feature of the conduct of Australian foreign policy over the last decade has been an active involvement in international institutions. Indeed, in a number of cases – such as the chemical weapons regime, the Antarctic Treaty System, and GATT – Australia has adopted a leadership role in creating, or influencing the course of, the international institution. Australia's extensive involvement with international institutions has had considerable impact on its domestic law and politics. '[T]he old culture in which international affairs and national affairs were regarded as disparate and separate elements ... is giving way to the realisation that there is an ongoing interaction between international and national affairs' (Mason 1996: 23). Such a transformation is not occurring without considerable public discussion on the merits of Australia's participation, the process by which Australia decides to become involved in particular institutions, and the impact of that involvement on the structures and process of Australian politics. After reviewing the nature of Australian participation in international institutions, this chapter will address three themes identifiable in public discussion regarding that role; these pertain to perceptions of a loss of sovereignty, of a democratic deficit, and of a worsening federal-state imbalance. Discussion will begin, however, by placing Australia's involvement in international institutions within the context of the process of globalisation.

Globalisation

Globalisation refers to the increasing levels of economic, social and political activity throughout the world that are not confined to national borders (*Trick or Treaty?* 1995: 8). According to Alexander (1996) this process of increasing interconnectedness and interdependence among States[1] 'presents the most dramatic potential for changes to humankind in the whole of recorded history'. States, which have traditionally been regarded as the key players in world politics are, to a greater and greater extent, subject to economic, political, social and cultural forces beyond their control. Of rising relative importance are other international actors: transnational corporations (TNCs), international non-governmental organisations (NGOs), and intergovernmental organisations (IGOs).

TNCs are corporations – such as General Motors, IBM, and Exxon – which operate across State boundaries. TNCs wield considerable and increasing economic power; by 1988, forty-one TNCs were among the world's 100 largest economic units, the top 792 companies each produced more than the economies of the world's forty-five smallest States (Papp 1992: 84–5). It has been estimated that by 2000 TNCs will produce two-thirds of the world's gross economic product (Papp 1992: 92).

NGOs operate internationally without formal ties to government. NGOs are probably not as powerful a force detracting from the pre-eminence of the State as the TNCs but are still influential, if only because of the staggering increase in their numbers since the Second World War, from 973 in 1956 to 4928 in 1994 (*Yearbook of International Organisations 1994–95*: 1625). Their aims and methodologies differ widely. Some, such as Greenpeace, seek direct influence on government policy, while others, such as certain humanitarian organisations, consciously seek to bypass governments; NGOs also include professional, scientific, and sporting bodies.

It is the intergovernmental organisations, however, whose relationship to the State is the most ambivalent. Intergovernmental organisations are organisations made up of States which choose to participate therein. Despite the potential threat to the State posed by intergovernmental organisations, States clearly see such participation as in their best interests. In 1994 there were some 263 such organisations (*Yearbook of International Organisations 1994–95*: 1625), their subject matter spanning virtually every aspect of international relations. This chapter concentrates on Australia's participation in IGOs and, conversely, their impact on Australia.

First, however, a word on terminology. 'International organisations' are physical entities, with a headquarters, staff, and so on. The term 'institutions' – or to use current terminology, 'regimes' – encompasses international organisations but is also often used to refer to patterns of cooperation between States which do not necessarily have these tangible manifestations; international institutions have been defined as 'sets of rules that may or may not involve international organisations' (Bernauer 1995: 351). Many such international institutions incorporate an IGO which carries out some of the activities with which the institution deals. International institutions or regimes are usually identified by the broad issue with which they deal –

for example, the law of the sea regime or the regime on the non-proliferation of nuclear weapons. An institution is founded by a treaty, an international legal document which functions as the constitution of the regime. For instance, the regime dealing with the non-proliferation of nuclear weapons was established by the 1968 Treaty on the Non-Proliferation of Nuclear Weapons; and the contemporary law of the sea regime by the Convention on the Law of the Sea of 1982. Such treaties set out how the participating States are going to solve, or at least manage, the issue that gave rise to the regime. They stipulate the scope of acceptable behaviour relating to that issue and thereby provide the basis on which States are to deal jointly with the issue in question.

Australia's pursuit of national interests through international institutions

Australia is currently a party to over 400 multilateral treaties (*Trick or Treaty?* 1995: 25), a number of which establish international regimes. Australia has been an active participant in the negotiation and operation of many of these institutions, often playing a much more decisive role in determining institutional outcomes than might be expected for a State of Australia's population, economic muscle and defence capabilities. The rationale for this active involvement in international institutions has been quite simple: policymakers have perceived it to be in the national interest. Australia is a 'middle' rather than a 'great' power; it is positioned some-where in between the most powerful and the weakest States in world politics. It is precisely because Australia does not enjoy high levels of political, economic or military clout that its policy makers have sought to enhance Australia's influence and its security – economic, military and environ-mental – through participation in international institutions.

Australia is not the only middle power to pursue its national interests through active involvement in international institutions. Other middle powers such as Canada and the Scandinavian States have also played substantial roles in the creation and operation of regimes in the post 1945 period. The nature of such activism has, however, changed over the years. In the immediate postwar era, the international agenda was dominated by geo-political security issues associated with the Cold War and there was little room for middle powers to manoeuvre. Not surprisingly, in these years middle powers tended to support the world order as it was being establish-ed under United States hegemony (Cooper, Richard and Nossal 1993: 19–20). In contrast, since the late 1980s middle power activism in inter-national institutions has often involved moving in different, though not necessarily conflicting, directions from that taken by the major powers. Three features of the global context have contributed to the changed nature of the middle power role (Cooper, Richard and Nossal 1993: 21). First, steadily increasing interdependence has given rise to a perceived need to be involved and to attempt to shape events and the rules of the game in a direction commensurate with our interests. Second, a changing global agenda has meant that security is now viewed much more broadly, to encompass economic and environmental factors. And, third, the relative decline of United States power and willingness to lead has opened up new opportunities for institutional leadership.

Of course, the form of leadership displayed by middle powers has generally differed from that traditionally associated with the great powers. Where middle powers have been able to assume a leadership role it has not involved domination so much as acting as a peer of other group members. Middle power leadership in international institutions characteristically involves fulfilling three functions (Cooper, Richard and Nossal 1993: 24–5): that of a catalyst, offering the intellectual and political energy to trigger an initiative and to take the lead in dealing with that issue; that of facilitator – planning, convening and hosting formative meetings, setting agendas and priorities, etc; and third, that of manager – finding practical solutions to stumbling blocks in the creation or operation of regimes.

While these activities are also carried out by great powers, the most powerful States have much bigger agendas and more pressures with which to deal. Middle powers are able to concentrate their resources on a few issues which they perceive as of particular importance to them, what Gareth Evans has referred to as 'niche diplomacy'. Annette Baker Fox (1980: 193) argues that middle powers in fact have the greatest freedom in policy choices – mistakes by superpowers may have global impact; smaller States often feel they have no room to manoeuvre. Indeed, Holbraad (1984: 69, 209) believes that middle powers have the most to gain from international organisations. In the last resort, great powers can do without them; and middle powers have more to lose from a state of lawlessness than smaller States. Australia has perceived it as in its best interests not only to be, but to be seen to be, a 'good international citizen'.

As Australia has increasingly been prepared to pursue an independent foreign policy its involvement in international institutions has been characterised by a considerable deal of risk taking (Cooper, Richard and Nossal 1993: 29). A great deal of effort has gone into coming to understand how other States and international institutions operate (Baker Fox 1980: 201). Since Australia is not part of any fixed regional grouping it has on occasion been able to act as an 'honest broker' between major powers with interests in our region and to build alliances with different sets of states with mutual interests regarding the particular issue in question.

Australia's formation and leadership of the so-called Cairns Group in GATT provides a good example of Australia pursuing its economic security interests through active involvement and initiative taking in an international institution. GATT, signed in 1947, served to establish what was to become the most significant multilateral forum dealing with international trade. The GATT regime of principles and rules regulating international trade and aiming to reduce levels of protection evolved through a series of negotiating 'rounds'. The agricultural sector had never been brought fully into line with GATT provisions and rules. Australia therefore undertook a major diplomatic initiative to establish and provide leadership to the Cairns Group of agricultural exporters, so named because its first (1986) meeting at ministerial level was held in Cairns, Queensland. The group consisted of Argentina, Australia, Brazil, Canada, Chile, Colombia, Fiji, Hungary, Indonesia, Malaysia, New Zealand, the Philippines, Thailand and Uruguay. Although a somewhat disparate group of States in terms of normal north-south, east-west divisions, all had a highly competitive, export oriented and, in most cases, lightly protected agricultural sector. Together they shared 26 per cent by value of world agricultural exports (O'Sullivan 1995: 9). The Cairns Group made it clear that agreement on other items in the Uruguay Round of GATT negotiations would depend on reform of agricultural trade. The strategy was successful; by the end of the round in 1993 all the GATT rules and principles that had previously applied to trade in manufactured goods had been extended to trade in agricultural commodities.

Let us now look in greater depth at two examples of Australia's efforts over the last half decade to pursue its security interests through initiative taking in international institutions.

International institutions and Australian military security: The chemical weapons convention

Chemical weapons are nothing new, the Greeks having used sulphur mixtures on the battlefield as long ago as 431 BC (Smithson 1992: 37). International attempts to limit or prevent their usage date from a 1675 Franco-German agreement not to use poisoned bullets (Smithson 1992: 37). The Gulf War gave fresh impetus to modern efforts to reach an agreement regarding chemical weapons, formal negotiations towards this end having begun within the Geneva based Conference on Disarmament in 1984. The basis for negotiations was the so-called 'rolling text', an evolving draft which was updated annually to indicate provisionally agreed elements and those on which disagreement remained.

Despite these efforts, progress towards a treaty was slow. States disagreed over whether the ban should be total and the nature of verification provisions. If very stringent they appeared as intrusive on national sovereignty; if too lax, the regime would not be deemed effective. During the 1980s Australia made a considerable contribution to the work of the conference. Australian involvement stemmed from the belief that disarmament questions should not be the exclusive domain of the great powers (O'Sullivan and Moules 1993: 60). In 1986 Australia chaired one of three working groups in the negotiations and reported on a trial inspection of an Australian civilian chemical plant. In 1989 Australia hosted a major international government–industry conference in Canberra which brought together chemical industry representatives and government officials. This was effective in mobilising widespread support for the view that a workable treaty on chemical weapons was indeed possible and desirable (O'Sullivan and Moules 1993: 60–4).

The end of the Cold War reinforced this view while the threatened use of chemical weapons by Iraq in 1991 heightened the sense of urgency surrounding such an agreement. In 1991 the UN General Assembly passed a resolution calling for the draft convention to be concluded in 1992, although progress within the negotiations made such an outcome appear improbable at best.

Australia's 'accelerated refinement' of the rolling text

It was in providing an impetus for the final negotiations that Australia made its greatest contribution to the development of a chemical weapons convention. Under the dedicated interest of Gareth Evans, Australian officials produced a model convention, which included compromise solutions to the outstanding areas of disagreement. Convinced of the possibility for a breakthrough in the negotiations, Australian officials discussed the text with officials in many State capitals and on 19 March 1992 Senator Evans presented to the Conference on Disarmament what he referred to as an 'accelerated refinement' (Evans 1992) of the rolling text.

The Chairman of the negotiating committee took up the Australian initiative to produce his own chairman's text which provided the basis for the final rounds of intense negotiations. On 3 September 1992 the annual report adopted by the conference contained the draft 'Convention on the Prohibition of the Development, Production, Stockpiling and Use of Chemical Weapons and their Destruction'. The text was unanimously endorsed by the UN General Assembly in November 1992 and was opened for signature on 13 January. As of March 1996, 160 States had signed the treaty and forty-nine had ratified it (given their final consent to be legally bound). The treaty will enter into force 180 days after sixty-five States have deposited their instruments of ratification. This is the first disarmament agreement negotiated within a multilateral framework that provides for the elimination of an entire category of weapons of mass destruction; its verification measures are also ground-breaking.

Many commentators have praised the Australian initiative that paved the way for the negotiating breakthrough that produced the Convention.

Ronald Lehman, Director of the United States Arms Control and Disarmament Agency referred to the Australian text as having been 'vital' (Letts and others 1993: 326) while the Russian federation's Disarmament Ambassador, Serguei Batsanov, paid tribute to Australia for having '[taken] the risk to be the first one to get outside a customary framework of the so-called rolling text and to propose a comprehensive and more simple and understandable draft of the Convention, thus opening up the road which ... led us to our present results' (O'Sullivan and Moules 1993: 57).

International institutions and Australian environmental security: The environmental protocol to the Antarctic Treaty

The Antarctic Treaty System (ATS) offers a good example of Australia's recent preparedness to adopt independent policies during the course of regime life. The ATS was established by the Antarctic Treaty, concluded in 1959. The prime issue addressed by the Antarctic Treaty was that of territorial sovereignty. Prior to 1959 seven States: Argentina, Australia, Chile, France, New Zealand, Norway, and the United Kingdom had asserted the right to govern a designated portion of the continent; parts of those areas claimed by Argentina, Chile, and the United Kingdom, overlapped. No State external to this group recognised the rights of any of the claimants while the United States and the Soviet Union, having made no formal claim, sought a multilateral solution to the question of sovereignty. The Antarctic Treaty offered a 'non solution' to the sovereignty issue by 'freezing' sovereignty claims for the duration of the treaty, purportedly to foster peaceful scientific cooperation on the continent. The solution was justified by the idea that science is non-political so that no activities which took place within the Antarctic regime would affect the legal position of any State, claimant or non-claimant.

The regime has evolved fairly smoothly, dealing with new sub-issues as they have arisen. In the early 1980s the parties to the Antarctic Treaty decided that the time had come to address the question of mineral exploitation. The issue of who could mine Antarctica, and where, confronted the sovereignty issue head-on because usually a territorial sovereign decides who can mine in its territory. If, for example, members of the ATS had decided that anyone could mine anywhere, the regime members would have been effectively denying the asserted sovereignty rights of the claimant States. If, on the other hand, the agreed solution had been that only the territorial claimants could mine in their respective pieces of territory, then it would be giving recognition to those claims. For these very reasons it was perceived as vital that a solution be found before any mining began.

Formal negotiations for an agreement on minerals began in 1982 and sessions were held each year until 1988. On 2 June 1988 the Convention for the Regulation of Antarctic Mineral Resources (CRAMRA) was concluded in Wellington, New Zealand (CRAMRA 1994). The agreed solution was to defer a decision as to whether any mining would be permitted but to provide stringent environmental safeguards should that decision be in the affirmative. A commission was to be established to decide whether mining would be permitted in any particular area, structured so as to give claimants considerable say, although the claimant involved would not get royalties. Members of the ATS congratulated themselves on again having provided for managing an issue before it had been brought to a head, in this case by the actual commencement of mining operations in Antarctica.

Australia and CRAMRA

But then came the shock. On 22 May 1989 Australia announced that it would not ratify the convention. This effectively placed a veto on the agreement.[2] Australia argued that any mining whatsoever was incompatible with protection of the environment. France followed suit the next month and support gradually increased for the idea that CRAMRA be abandoned in favour of Antarctica being declared a 'nature reserve, land of science'. On 4 October 1991 the ATS concluded the Environmental Protocol to the Antarctic Treaty which banned any activities relating to mineral resources other than scientific research, while making provision for the decision to be reviewed in fifty years' time.

Australia's actions in this process were decisive in having the regime abandon the minerals convention. It is not usual for a State that has negotiated a treaty then not to ratify it; Australia's move was bold and received a lot of criticism at the time. Prior to the 1980s Australia had played an influential, though generally undistinguished, role in Antarctic affairs, participating actively but not seeking a leadership role (Beck 1990: 106). Australia had not taken policy decisions that would have left it isolated in the Antarctic community. In the case of CRAMRA, however, the Australian position was in direct conflict with that of both the United States and Britain, two of the most influential States in the regime. At the time it was widely thought that Australia would back down when faced with strong opposition. Those in favour of CRAMRA argued that, should the ATS members ever decide to permit mining, it was better to have stringent environmental safeguards in place than nothing.

Australia and France lobbied for support for their proposals, the prime ministers of both countries taking it up as something of a personal crusade (Elliott 1994: 182). Between November 1990 and October 1991 four sessions of the Eleventh Special Consultative Meeting were held, by the end of which consensus had been reached on a new 'comprehensive' environmental agreement. When the first session began Australia and France had been joined by Belgium and Norway in a formal coalition referred to as the Group of Four (Elliott 1994: 187). Through ongoing efforts at coalition building this group grew until it was Britain and the United States which were isolated in their negotiating position and eventually yielded. The final act of the special consultative meeting was adopted in Madrid on 4 October 1991 and the Protocol on Environmental Protection to the Antarctic Treaty was opened for signature until 3 October 1992. A voluntary moratorium on mining is to continue until the protocol comes into effect.

There was undoubtedly more than one domestic reason for Australia's actions (see Bergin 1991). Outwardly, Australia argued that its actions were inspired by the need to protect the Antarctic environment, though cynics have suggested that it had more to do with the increasing electoral importance of the Green movement at a time when the Hawke government was about to face an election. Certainly there was pressure from NGOs, including Greenpeace, the Australian Conservation Foundation, and others, which joined together to form the Antarctic Southern Ocean Coalition. In addition, Australia had not been entirely happy with the manner in which CRAMRA managed the original regime issue of sovereignty. Australia felt that not enough had been done to respect its sovereignty, and was particularly unhappy at the lack of anti-subsidy provisions in the agreement.

Australia's participation in international institutions as a source of domestic controversy

The period of increased Australian initiative-taking in international institutions since the late 1980s has been an exciting one in Australian foreign policy. Coupled with the increase in the number of international regimes and the whole process of globalisation, of which that is a part, it has, however, increased domestic controversy regarding Australia's participation in multilateral treaties and institutions. There have been three persistent themes in the public debate. The remainder of this chapter will address each in turn.

Loss of sovereignty

There is a feeling among many Australians, often played on by the media, that the nation is being increasingly governed from without by international institutions so that we are losing control over our own political processes and law. The assertion is not without some foundation. International law has had an increasing impact on Australian law, particularly that dealing with international trade, the environment and human rights (Mason 1996). Concern over a perceived loss of sovereignty has been heightened by the fact that the High Court of Australia, the highest court of appeal in the Australian judicial system, has displayed an increasing preparedness to draw on international law in arriving at its decisions. Justice Michael Kirby, one of Australia's greatest advocates of the use of international law to fill gaps in the common law or to assist in the interpretation of ambiguous statutes, is the most recent appointee to the court. The *Mabo* decision is one notable example of the use by the High Court of international law as an avenue to effecting change in Australian common law. This decision of 3 June 1992, the first Australian judicial recognition of a native title to land, was justified by the finding that Australia had not been *terra nullius* (a term of international law) at the time of European colonisation, a finding which was, in turn, justified by the 1975 *Western Sahara* decision of the International Court of Justice (Scott 1996).

International law may also exert an indirect influence on the Australian legal system, a High Court decision being influenced, for example, by a treaty which Australia has ratified but not yet incorporated by statute into municipal law (Opeskin and Rothwell 1995: 24ff). This has been highlighted by the recent *Teoh* case,[3] in which the court made it clear that a treaty which Australia had ratified but not yet incorporated by statute into municipal law would give rise to a 'legitimate expectation' that its terms would be taken into account in administrative decisions by government officials. In *Teoh*, the High Court found that Australia's obligations under the Convention on the Rights of the Child, a treaty that the government had not yet legislated to implement, gave rise to a 'legitimate expectation' that the rights of Mr Teoh's children be taken into account in a decision by a Commonwealth immigration officer regarding the deportation of Mr Teoh.

Alarmed by the possible implications of this ruling, the government sought to reinforce the traditional assumption that treaties do not automatically become part of Australian law but require the passage of appropriate legislation. The Administrative Decisions (Effect of International Instruments) Bill 1995 provided that, even where the government has signed and ratified a treaty this should not necessarily give rise to the expectation that the terms of the treaty will be taken into account by an administrative decision maker. This so-called 'anti-Teoh legislation' lapsed with the election of March 1996.

The *Toonen* case has also highlighted the question as to whether Australia is losing sovereignty to the international institutions in which it is involved. From 1988 onwards the Tasmanian Gay and Lesbian Rights Group (TGLRG) engaged in a concerted attempt to achieve the repeal of Tasmania's anti-sodomy laws (Tebensel 1996: 15).[4] When efforts to have reforming legislation passed through the Tasmanian parliament appeared futile the TGLRG decided to take the issue to the UN Human Rights Committee. Under the International Covenant on Civil and Political Rights (ICCPR), individuals can take cases of alleged human rights violation directly to the committee, so long as domestic avenues to redress the alleged violation have been exhausted and the case is not under investigation by any other international body (Morris 1995: 101). The Human Rights Committee can then decide whether to investigate the case and issue an advisory opinion.

On 25 December 1991, the day on which Australia's ratification of the First Optional Protocol to the International Covenant on Civil and Political Rights came into force, Nick Toonen, a gay rights activist, lodged a complaint with the Human Rights Committee, arguing that Tasmania's laws prohibiting sexual behaviour between consenting adult males in private contravened three rights under the ICCPR: those to privacy, to equality before the law, and to not be discriminated against (Morris 1995: 102). Asked to respond, the federal government concurred with Nick Toonen that Tasmania's laws violated the right to privacy and agreed to accept a UN Human Rights Committee finding (Morris 1995: 110). On 8 April 1994 the UN Human Rights Committee informed the Commonwealth government of its finding that Tasmania's anti-sodomy legislation left Australia in breach of its obligations under the ICCPR and that an effective remedy would be to repeal the relevant sections of the legislation.

Accordingly, when it became apparent that the Liberal government in Tasmania refused to repeal those sections the Commonwealth parliament passed the Human Rights (Sexual Conduct) Act 1994. Section 4 of this Act provided that sexual conduct between consenting adults in private is not to be subject to arbitrary interference with privacy as understood in article 17 of the ICCPR. A number of commentators (such as Mason 1996: 28) and participants saw this incident as evidence of international institutions exerting too great an influence on Australian politics and law, despite the fact that Australia had been placed under no legal obligation to change its laws on the basis of the UN committee's findings; the committee can only exert pressure of a political or moral nature. Senator Eric Abetz (Liberal, Tasmania), for example, argued that 'Labor has decided to act against Tasmania's democratically instituted laws on the strength of the pontifications of the United Nations rabble sitting on the other side of the world' (*Sunday Age*, 11 December 1994); while Geoffrey Barker asserted that Australia taking action on the basis of the findings of the UN Human Rights Committee was the contemporary equivalent of the Privy Council previously acting as our highest court of appeal (the *Age*, 21 April 1994: 13; see also Fraser, the *Australian*, 17 August 1994: 13; McGinness, the *Australian*, 20 April 1994: 11).

Perhaps the most obvious way of refuting the 'loss of sovereignty' claim is to point to the fact that the very act of signing and ratifying an international agreement is an act of sovereignty. More fundamental yet is the point that, even if some control over Australian law and politics is being ceded to international institutions, such institutions have become an intrinsic feature of world politics. It is highly unlikely that Australia's national interests would be any better served by opting out of the international system even if this were possible. As Alston (1995: 25) has recently argued, it is time for the debate on globalisation and Australian multilateral treaty participation to move on, so that the focus can shift from form to substance: 'rather than indulging in the almost xenophobic rhetoric to which some political and other community leaders have been prone, there needs to be a serious substantive discussion on the merits of individual issues as they arise'.

A democratic deficit

The second broad theme in public debate on Australia's contribution to multilateral treaty making and participation in the institutions to which they often give rise or of which they are a part, relates to the extent to which parliament and the general public should play a role in decisions regarding participation in international institutions. The Australian constitution does not explicitly state the powers of the executive. The power to enter into a treaty is, though, generally regarded as falling within the domain of the executive as provided for in section 61 of the constitution.[5]

In practice it is the minister for foreign affairs, on the advice of the Department of Foreign Affairs and Trade (Mason 1996: 21) and other ministers, to whose portfolio the subject matter is relevant, who decide on the instructions to be given Australia's negotiating delegations to international conferences and whether to ratify the ensuing treaty. Where decisions involve new policy or significant variations to existing policy, significant expenditure or new legislation, they are taken to cabinet. The governor general, acting on the advice of the executive council, must then approve any recommendation before action is taken in the international arena to sign a treaty or take action subsequent to signature. While there is little doubt that treaties receive 'detailed and exhaustive scrutiny by the relevant members of the Government before action is taken to make Australia a party' (O'Sullivan 1995: 3), many commentators and parliamentarians believe that the lack of an explicit legal role for parliament leaves a 'democratic deficit' in the process of Australia's treaty involvement.[6]

As with the loss of sovereignty theme this argument can, at least in theory, be easily contradicted. The executive is accountable to the people through the process of election. It has, furthermore, been government policy not to ratify an international agreement until Australian legislation complies with the obligations (*Trick or Treaty?* 1995: 229–30). It is also true, however, that this has not always happened in practice, a number of treaties having been ratified without legislation in place to implement their terms or existing legislation amended to accommodate the requirements of the treaty.[7] Adherents of the democratic deficit criticism further maintain that, even if parliament were required to approve the terms of a treaty before ratification, the fact that multilateral treaties are unlikely to become an election issue would still leave a 'democratic deficit' in the sense of no electoral mandate from the people.[8]

There have, over the years, been some moves to increase parliamentary participation in treaty decisions. In 1961 Menzies introduced a practice of tabling treaties twelve sitting days prior to their ratification[9] (this may well be much more than two weeks before ratification as parliament does not sit every day). But adherence to this procedure gradually slackened, it becoming standard practice for the Department of Foreign Affairs and Trade to provide a list of treaties ratified by Australia every six months, which meant that many treaties were not tabled until after ratification (*Trick or Treaty?* 1995: 5). More recently, the government announced in October 1994 that all multilateral treaties would, if possible, be tabled before ratification and that a schedule of multilateral treaties under negotiation would also be tabled (*Trick or Treaty?* 1995: 25). At the hearing of the Senate Legal and Constitutional References Committee on the Commonwealth power to make and implement treaties on 14 June 1995, the Department of Foreign Affairs and Trade agreed to table treaties more frequently than six months where there was significant interest in the treaty, but no particular urgency.[10] In 1995 Senator Bourne introduced the Parliamentary Approval of Treaties Bill 1995 which provided, *inter alia*, for notification of Australia's intention to enter into a treaty to be published in the *Gazette* and tabled in each house of parliament. Were a member of either house to request that the treaty be considered by that house, the treaty could not be ratified until approval was subsequently given. The bill was not voted on before the federal elections of March 1996. At the time of writing the bill had been reintroduced onto the agenda for debate but no date for such debate had yet been set.

One of the early initiatives of the incoming Coalition government was to announce a number of reforms to the treaty-making process which were designed to overcome the identified democratic deficit. On 2 May 1996 the Minister for Foreign Affairs, Alexander Downer, and the Attorney-General, Daryl Williams, tabled the government's response to the report of the Senate Legal and Constitutional References Committee and announced that treaties were to be tabled in parliament at least fifteen sitting days before the government took any binding action. Together with the treaty there would be tabled a 'National Interest Analysis' to facilitate parliamentary and community scrutiny of the treaty's provisions and their likely impact on Australia. The government also proposed the establishment of a Joint Parliamentary Committee on Treaties to consider the tabled treaties, their National Interest Analyses and any other questions relating to international instruments referred to it by either house of parliament or a minister. In response to a further recommendation of the Senate Legal and Constitutional

References Committee the incoming government was also to establish a Treaties Information Database to be available free of charge to the public, interested NGOs and industry. A new Treaties Secretariat in the Department of Foreign Affairs and Trade would coordinate the implementation of these reforms (Downer 1996).

The whole question of a greater treaty role for parliament – whether it be given an actual veto over treaty participation or merely greater opportunity to debate the terms of treaties – is one which is likely to be the subject of ongoing debate in the remaining years of the decade.

A federal imbalance

Australia has a federal system of government in which power is shared between levels of government. The powers of the Commonwealth government are set out in section 51 of the constitution, leaving the states to deal with all other matters. Where a federal and state law conflict, the federal overrides that of the state. The constitution makes no specific reference to treaties, but section 51 provides that the parliament has the 'power to make laws for the peace, order, and good government of the Commonwealth with respect to' a number of subjects, one of which is 'external affairs'. What the constitution leaves unclear is whether the Commonwealth has the power to legislate to implement treaties whose content would otherwise be the domain of the states.

It was not until 1983 that the High Court gave an unequivocal ruling on this question. The *Tasmanian Dams* case[11] concerned the decision by the Tasmanian government to build a dam on the Franklin River in Southwest Tasmania. The Commonwealth government, with the cooperation of the Tasmanian government, had previously listed the relevant area under the Convention for the Protection of the World Cultural and Natural Heritage.[12] In March 1983 the Commonwealth government passed legislation relying on the external affairs power (among others) to prevent construction of the dam. The Tasmanian government took the issue to the High Court which decided in favour of the Commonwealth. A majority of the judges stated quite clearly their view that the external affairs power supported Commonwealth legislation to implement any treaty obligations, no matter its subject matter (see Burmester 1989: 197; Durack 1994: 5; Ravenhill 1990: 88).

The combined impact of the *Dams* case and the increasing number of treaties pertaining to fields such as human rights and the environment, which are areas traditionally the domain of the states, has been to greatly increase the legislative power of the Commonwealth at the expense of the states. Indeed, since international law now encompasses virtually every subject matter of politics the legal basis exists for the Commonwealth to override virtually every piece of state legislation to the extent that states could theoretically become redundant. As Sir Harry Gibbs, then Chief Justice of the High Court, has commented:

> [T]here is almost no aspect of life which under modern conditions may not be the subject of an international agreement, and therefore the possible subject of Commonwealth legislative power. Whether Australia enters into any particular international agreement is entirely a matter for decision by the executive. The division of powers between the Commonwealth and the States which the Constitution effects could be rendered quite meaningless if the federal government could, by entering into treaties with foreign governments on matters of domestic concern, enlarge the legislative powers of the Parliament so that they embraced literally all fields of activity ... Section 51(xxix) should be given a construction that will, so far as possible, avoid the consequence that the federal balance of the Constitution can be destroyed at the will of the executive.[13]

In political terms such a scenario is extremely unlikely. Where the subject of a treaty is already being dealt with by state governments the Commonwealth would generally prefer to draw on the administrative machinery already in place rather than undergo the expense of duplicating it (Opeskin and Rothwell 1995: 16). Perhaps more significantly, even the Labor Party, which is more centralist that the conservative parties, recognises the electoral unpopularity of using its powers to override state legislation.

In the case of the Toonen affair, the Commonwealth Labor government was particularly wary of criticism that in pursuing its perceived international obligations it would ride roughshod over state interests. The government declined to take any immediate action following the advisory opinion of the UN Human Rights Committee, the federal Attorney-General, Mr Lavarch, stating that he was 'very loath to rely on external powers' and was 'not going to rush in with legislation. We'll give Tasmania a fair time to look at the decision' (the *Age*, 12 April 1994: 1). When the government did then go ahead and introduce the Human Rights (Sexual Conduct) Act 1994 there were immediate charges of interference with states rights. Mr Downer, as Opposition Leader, commented that '[t]he federal system of government is again under attack by Labor's centralist grab for power, and the external affairs power is seen by it as an important means of achieving its centralist goals' (the *Age*, 31 October 1994: 1); while the Tasmanian Attorney-General, Mr Cornish, said that Tasmanians would not want big brother in the form of the federal government telling Tasmanians that their law must be changed (the *Age*, 16 April 1994: 19).

To better protect state interests moves have been made to increase the involvement of states in decisions regarding the negotiation and ratification of treaties. In 1982 the premiers and Commonwealth reached agreement on a set of 'Principles and Procedures for Commonwealth-State Consultation on Treaties' which was revised the following year and again in 1991–92.[14] This allows for the states to give input to the Commonwealth but the states have no capacity to prevent the Commonwealth from going ahead. In 1992 a Standing Committee on Treaties, consisting of senior Commonwealth and state/territory officers, was established. It meets at least twice per year, prior to which the Commonwealth circulates a list of treaties regarding which action is proposed during the next six months. In addition, some Australian negotiating delegations now include a state representative, as was the case, for example, with the inclusion of a Tasmanian representative in the delegation to the Antarctic minerals negotiations. Such state representatives are not entitled to speak for Australia but are simply there in an advisory capacity and for the information of the states.

While most of the reforms of the treaty making process announced by the incoming minister for foreign affairs and the attorney-general on 2 May 1996 related to the issue of a democratic deficit in the treaty making process, one did involve Commonwealth support for the creation of a Treaties Council as an adjunct to the Council of Australian Governments. This council is intended to have an advisory function. According to the new foreign minister in the Coalition government after the 1996 election, Alexander Downer, the establishment of a Treaties Council together with the commitment to prepare National Interest Analyses for all future treaty actions 'herald[s] a new phase in Commonwealth-State consultation on treaty-making' (Downer 1996).

Conclusions

Australia generally has little control over the processes of globalisation; the Australian government – like all national governments – has been under increasing challenge from the expansion in the number of NGOs, TNCs and IGOs and in the range of their activities in recent decades. Since it has not been realistic to consider opting out of the system of international politics, Australian governments have sought to ensure that the establishment and evolution of international institutions accord as closely as possible with their perceptions of the country's best interests. As this chapter has documented, Australian officials have been remarkably successful in this process over the last five to ten years, as exemplified by the Australian contribution to the emergence of the Chemical Weapons Convention, and its role within GATT and the ATS.

Former Minister for Foreign Affairs, Gareth Evans, argued strongly for Australia's continuing to take a proactive role in international institutions:

> Our future prosperity and security rely, to a large extent, on our playing an active and positive role on the international stage. Our contribution to international peace building and the international rule of law, our activism in inter-

national forums, and our commitment to establishing and maintaining global standards are what will keep us afloat in a sea of changing power relationships. Policy makers cannot try to disregard international developments such as these – rather they must try to influence those developments to promote and protect national interests. (Evans 1995: 6)

Australia's involvement in international institutions has not, though, been without its critics. Three negative domestic impacts of this involvement were identified in this chapter – the perceived democratic deficit, the worsening federal–state imbalance (Evans dubbed this the 'national conspiracy theory' (Evans 1992: 1–2)) and the supposed loss of sovereignty (or what Evans has dubbed the 'global conspiracy theory'). While all contain some degree of truth, the extent of the problems has tended to be exaggerated in much political debate. It is, for example, realistic to expect that if Australia is to be actively involved in international institutions then those institutions will come to exert some degree of influence on Australian politics and society. But to the extent that involvement in an international institution produces a loss of sovereignty, that loss is itself the result of the decisions of a sovereign government.

The Coalition government elected in March 1996 has taken steps to reduce the perceived negative impact of Australia's involvement in international institutions and has been critical of what it regards as the previous Labor government's preoccupation with multilateralism. Australian participation in international institutions and the impact of that participation on domestic law and politics is likely to be the subject of ongoing and at times vigorous debate in the years leading up to the centenary of federation on 1 January 2001.[15]

Notes

The author would like to thank Prudence Gordon, doctoral student at the ANU, for her valuable research assistance.

1 In this chapter, 'States' refers to the subjects of international law, known colloquially as countries (for example Australia), while 'states' refers to subnational units (such as Queensland or New South Wales).
2 See article 62.
3 *Minister for Immigration and Ethnic Affairs v Teoh* (1995) 183 Commonwealth Law Reports, 273.
4 See sections 122 and 123 of the Tasmanian Criminal Code of 1924 (amended 1987).
5 Section 61 provides: 'The executive power of the Commonwealth is vested in the Queen and is exercisable by the Governor-General as the Queen's representative, and extends to the execution and maintenance of this Constitution, and of the laws of the Commonwealth.'
6 The term 'democratic deficit' was apparently coined in the context of European Union institutions – submission by K. Baxter to *Trick or Treaty?* 1995, submission no. 111, vol. 7, 1435.

7   Examples include the Convention on the Rights of the Child and the International Labor Organisation Convention No. 158 on the termination of employment (Twomey 1995: 12).
8   See *Trick or Treaty?* 1995, submission no. 103, vol. 6,1310 by Professor G. de Q Walker. A number of industry associations have called for greater industry and community participation in Australian treaty-making. See 'A Proper Role for Parliament, Industry and the Community in Australian Treaty-Making', Background paper produced by, *inter alia*, the Australian Mining Industry Council and the Business Council of Australia, January 1994.
9   Commonwealth of Australia, *Parliamentary Debates 1961*, third session of the twenty-third parliament, 10 Eliz. II, Vol H of R 31, 1693.
10 *Hansard*, SLCRC, 14 June 1995, 691, per C. Lamb quoted in *Trick or Treaty?* 1995, 248.
11 *Commonwealth v Tasmania* (1983) 158 Commonwealth Law Reports 1.
12 On 22 September 1981 the Tasmanian government requested that the Commonwealth nominate the area concerned. However, shortly before the Commonwealth did so, in December 1982, Tasmania tried, unsuccessfully, to withdraw its consent to the proposal, see Crock 1983, 256, footnote 4.
13 *The Commonwealth v Tasmania* (1983) 158 CLR 1 at p.100.
14 This is reproduced in an Annex to Department of Foreign Affairs and Trade, *Negotiation, Conclusion and Implementation of International Treaties and Arrangements*, Canberra, August 1994, 26–9.
15 Much of this debate involves the question of constitutional change. See, for example, Durack 1994 and Gibbs 1994.

References

Alexander, D. (1996), 'Guest Editor's Introduction: The Progression of Globality', *Social Alternatives*, 15:1 (January), 5.

Alston, P. (1995), 'Reform of Treaty-Making Processes: Form over Substance?' in P. Alston and M. Chiam (eds), *Treaty-Making and Australia: Globalisation versus Sovereignty?*, Sydney: Federation Press in association with Centre for International and Public Law, ANU.

Australia and International Treaty Making: Information Kit (1994), Canberra: Department of Foreign Affairs and Trade.

Baker Fox, A. (1980), 'The range of choice for middle powers: Australia and Canada compared', *Australian Journal of Politics and History*, XXVI: 2, 193–203.

Beck, P. (1990), 'Australia's New Course in Antarctica' in W. S. G. Bateman and M. W. Ward (eds), *Australia's Maritime Interests – Views from Overseas*, Canberra: Australian Centre for Maritime Studies, 102–19.

Bergin, A. (1991), 'The Politics of Antarctic Minerals: The Greening of White Australia', *Australian Journal of Political Science*, 26, 216–39.

Bernauer, T. (1995), 'The effect of international environmental institutions: how we might learn more', *International Organization*, 49, 2 (Spring), 351–77.

Burmester, H. (1989), 'A Legal Perspective', in B. Galligan (ed.), *Australian Federalism*, Melbourne: Longman Cheshire, 192–316.

Byrnes, A. and Charlesworth, H. (1985), 'Federalism and the International Legal Order: Recent Developments in Australia', *American Journal of International Law*, 79, 622–40.

Shirley V. Scott   289

Cooper, A. F., Richard A., and Nossal, K. R. (1993), *Relocating Middle Powers: Australia and Canada in a Changing World Order*, Vancouver: UBC Press.

CRAMRA (1994), 'Convention on the Regulation of Antarctic Mineral Resource Activities', reprinted in *Handbook of the Antarctic Treaty System*, 8th edn, Washington, DC: US Dept of State, 203–39.

Crock, M. (1983), 'Federalism and the External Affairs Power', *Melbourne University Law Review*, 14: 2 (1983), 238–64.

Downer, A. (1996), 'Reform of the Treaty-Making Process', Statement delivered 2 May.

Durack, P. (1994), *The External Affairs Power*, Perth: Institute of Public Affairs.

Elliott, L. M. (1994), *International Environmental Politics: Protecting the Antarctic*, London: St Martin's.

Evans, G. (1992), Address to the Conference on Disarmament in Geneva, 19 March, extracted in Department of Foreign Affairs and Trade, *Backgrounder*, 3: 5, 27 March, 3.

Evans, G. (1995), 'International Treaties: Their Impact on Australia', Keynote address, International Treaties Conference, Canberra, 4 September.

Gibbs, H. (1994), 'Federalism in Australia', The Sir Robert Menzies Lecture 1993, Melbourne: Sir Robert Menzies Memorial Trust.

Holbraad, C. (1984), *Middle Powers in International Politics,* London: Macmillan.

Letts, M., Mathews, R., McCormack, T. and Moraitis, C. (1993), 'The Conclusion of the Chemical Weapons Convention: An Australian Perspective', *Arms Control*, 14, 3 (December), 311–32.

Mason, A. (1996), 'The Influence of International and Transnational Law on Australian Municipal Law', *Public Law Review*, 7: 1 (March), 20–32.

Morris, M. (1995), *The Pink Triangle: The gay law reform debate in Tasmania*, Sydney: UNSW Press.

Negotiation, Conclusion and Implementation of International Treaties and Arrangements (1994), Canberra: Department of Foreign Affairs and Trade.

Opeskin, B. R. and Rothwell, D. R. (1995), 'The Impact of Treaties on Australian Federalism', *Case Western Reserve Journal of International Law*, 27, 1–59.

O'Sullivan, P. (1995), 'Australia's capacity to influence treaty outcomes', Paper presented to the International Treaties Conference, Canberra: 4–5 September.

O'Sullivan, P. and Moules, B. (1993), 'The Australian Contribution to the Conclusion of the Negotiations for a Chemical Weapons Convention', *Disarmament: A periodic review by the United Nations,* XVI: 1.

Papp, D. S. (1992), *Contemporary International Relations: Frameworks for Understanding*, 3rd edn, New York: Macmillan.

Ravenhill, J., (1990) 'Australia' in H. J. Michelmann and P. Soldatos (eds), *Federalism and International Relations: The Role of Subnational Units*, Oxford: Clarendon.

Scott, S. V. (1996), '*Terra Nullius* and the *Mabo* Judgment of the Australian High Court: A Case Study of the Operation of Legalist Reasoning as a Mechanism of Political-Legal Change', *Australian Journal of Politics and History*.

Smithson, A. E. (1992), 'Chemical Weapons: The End of the Beginning', *The Bulletin of the Atomic Scientists*, (October), 36–40.

Tebensel, T. (1996), 'International Human Rights Conventions and Australian political debates: issues raised by the "Toonen Case"', *Australian Journal of Political Science*, 31, 1, 7–23.

Trick or Treaty? (1995), Commonwealth Power to Make and Implement Treaties Report by the Senate Legal and Constitutional References Committee, Canberra: Senate Legal and Constitutional References Committee Secretariat.

Twomey, A. (1995), 'Procedure and Practice of Entering and Implementing International Treaties', Parliamentary Research Service Background Paper No. 27, 1995, Canberra: Department of the Parliamentary Library.

Union of International Associations (ed.) (1995), *Yearbook of International Organizations 1994–95*, Vol. 1. 31st edn, Munchen: K. G. Saur.

Waters, M. (1995), *Globalization*, London and New York: Routledge.

Index

291